The GIRLS *of* ATOMIC CITY

★ ★ ★ ★ ★

THE UNTOLD STORY OF THE WOMEN WHO HELPED WIN WORLD WAR II

★ ★ ★ ★ ★

DENISE KIERNAN

A TOUCHSTONE BOOK
Published by Simon & Schuster

New York London Toronto Sydney New Delhi

Touchstone
A Division of Simon & Schuster, Inc.
1230 Avenue of the Americas
New York, NY 10020

Map on pp. xviii–xix reproduced from *Manhattan: The Army and the Atomic Bomb*
(Vincent C. Jones, Washington, DC: U.S. Government Printing Office, 1985).

All photos are by James Edward Westcott, courtesy of the National Archives,
with the exception of: insert page 1, top left, courtesy of Celia Klemski;
insert page 1, top right, courtesy of Colleen Black; insert page 1, bottom, courtesy
of Jane Puckett; insert page 16, top left, courtesy of the author; insert page 16, top
right, courtesy of the author; insert page 16, bottom, courtesy of Jack Parker.

First Touchstone hardcover edition March 2013

TOUCHSTONE and colophon are registered trademarks of
Simon & Schuster, Inc.

For information about special discounts for bulk purchases,
please contact Simon & Schuster Special Sales at
1-866-506-1949 or business@simonandschuster.com.

The Simon & Schuster Speakers Bureau can bring authors to your live event.
For more information or to book an event contact the
Simon & Schuster Speakers Bureau at
1-866-248-3049 or visit our website at www.simonspeakers.com.

Designed by Ruth Lee-Mui

Manufactured in the United States of America

10

ISBN 978-1-4516-1752-8
ISBN 978-1-4516-1754-2 (ebook)

For Joe

Contents

Introduction

There have long been secrets buried deep in the southern Appalachians, covered in layers of shale and coal, lying beneath the ancient hills of the Cumberlands, and lurking in the shadow of the Smokies at the tail end of the mountainous spine that ripples down the East Coast. This land of the Cherokee gave way to treaties and settlers and land grants. Newcomers traversed the Cumberland Gap to establish small farms and big lives in a region where alternating ridges and valleys cradle newborn communities in the nooks and crannies of the earth. Isolated. Independent. Hidden.

In 1942, a new secret came to this part of the world. The earth trembled and shook and made way for an unprecedented alliance of military, industrial, and scientific forces, forces that combined to create the most powerful and controversial weapon known to mankind. This weapon released the power present in the great unseen of the time, unleashing the energy of the basic unit of matter known as the atom.

Author H. G. Wells might have called them Sun Snarers, the people who descended upon the valleys and ridges.

"And we know now that the atom, that once we thought hard and impenetrable, and indivisible and final and—lifeless—lifeless, is really a reservoir of immense energy . . . ," Wells wrote in his 1914 book, *The World Set Free*. This lesser-known title by the *War of the Worlds* author describes the harnessing of the power of the nucleus: "And these atomic bombs which science burst upon the world that night were strange even to the men who used them."

Wells wrote this long before the neutron was discovered, let alone fission, and his work began to popularize the phrase "atomic bombs" before those devices ever took form beyond the author's pages. But years earlier, people in the mountains claim another prophet lay on the ground, overcome with visions of a project that would bring the snaring of the sun to the hills of Tennessee.

They say a prophet foretold it.

A general oversaw it.

And a team of the world's greatest scientific minds was tasked with making it all come together.

But it was the others, the great and often unseen, who made the visions of the Prophet and the plans of the General and the theories of the scientists a reality. Tens of thousands of individuals—some still reeling from the Depression, others gripped by anxiety and fear as loved ones fought overseas in the most devastating war any of them had known—worked around the clock on this project, the details of which were not explained. For the young adventurers, male and female, who traveled to Oak Ridge, Tennessee, during World War II, doing their part meant living and working in a secret city, a place created from the ground up for one reason and one reason only—to enrich uranium for the world's first atomic bomb used in combat.

Roots have always run deep here. They were dug up and scattered when the strangers with the project came to the foothills of the Cumberlands, but the newcomers, too, could not resist the pull of the earth and dug their own roots down deep into the Tennessee clay, soaked by mountain rain and baked by a thousand suns. Permanent. Enduring.

Many of these workers on this secret project hidden in the hills were young women who had left home to fight the war in their own way. They left farms for factories willingly, wrote letters hopefully, waited patiently and worked tirelessly.

A number of these women—and men—still live in Oak Ridge, Tennessee, today. I have had the fascinating and humbling privilege of meeting them, interviewing them, laughing and crying with them and hearing firsthand their tales of life in a secret city while working on a project whose objective was largely kept from them. Over the years they have graciously given me their time and suffered through repeated questions and what must have seemed like insane requests to recall moments from their day-to-day activities roughly 70 years ago. They did so happily and enthusiastically and never, ever with even the slightest bit of bravado. That is not their style. I did not only learn about life on the Manhattan Project. I also found myself taken aback by their sense of adventure and independence, their humility, and their dedication to the preservation of history. I wish I could include each and every one of them in these pages, but I cannot. I hope those who find themselves only in the acknowledgments will accept my thanks in place of my prose. I feel exceptionally lucky to know those who continue to live on, and miss those who have passed since I began working on this book.

Without them, this sun-snaring—this Manhattan Project—would not have achieved its objectives, and because of them a new age was born that would change the world forever.

These are some of their stories.

—Denise Kiernan,
summer 2012

Principal Cast of Characters

PEOPLE
(THE WOMEN, IN ORDER OF APPEARANCE)

Celia Szapka

A secretary transferred from the Manhattan Project's original offices in New York City, Celia grew up in the coal-mining town of Shenandoah, Pennsylvania.

Toni Peters

A secretary from neighboring Clinton, Tennessee, Toni heard about the Project from its beginnings, when the government seized her aunt and uncle's farm to make way for the secretive town.

Jane Greer

A statistician-mathematician from Paris, Tennessee, Jane oversaw a team of young women who crunched numbers around the clock to track the production rates of the Y-12 plant.

Kattie Strickland

A janitorial services worker from Auburn, Alabama, Kattie came to Oak Ridge with her husband to work at K-25.

Virginia Spivey

A chemist from Louisburg, North Carolina, Virginia came to Oak Ridge after graduating from the University of North Carolina. She worked in the chemical department of Y-12 analyzing product.

Colleen Rowan

A leak pipe inspector at the K-25 plant, Colleen left Nashville, Tennessee, for Oak Ridge, along with more than 10 members of her extended family.

Dorothy Jones

A calutron cubicle operator from Hornbeak, Tennessee, Dot was recruited right out of high school.

Helen Hall

A calutron cubicle operator and sports fanatic from Eagleville, Tennessee, Helen was recruited from the small coffee shop and pharmacy where she worked.

Rosemary Maiers

A nurse from Holy Cross, Iowa, Rosemary came to Oak Ridge to help open the very first clinic.

OTHER WOMEN OF NOTE

Vi Warren

A columnist for the *Oak Ridge Journal* and wife of the Project medical chief, Stafford Warren.

Ida Noddack

German geochemist who suggested the possibility of fission years before its discovery.

Lise Meitner

Austrian physicist who escaped Nazi Germany and was part of the team that discovered fission.

Leona Woods

American physicist who worked on the first-ever sustained nuclear reaction.

Mrs. H. K. Ferguson

Representing the H. K. Ferguson Company, principal contractor for the S-50 plant. Her real name shall be revealed. . . .

Joan Hinton

American physicist who worked with Enrico Fermi's team at Los Alamos, New Mexico.

Elizabeth Graves

American physicist who worked on the neutron reflector that surrounded the core of the Gadget.

PEOPLE (THE OTHERS)

The General

General Leslie Groves, head of the Manhattan Project.

The Scientist

Robert Oppenheimer, laboratory director of the Manhattan Project at Los Alamos. "Coordinator of Rapid Rupture."

The District Engineer, or The Engineer

Col. Kenneth Nichols, administrative head of the Manhattan Project.

The Secretary

Secretary of War Henry Stimson.

The Photographer

James Edward "Ed" Westcott, official photographer for Clinton Engineer Works (CEW) during World War II.

Eric Clarke

Chief psychiatrist for the Manhattan Project at Oak Ridge.

Ebb Cade

A construction worker at K-25.

Stafford Warren

Chief of the medical section of the Manhattan Project.

Enrico Fermi

Also known as Henry Farmer and the Italian Navigator. Italian physicist and head of the physics group at the Chicago Metallurgical Laboratory; assistant laboratory director at Los Alamos.

Ernest Lawrence

Also known as Ernest Lawson. American physicist who developed cyclotrons and calutrons for the electromagnetic separation process. Head of the Berkeley Radiation Laboratory for the Manhattan Project.

Niels Bohr

Also known as Nicholas Baker. Danish physicist who contributed to the modern understanding of the structure of the atom and to the field of quantum mechanics.

Arthur Compton

Also known as Arthur Holly or Holly Compton or Comus. American physicist and head of the Chicago Metallurgical Laboratory.

PLACES

Oak Ridge, Tennessee

Also known as Site X, Kingston Demolition Range, Clinton Engineer Works, and the Reservation. The designation "Clinton Engineer Works" referred to the entirety of Site X in Tennessee, while "Oak Ridge" referred more specifically to the "Townsite" and other residential, nonplant areas of the site.

Y-12

The electromagnetic separation plant at Oak Ridge, home of the calutrons.

K-25

The gaseous diffusion plant at Oak Ridge and, for a time, the largest building under one roof in the world.

X-10

The pilot reactor at Oak Ridge for producing plutonium upon which the reactors at Hanford, Washington, were based.

S-50

The liquid thermal diffusion plant at Oak Ridge.

Los Alamos, New Mexico

Also known as Site Y or the Hill. Manhattan Project site where the Gadget was designed.

The Chicago Metallurgical Lab, University of Chicago, IL

Also known as the Met Lab, site of Chicago Pile-1 and the first ever sustained nuclear reaction.

Hanford, Washington

Also known as Site W. Site of the Project's full-scale plutonium production facility.

THINGS

The Gadget

The atomic bomb, both implosion and gun models. "It."

Tubealloy (Tuballoy, Tube-Alloy)

Uranium. Sometimes referred to as "alloy" or "Product" in its enriched form, which was used as fuel for the atomic bomb.

49

Plutonium. Element 94. Also referred to as "Product" or "material" in the context of fuel for the atomic bomb.

The Project

The Manhattan Project. More formally known as the Manhattan Engineer District (MED). The MED originally referred to the geographical designation of the Project's initial headquarters in New York City but came to include all Manhattan Project sites.

Author's note: The information in this book is compartmentalized, as was much of life and work during the Manhattan Project.

CLINTON ENGINEER WORKS
Tennessee
1943 - 1945

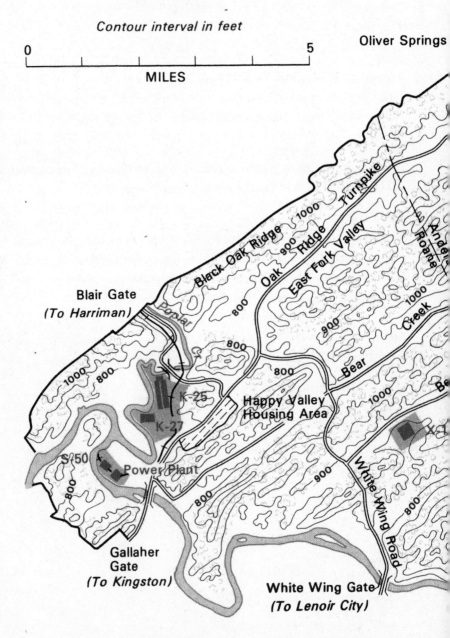

Contour interval in feet

0 |___|___|___|___|___| 5

MILES

Oliver Springs

Blair Gate
(To Harriman)

Black Oak Ridge

1000

Oak Ridge

Turnpike

900

East Fork Valley

Anderson
Roane

1000

Poplar

Creek

800

800

800

800

1000

Bear

K-25

Happy Valley
Housing Area

Be

K-27

1000

S-50

X-1

800

Power Plant

800

White Wing Road

800

800

Gallaher
Gate
(To Kingston)

White Wing Gate
(To Lenoir City)

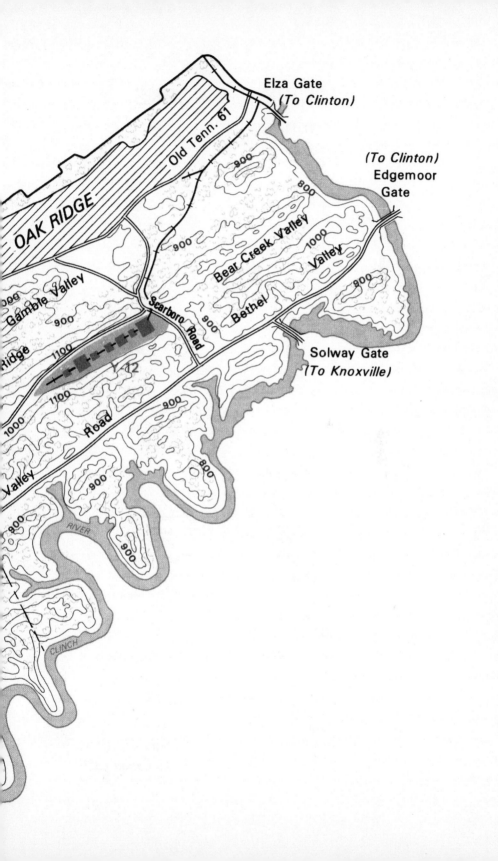

Elza Gate
(To Clinton)

(To Clinton)
Edgemoor
Gate

OAK RIDGE

Old Tenn. 61

900

800

900

1000

Bear Creek Valley

Valley

Bethel

900

Gamble Valley

900

Scarboro Road

900

Solway Gate
(To Knoxville)

Ridge

1100

Y-12

1100

1000

900

Road

900

800

Valley

900

900

RIVER

900

CLINCH

The GIRLS *of* ATOMIC CITY

Revelation, August 1945

That morning, the excitement coursing throughout the complex known as the Castle was infectious. The words no one was supposed to speak, the words many had not even known existed, ricocheted off walls and flew freely from the mouths of even the least informed inhabitants of Site X.

Toni was beside herself. How could she not be? Phones rang, women gabbed uncontrollably, giving not a thought to what they were allowed to say, and no one tried to stop them. The merest details gleaned from newspapers, the radio, or flapping gums were making their way down the halls, into corner offices and throughout the secretarial pool. Slowly the entire Reservation was igniting, ripples of information expanding outward via word and wire. For every voice that uttered the News, at least two more spread it from there forward, faster this time, exponentially increasing the radius of those in the know.

Rosemary was glued to the radio, packed into her boss's office with the others who had abandoned their stations. Colleen and Kattie were at work, too, miles away in the cavernous factory whose purpose was now all too clear. Jane heard such a ruckus outside her office that she threw open the window, waiting for the did-you-hear-don't-you-know shouts to waft up from below. Virginia and Helen had taken long-planned vacations, but the news managed to reach them, too, hundreds of miles away. And Celia and Dot were at home; they were, after all, housewives now. A lot had changed in two years.

Did Chuck already know? Toni wondered.

She had always assumed he would know before her, but no matter. She *did* know and there was no doubt about it. She needed to hear what he thought. Everything would change now.

Wouldn't it?

But when Chuck answered the phone and Toni blurted out the truth, she heard nothing in response.

"Chuck! Chuck! Did you hear me?!"

All she heard was a click at the other end of the line.

Chuck had hung up on her without speaking a word.

She wasn't supposed to know.

Was she?

She had spent years not knowing, wondering, sometimes guessing, and then giving up. She had accepted the need and duty to *not* know, and now this. Today, for no apparent reason, without any warning and out of the sweltering summer blue, came the Secret. Toni had spoken the word that, until this day, was not to be spoken. A word to change the world.

Either she was right, or she was in big trouble.

CHAPTER 1

★ ★ ★ ★ ★

Everything Will Be Taken Care Of

Train to Nowhere, August 1943

Southbound trains pierced the early morning humidity. The iron and steel of progress cut through the waking landscape.

Celia sat in her berth, the delicate folds of her brand-new dress draping over her knees as she gazed out the window of the train. Southbound. That much she knew, and that she had a sleeping berth because it was going to take a while to get to her destination. Towns and stations simmering in the August heat rippled past her view. Buildings and farms bubbled up above the horizon as the train sped by. Still, nothing she saw through the streaked glass answered the most pressing question in her mind: *Where was she going?*

Already many hours long, Celia's trip felt more endless because her final stop remained a mystery. She had no way to measure the distance left to travel or to let her subconscious noodle over what portion of the trip had already elapsed. There was only the expanding landscape and the company of a small group of women, previously unknown to her, but with whom she was now sharing this secrecy-soaked adventure. Celia had quite willingly embarked on a journey without first obtaining much tangible information. So she sat, waiting to arrive at the unknown.

A wavy-haired 24-year-old, Celia was always up for a change of scenery, and this trip was not her first. Her hair was a deep brown, not quite as black as the coal ash that coated life in the Pennsylvania town that she had left behind: Shenandoah. It was a town about 100 miles and roughly the equivalent in light-years from Philadelphia, and which writer George Ross Leighton referred to as "a memorial to the age of rampant industry." He described her "once-prosperous" hometown as one that was, in many ways, reminiscent of so many other American towns: past its prime, fighting to survive, and abandoned by the business that had spawned its heyday, a business that kept the lion's share of profits far from the reach of the rock-shredded, blackened hands that had built it. It was already a region in decline, even back in 1939. But that mining town had given Polish families like hers—and Czechs, Russians, Slovaks—work. Sometimes it was steady, most times not, but it was a chance at a decent living.

Land of anthracite! Celia's hometown was like many mining towns in the east, its lifeblood linked to the precious rock buried down deep in the surrounding hills and valleys; a high-carbon, low-impurity, more lustrous incarnation of mineral coal. Locked in the bonds that held it together was energy itself. It could be released in dreamy blue flame and bestow its power on its liberators. But soon the allure and sheen of coal had given way to grime and neglect, much as the banking room of the Shenandoah Trust, a victim of the Great Depression that was still fresh in folks' minds, had given way to Stief's Cut Rate Drug and Quick Lunch. Rather than thriving, the town was choking. Rusted smokestacks punctuated the now-polluted horizon, redbrick edifices had surrendered their vibrancy to the soot of an overworked earth, all dingy reminders of an industry that once ran rampant and now hobbled on its last legs.

That was behind her now. Every passing moment separated Celia from what could have been an ash-covered existence as the wife of another miner. She had never wanted that future but only recently realized that it was not carved in stone. As for her new employment and soon-to-be home, "secret" was the operative word. It was repeated frequently, and rendered the most innocuous of questions audaciously nosy. When Celia had asked the obvious—*Where am I going? What will I be doing?*—the answer was that she was not allowed to know any more than she had already been told. She would be given only the information that she needed to get where she was going. Asking questions was frowned upon.

She had gotten a taste of this "don't ask" world of work during the short time she had spent working as a secretary for the Project in New York City. Secrets were secret for a reason. She had to believe that. If there was a need for her to know something critical, she would be told when the time was right. Whatever "it" was, it must have been very important. That said, hopping a train with her one, simple suitcase in hand had felt more than a little odd. Would she know her stop? Would something jump out at her from the landscape, some detail of its appearance crying out to her, "Yes, Celia Szapka! This is it!" Then again, she had never ventured south and she was now southbound. That much she knew.

Everything will be taken care of . . .

Celia had chosen to trust her boss, and so far what little he told her had proven true. The limo had picked her up the morning before from her sister's home in Paterson, New Jersey. She sat alone in the car and the driver made no other stops as the car motored south through the industrial heart of the Garden State before arriving at the train station in Newark. There she boarded the train, situated her scant belongings in her prearranged berth, and waited to depart. Once at the station, she had been joined by other young women, most seeming to be about her age, and none of them any more informed than she was. Celia was somewhat relieved to know that she was not the only one being kept in the dark. She and all the other young (and she assumed single) women sitting around her were heading in the same direction. They were All in the Same Boat.

Neither Celia nor any of the other girls sitting on the train would complain about the secrecy. Complaining was not in fashion in 1943, not with so many sacrifices being made thousands of miles away, across oceans she had never seen. So much loss of life and family. How could she or anyone else heading to a good, safe job complain? The war permeated every aspect of existence, from sugar, gas, and meat rations to scrap metal drives and the draft. Businesses across the country were abandoning the manufacturing of their usual wares—from kitchen appliances to nylons—in order to churn out everything from tires and tanks to ammunition and airplanes.

Details of battles and news of troop movements did little to shorten the excruciating lapses in time between letters arriving from abroad, or to relieve the sadness for losses suffered by friends, which were sometimes followed by a twinge of guilt-laden relief when news of the dead had spared your home yet again. Small flags of remembrance, a star for each loved one, marked the homes of those affected by the war. So many stars hung in so many windows, stitched carefully by nervous mothers, sisters, and sweethearts. No matter the town, a walk down any residential street was sure to turn up blue-star banners waving alone in living-room windows, requesting silently to passersby to pray for the safe return of the brother, father, or husband that each five-pointed fabric memorial signified. And every Blue Star Mother lived in fear that her star's color might one day change, might be rendered gold by an unwanted telegram or a knock at the door, that what once hung as a sign of support and concern would be transformed into a symbol of mourning.

Everyone's patience and nerves were being tested, and Celia's were no exception. Certainly the Szapka family had endured their share of difficulties. Despite it all—the tight money, her father's long hours in the coal mines, the ceaseless work at home—they persevered. Complaining would not help secure the safe return of her brothers Al and Clem. It wouldn't make her father's work any more steady or do anything to clear his persistent cough, which seemed to be getting worse with each labored breath.

In summer, the mines had no work for her pa. The proud Pole, never one to take a handout no matter how tough things got, refused to go on the dole. So with little money to feed their kids, Celia's parents packed Celia and her three brothers and two sisters—when they were all at home—off to their grandmother's house in New Jersey. Memories of those summer visits to Grandma were not filled with hopscotch, swimming, or cookie-baking. Celia was put to work, cleaning and scrubbing floors. Her grandparents looked after her and her siblings, making life a little easier on her parents until the mines opened back up and it was time for the kids to go back to school. But there would be no mining work for her brothers. Her parents never wanted that for their sons. They were all gone now: Al to the Philippines and Clem off to Italy. And Ed, lovely Ed, her oldest brother and her favorite, was in the tiny town of Vernon, Texas, the only place he could get his own Catholic parish.

And this was how Celia was doing her part. She quickly learned that all the women on the train had been told that their new jobs served one purpose only: to bring a speedy and victorious end to the war. That was enough for her.

★   ★   ★

It had taken several years to break the bonds with Shenandoah and her mother. The year Celia had graduated high school, her mother sent her to New Jersey—"that's where the jobs are"—to live with her older sister in Paterson. But that was about as far as Mother wanted Celia to travel. Celia got a job making three dollars a week as a secretary and hated every minute of it. She wanted badly to attend college, but there was no money. Her parents believed her younger sister, Kathy, needed the leg up more than Celia did. At three dollars a week, Celia knew she wasn't going to be able to set money aside for college anytime soon. That prospect looked no more promising in Paterson than it had back in Shenandoah.

Then a new opportunity presented itself. Celia's cousin told her about the civil service. There would be classes, he explained, and then a test. Jobs could be anywhere, he said. Sometimes the government sent you overseas to places like Europe. *Europe.* The possibility alone was enough to get Celia to class. *Besides,* she thought, *what's the harm in taking a test?*

Sure enough, within three weeks the first offer came through: to work for a reconstruction finance company. Celia wasn't exactly sure what that was, but it didn't matter: Mother forbade it.

You're not going away. You're too young. We need you close to home . . . Her mother spouted a litany of reasons why Celia should not be allowed to explore the best opportunity that had ever come her way. Celia's older sister was married. Her younger sister was going to go to college. Celia was stuck in the middle, the grip of the Keystone State unrelenting, suffocating. At her mother's insistence, Celia declined the offer. Then another job offer arrived, this one with the State Department in Washington, DC.

This time when the letter landed in Celia's lap, Celia's recently ordained brother was home visiting from Texas. How she'd missed him. Seven years her senior, Ed had moved away when Celia was still in elementary school. She'd cried for days. Maybe you're not supposed to have favorites, but Celia didn't care. Ed was hers. Mama had always said the pair were cut from the same cloth. Ed saw Celia's eyes light up when she received the State Department letter and her face begin to fall when Mama started to protest about Washington being too far afield. Celia had gotten over not being able to go to college, she'd gotten over saying no to the last job offer, she thought she'd get over this, too.

But Father Ed wasn't standing for it. And tough-but-loving Mary Szapka was no match for a priest on a mission. The discussion was heated but short, and it was decided: Celia was going to Washington to take that job, Ed said. "And I'm taking her."

Washington had been a spectacular experience, one that had reshaped Celia's ideas about her own future. She adored living in the boardinghouse on E Street, having roommates her own age, working for the State Department. And the salary! By the time she left DC she was earning $1,440 a year! She never thought she'd ever see numbers so big on a paycheck that had her name on it, let alone at 22 years old. She shared a bedroom in a boardinghouse with five other girls and each day made her way down the grand sidewalks of the nation's capital to work. There, the office she shared with the other secretaries had a small balcony with its own view of the White House Rose Garden. Celia would walk out there on her breaks, and on a few lucky occasions, she and the other young women spied President Roosevelt down below, as he slowly made his way around the manicured grounds. The girls would wave excitedly. Once he even waved back. The President of the United States. Imagine that.

Those years in Washington had loosened Celia's ties to home, but her mother kept on tugging. When her boss, Ambassador Joseph Grew, wanted Celia to transfer to Australia—a big vote of confidence in Celia's abilities—that tug turned into a yank. But Celia couldn't return home. Not anymore. She'd seen too much, done too much, earned too much. Any future in Shenandoah seemed dismal, certainly devoid of any intrigue. There had to be a better way to pacify her mother and not abandon everything she had already built for herself. She had to see about getting a job *closer* to home—just not *at* home.

New York City. When Celia's transfer came through all she knew about her job was that it was for the war effort, it was *not* in Shenandoah, and her mother couldn't complain that it was in Australia. She was living back in New Jersey again, but this time it was different. She was a real working woman now, joining the hordes of other Jerseyites who took the train every day across the Hudson and into Penn Station.

Celia adored Manhattan—the noise and grime and glitz and crowds. Her walk from the train to her office was filled with shops and people and a constant buzz that sustained her every step. Sometimes after work, she walked along Fifth Avenue, or strolled through Times Square. Shenandoah was again a memory.

At first glance, there was nothing particularly noteworthy about the Arthur Levitt State Office Building at 270 Broadway in New York City. Standing across from City Hall Park, it was a large office building in a sea of large office buildings cramming the twisting streets of lower Manhattan. By the time Celia boarded her southbound train in August of 1943, the 18th floor of 270 Broadway had been the home of the North Atlantic Division of the Army Corps of Engineers and the first headquarters of the Project for nearly a year.

The 270 building wasn't the only site on the island that played a role in the Project for which Celia now worked. All across New York City, other pieces were falling into place. The Madison Square Area Engineers Office at 261 Fifth Avenue was charged with securing materials. Research was happening in Pupin Hall at Columbia University. The Baker and Williams Warehouses offered temporary storage for tons of processed material from the Eldorado Mining and Refining Limited company in Canada, material that was the key to the Project. This material was not the kind of ore from Celia's corner of Pennsylvania, but another rock altogether. This ore was called Tubealloy by many in the Project, its real name no longer to be spoken aloud or written down. Tubealloy was the element upon which all the Project's hopes depended, and huge quantities of it were stowed away across New York Harbor, in the Archer Daniels Midland warehouses on nearby Staten Island.

Tubealloy was why Celia's job existed, though she knew no more about it than the average New Yorker bumping and bustling past her on the overrun train platforms. But all across the island, in anonymous buildings and offices, countless people were quietly dedicated to finding, extracting, and purifying the Tubealloy needed for the Gadget.

Celia quickly became accustomed to secrecy in her secretarial post. She signed many papers, offered her fingerprints willingly, and endured not a few lectures about the importance of never discussing anything that she did at work. She could still hear her mother's voice warning her about the dangers of contracts.

"Be sure you read everything you sign! You might sign your life away!" she said.

Celia had responded with the customary "Oh, Mom . . ." But she had, nevertheless, read everything that she had signed. It all seemed natural to her somehow, as though the absence of detail implied the job's importance.

This latest, peculiar transfer had come shortly after Celia had relocated to the Project offices in New York City. Only four months had passed when Celia's boss, Lt. Col. Charles Vanden Bulck, called Celia into his office and asked her if she would be willing to transfer yet again. The offices were relocating, he explained, and he needed to know if she was willing to go along with them.

"Where are we going?" Celia asked.

"I can't tell you."

Celia wasn't quite sure what to make of this and pressed a bit, wanting to know at least what direction she was headed. If it was far, she was going to hear it from her mother.

"It all depends on how far away it's going to be," she tried to explain.

But Vanden Bulck still would not say. All he would tell her was that the move was for an important project and that the destination was top secret.

"Well then, what will I be doing?" she wondered.

Again, no real details. She wasn't quite ready to give up yet. They had to tell her *something*.

Didn't they?

"For how long?" she finally tried. If she were going away again, her mother would at least want to know how long she would be gone. Surely they could tell her that much.

"Probably about six months, maybe nine," was the answer.

There it was, her official offer: some kind of new job in some kind of place and probably for about six, maybe nine, months. Perfect. Her mother would love it.

"How am I going to get there?"

"We'll pick you up and you'll go by train. Everything will be taken care of."

Celia signed on.

She would explain to her mother that it was for the war, for Clem, and for Al. Mama couldn't say no to that.

My God, it was a job! A good job, a well-paying job. There were worse fates than a bit of secrecy as far as she was concerned. Other women in other cities were doing what they could, moving into the workforce in record numbers. A cover of the *Saturday Evening Post* in September 1943 would depict a Stars and Stripes–clad woman, marching forward, toting everything from milk, a typewriter and a compass to a watering can, telephone, and monkey wrench. Women's roles in the workforce were expanding exponentially. And with not one but two brothers fighting overseas, Celia felt something that overrode any misgivings: Purpose. Duty. If doing her part meant leaving home for some unknown, godforsaken place, then that's what she would do.

★　　★　　★

Now the tracks stretched out before the train, the distance that separated Celia from her parents was the greatest it had ever been, and was growing still. She had managed to get some sleep during the night as the rickety sway and swivel of the train rocked bodies gently to and fro. She had made some new friends on the journey. But it was past dawn now and she was getting anxious. She was wearing her new dress, the one her sister Kathy had bought for her. The dress was black and white, with a straight skirt—not too long but certainly not too short. It may not have had a designer label, but it was the fashion of the moment. A smart hat sat atop her meticulously groomed locks, and she wore the coveted I. Miller shoes that she had bought for herself near Times Square in honor of this new clandestine assignment. Wherever she was going, she wanted to look her best. "Don't hold her back," Father Ed had said to her parents. She wouldn't be here without him. She had the chance to make something of herself. She wasn't going to waste it.

Soon a slight buzz grew into a full chatter that bounced off the sleepy bodies in the train car. The gaggle of girls began whispering to each other that the train was slowing and that they were all getting off at the next stop. Celia looked out the window and soon the sign hanging above the station platform came into view: Knoxville, Tennessee.

Is this it? she wondered.

Celia gathered her bag and followed the other women as they made their way through the car, down the stairs, and onto the platform. August smacked her unceremoniously in the face, a humid stagnant "hello" greeting her as she exited the train. It was quite an exodus. It appeared to Celia as if everyone had gotten off the train.

A man approached them explaining a car was waiting to take them the rest of the way.

Everything will be taken care of . . .

Celia piled into one of several vehicles parked outside the station, bursting to know their next stop. But it was early still—right around six o'clock in the morning—and the official-looking man who had come to fetch them said they were all going for breakfast.

The downtown buildings loomed high for Knoxville but not so much in Celia's eyes, accustomed as she was to the cloud-grazing rooftops of New York City. The car turned down Gay Street, one of Knoxville's main drags. The streets were starting to awaken. Deliverymen carted what rationed meats and sundries were available to the shops vying for their share, the bark of a newspaper vendor cut through the early morning hum and shuffle of workers heading off for the early shift. The town car slowed and halted at 318 North Gay Street. Celia looked up. Nestled beneath the Watauga Hotel sat the Regas Brothers Cafe.

She exited the car and entered the restaurant, a long, large, open space with soaring ceilings. Booths lined one wall and a long counter anchored the opposite side of the room, its length measured by 18 swivel stools. Six larger tables stretched between them down the middle of the room, draped in starched white tablecloths and flanked by arched, cane back chairs. Men in crisp white shirts, long ivory aprons, smocks, and narrow, black ties hurried across the polished tiled floors. Celia and the other girls sat at the counter pondering the menu.

One menu item puzzled them. Like Celia, most of the women hailed from Pennsylvania, New York, and New Jersey. None had heard of any such thing as "grits." At the Szapka house, it was Polish food three times a day, and that suited Celia just fine. Even when things were tight—and they almost always were—her mother put a good meal on the table. Neighbors who lacked Mary Szapka's baking prowess shared extra butter and flour in exchange for a share of the treats that popped out of the Szapka oven. And whenever Celia's mother sent Celia to the butcher with a dollar—"Get as many potatoes as you can!"—the butcher, who had known Celia her entire life, always threw in a few extra. Potato pancakes, potato pie, potato dumplings. Potatoes.

When Celia heard the word grits, her curiosity was piqued by anything that was not of spudlike origin. A tall black waiter in a long white apron gave the girls a simple and straightforward description: Grits were little white things made from corn. And you put butter on them. *Just like potatoes.* The waiter encouraged Celia to give them a try. The bowl of hot, butter-soaked hulled corn arrived and Celia put a steaming, slippery spoonful in her mouth, enjoying the first taste of her new life.

Once the women had finished their morning meal, they piled back into the limo again. The driver, pleasant enough yet wordless, drove on. Knoxville soon disappeared behind them. The landscape opened wide in every direction, framed by the low rolling hills that marked the timeless tail end of the Smokies. The rising sun of the East crept farther up the backdrop of morning sky behind them.

Though these country roads were far from where Celia had started off in Pennsylvania, their history, too, was being shaped by a burgeoning industry, one also built upon a rock—not as lustrous as anthracite, but one that held tremendous power. This rock, unknown to most Americans, was recasting not only this once-quiet slice of Appalachian farmland but the landscape of warfare forever.

Celia did the only thing that she could: wait.

While she did, other women on other trains kept pulling into the very same station, their routes like veins running down the industrial arm of the East Coast, extending from the heart of the Midwest, the precious lifeblood of a project about which the women knew nothing, all of them coursing toward a place that officially did not exist.

TUBEALLOY

★ ★ ★ ★ ★

THE BOHEMIAN GROVE TO
THE APPALACHIAN HILLS,
SEPTEMBER 1942

"Weaving spiders, come not here."

This has been the motto of the Bohemian Club since 1872, and is emblazoned on the plaque outside its San Francisco headquarters. It was not long before this exclusive, invitation-only, all-male organization, originally founded by journalists, had a waiting list decades long and boasted a membership of US presidents, industry magnates, and cultural tastemakers. However, San Francisco was not the place to be. That honor fell to the Bohemian Grove. About 70 miles north of the city by the bay, on a secluded 2,700-acre parcel nestled deep among towering redwoods, the Bohemian Grove was the club's annual summer encampment, its most enticing and intense gathering. It was here, far from the prying eyes and ears of the uninitiated, that members of the Project had come to meet in September of 1942.

The summer encampment kicked off with the opening ceremony, a ritual known as the Cremation of Care, which featured hooded, torch-bearing men, setting fire to an effigy dubbed "Dull Care," in a ritual described as having Druidic and Masonic overtones—Mardi Gras–style fun to some, creepy to others. The focal point of this fiery fete was the altar of the Great Owl of Bohemia, which stood at the end of the Grove's lake. An imposing, roughly carved wooden owl, symbol of the Bohemian Club, hovered forty feet high atop an altarlike, semicircular stone platform, watchful in its way. The remainder of the two-week, three-weekend encampment had something for everyone: performances, plays, and concerts. Swimming and skeet shooting. Long lunches, lots of liquor, lectures, blazing bonfires, and bonhomie. Nonmembers lucky enough to receive an invitation to the exclusive enclave received written instructions beforehand: no cameras, no recording devices, and so on. Bohemian Grove was—*is*—viewed, by many, as a kind of ritual male bonding deep in the woods, the kind that members believed unattainable in the outside world.

Bohemian Grove attendees were organized into distinct groups of "camps": Hillbillies. Poison Oak. The elite Mandalay. Some camps were known for a particular drink that was always on hand, or a historical artifact that they proudly held in their possession. These groups of men often shared some sort of association, occasionally related to the business they were in. The Pleasant Isle of Aves camp, for example, boasted almost exclusively members that had some sort of association with the University of California at Berkeley.

While the "no women" rule was hard and fast, the "no weaving spiders" directive—no business—was oft flouted. The group of Project associates meeting at the Bohemian Grove not quite a year before Celia and others like her boarded southbound trains for an unnamed station in the long shadow of the Smokies had come to do just that.

It wasn't the first time that Ernest O. Lawrence, the prairie-raised former aluminum salesman and Nobel Prize–winning physicist from Berkeley, had entertained military guests at the Grove Clubhouse overlooking the Russian River. But the stakes were higher now and the group assembled far more influential. Among those gathered were members of the University of California radiation, or "Rad" lab, the director of Standard Oil, Project scientists James Conant and Arthur Compton, and the slight-of-build, large-of-brain J. Robert Oppenheimer, a scientist with a penchant for broad-rimmed hats and Eastern philosophy.

Soon-to-be District Engineer Kenneth Nichols attended—then an Army lieutenant colonel. The bespectacled engineer was emerging as the General's right-hand man and was learning, as best he could, how to manage and maneuver the General's seemingly unreasonable-bordering-on-unrealistic expectations, without which the impossible goals of the Project might not become reality.

He had news for the group gathered among the redwoods: Edgar Sengier, a Belgian businessman, had a tremendous supply of high-quality Tubealloy his company was willing to sell.

Decision made: Buy it. All of it. Secure more if possible. Lock it down.

Also up for discussion among the men was the location of Site X. It appeared that a spot in Tennessee held the winning lottery ticket, but this needed to be finalized.

Decision made: Buy it. Do whatever necessary to secure the land. Prepare to break ground as soon as possible.

Virtually no one in East Tennessee knew their region was even under consideration as part of any groundbreaking wartime venture, including those who would come to inhabit and work at the soon-to-be-built Reservation. Another version of this story, one perhaps steeped more in lore than location, holds that Site X was selected in a back-room deal in Washington, DC. As the story goes, Secretary of War Henry Stimson had approached Tennessee senator Kenneth McKellar, chair of the Senate Appropriations Committee, asking if he might figure out a way to "hide" $2 billion for the funding of a secret war project. The dapper and oft-bow-tied McKellar had served longer in both houses than anyone else in Tennessee history—heck, practically anyone in the United States. McKellar wanted to help, but so much money? McKellar took his concerns directly to President Roosevelt and met with him at the White House. The request was the same: This project could bring a speedy end to the war. So when Roosevelt reiterated, "Can you hide $2 billion for a secret project that we hope will end the war?" Senator McKellar deftly replied, "Well, Mr. President, of course I can. And where in Tennessee do you want me to hide it?"

Regardless of how it happened, more than half of the $2 billion eventually appropriated for the Project would go to Site X, whose primary function would be enriching Tubealloy to serve as fuel for the Gadget that this group gathered at the Bohemian Grove hoped would end the war.

The man at the center of the Project, the General, did not attend the Bohemian Grove meeting but would officially take over the Project mere days later, on September 17, 1942. The bright star of the Army Corps of Engineers, the General had been the mastermind behind the speedy construction of the Pentagon. He was also known to have a personality and management style that strained the bounds of polite discourse much the way his expanding midsection was straining the bounds of the belt on his always perfectly pressed, Army-issue khakis.

Within days of taking the helm of the Project, the General finalized movement on the Tennessee site and dispatched the Engineer to meet with a polite yet somewhat reticent Edgar Sengier at his offices in the Cunard Building at 25 Broadway in New York City.

Did this man have authority to deal? wondered the cool, dapper Belgian with the thinning hair and impeccable styling.

This was not the first visit Sengier had had from a military man curious about his holdings. And this man, though professing to be with the military, was dressed in civilian garb. The meeting was brief and to the point. The Engineer was pleasantly surprised to learn that Sengier's mining company, Union Minière du Haut Katanga, had roughly 1,200 tons of high-grade Tubealloy ore sitting that very moment on Staten Island and much more where that came from: the Belgian Congo. Sengier had left Brussels for New York in 1939, shortly before the Germans invaded Belgium and Hitler's shadow looked as though it might fall on Africa. Sengier moved not only himself but his ore as well to the United States, shipping container after container across the Atlantic to New York. This material, once considered handy for dyeing Fiesta ware, regarded by some as mere garbage, a geological nuisance that got in the way of mining more important materials like silver, now was the sun at the center of the Project's secretive solar system.

Roughly 30 minutes and an eight-sentence scribbling on a yellow legal pad later—with a carbon copy left behind for Sengier's files—the Engineer walked out onto the noisy Manhattan streets carrying a piece of paper that gave the US government access to the richest Tubealloy ore ever tapped on planet Earth, a geological freak of nature, really, boasting nearly 65 percent purity. It was from deep in the mines of Shinkolobwe, a name that means "fruit that scalds."

Within days, the Project arranged for the purchase of Sengier's Staten Island stash and another 3,000 tons still waiting in Africa. The price was $1.60 per pound, of which $1.00 went to Sengier and another $0.60 going to initial processing at Eldorado in Canada. Office buildings, the shipping containers, the storage facilities: All were now hidden in plain sight, shrouded by the asphalt chaos of New York City and its environs, all right under the noses of millions of Americans.

The ore score was a real boon for the Project. The materials were coming together, but the scale was about to expand drastically. A month later, in November 1942, the Project chose Site Y, a spot 35 miles northwest of Santa Fe, New Mexico, for development of the Gadget itself: Los Alamos. The General had heard from his newly appointed Site Y head that his team of scientists in the desert would need much more enriched Tubealloy than they had originally estimated, if they hoped to get the Gadget designed and tested in time—that is, before the Germans figured out how to do it.

The spiders were weaving, Site X and Site Y were secure, and the Project had a line on a supply of Tubealloy and plans for gargantuan plants of never-before-imagined size and scope.

Now all they had to do was find enough bodies to fill them.

CHAPTER 2

★　★　★　★　★

Peaches and Pearls

The Taking of Site X, Fall 1942

In the Hills of Tennessee, where man has harnessed the power
of rivers, there resounds again the roar of tractors and bulldoz-
ers, the thud of hammers, and buzz of saws. This time, however,
American Brain and Brawn is transforming a peaceful tract of
farm land into a thriving modern community. The "old-timers"
at Oak Ridge (those of us who have resided here two weeks or
longer) have already been instilled with a feeling of civic pride in
the rapid strides made in establishing and improving Oak Ridge.

—*Oak Ridge Journal*, September 4, 1943

Toni Peters had no doubt that something big was going on over there
near the Black Oak Ridge, and today she was finally going to find out
just what it was.

Sure as the day is long, she—and everybody else in her hometown
of Clinton, Tennessee—knew that whatever was being built along the
Clinch River was not your run-of-the-mill wartime factory.

No, sir, not with the nonstop comings and goings. This was not
the refurbishing of a cannery to make airplane parts or an assembly
line pumping out shell casings. No one seemed to know what was
going on, not even the people already working there. Lines of packed
train cars snaked through the land and convoys of overloaded trucks
headed into that strange new Reservation. But nothing ever seemed
to come out: no tanks, no munitions, no jeeps. The perpetual rumble
and hum of transport and construction seemed to carry on the wind,

landing in Clinton's ears, teasing those who lived there with its incessant song of mysterious progress.

During the past year, Toni's senior year of high school, work seemed to shift into high gear, and chatter about the war project just 10 miles down the road followed suit. The class of 1943, Toni among them, hoped there might still be jobs available after graduation. The people of Clinton were right next door to something of a size and scale that their little corner of the state had never seen.

Everything's goin' in and nothin's comin' out. . . .

That was the talk around town, from the drugstore to the hosiery factory. That, and talk of jobs. But that was just talk. Today was Toni's birthday. She was going to find out for herself what was going on behind those fences.

Toni's family had learned early on about the new development in their corner of East Tennessee. Aunt Lillie, her mama's sister, had found out firsthand. Whatever the government was building was far too grand to squeeze in between the existing lives and lands already carved into this corner of Southern Appalachia, and Aunt Lillie and Uncle Wiley's peach farm in the community of Wheat was smack dab in the line of bureaucratic wartime fire.

The Army Corps of Engineers had been scouting the land since that past spring. They began surveying in earnest, walking property lines, and trying to make sense of boundaries that had lasted centuries but had never needed to be stated. The Project found the region appealing for a number of reasons. The Southern and the Louisville & Nashville railroads conveniently tracked along the northern reaches of the 83,000 acres that the Project was initially eyeing. The land backed up to an elevated crest called the Black Oak Ridge. The site skirted past the towns of Oliver Springs and Kingston, Harriman, and Clinton. Smaller established communities such as Wheat, Elza, Robertsville, and Scarboro were in an area that offered a lot of land at little cost. It was generally secluded, far enough from the coasts to avoid an easy attack, but easily reached by New York, Washington, and Chicago. The plants would fit snugly into the valleys between the ridges. And the Smokies stood starkly to the east like an ancient wall of secrecy, a towering guard all its own. The mild climate was a fit as well. Plants needed to be constructed at blistering speed, requiring as close to year-round work as possible. Finally, the Norris Dam and the bottled-up energy of the Clinch River could provide a tremendous supply of electricity—the kind that was particularly suited to a colossal military reservation like Site X.

★ ★ ★

Surveyors. They had been East Tennessee's harbingers of doom for at least the last two decades, longer than that if you were Cherokee. At the first sighting of a tripod or transit, alarm bells should have sounded. The last time surveyors had taken to walking the back roads of Anderson and Campbell Counties, back in the early 1930s, the massive Norris Dam soon followed, spanning the Clinch, a tributary of the Tennessee, which had long supplied families near its banks with food and more. Most locals kept a fish gig or two on hand for spearing catfish, but the Clinch had also been known for the freshwater pearls that the mussels it nourished consistently produced. Toni's town of Clinton played a key role in that iridescent industry. Market Street was home to pearl hunters hawking the gems and shells—ideal for buttons. With pearls going for as much as $100 a pop, it was enough to send anyone wading into the nearby waters, grasping hopefully for the molluskan riches.

At 265 feet high and 1,860 feet across, the Norris Dam reshaped the region. The project was a product of Roosevelt's New Deal and the first of its size and kind constructed by the Tennessee Valley Authority. It took three years to build. A new town was established just for the construction workers. The hydroelectric power the dam would supply would change the lives of the people living in and around East Tennessee, bringing jobs in the short run and electricity in the long.

Toni was about nine years old the first time she ever lay eyes on the dam, a favorite family destination. Benjamin Peters, a local printer, loved herding his children into the car to seek out nearby adventure. Sandwiches were packed, and Toni, Rooie, Tincy, Silver Buckles, and Dopey—nicknames only for the Peters children—would sit and gaze at the massive machinery, unearthed clay, and seemingly tamed river, the dam feeling much like a bit on a horse just waiting to bolt. Countless bodies streamed efficiently like fire ants along a freshly poured concrete hill. She could still hear her father's favorite call to arms:

"Honey, get the kids! We're going to that dam site!"

The dam's construction and the resulting flooding called for the relocation of living and dead alike: nearly 3,000 families and 5,000 graves had to be relocated. And for some, the arrival of Norris Dam was not the first time land had been taken from them, with the Great Smoky Mountains National Park having already moved some residents from their ancestors' lands years earlier. And the water, once released from Norris Lake, was much too cool for mussels accustomed to more tepid and shallower waters. They slowly began to die out, taking their pearls with them. Clinch River pearls began to pass into memory, after making it as far as the Paris Exposition of 1900, where they lent a touch of Appalachian glitter to the "City of Light."

But the Smokies and the Norris and the end of the pearling industry were merely setting the stage for this, yet another uprooting of life, another rerouting of history.

Around October of 1942, after surveyors weighed acreage, homes, and outbuildings, reducing lives and livelihoods to a statistical formula, the notifications came. Declarations of Taking. Notices of Condemnation. Requests to Vacate. News came in varying forms, no one any easier to digest than another. Always there was the feeling of being sucker-punched, leaving you breathless, doubled over, gasping for options. In some cases children were sent home from school to deliver the bad news: The government said they had to find a new place to live. Other families came home from work or back from the fields to find the notices tacked up to their doors or trees, stating abruptly that the land belonged to the United States of America and was going to be used to establish something called the Kingston Demolition Range. Other families received the gut-wrenching news via mail or messenger—a knock at the door jarring them from the already taxing daily reality of raising food and children. The name "Kingston Demolition Range" was itself a form of motivation. One woman reported being told that staying in her home would be risky, as they might well be dropping bombs in the area.

The amount of time given to families to vacate their homes ranged widely. The lucky ones got as much as six weeks, maybe more. Others had to be packed up in two or three weeks. Parlee Raby of Oliver Springs received this notice from the Land Acquisition Section of the Corps of Engineers for the Kingston Demolition Range, dated November 11, 1942:

The War Department intends to take possession of your farm December 1, 1942. It will be necessary for you to move, not later than that date.

In order to pay you quickly, the money for your property will be placed into the United States Court at Knoxville, Tennessee.

The Court will permit you to withdraw a substantial part of this money without waiting. This may be done without imparing [sic] your right to contest the value fixed on your property by the War Department.

It is expected that your money will be put in court within ten days, and as soon as you are notified, it is suggested you get in touch with the United States Attorney to find how much can be drawn.

Your fullest co-operation will be a material aid to the War Effort.

Very truly yours,

Fred Morgan

Project Manager

After the notifications came the negotiators from the Corps of Engineers Land Acquisition Section, who set property prices based on the earlier assessments. Reimbursements were hardly fair from a strict land-value point of view, even less so if stress and strain were taken into consideration. The shock and loss of individual homes was difficult enough, especially for residents getting on in years, but this was the loss of schools, churches, family farms, shops, and long-traveled stretches of familiar road. The Taking encompassed large tracts of land and small farms, ramshackle hovels, and expansive homesteads, hills with memories, crops, and orchards. A man named Van Gilder lost 1,000 acres. The Brummitt family was promised $900 for 40 acres and did not receive all of it. The Irwin family was offered $10,500 for their Gamble Valley farm, which included a large antebellum home, a five-room framed house, two tenant houses, barns, outbuildings, crops, and equipment. The amount offered could not buy *half* of what was "bought" from them. Entire communities and the ways of life that infused them were to be wiped away in a matter of weeks. For some residents of East Tennessee, this was the *third* time they were evicted from their lands—both the Great Smoky Mountains National Park and Norris Dam having already claimed their share years earlier.

To estimate those displaced, the number of parcels was multiplied by average family size, give or take a few. There were in the neighborhood of 800 parcels, putting the estimation at around 1,000 families and 3,000 people.

But the real number of the displaced may have been much higher. Tenant farmers and sharecroppers living in outbuildings and on the lands of others didn't figure prominently into the calculations, making it harder to estimate the true number of displaced residents. They were to be as overlooked and undervalued as the land itself and the history that infused it for centuries.

The majority of evicted families accepted the terms offered them on the spot. Officials had strongly suggested that each additional day that they held out reduced the chance that they would see any money at all. There were those who protested and organized meetings, and some even saw the amounts paid them by the government increased a bit. But they had to move all the same.

It was not that they didn't support the war effort. These were patriotic people, some of whom could trace their families back to the founding of the United States, whose ancestors had fought in the American Revolution. Some were Scots-Irish and Dutch who had made their way south seeking better climate and more arable lands. They had survived the Great Depression. Maybe just barely, but they had survived it. War was a time of sacrifice for all. But their country was asking more of them than just some rusty coffeepots for a scrap-metal drive. It was asking for their homes, their lands, and their livelihoods. It wasn't just the structures, but the sum of all the work, love, and life they'd known. They would have to hand over secret hiding places passed down among children, onetime saplings that now towered over their homes, dozens of cemeteries in churches and backyards commemorating lives past, children lost to fever, men lost to other wars in other times.

It was even harder for those who had, from a strictly monetary point of view, "less" to lose. Many had no cars or trucks to move what meager possessions they had. Some owned one pair of shoes, others none at all. The government offered no money to move, and if residents used the money they were going to receive for their homes, what would they live off? How could they eat? This wasn't industrial-scale big tobacco or cotton farming. This was subsistence, put-food-on-the-table farming. These people weren't asking for anything much; they only wanted to feed their kids, work their land, and then one day be buried beneath it alongside their spouses, parents, and grandparents.

As the Taking continued through the end of 1942 and into 1943, the 83,000 acres that the Land Acquisition Section had originally scouted for Site X was, in the end, closer to 56,000 acres or about 92 square miles, stretching roughly 17 miles long and averaging 7 miles wide. That number would eventually swell to approximately 59,000 acres, growing out of the Cumberland Foothills, punctuated by ridges like the Pine and the Chestnut. The Site was cradled on three sides by the Clinch River. Roughly 180 structures were spared, and were put to various uses before, during, and after the completion of Site X, from housing to storage.

Toni's aunt Lillie and uncle Wiley lost their home and peach orchard. Nearby Roane County had been the peach capital of the United States in the 1920s and into the '30s, until severe cold destroyed the crops almost irreparably. But that little peach orchard meant something deep and real to Toni and her entire extended family beyond property and income. The orchard meant summer to

Toni—the smell, the taste, the fuzzy, sticky feel of high summer. It meant standing alongside her brothers and sisters, a roadside crew, helping Aunt Lillie and Uncle Wiley pick the juicy golden fruits. You wanted to get them just right. You couldn't pick them too late and too soft, because you wanted them to last, to keep their shape and flavor in the heat of the sun and to stay perky and firm enough for pie. But you didn't want to pick them too soon and too hard, either. You had to let the sugars develop, let the flesh of the fruit yield just enough to unleash a syrupy-sweet-tangy trickle from the first juicy bite, sending the success of a season's worth of sun and rain flowing down your chin.

The gang of Peters children would pluck them, eat them, can them, and often sell them. After picking, Toni and Dopey would sort the peaches according to quality and line the sorted bushels along a small stretch of Clinton Highway. Their handmade sign advertised their offerings: one dollar a bushel for "good" peaches, 75 cents a bushel for "not quite as nice," 50 cents for "poor" peaches, and finally, at the bottom of the bushel, downright "bad" peaches offered to passersby for 25 cents a bushel. But even the bad ones were still worth snagging; they were fine for a batch of peach butter. Those summer morning breakfasts were filled with sliced peaches soaking in sugar and milk.

These sweltering ambrosial mornings were a gift offered up freely by a land that had long responded in fruit and grain to the care Aunt Lillie and Uncle Wiley gave. But no more. Toni's aunt Lillie and uncle Wiley moved to a nearby farm to stay with relatives and figure things out. They were lucky to have their people nearby. For Toni, the peachy days of high summer were gone.

★　　★　　★

They say the Prophet had seen it coming.

A popular story goes that an old man of the mountains by the name of John Hendrix had had visions before, but this one was bigger, more elaborate. He was around 50 at the time and had come from the woods near his home in the vicinity of Scarboro and Robertsville, where he had slept forty nights on the forest floor—as a voice had instructed him to do. When he finally emerged from the woods, he shared his vision with anyone who would listen.

"Bear Creek Valley some day will be filled with great buildings and factories and they will help toward winning the greatest war that ever will be," he said to those gathered at the local store, where he often shared his visions. Most just humored him. This one was so rich in detail, though. The life-worn man of the earth went on to talk of a city built on Black Oak Ridge, of railroad spurs, and of countless people and machines.

"I've seen it," he said. "It's coming . . ."

John Hendrix died in 1903. Now almost 40 years later, few had seen it coming.

Construction began on Site X in late 1942, the detritus of rapidly uprooted lives still scattered over the ground, reminders of what was. Fences of abandoned farms lay tangled and splintered; cattle roamed free, disoriented. Construction workers and scavengers made their way through vacated lands, finding books, photos, shoes, pans, tools, and more lying abandoned in the dust. Sacrificed memories, casualties of the war.

Prices on *available* land—now a scarcer and more valuable commodity—took off for the rafters, inflating beyond most folks' fiscal grasp. The evicted had to compete with new workers arriving to the area in droves, drawn from other regions in the South by news of upcoming construction jobs at this big, new site. So many locals soon found themselves applying for work at the project that had evicted them in the first place. Reduced to renters and wage earners, these displaced people would work at Site X, on lands they once held as their own.

In August 1943, long after construction had begun and as people like Celia began making their way to the Reservation, a House Military Affairs subcommittee held an open investigative committee to address ongoing complaints of the dispossessed who felt they were not fairly compensated for their property. Congressman John Jennings Jr. was in attendance as locals stated their cases, often loudly, their dusty faces streaked with tears. But there was little to be done.

The governor himself, Prentice Cooper, was not informed about the Project until 1943, after land had been acquired, razed, and reshaped for what was to come.

By fall of 1943, three plants, code-named Y-12, X-10, and K-25, were under way and thousands of construction workers were laying foundations and erecting colossal structures at what was *now* called the Clinton Engineer Works. Toni's family had been lucky, all things considered. Tinier communities had been all but erased from the landscape. Downtown Clinton remained intact. No one had taken Toni's home. Kids were still playing Red Rover, joyriding in borrowed cars, and sneaking around for a puff or two of some rabbit tobacco. The Five and Ten Cent Store where Toni worked summers making $1.42 a day and spending 25 cents of that on a hamburger at lunch remained a place to enjoy a gossip or a dance in front of the jukebox. Hoskins Drug Store was busier than ever, and the Clinton Theater, where she had delighted in seeing every Laurel and Hardy film she possibly could, was still taking tickets. The pearl hunters might have been gone, but Market Street cut a fine figure through town and was home to whoever had something to sell.

Toni knew there was no money for college, so she never bothered asking. Mama always said once school was finished, it was time for kids to start paying rent. After graduating in spring 1943, Toni had taken the job at a local law office and stayed with her sister Tincy, who had eloped with the love of her life. It was a house of drinking, laughing, smoking, and ceaseless carrying-on. But no matter what kind of nonsense transpired, or what wet roadhouse in their dry county Tincy and the gang returned from, late night carousing always ended in a stop by Toni's room. Toni would wake to the sound of doors and giggles, shadows in the hall, a warm hug from her sister, and a hot Crystal's hamburger in a grease-stained paper bag.

But Toni was ready for something new. Her personality had gotten her as far as her smarts. Her shoulder-length waves framed a face perpetually highlighted by an impish grin. Her father had taught her that excitement could be found just around the bend. *"Man decides to hold his own funeral before he dies . . . ,"* her father once read in the paper.

"Kids! Get in the car!" Off they went to a stranger's "living" wake. Now it was Toni's turn to seek adventure. She was going to join the girls who had gone to look for jobs at that big site down the road.

Toni could not help but be influenced by the new expectations of the young women of the time. This was the era of Rosie the Riveter, when a song by Redd Evans and John Jacob Loeb gave voice to more than one million women who had already joined the workforce, bandanas in their hair, grease on their smocks. Then artist J. Howard Miller, commissioned by Westinghouse to create a series of posters, gave Rosie a face after seeing a photo of Geraldine Hoff, a 17-year-old Lansing, Michigan, cellist-cum-factory worker. Miller's poster caught the eye of artist Norman Rockwell, and his take on the war's working woman graced the cover of the *Saturday Evening Post* on May 29, 1943, forever linking Rosie's name to the image inspired by Geraldine. Clad in denim coveralls, an American flag waving behind her, the woman sits, sandwich in hand, a riveting gun and lunch pail inscribed with "Rosie" in her lap. Goggles and a welder's shield frame her proudly smudged face as a copy of *Mein Kampf* ably props up her tired feet.

Rockwell famously painted the world not as it was but as he would have liked it to be, he said. His was a more comforting vision of a world in conflict, a vision that focused on determination and stick-to-it-iveness, on family and home, even as that home, that way of life, felt threatened.

Rockwell's vision would be echoed more locally in the images of a young, unknown photographer who had been hired to document Site X for the Project from the very beginning of things, as ground broke and fences grew. Twenty-one-year-old James Edward "Ed" Westcott was tall and thin, pressed shirts hanging off his wiry frame. Hair parted deep on one side fell in a slick swoop along his put-you-at-ease face, a camera permanently suspended from his long, thin neck. Given unlimited access, he spent his days prowling every inch of Site X and the lives of the people who were moving there to make it home. His lens captured the grand and seemingly mundane, the towering edifices under construction, the somber and smiling faces of the displaced seeking work. As the Reservation grew and the new-comers settled in, he would portray Site X as the Project envisioned it, and as those who traveled there wanted it to be. He snapped the rising town's pioneering spirit and the expressions of a newfound camaraderie among those for whom family and home were far away. Maybe here life could be the way everyone would like it to be, a view of prosperity and hope, of digging in and smiling down any adversity, a sentiment shared by many who survive the most difficult of times.

Bad peaches can always make peach butter.

Today was Toni's 18th birthday. She was old enough to go and do and be whoever she wanted. She was heading down the road, straight through those armed gates, past that barbed-wire fence and right into that place she had heard so much about. Adventure could be right around the corner.

She was going to that damn Site.

TUBEALLOY

★ ★ ★ ★ ★

IDA AND THE ATOM, 1934

A brilliant 38-year-old German geochemist named Ida Noddack had read Italian physicist Enrico Fermi's paper "Possible Production of Elements of Atomic Number Higher than 92," in *Nature*, with great interest, as had the rest of the international scientific community in 1934.

Ida, however, was not on board with Fermi's conclusions in this case.

Fermi's groundbreaking work was identifying "new radioactive elements produced by neutron bombardment." Neutrons had changed the physics game, and Fermi was doing more than anyone at the time to analyze the impact that these tiny, subatomic particles had on other elements.

An *atom*, the basic unit of existence of the material world, contains a central *nucleus* made up of *protons* and *neutrons*, with *electrons* orbiting around it. Ernest Rutherford first proposed that the atom contained a small, positively charged center orbited by electrons. He later theorized about the existence of neutrons, and was soon proven correct. Protons possess a positive charge, electrons a negative one, and neutrons are the Switzerland of atomic particles: neutral.

The number of protons in an atom determines its *atomic number* and, in a sense, its identity. It also determines where that element lives on the periodic table. The number of *neutrons* present in an atom determines the *isotope* of that element. Some elements have only one isotope, while others have several. Carbon 12 and carbon 14 are two isotopes of that abundant element. Both are still carbon, both have six protons, but they behave differently because they contain differing numbers of neutrons.

The advantage to being neutral on the atomic level is similar to that of being neutral politically: You can enter charged situations more easily.

Neutrons can more easily slip into the positively charged nucleus of another atom than can positively charged particles or protons. And they can do so at slower speeds.

Why encourage neutrons to enter the nucleus of another atom? To see what happens, of course. In 1934, this is precisely what Fermi had been doing in his famed laboratory at the Institute of Physics at the Università di Roma La Sapienza. He and his team, known as *i ragazzi di Via Panisperna,* were bombarding elements all the way up the periodic table with neutrons to see how they behaved.

When a nucleus absorbed another neutron, radiation was often emitted and new isotopes formed. These new isotopes tended to be in the same neighborhood of the periodic table as the element that had been targeted.

But when Fermi got to the largest naturally occurring element on the periodic table, element 92 (later referred to as "Tubealloy" by the Project), things got interesting.

When Fermi bombarded element 92 with neutrons, several different products were observed, but he and his team could not identify all of them. He worked his way down the periodic table from 92, comparing the products of his experiment to the attributes of elements 91, 90, and so on, down to lead, atomic number 82.

No match.

Fermi concluded that the unidentified fragments in the resulting postbombardment mix might have been from a new element, even heavier than element 92: an element with an atomic number of 93 or beyond.

Why did he stop at lead? Ida Noddack wondered.

Ida was a woman with more than just a passing knowledge of the periodic table. She had long studied Mendeleev's organizational chart of known elements and devised her own version in 1925. Head down in her lab, dark hair pulled back in a chignon, she worked alongside and eventually married chemist Walter Noddack, with whom she had discovered element 75, rhenium, named for her homeland, the Rhine Valley. In her opinion, Fermi stopped his comparisons too soon.

She deemed Fermi's work inconclusive, and in late 1934, she published her views on Fermi's findings in an article titled "Über Das Element 93" (On Element 93), in which she proposed an idea that seemed unrealistic to most, preposterous to others.

Ida wrote that while doing this sort of experiment, it could be assumed that "some distinctly new nuclear reactions take place which have not been observed previously . . . When heavy nuclei are bombarded by neutrons, it is conceivable that the nucleus breaks up into several large fragments, which would of course be isotopes of known elements but would not be neighbors."

Fermi and the rest of the physics community disregarded Ida Noddack's take. Her paper was both ignored and on occasion mocked. However, Noddack's proposed, and subsequently dismissed, theory—that the nucleus might actually be able to *split*—was not wrong.

Ida Noddack was simply ahead of her time.

CHAPTER 3

★ ★ ★ ★ ★

Through the Gates

Clinton Engineer Works, Fall 1943

> We were indignant when we had to sneak out of our home com-
> munities without telling our friends where we were going and
> what for. If it was all so important, why not impress the friend by
> giving them the "dope." What was it all about anyway?
>
> —Vi Warren, *Oak Ridge Journal*

Kattie leaned back in the car, exhausted. Not too much farther to
go now. Her brother-in-law Harvey was driving and she and her husband, Willie, sat watching out the window as Alabama eventually
turned into Tennessee. They'd rest once they got to Chattanooga, but
then tomorrow they had to press on. Willie had been away from home
and from Kattie for a while now, but that was all changing.

These were the times for men to be away from home. Kattie knew
that. At least he wasn't off fighting. Willie had done what was best
for the family and now she was traveling more than 300 miles to do
the same, to move to the Clinton Engineer Works, a place she'd never
laid eyes on, a place not on any maps. Good work, good money.

"Ain't here yet," the cashier used to chirp every time Kattie strode
eagerly into the Western Union office in Auburn, Alabama. Kattie
would circle back later, anxious to receive the $50, $70, or sometimes
even $100 that Willie sent home like clockwork.

And he was sending that money right into the hawk's hands. Kattie's grasp on money was fierce. She didn't let go unless she put food
on the table or savings in the bank. When she got to Tennessee she

would be doing the sending, too. Sending money home to those precious babies she was forced to leave behind.

Harvey had gone to Tennessee first, then returned to town with word of a big war site that was hiring at rates they were never going to see in Auburn. It was all right, Harvey had said. And they badly needed workers. So Willie went along with him, and when he finally came back to Alabama for a visit, he told Kattie that she should come with him to Tennessee. There was work for her, too.

Kattie's mama—who'd always liked Willie—had to disagree. Kattie was the only child of her parents' nine boys and girls left at home to help out, though she now had kids of her own. Kattie had been working at the library at the university, dusting every corner, every shelf, then returning home to help her mama and take care of her own four children. But it was hard to argue with this Tennessee money, and finally Kattie's mama gave in. No one would dare raise a word against bringing more dollars home.

She hadn't the faintest idea what to expect from this new place. All Willie had seen was his hut, the construction site, and the cafeteria, so he hadn't much to tell. Hard work didn't scare her, that was sure. She had seen hard. Picking pound after pound of cotton in the afternoon, cooking supper with Mama in the evening, getting up the next day to milk four cows—one cow so feisty she could, as Kattie liked to say, kick the sweetnin' outta ginger cake. (Her brother Commodore had to tie that cow up before Kattie would take one step toward those angry udders.) In her younger days it was then off to school where incorrectly answered math problems meant a heavy-handed smack. When she was a child, she didn't know which was worse, her switch-happy teacher in the one-room schoolhouse or that cow. Both had to be faced every day. *That* was hard. Picking an entire bale of hay alone was hard. Moving constantly from field to field, crop to crop, even as a child, was hard.

Whatever this new place in Tennessee had to dish out, she knew she could handle it. Auburn was moving farther and farther behind her, and along with it the towns and roads she'd known all her life, the fields of corn where she'd learned to husk in a flash, saving the long silky strands of maize to make wigs for dolls who'd long lost their original coifs. Mama. Even that darn cow was miles away now.

But that's not what was making Kattie cry as the car wound its way along the twisting roads of northern Alabama. With every passing mile, she was that much farther away from her babies. Leaving her children behind, children she'd been told were not welcome at this new place, not if your skin was black, anyway. That was hard.

★   ★   ★

Celia stared out of the window of the large town car as it bounced along the unpaved road and stopped at a gate flanked by a barbed-wire fence extending in both directions, vertically accented by observation towers. The car stopped. Armed guards in military uniforms approached. The driver got out of the car, and returned after a quick chat and a flash of some paperwork. The guards waved the car on.

Celia watched as the first glimpses of her new—Should she call it a town? A camp? An outpost?—passed slowly by. Military. That presence was immediately clear. Though Celia had had her share of protocol and security measures in Washington and New York, this was different. The car couldn't have moved much more quickly, even if the driver had wanted it to. The mud made sure of that. Celia had never seen so much in her life. Having grown up in a mining town, she knew from dirt. She had known a life of soot, lustrous or not, settling in, on, and around every nook and cranny and every seam of your dress.

But *this* was like a raw pit of gummy earth. She and the other girls were still tired from the long train ride and intermittent sleep. Breakfast, though welcome, had only served to prolong the mystery. They had all been anxious to see where they were going to be living and working. Right now, gazing out the car window as wet, sticky earth sprayed up from the rain-soaked tires, it did not look good. Their first impressions were clay colored. They weren't arriving as much as sinking into a sopping sea of mud.

Construction went on in every direction. The fences had been some of the first things to go up, and crews repurposed the barbed wire taken from many of the farms and homes that had been moved off the land. Celia couldn't see any sidewalks, only wooden planks laid over the newly excavated ground. There were some houses, virtually identical, sitting side by side and lining the dirt roads. There were larger buildings, mostly white, similar in style and shape, not like the brick and stone and shingle of every other town she'd seen, or the soaring concrete and steel of the city she'd just left. Though the town was brand-new—less than a year old—somehow the mud managed to make everything seem run down. Wherever they were, it didn't look finished. Why on earth would her bosses have decided to move the offices from New York City to . . . to . . . wherever this was? But if Celia wondered about the reason for the move, she never asked. She had worked for the Project long enough to know that much.

She also knew well the futility of asking the driver where they were headed. But then he finally spoke up: "You're going to work first," he said.

He took a turn off the main road, headed up a small incline, and finally came to a stop. Celia looked out the window and across a small expanse of grounds to the building that was going to be her new office. It looked like an H from where she sat, one long, narrow white building with a pitched roofline set perpendicular to a pair of two-story buildings on either side. Celia glanced down either side of the central structure. The complex didn't look completed yet—the land surrounding it still resembled a construction site—but it was. Between the car and the squat white building was nothing but more mud. The sun was a bit higher in the sky now, but had done precious little to dry up the mess.

Celia was collecting herself and her bag when a collective gasp emanated from the other women in the car.

Celia turned. She stared, astonished, as one of the girls stepped out of the car and began sinking, as if in quicksand.

Foot! Ankle! Midcalf . . . ?

The young woman finally managed to extricate herself, but her shoes were certainly ruined, if she could even manage to retrieve them. Celia watched as the next woman bravely exited and tried to avoid a similar plight. No dice. After a few steps she, too, began to lose her footing in the morass of unavoidable muck.

Celia was horrified. Imagine wearing their best clothes and shoes and having them ruined on the first day at a new job! But her pity was soon replaced by concern for her own hard-earned ensemble: The dress her sister had bought her and these precious I. Miller shoes.

There is no way I am stepping out of this car in my new shoes.

She had never in her life had such an expensive pair, and she had bought them herself. She wanted to make a good impression and was not about to sacrifice her footwear to the elements.

The driver waited.

"I can't!" she said. "I paid twenty-three dollars for these shoes!"

Celia sat, adamant, not about to step one foot out of the car. The driver exited the vehicle, marched around to Celia's door, and flung it open. Then he offered Celia the only solution he could think of: He snatched her up and carried her across the muddy expanse, safely depositing her at the door of the administration building.

Relieved, Celia strolled past her travel mates, who were washing their feet and footwear in small sinks that were conveniently located right inside the door. She met briefly with Lieutenant Colonel Vanden Bulck and was introduced to two civilians, Mr. Smitz and Mr. Temps.

She received two distinct identification badges. One was a "Townsite Resident's Pass"; the other was a badge that specifically allowed her entrance into this, the administration building, or "Castle on the Hill," as she'd heard it called. She peered at the badges. Across the top of the resident badge, beneath the date of issue and her ID number, was written in large letters "Clinton Engineer Works." Her age, height, weight, and eye color were listed. The pass stated that she was "a resident of Oak Ridge Tennessee," and was "authorized to enter and leave the reservation only through gates on Highway no. 61 (Clinton, Elza, or Oliver Springs)."

Celia signed her new badge alongside the signature of a "Protective Security Officer." The badge had to be worn and visible at all times. Now, at least, one of her questions was answered: She was a resident of Oak Ridge, part of the Clinton Engineer Works.

A short while later, carrying her suitcase and clutching her oh-so-precious and still unsoiled shoes in hand, Celia carefully made her way out of the Castle and walked barefoot across Tennessee Avenue toward dormitory W-1, the first and currently only women's dorm built in Townsite. Celia wasn't the only woman in the small lobby looking for a place to live, and space was scarce. The housemother mentioned that one woman had a double room she was looking to share. And that's how Celia introduced herself to Maybelle Panser from Wisconsin.

Maybelle led Celia upstairs to the second floor of the two-story building. The room had two single beds, a night table positioned between them. There were two small dressers and a very tiny closet of sorts, in front of which hung a cloth curtain rather than a door. Everything was brand-new. The mattress didn't seem too bad. The room had a single window, and when Celia looked out she could see the Castle. Communal bathrooms were down the hall. Unpacking was a breeze, as Celia had not brought much with her. A few changes of clothes and makeup, of course, but only the basics: some pancake, a little lipstick, her eyebrow pencil, and powdered blush. The I. Miller shoes went straight into the closet, where they would stay.

The housemother was strict, and curfew was 10 PM unless you had permission otherwise or had shift work. Celia thought the cost for the rooms was reasonable. She and Maybelle would each pay $10 a month to share the space. Downstairs in the lobby, everyone had their own mail slot for letters and other messages. She had promised her mother and her brothers that she would write. She had yet to figure out how they were supposed to write her back.

★　　★　　★

After hearing so much about the Clinton Engineer Works, Toni was now seeing it firsthand. The guards with guns checked that she did, in fact, have an interview, and let her pass. The construction, the people—it amazed her that all this activity was right down the road from

Clinton. There was one last pearl to be plucked from the Clinch: The world was her oyster.

Guards directed Toni to the administration building for her interview. The Project was recruiting as heavily as ever, with offices in Knoxville for the different contractors who ran various plants and administrative operations. Toni found it oddly quiet when she entered the Castle, a contrast to the buzz outside. She wondered if she was the only one being interviewed for the job. That would be a stroke of luck. Toni had taken bookkeeping courses and had become, she thought, a darn good typist. At the very least she had to be able to get a job as a secretary. She didn't want a factory job if she could avoid it.

A Mr. LeSieur greeted her with a welcoming smile that put her at ease. But moments later, it became clear that Mr. LeSieur was not going to be interviewing her. Instead, he walked her down the hall and into the office of Mr. Diamond, whom Toni immediately pegged as a big ol' Yankee. Toni had never met one up close before, but she had heard plenty about them. It wasn't unusual for northern buyers to be spotted in Clinton haggling with pearlers on Market Street.

Mr. Diamond had a massive, booming voice and a belly to match. Right off, Toni could tell that there would be no introductory niceties, no how-do-you-dos or where-are-you-froms with Mr. Diamond, that southern sort of conversational two-step that was second nature to her, and only polite.

Mr. Diamond got right down to it.

"Do you take dictation?"

"Yes, sir, I do."

Mr. Diamond shoved a pad at Toni and began to speak.

It wasn't like anything Toni had ever heard before. She leaned forward, every muscle in her body, up to her freshly scrubbed ears, tensed in concentration as she listened so hard she thought she would sprain something. She felt totally lost, like she was riding some sort of syllabic roller coaster, trudging blindly on an endless scavenger hunt in search of the letter R.

Goodness, Lord, what on earth is that man saying? Is he speaking English?

Mr. Diamond finished and looked up at Toni. Toni looked down at her pad. The transcription looked more like an unfinished game of hangman—just about every third word was a gaping blank space. Toni had no choice. She showed Mr. Diamond what she had done.

"No, no, no!" he barked. "Tran-SCRIBE it!"

Toni said nothing, but Mr. Diamond's tone was wearing on her. Though she didn't understand everything he said, his exasperated snarl communicated volumes.

"Well," he continued in a huff. "Can you at least type?"

"Yes, sir," Toni answered. "*And* I can take dictation, too. I couldn't understand a word you said!"

"I didn't understand a word you said, either!"

That was that. Interview over. Mr. Diamond called out to Mr. Le-Sieur: "Come get Miss *Pee-tuhs*!"

Mr. LeSieur escorted Toni out and asked her to sit down and wait for a moment.

I can work for anybody, Toni thought to herself. *I don't have to work for him. There are plenty of jobs.* Maybe, just maybe, she would take a factory job if she had to.

They kept her waiting, and waiting . . .

Heck—enough of this.

Toni got up on her feet and was ready to storm out the door. But Mr. LeSieur appeared suddenly and stopped her.

"Mr. Diamond wants to know if you can start on Monday."

★　　★　　★

DO YOU KNOW . . . That owing to, shall we say, circumstances over which we have no control, the *Journal* cannot print the names of any persons in its columns for the present. This will explain our failure to publish various news items contributed, bowling scores—We are unique—the only newspaper in the country without any news.

—*Oak Ridge Journal*,
October 17, 1943

Jane unfolded the thin, brownish onionskin paper. A telegram. Finally. The Clinton Engineer Works and Tennessee Eastman Corporation had deigned to write to her family's elegant home in Paris,

Tennessee, with instructions. She'd thought the interview with Mr. Powers had gone well, and the offer of work had come the first week of October. But that hadn't been the end of it.

"We are at present making the necessary investigation and on receipt of a satisfactory report from this investigation, you will be immediately notified to report for work."

Investigation? Jane wondered. *What kind of investigation?*

It was all very hush-hush. Daddy had heard from a few of the neighbors that men had come around asking a lot of questions about Jane. They were "Secret Service." That's what everyone in town kept calling them, anyway. That, or FBI.

What kind of girl was this Jane Halliburton Greer? Was she wild? How did she do at school? Did she drink? Really now, tell the truth. And what about that family of hers? Any rotten apples there? High school teachers, college professors, neighbors—everyone, it seemed, got a visit.

Jane didn't know the specifics about the Project, but it was clear that whatever it was she would be doing must be important, or else why all the fuss?

A petite 22-year-old, Jane carried herself with a down-to-earth air, despite her family's long history in Middle Tennessee. She wore her dark brown hair parted on the left, undulating tousles washing past her prominent cheeks, ebbing again at her gymnast's shoulders, before landing with a final bounce at the top of a spine that exhibited the kind of impeccable posture grown out of a lifetime of grooming and horseback riding. Whatever bad things the "FBI men" might have been looking for they apparently didn't find because now, in front of Jane, was the final word. She was to report to work at 204 Empire Building on Market Street in downtown Knoxville. She would work as a statistician, and the pay was good. She would earn $35.00 per week to start, three dollars more a week than General Electric had offered her. She was expected to work 48 hours each week. So factoring in overtime, the total would come to $45.50. Nice.

But it all wasn't about the money. She wanted to work close to home, and this was a good job doing what she had studied to do.

Not what she had *wanted* to do, of course, but what she had ended up doing. Several years earlier, she had decided to become an engineer. And she had worked hard at Judson College in Alabama to take all the right courses that would allow her to study engineering once she'd transferred back home to attend the University of Tennessee. But come registration day, a university official rudely yanked her out of line where she stood waiting to register for the School of Engineering.

"We don't matriculate engineering as a major for females," he told her.

Jane stared, heat rising up through her cheeks, speechless. Angry. Who did he think he was to tell Jane Halliburton Greer what she could or could not do?

"See that man standing over there?" the official said, gesturing to a professor Jane would soon learn was one Dr. Paul Barnett. "He's a statistician. You can study statistics."

And just like that, all her hard work, all the course choices and the studying and the stellar grades she'd earned at the junior college didn't matter. No engineering, no matter what. She was going to study statistics. Jane finished her two years in the Department of Business Administration with a degree in governmental economics, after taking all the statistics courses they had, and some math and physics to boot—the first woman ever to do so at the University of Tennessee. The work had paid off. The job offers that came her way were certainly good ones, and there was some dismay, especially on the part of George Washington University in Washington, DC, as to why she decided to accept a job in the sticks outside Knoxville. GWU had even offered to bring her up to Washington, show her around.

"I find it a little hard . . . to decide exactly upon what basis you have made your decision to accept the offer of the Clinton Engineering Works but I have a feeling that you have decided largely upon the basis that you will be able to stay near to home," the GWU official wrote snippily. "Yet I seem to gather from your letter that the type of work which you will be doing for them is not entirely to your liking, and what you actually would prefer would be to have a project like ours located where the Clinton Engineering Works now stands."

She *did* want to be near home, but not because she didn't want to travel. Not Jane: She had always been ready to pack a bag, see the world. But her father, who had his own transfer and storage business in Paris, Tennessee, was a widower now. It was still hard to believe her mother had already been dead several years. If she had the opportunity to use her degree to help the war and stay nearby home, she was obligated to do that. Obligated to her daddy and to her deceased mother, Hattie Newell.

Once in Knoxville, Jane received her pass—No. 2449—and had plenty of papers to sign, lots of fine print to read. Her agreement stated that she would not "at any time disclose either orally or in writing, or otherwise, to any person except such as shall be designated in writing by the general manager of Tennessee Eastman Corporation, any knowledge or information which I may have acquired while in the employ of Tennessee Eastman Corporation, or elsewhere, or which I may hereafter acquire while in such employ, pertaining to any of said work done directly or indirectly for the United States Government . . ."

Boy, those government folks sure could blather on.

She signed without hesitation, like most everyone else. She took a bus to the Clinton Engineer Works, where an old college friend, Doris, met her. Doris had accepted a similar position and had moved in, expecting to room with Jane. But limited space had already forced Doris to take in someone else. Housing employees were continually shuffling people around, converting single rooms into doubles, improvising in the face of an ever expanding workforce. There wasn't a spot for Jane yet, so she would have to stay temporarily at the Site's one "hotel" of sorts, the Guest House. It was a long, two-story building with two wings that extended out in either direction from a central entrance marked by four large white columns. It was right in the middle of Townsite, near the bus depot and cafeteria.

But when Doris showed up to gather Jane and take her to the Guest House, she wasn't alone. She had brought along the fellow she had been dating, a man named Jim, whom Doris said she had met on the bus. Exiting the car at the Guest House, Jane stepped onto what she believed to be solid ground, only to find herself sinking fast, like so many women before her. Doris and Jim didn't seem at all surprised. Jim helped her get her footing and retrieve her shoe, and Jane watched as he carried her suitcase inside. Jane was still dating someone from back at UT in Knoxville, but couldn't help but notice the polite young man. Up the stairs that handsome man went, where larger guest rooms had been crammed full of Army cots to accommodate Jane and others who were waiting for housing, waiting for training, waiting for the next dorm to be built. But waiting looked like it would be a real pleasure with interesting work, good pay, and a town full of mannerly young men at your beck and call.

★   ★   ★

When news of the big war factory in Tennessee spread as far south as Kattie's home in Auburn, Alabama, it hadn't arrived by word of mouth alone. Recruiters had set off throughout the rural south seeking laborers by the droves. J. A. Jones Construction, responsible for the construction of the gargantuan K-25 plant where Willie worked, hit Georgia, Alabama, Arkansas, and Mississippi for as many workers as they could get their hands on, sometimes bending rules established by the War Manpower Commission (WMC)—one of several acronym-wielding labor bureaucracies that had been established to regulate the recruiting and distribution of the workforce throughout a country desperately in need of war workers. Complaints were filed, one by the WMC stating that a J. A. Jones recruiter, in an act of "labor piracy," had pulled up to a United States Employment Service office in Mobile, Alabama, with a large truck and left with 40 black workers bound for jobs in Tennessee.

In 1942, presidential Executive Order 8802 stated that "there shall be no discrimination in the employment of workers in defense industries or government because of race, creed, color or national origin." The Fair Employment Practices Committee had also been established to address discrimination in wartime industries. But that did not mean an end to segregation in a Jim Crow state like

Tennessee. Though the government had the opportunity to establish the Reservation as a completely desegregated zone, it did not; black residents on the grounds of the Clinton Engineer Works would be primarily laborers, janitors, and domestics, and would live separately, no matter their education or background. This would prevent noted mathematician, physicist, and engineer J. Ernest Wilkins Jr., who was working at the Metallurgical Lab at the University of Chicago, from being transferred to Oak Ridge.

In September 1944, Hungarian physicist Edward Teller wrote Harold Urey, director of war research at Columbia, of Wilkins's abilities and the problem his race would present in a transfer to Site X.

> Mr. Wilkins in Wigner's group at the Metallurgical Laboratory has been doing, according to Wigner, excellent work. He is a colored man and since Wigner's group is moving to "X" it is not possible for him to continue work with that group. I think that it might be a good idea to secure his services for our work.

★　　★　　★

Kattie, Willie, and Harvey entered CEW on the Kingston side, arriving from the southwest, and drove up to the gate. Harvey and Willie knew the drill now. Guards stopped the car and directed the trio up a short road to a processing building where Kattie could retrieve her official working papers. She returned to the gate, showed the guards, and—badge in hand—was now allowed full entrance onto the Reservation.

Harvey and Willie took her next to the Camp Operations Office for the K-25 plant where, Kattie learned, she would begin working as part of the janitorial service. She had never glimpsed anything like K-25 in all her life. The building wasn't even finished yet and it was already the biggest thing she had ever seen. The building was so long that she couldn't even see where it ended, *if* it ended. And the construction workers milling around were still adding to it.

Kattie's new living assignment, on the other hand, was notably smaller: a 16-foot-by-16-foot "hutment," a square plywood box of a structure that had a potbellied stove sitting right smack-dab in the middle, its stovepipe heading out through the low roof. There were no real windows, no glass, only shutters. And she would be sharing the 256-square-foot space with three other women, not with Willie. Despite their marriage license and four children, black couples were not permitted to live as man and wife on the Reservation.

Kattie got to work settling in. She had packed quickly, bringing only one bag and one trunk full of khakis and shirts. It was getting to be that you couldn't tell the women from the men anymore, Kattie thought, what with the way women were dressing when they went to work these days. She had also brought along something for church, just in case. She sure hoped there would be somewhere to go to church. But despite her meager belongings, there was barely enough room in the hutment to store what she had. It was rickety, it was small, but it would do. And it would only cost her $1.50 a week to live there. Here, she would earn better pay than she had ever known. What was left after she covered her basics would go back to Alabama, to her children.

Whatever this place was, she would find a way to make it home.

★   ★   ★

Despite great effort, the Project was facing stiff competition for labor. Men had volunteered to fight, others were drafted. Patriotic duty called for every able-bodied individual left at home to work in war-related industries. Skilled tradesmen such as electricians and plumbers were in such high and constant demand that they were often brought down to Tennessee from cities in the Northeast. But secrecy was a hindrance and advertising a challenge for the Project as it competed with other wartime industries for workers. While other outfits could advertise exactly the type of jobs that were available— *"Build bombers in Tacoma! Munitions plant in Chicago seeks pipe-fitters!"*— the Project had to pull its punches. Job notices were necessarily vague, describing posts in the most basic terms: carpentry, drivers, plumbers. The work was of vital need for the war effort. Full stop. Contractors rarely mentioned the specific location or additional details regarding specific tasks.

There was, however, on-site housing, a free bus system, and for white workers with families, there were even schools. The federal restrictions put in place to prevent employers from snatching workers from other jobs forbade offering better wages, for fear of inflation. But at times the Project did just that, enticing workers with excellent pay, dorms, cafeterias, and low rent. The advertisements could not mention, however, that workers were being hired to help create a device the military hoped would decisively end the war.

There were some perks that the Army could offer that other companies could not, not the least of which was deferment of military service. And as individual contractors like DuPont pulled employees from other locations to come to work at the Clinton Engineer Works, the government was pilfering labor from its own ranks as well, sometimes zeroing in on boys as they were preparing to be shipped overseas, only to suddenly find themselves reassigned to a completely unexpected post.

Formed in May of 1943, the Special Engineer Detachment was one way that the Project dealt with a lack of technically trained labor. Army men with special skills—a background in chemistry perhaps, or engineering experience—could be directly assigned to the Project. The program's initial roster contained 334 names, but that wasn't nearly enough. As fall neared, the SED's search expanded into the realm of academia as potential draftees with the right skill set were recruited. Then the Army expanded its reach still further to include the Replacement Training Centers and the Army Specialized Training Program. Many of these recruits still wore their uniforms in and around Clinton Engineer Works and lived in specially designated barracks.

The Project pulled out all stops in an effort to locate educated soldiers who could be sent to CEW. It even reached out to colleges and universities, asking for the names of any graduates who had been drafted so that it could track the young men down and reroute them from wherever they were headed to Oak Ridge—or, as some of the northerners had affectionately begun to call it, Dogpatch.

Captain P. E. O'Meara, Town Manager

Corps of Engineers, U.S.A.

Oak Ridge, Tennessee

Dear Sir:

My compliments to you sir for your very fine "message" in the October 16th issue of the Oak Ridge Journal. I think it's darn near time
that some got up and gave the Army a great big cheer for the swell job
they have done here, and stop finding fault.

The other morning, while waiting for the Cafeteria to open, one of
the "patriots" was complaining about having to stand out in the cold. I
wondered to myself if this chap had ever read an eye witness account of
the invasion of Attu. . . .

Sure, we would all like to be home with our families, so would those
kids who "hit the beach" at Salerno—some of whom will never come
home.

There's only one thing wrong with your message, Captain—you hit
them with a powder-puff.

> Sincerely,
>
> W.J. O'B.
>
> Dorm M-6

★　　★　　★

"What godforsaken place have you brought me to?"

Celia had to laugh at the outburst, one sister howling at the other
as they stood in the dorm lobby.

Fresh off the bus and just processed, the pair were still gawking
at their new surroundings. New arrivals didn't stick out for long.
With the number of people constantly swarming in from all over the
country, it had taken Celia only a few weeks before she began to feel
like part of the old guard. It wasn't like other small towns, where you
spent your entire life surrounded by the same faces, where brothers
and sisters and parents and grandparents had known each other for
generations. There was no established cadre of locals who could trace
their roots back to Oak Ridge.

If there were no locals, there were no outsiders. Everyone was from somewhere else. Everyone was anxious to meet new people.

Some took to the Reservation immediately. Others found the surroundings a little more raw than they had anticipated. There was always a sympathetic ear close by, a make-the-best-of-it spirit infusing the brand-new yet dust-covered town.

We can do it! That's what Rosie would have said.

Stop your belly-achin'! That's what Appalachian folk would say.

None had figured the Clinton Engineer Works into his or her plans. How could they have? Nonetheless, this is where they were going to make their stand: together, knee-deep in mud, for the remainder of a hellish war that seemed to have no end. They were told they were going to help bring that end about. They had to believe that was true. And no matter what, they were All in the Same Boat.

Summer's searing edge was softening into an autumn much warmer than those in Pennsylvania, but still a welcome relief. Celia thought it must have rained every single day that first August of 1943. Hot summer rains exploding into the middle of a steamy southern afternoon, tearing through the sky and sun and leaving in their wake a sultry memory. Steam rose off concrete and tar, mud swirled beneath ever-present wooden sidewalks, cutting rivers into recently denuded soils. Real "frog stranglers"—that's what the locals sometimes called a good downpour. Luckily, the few shops, cafeteria, rec hall, and bus were close by, because the only real deterrent to walking remained mud, which Celia soon learned was not the result of some sort of climatological fluke. It was there to stay, occasionally upstaged by its dryer, hack-inducing cousin, clay dust.

"You've got a case of the Oak Ridge croup . . . ," more than one doctor would quip in the face of a wheezing patient.

The main cafeteria was a short walk from the dorm and right on Celia's way to the Castle on the Hill. The food served up there was basic, affordable, plentiful, but a far cry from her mother's cooking. The cafeteria also served as a coffee klatsch/sing-along lounge for not just women, Celia noticed, but many, many, oh-so-many young, single men that had come to work all day, every day, on whatever it was this place was working on.

On her drive in that first day, Celia hadn't noticed any stores lining the dirt roads, but with so much construction and all the buildings cut from the same prefab construction cloth, it was hard to tell what was going up where. Williams Drugstore and a few other shops had since opened in Jackson Square, the shopping and cafeteria complex in the middle of Townsite. And there was even a pint-sized version of Miller's of Knoxville and a grocer that boasted rationed *and* unrationed picnic lunches, along with potted meats and far-from-Vienna sausages. That month's *Journal* advertised rayon panties—*with elastic bands!*—dickies, and even 25-gauge rayon hose. But if a gal wanted to do some serious shopping, Knoxville was the place to go. Twenty miles away was not a quick trip. There were buses moving in and around the area 24 hours a day, bringing workers who lived off-site onto the Clinton Engineer Works, and transporting Townsite residents to and from Knoxville and surrounding towns. But cars were better, faster, and less crowded.

Celia, like most residents, did not have one.

So when Lew asked her if she was interested in taking a drive over to Knoxville to pick a friend up from the train station, Celia jumped.

She'd met Lew Parker at one of Father Siener's youth group meetings. Celia was always hearing about this or that different "group" forming. Was this what college was like? Maybe she hadn't missed much after all. Attending mass had helped ease Celia's transition and proven a boon for her social life. There were, she soon learned, plenty of good Catholic boys to be found.

When she first arrived, there was no church, but she had heard that one was being built. She met Rosemary Maiers, a young nurse recently arrived from Chicago who was helping to get the clinic up and running. The two went to mass wherever they could. In the very early days, all denominations had to make do: Services in the rec hall could be conducted by topping off a couple of 3.2 percent beer kegs with some plyboard and covering it with a simple tarp. Instant altar. Mass was held at Father Siener's home on Geneva Lane, his living room converted to a small chapel.

The Chapel on the Hill was finally dedicated at the end of

September and copies of keys were passed around to various religious representatives, all of whom offered prayers and invocations for the single, wooden white building that would serve Jews, Catholics, Baptists, Episcopalians, and more. But Celia still liked the intimacy of Father Siener's house best. Potlucks and prayer groups, the familiar rise-and-fall cadence of the Latin mass, the kneel-sit-stand-kneel Catholic calisthenics that were soothing in their repetition. That's where she had met Lew.

Lew had been working for DuPont in Alabama before the company transferred him to CEW, where it was managing the X-10 pilot plant. Now his old roommate, whom he'd convinced to apply for a transfer as well, was arriving at the train station. Afterward, Lew told Celia, "we'll all go to dinner at the Regas." Done deal. Even if it was only a quick drive over and back, Celia thought, at least she'd get a good meal.

They picked Henry up at the station, and soon Celia and the two men were at dinner. Celia listened as the friends played catch-up, but couldn't help but notice a definite shift in her mind from one to the other.

Who is this guy? she wondered. Easy on the eyes, polite.

During the long car ride home, Celia listened as Henry sat in the backseat and talked about some girlfriend he had left back in Alabama, about his family.

What's that? Polish? He's Polish?

Maybe he would ask her out, Celia thought. She hoped Lew wouldn't mind. He seemed to be getting serious, but serious was not for Celia. There were too many available men behind these fences. Dating around was the ticket. Lew drove through the gates and back into Townsite, dropping Celia off at her dorm. She said good-bye to both men, hoping that wouldn't be the last time she'd hear from that charming Henry Klemski.

★   ★   ★

In the meantime, Celia had no trouble keeping herself occupied. She worked from 8 AM to 4:30, Monday to Friday, overtime when needed. She was happy not to have shift work, unlike women she'd met in the dorm or cafeteria who worked in the factories and had changing schedules that sometimes required them to work through the night. Nothing ever seemed to shut down here.

The short distance between her dorm and the Castle on the Hill remained a sticky obstacle course to be maneuvered at least twice a day. And vanity be damned, the I. Millers were gathering dust in the tiny closet she shared with Maybelle. She more regularly opted for a trusty yet fashionable pair of ladies' saddle oxfords—*Now available at Miller's in Jackson Square, shoppers!*—but even those weren't immune to the pervasive shoe-sucking gunk. It wasn't long before, on her way to work, she stepped right where she should have stepped left and found herself knee-deep in the mire. By the time she managed to extricate her foot from the soppy goop, her brand-new saddle shoe was no longer attached to it. She felt sick. Hard-earned money sucked into the earth.

Days were busy at the Castle on the Hill, now headquarters for the entire Project. The day Celia arrived, August 13, 1943, Kenneth Nichols (now a full colonel) had officially taken over as District Engineer and was in charge of all things administrative for all the Project sites. Celia was in the secretarial pool that served Lieutenant Colonel Vanden Bulck, Colonel Nichols's righthand man, but spent most of her time working with Mr. Smitz. Typing up letters and memos and taking dictation occupied a sizable slice of Celia's time, though the office also handled some sort of insurance, hazard insurance, based on the little she had seen, taken out for individuals working at the CEW. There was a lot she didn't know. She had heard about the big factories located elsewhere on the Reservation, but she had never actually seen them. Lew worked in one, she thought; Henry, too. She saw people getting on buses labeled Y-12, K-25, and X-10, which she guessed were the factories. But you didn't go anywhere your pass didn't permit you. If you did, at the very least you'd get a good talking-to. At the most, there might be one last bus ride—right off the Reservation for good. And, she had been told, people were watching, to make sure you didn't shoot your mouth off about what you did and where you did it.

When necessary, she also filled in for Lieutenant Colonel Vanden Bulck's personal secretary, Sherry. So it wasn't much of a surprise when she was called in to take Sherry's place one morning. She walked into Vanden Bulck's office to find the colonel and another man awaiting her.

"Sherry's not here," Vanden Bulck said. "I've got someone visiting me and I want you to take dictation from him."

Celia stood, her notepad and pen at the ready.

General Leslie Groves stepped forward. To Celia's eyes, he was a military man in uniform, maybe in his late forties. He had a thick swath of wavy hair combed straight back over his head, with a small streak of gray sprouting over one eye. His mustache was thick but tidy, like the rest of his appearance, and his midsection ample. There was no reason for Celia to recognize this particular man, of course. They had never met before, their paths had never officially crossed in Manhattan, though they had both been there. Still, she could tell he was important by the way everyone was scurrying around him, looking at him. There were few other visual clues. His uniform bore no name tag. And Vanden Bulck didn't bother to introduce Celia to the big man, either.

Celia didn't ask who the man was, why he was there, or what all the multicolored stripes on his uniform meant. But she liked something about him immediately. He smiled at her and was polite and had a serious sort of warmth when he spoke. But that wasn't enough. Celia liked to know how to address people. That's how she had been raised. So she asked Lieutenant Colonel Vanden Bulck's nameless friend what she should call him.

"Just call me GG," he said.

★   ★   ★

Christmas 1943. "I'll Be Home for Christmas" wafted from radios across the country, its wistfully hopeful lyrics striking a somber chord for those who knew loved ones remained thousands of miles away as the 25th rolled around. Mothers scoured the few stores that had opened in the Townsite area of Clinton Engineer Works for anything that might pass for a present. A new game called Chutes and Ladders was all the rage, but wartime and rations had affected children, too. Any child who longed to see a brand-new Lionel Train chugging around the base of their Christmas tree would be disappointed: the company had ceased production of metal trains in order to build compasses for the war. They offered only paper train sets this year, a dollar apiece, that were notoriously frustrating to put together, with their flaps and perforations. Chemists and cubicle operators sat in cafeterias that remained in operation as if the holiday didn't exist, toasting each other with contraband booze that quickly dissolved the feeble glue holding together tiny cone-shaped paper cups designed for water and nothing more.

December. A month of personal evaluation and remembrance, one that would now live in infamy. For the Project, it was a month that had historically brought shifts in fortunes.

Just a year earlier, in December 1942, Project scientists had ushered in a new age of power, one they were rapidly working to fully understand.

December 7, 1941, brought Japan to the shores and skies of Pearl Harbor and brought the United States into World War II.

But in December 1938, events had transpired that would send the first ripples across the Atlantic of the unleashed power of what the Greeks called *atomos*, news that had resulted in the birth of the Project.

TUBEALLOY

★ ★ ★ ★ ★

LISE AND FISSION, 1938

Four years after Ida Noddack had challenged Enrico Fermi's findings, another female scientist was struggling to make sense of unexpected data. December snow crunched beneath Lise Meitner's feet as she walked steadily alongside her nephew Otto Frisch over frozen Nordic ground. The Austrian physicist kept up on foot as Frisch glided along on cross-country skis through the woods near the coastal village of Kungalv, Sweden.

Lise was frozen in thought, icy cold air needling nostrils and skin and eyes, infusing the already tense atmosphere with a frigid alertness. Night was falling on 1938, a year in which the radio broadcast of H. G. Wells's fictional *War of the Worlds* had terrorized Americans, and another very real world war was fast becoming fact. A man named Adolf Hitler had just been named *Time* magazine's "Man of the Year." Lise mulled over the latest advancement in her field of physics, and its potential ramifications on an increasingly unstable political landscape, one which had led to her own exile from Berlin months earlier.

Lise had recently received a letter from her now long-distance colleague, Otto Hahn, a radiochemist at the Kaiser Wilhelm Institute for Chemistry, in Berlin. She had just seen Hahn a month ago in Copenhagen. Mere exile wasn't enough to keep the shy but driven woman from consorting with her old team, even if at a great distance. She had little choice: Once Austria had been annexed by Germany she began to abandon hope that her Austrian citizenship and scientific standing could protect her from the likes of SS head Heinrich Himmler, on whose radar she had eventually landed. Though she had been baptized at birth and long considered herself a Protestant, she was, in the eyes of the Nazis, a Jew.

She had waited too long to leave, perhaps, keeping her head down and buried in her work, as the political situation deteriorated around her. Once the Anschluss and concerned friends convinced Lise it was time to flee, she boarded a train for Holland. The reason for travel given to all but a handful of those closest to Lise was vacation. She had an invalid passport, prompting friends to pull whatever strings they could with political contacts in Holland and officials with Dutch immigration. Hahn had given her a ring that belonged to his mother, feeling it might be useful in case of an emergency. On the way to the station, she wanted desperately to turn around and go back. As the train approached the Dutch border, Lise's anxiety grew. The train stopped. Patrolmen walked through the train. Her friends' efforts had been successful, and Lise passed into Holland without incident. She eventually made her way to Sweden, where physicist and friend Niels Bohr had secured a spot for her in the laboratory of Karl Manne Georg Siegbahn at the Physics Institute of the Swedish Royal Academy of Sciences.

Lise was grateful for the position but missed her daily interaction with Hahn and the third member of their team, chemist Fritz Strassmann. She would sing quietly to herself in the lab as she did her experiments alongside Hahn, a man with whom she'd worked for decades, a man who knew her back when she was banished to research in a basement workshop because a superior thought women in the chemistry labs were dangerous—their hair might catch on fire. She corresponded with Hahn and had arranged for their clandestine Copenhagen meeting to discuss their ongoing work. The Meitner-Hahn-Strassmann team were still focusing much of their research into the bombardment of Tubealloy with neutrons, spurred on as many in their field were by the work of Enrico Fermi. Fermi had just been awarded the 1938 Nobel Prize for his work on nuclear reactions with slow neutrons. Lise's lab was among others now firing up the neutrons, publishing their results. Bombardments away.

Ida Noddack's husband, Walter, mentioned to Otto Hahn that Hahn should incorporate Ida's critique of Fermi's work in his publications and talks on the topic. Hahn was unimpressed, saying he didn't want to make Ida look "ridiculous." Her "assumption of the bursting of the . . . nucleus into larger fragments was really absurd."

However, the results of Hahn and Strassmann's latest experiment had turned Lise's holiday stroll in the woods of Kungalv into a mental marathon. They needed answers. And Hahn thought Lise would be the one with the smarts to provide them.

THE "LIQUID DROP" MODEL

Hahn's letter to Lise had arrived on the shortest day of the year, rendered even more brief by both latitude and urgency. After bombarding Tubealloy with neutrons, Hahn and Strassman had found isotopes of barium of all things, an element just about half the size of Tubealloy. How could that have happened? Tubealloy couldn't have split apart, could it? Lise had written Hahn back immediately. She, too, found the results "amazing."

"Perhaps you can suggest some fantastic explanation," Hahn wrote in response. "We understand that it really can't break up into barium. . . . So try to think of some other possibility. . . . If you can think of anything that might be publishable, then the three of us would be together in this work after all."

Lise sat and sketched in the woods, working to give shape to the physics storming through her winterized mind. Her 34-year-old nephew, Otto Frisch, the better artist and himself working in nuclear physics with Bohr in Copenhagen, refined the images. Frisch hadn't wanted to discuss Hahn's findings at first. This visit in Kungalv, Sweden, with his 60-year-old aunt was for the winter holidays, and he had his own experiments to ponder. But Lise wouldn't drop it. She found her thoughts inspired by Bohr's "liquid drop" model of the nucleus—a model that hadn't been available for consideration when Ida Noddack put forth her views on Fermi's findings.

Nobel Prize laureate Niels Bohr had already contributed much to the understanding of the atom. He first introduced the theory that electrons traveled in specific *orbits* around the nucleus. These were also called at different times and under different circumstances shells, clouds, or energy levels. (Visual interpretations of Bohr's model of the atom would inspire Styrofoam ball mobiles and science-fair entries for decades to come.)

His *liquid drop* model was exactly as it sounded: The nucleus of an atom shouldn't be viewed as a hard, spherical entity, but was more akin to a drop of liquid, capable of moving, elongating . . . *dividing*? If a nucleus *did* divide, the tremendous energy that held the atom together would be released in the process. That energy would be proportional to the mass of the nucleus. Lise had attended Albert Einstein's lecture in Salzburg in 1909, where he discussed a revolutionary concept: the conversion of mass into energy.

$E = mc^2$

Using this and various other formulae—Lise's nephew was amazed at the equations his aunt kept effortlessly on call in her mind—the two scientists scribbled and computed. They estimated that the division of a nucleus of Tubealloy would result in not only the emission of other neutrons but a release of energy in the neighborhood of 200 million electron volts *for each individual atom.*

That was enough power to be noticed. Frisch would later describe this as enough energy to make a grain of sand, visible to the human eye, jump. And one mere gram of Tubealloy—one-fifth of a teaspoon, less than what one would spoon into a cup of coffee—contained an estimated 2.5×10^{21} atoms. That's 2.5 sextillion, or 25 followed by twenty zeroes.

In one gram.

Forget jumping grains of sand—that was enough energy to displace a chunk of desert.

THE PROJECT IS BORN

Back in Stockholm, Lise wrote Hahn that she was "fairly certain now that you have a splitting towards barium . . ."

For Hahn, publishing with his longtime, yet exiled, non-Aryan collaborator posed difficulties. Lise understood at the time. She knew that while isolating evidence was essential, being able to explain what you have witnessed was equally as crucial if not more so. So she and her nephew did. She helped put into words what Fermi had seen years earlier but failed to fully explain, what Noddack had deemed possible when everyone else doubted her. Hahn and Strassmann had found the evidence, but Lise made sense of it.

Fission.

That's what Lise and Frisch decided to call it.

Frisch got word to Bohr just prior to Bohr's boarding the ship *Drottningholm* bound for America. There he would discuss the findings with all the right members of the scientific community. In January 1939, Hahn and Strassmann published—without Lise—in the scientific journal *Naturwissenschaften* a paper describing what they had witnessed. Their findings arrived in the United States shortly after Bohr's ship. Lise collaborated with Frisch over the phone—he in Copenhagen, she in Sweden—and composed their own paper explaining what Hahn and Strassmann had observed, which was published in the British journal *Nature*. It was the first theoretical interpretation of the fission process. Much research followed under the flags of several nations, and the emission of neutrons during fission was confirmed—as was the release of cosmically confounding amounts of energy that went along with it.

Bohr's ship was met by Enrico Fermi and his wife, Laura, who had arrived in the United States earlier that month with their family. After picking up Enrico's Nobel Prize in Stockholm they had just kept going. Laura was Jewish, and Benito Mussolini's Italy was not safe for her, no matter who her husband was. Also in the United States, Hungarian physicist Leo Szilard and others believed secrecy was now needed: The scientific community should work to keep any further discoveries quiet. There was a war on. Szilard and another Hungarian physicist, Eugene Wigner, met with Albert Einstein in Princeton, explaining the snowballing developments in the field of nuclear physics and convincing the genius professor with static-electric locks that President

Roosevelt needed to support Tubealloy research efforts in the United States. They warned that Germany was already conducting their own research and drafted a letter saying so. Einstein put his signature to it. Alexander Sachs, an economist and a friend of the president, delivered it.

Shortly thereafter, in October 1939, the first of a long line of committees and advisory groups and classified brain trusts that would eventually evolve into the Manhattan Engineer District and the Project was formed and given a paltry $6,000 in funding. On December 6, 1941, one of these administrative incarnations—the S-1 Section of the Office of Scientific Research and Development—met and proposed not only another administrative reorganization, but more importantly an "all-out" effort to work on unleashing this new power. If anyone present had had any misgivings about committing time, money, and manpower to what would become the Project, they may likely have changed their minds the very next day, December 7, 1941.

The snowy realizations of an exiled female Austrian physicist had resulted in an unprecedented mobilization of military, industrial, and scientific worlds. Fast-moving bullets and slow-moving neutrons were aimed toward a single objective: a victorious end to the war. Ida Noddack's theories and Lise Meitner's explanations had resulted in a chain reaction of their own, science colliding with military and industry, splitting into compartmentalized and mobilized units, each moving along its own trajectory, ready to make sand jump in the desert.

* ★ ★ ★ ★ ★

Bull Pens and Creeps

The Project's Welcome for New Employees

Perhaps we just don't know where to begin. Judging from pre-war
standards, a three-year accumulation of shop-talk should add up
to quite a total for the average man.

—Vi Warren, *Oak Ridge Journal*

Virginia Spivey was stuck in limbo, the kind that existed for those
lacking appropriate paperwork—and in triplicate. If there were a
penance designed specifically for the shy-yet-spunky, 21-year-old
woman, it came in the form of a daily challenge to devise something
of value to teach the other fidgety individuals who were stuck with
her in a place called the "bull pen."

Before new arrivals to CEW could be given free reign to work at
their new jobs, the appropriate clearances had to be earned, physicals passed, photographs and fingerprints taken, urine collected,
and stacks of "I swear I won't talk" papers signed. They could move
into housing, but it was life in the bull pen until job clearance came
through. The amount of time this process took depended on the individual and the job. Someone working in an area of a plant that was
a degree closer to the Secret required much higher clearance than
someone working in the cafeteria.

Until the precious stamp of approval arrived, life went on. People
got settled in their trailers, houses, or dorms, and many spent their
days in the bull pen near the Castle. There they smoked, read, possibly learned skills that may or may not have anything to do with the

new job they had yet to secure, or they sat idly by, waiting for their chance to move on.

The mind-your-own-business ethos permeated life at CEW. The moment you passed through the guarded gates, the veil of secrecy descended: No specific information about the world within the gates, no matter how mundane, was to be shared. When in doubt, shut your mouth.

New residents were often briefed unofficially by "old-timers" who had lived on the site for at *least* a few weeks. Signs and billboards posted throughout the Reservation reminded all to mind their "loose lips." The following appeared on the first page of the resident's handbook:

> This military area contains a vital war project. Like other installations contributing to the war effort, its security depends upon the whole-hearted cooperation of all concerned in the observing of regulations designed to safeguard the place, the people having access to the area and the information, material, and operations pertaining thereto.
>
> Accordingly, a safe rule to follow is that What you do here, What you see here, What you hear here, please let it stay here.

Background checks were only one step and did not always guarantee employment. Officials also used the waiting period and training process to screen people's behavior.

One story described a locksmith who sat bragging about his lock-picking prowess to the rest of his training group. He was chomping at the bit to get into those plants so that he could show the military just how lax their security was.

He promptly disappeared from Y-12 training classes.

Others might be dismissed for problems at home, the personal kind that most individuals would consider none of an employer's business. But this was no ordinary employer. Money issues, for example, might make someone more likely to do or say things for personal profit. Despite the Project's desperate need for labor, empty chairs routinely appeared with no explanations given.

Some new recruits viewed orientation films depicting the enemy cloaked in blazing terror. Others were asked questions like:

Do you drink? How often?
   If someone close to you revealed a secret, would you report them?
   Have you ever belonged to any group with communist ties, or that opposes the democratic form of government?

Someone was always watching. One man training to be a supervisor at the Y-12 plant was told that one in four persons here was FBI. Those who worked in processing sometimes broadcasted anecdotes meant to drive home the "zip it" message for new recruits. These were specific enough to be believable, yet vague enough to leave you wondering about the fate of the offending individual.

A woman thoughtlessly wrote her family describing the size and number of facilities in her new town . . . Someone kept a diary . . . A man told a friend about the type of machinery he saw in his plant . . .

During processing and training, individuals, no matter the rung they occupied on the information ladder, were given just enough detail to do their job well, and not an infinitesimal scrap more.

While waiting for his Q clearance, one young scientist in training received a refresher course about topics he'd studied in high school. During the briefing, he asked the instructor to clarify one of his statements. The response from the instructor was clear: Curiosity for curiosity's sake was not appreciated. If the young man wanted to stick around, he had better shift his focus to his work and trust that everything he needed to know would be told to him precisely when he needed to know it.

★   ★   ★

Oddly enough, Virginia had already received clearance. She had answered the questions, signed the forms and gone through the rigmarole when she came to CEW in December 1943 for her interview. At the time, she was still in school and not available to work. Now, no one seemed to know where her clearance was. She was assigned a dorm room in the newly established West Village, and each day she reported to the bull pen. Because she had a college degree, she was thrust into the unexpected role of teacher.

Back at the University of North Carolina, Virginia had specifically decided *not* to teach. Initially majoring in English, the first teaching course she took at Chapel Hill changed her mind. She found it rote and uninteresting. But she had always been inclined toward science; she found it endlessly fascinating. There was always something new to learn, always something that had applications to what was going on in the real world, *today*. She switched to chemistry and never looked back.

A recruiter came to speak to Virginia shortly before graduation. Virginia listened as the woman described a 90-square-mile area, with plants operating for the war effort and free buses running all night and day. There Virginia could put her science background to use. This magical place was in Tennessee, and Virginia was invited to come out for an interview over Christmas break.

It had been Virginia's first train trip. She left home in Louisburg, North Carolina, where she had been spending Christmas with her family, and caught the bus to Greensboro. She spent the night with some friends at Greensboro College and caught a cab to the station the next morning. The train headed west and the flat Piedmont terrain exploded upward as they got closer to Asheville in the mountains of Western North Carolina. She had driven through Asheville before with her family. The Blue Ridge scenery was so different from her usual sea-level surroundings. Wisps of cloud clung to the rugged slopes of the Smokies, seeming to dance alongside the car just beyond the window. "Roll your windows down," her father used to say, "and wash your hands in the clouds."

Virginia's friend Johnny, who had already begun work at CEW, met her at the Knoxville station, flower in hand. It was late, and she went straight to a boardinghouse in downtown Knoxville where the recruiter had arranged for her to stay. Virginia's friend Virginia Kelly, also from Chapel Hill, had made the trip down from her hometown of Rochester, New York. The city appeared booming, jam-packed. Virginia was glad to have someone she knew to share the experience with.

Breakfast couldn't have come soon enough. Not knowing how much a meal would cost in the dining car, Virginia had ignored the porter's call to dinner and gone to bed hungry. Afterward, a car whisked the girls away to a Knoxville office where they were given physicals. Then the driver took the two Virginias down the highway through guarded Edgemoor Gate, onto the Reservation and straight to the Y-12 plant. Virginia enjoyed the view on the way in, passing along the frosted Clinch. Once through the gates the palette shifted. Slushy construction trails sprouted where wide tires had cut into the frozen earth.

The interview at Y-12 was mercifully brief and offered little more information than the recruiter who had visited campus. Virginia was offered a job and had accepted it. She was going to be a lab assistant on a very important war project. She would start after graduation.

Now after arriving at CEW no one could find Virginia's paperwork. Officials instructed Virginia that the other workers in the bull pen with her needed to be trained. For what, specifically? The officials couldn't say.

Virginia racked her brain to come up with interesting and impromptu lessons. The individuals were as varied as the jobs they were going to fill and they had arrived from farms across the state, and states across the country. Southern. Northern. Educated. Dropouts. City. Country. Male. Female. Virginia thought some looked bored to death no matter what she had planned for the day. Others were surprisingly interested. Virginia made the best of the uninspiring surroundings. She even performed small chemical experiments, designed to help explain, for example, how reactions took place and what "gases" were. She trotted out the old chemistry class standby of baking soda and vinegar. The hydrogen in the vinegar slammed into the bicarbonate of the baking soda, the resulting acid transformed into carbon dioxide and water, releasing a bubbling over of foaming energy, a visual show of new expanding forces resulting from the collision of two quiet and inert ones.

Virginia taught everyone how to read water and electric meters. Some had never used or even seen a yardstick or meterstick before, and Virginia explained the difference between the two. If nothing else, it gave her something to do besides sit and wait. Occasionally someone would stand up and wander out of the room mid-lesson. Sometimes they would come back in an hour, sometimes never.

There were a fair number of young women, many still in their teens, who had just strolled out of rural Tennessee high schools. Another part of the training was to show this fresh-faced group how to read dials and gauges and what, precisely, dials and gauges were. Virginia didn't know why the women would be reading the instruments, so the instructions covered basic concepts. All the better, considering the limited education some possessed. She explained what she considered to be the rudimentary movements and logic. Some dials, gauges, and knobs move in both directions, she explained, around a zero or central position, and not just simply from left to right, from smaller to bigger. That idea was slightly counterintuitive, especially for an 18-year-old coming from a home that lacked plumbing or electricity. But Virginia loved meeting so many new people and found many of the women to be attentive and quick learners.

One of the bull pen regulars was a man named Mac Piper, who had been paying particularly close attention to Virginia. He introduced himself and explained that he was going to be a personnel head for the division at Y-12, to which Virginia was originally assigned. Mac wanted to know if Virginia would like to work as his assistant. The job would be in human resources and not a lab. But she needed to get out of the bull pen. This offer seemed to be the quickest path to freedom. She took it.

This wasn't the first time things hadn't gone the way Virginia had planned. She had learned early on in life to make the best of what came your way, even if it was painful or seemed unfair. She had seen both. This was just an unexpected twist in the road and she would happily follow it.

★ ★ ★

Dorothy Jones must have spent six weeks in training working on those darn machines. She had just graduated high school, finally free of schedules and teachers and yet here she was—back in class again.

Dot knew the panels in front of her weren't the real thing. But she wouldn't see the real thing until training was over and her building at the plant was ready. In the meantime, she learned about knobs and dials, the likes of which she had never seen back in Hornbeak, Tennessee. Her quiet little hometown in the sparsely populated northwest corner of the Volunteer State sat roughly 20 minutes from the state line, where the Mississippi snaked in and out along the southernmost foot of the state of Missouri.

The Project liked high school girls, especially those from rural backgrounds. Recruiters sought them out relentlessly, feeling young women were easy to instruct. They did what they were told. They weren't overly curious. If you tell a young woman of 18 from a small-town background to do something, she'll do it, no questions asked. Educated women and men, people who had gone to college and learned just enough to think that they might "know" something, gave you problems. The Project scoured the countryside of Tennessee and beyond looking for recent graduates.

Dot had no fixed plans beyond high school, and she wasn't alone in that respect. She could only think of two or three kids from her graduating class of 12 or so who were going to college. When the job notice went up at school, she jumped at the chance to take the short, handwritten test the recruiters administered. She was shaking in her boots when she took it and couldn't remember much of it, but it had been blissfully free of math.

For the life of her she couldn't figure out why more students weren't meeting with the recruiters, why anyone would want to stay in Hornbeak for the rest of their lives. She had always dreamed of traveling, of flying off to somewhere like Paris, even though she had no idea how she would ever make it happen. She wanted to marry well, someone with a college degree, someone who would be a good supporter. It all seemed so far removed from her life on the farm. But she dreamed anyway. Why deny yourself that? And why not leave? How often did opportunities like this come along in Hornbeak? Opportunities to go and do something, anything, to go somewhere—else.

Wanting to leave home didn't mean Dot wasn't scared. She had been surprised how quickly she got the news that they had already found her a position. Her father drove her in their truck to the bus stop in Nashville. When she arrived in Knoxville there was a bus waiting to take her through the dusty gates and onto the Reservation where she would build a new life. She was the only person—male *or* female—who had made the trip from Hornbeak to Knoxville to work.

But it wasn't exactly what she was expecting.

When she first spied the guards and the fences and the Wild West–looking, mud-covered, half-built town that had sprung up in the Cumberland Foothills, she thought, *If I had enough money I would turn around and go back home!* The recruiters and the handbook and the billboards had rattled her. Dot worried she would say something wrong, sure she'd slip up and be arrested or shot. She was a country girl far out of her comfort zone.

Good gracious—at least Hornbeak had sidewalks.

But she soon got comfortable. There were other girls in the dorm just like her—out of their element, waiting for clearance, enduring training on fantastical machines. And there were women who seemed very much on the ball, or at least they acted like they were.

She missed her mama, though. A good ol' plump woman with a welcoming lap no matter your age, a soft bosomy shelf that held the answer to any crisis, a pillow for your troubles. But Dot wouldn't run home. Her parents were happy that she found a good job. She had always been useless on their farm and she knew it. Simple tasks like making runs down to the pump for water turned into long spells of sitting by the radio and listening to soap operas.

Dot, the baby of seven and Farmer Jones's youngest daughter, was the last to leave home. Her sisters had left town to find work. Her brothers had been long gone, off to war, Woodrow and David in the Army, and Shorty . . . Shorty had been a deck gunner for the Navy. She had always looked forward to the crazy postcards he'd mail home to her. Her favorite was a photo of Shorty—no doubt drunk as a skunk—wearing his fancy Navy whites up top and a grass skirt down below that he'd mailed her all the way from Hawaii.

He had been only 23 years old when her family got the news, right before Christmas.

Believed to be among the missing . . .

That's all she and her parents were told. No one ever came right out and said he was dead. But they all knew, even before word arrived. Once the world learned the fate of the USS *Arizona*, she and her family knew. He was probably still there, with so many others, trapped beneath the murky waters.

"Somewhere in East Tennessee" was more than a job. Dot felt it was a way to help end the war that had taken Shorty from her. The last time she'd gotten one of his postcards, Shorty still called her "Baby." Funny, she thought. He was the one who never really got to grow up.

★   ★   ★

Spring was in the air, Townsite was growing by leaps and bounds— *"McCrory's 5, 10, & 25 Cent Store Now Open in Jackson Square next to the Ridge Theatre!"*—and *The Oak Ridge Journal* paused to ask residents, "Does Your Tongue Wag?"

. . . Specialists in Axis espionage and sabotage activities are standing before their leader . . . they are about to embark on a vital mission for Naziland . . . and here are typical instructions to enemy agents . . .

We have reports that somewhere in the American state of Tennessee there is a new war project about which you MUST get DETAILED information . . .

Talk and listen: Get public opinion and current speculations about the work being done. . . .

The natives and workers will aid you—they will talk, talk, talk. Listen. Some will tell you because they are unsuspecting, have faith in everyone they meet, others are plainly ignorant that they are giving information. . . .

Search discarded plans and trash. Listen to every possible conversation—these Americans talk constantly about their work . . . psychological sabotage is your weapon of which our Dr. Goebbels is the master. When you hear a rumor spread it to every ear that will listen . . . bad food, mud, sickness, poor pay, strikes, waste, discrimination, race prejudice and persecution—make the place sound so dirty and miserable, so poorly managed and inefficient that no decent person would want to remain there. . . .

Make them hate the state of Tennessee until they leave in droves. . . .

Let the looseness of their tongues and the softness of their brains do your work for you. Bring me the report that this project in Tennessee will be entirely useless to America. Heil Hitler!

★   ★   ★

A sudden knock came at the door.

Helen looked up, startled, as she sat in the middle of her dorm room floor folding laundry. She wasn't expecting anyone to come calling.

It must have been a mistake.

Helen had returned home from another interminable day at the bull pen—still no clearance, still no word on when she would be officially starting her new job. She got back to the dorm as quickly as possible to get her laundry done before the washing rooms got too crowded with girls rinsing out their unmentionables for the next day.

She had heard the laundry service was not to be trusted.

Then the knock came again, more insistent this time. Whoever was out there wasn't going away. Helen stood up and crossed the room, gingerly avoiding the carefully stacked laundry, and opened the door. It was her dorm mother.

"There are two men downstairs here to see you," she said.

"I'm not expecting anyone," Helen replied. "I don't know any men."

"Are you Helen Hall?"

"Yes, I am."

"Well, they asked to speak to you. You need to come downstairs."

Helen did as she was told. As she walked down to the small lobby of her dormitory, her mind began to race.

Who could these men be and what do they want? she worried. *Have I done something wrong already? Oh, no, I hope I haven't already made a mess of things.*

Once in the lobby the dorm mother pointed out the two men. Helen looked at them. They wore dark suits, and once Helen got a look at their faces she was sure beyond a doubt that she did not know them.

Helen walked over.

"I'm Helen Hall," she said, and waited.

The two took a few furtive glances over their shoulders, seemingly surveying the other young women and visitors gathered in the lobby—people picking up mail, using the phone, chatting.

"Would you mind if we stepped outside to speak?" one of the men asked.

Helen agreed. What else could she do?

The three exited the dorm. It was dark. She may have been a small-town girl, but she knew that speaking in the dark with strange men was not advisable. But these were clearly Very Important Men.

The men began to speak.

Helen listened, and she soon learned that she wasn't in trouble—that wasn't it at all. The real reason they wanted to speak to her was almost as disconcerting.

Would she mind, the two men wondered, *paying very close attention to what the people around her were doing and saying?*

Helen kept listening.

The men wondered if she would be willing to listen to conversations taking place around her at work and in the cafeterias. She should also pay particular attention to any individuals who seemed to be speaking out of turn, maybe talking a bit too much about what they did at the plant, for example.

All she had to do was write down all the relevant information she had gathered—names, dates, locations, what was discussed—and deliver it to them. She wouldn't have to give it to them in person. Her notes would be delivered to an unmarked box that no one else would know anything about.

It would all be completely confidential.

As they spoke, it dawned on Helen that she, an 18-year-old girl from Eagleville, Tennessee, recruited from a diner-drugstore in Murfreesboro to come work at a war plant she'd yet to lay eyes on, was being recruited to spy.

The two men stood waiting for Helen's answer.

Well? Yes or no?

It was very important, they stressed, to the work they were doing there. It was important to the war effort.

She did *want to do her part to help, didn't she?*

The men handed Helen a stack of blank envelopes preaddressed to the ACME Insurance Company in downtown Knoxville and told Helen that she could fill them in with all the pertinent information. They told her where the drop box was located. Not to worry. It was all quite anonymous. She would be able to leave information there without arousing suspicion from anyone at all.

Though the men were asking, Helen didn't feel she had a choice. She did the only thing she felt she could do:

Of course she would help, she said.

She took the envelopes. The two men thanked her and walked off into the darkness. She turned and went back inside her dorm.

She made her way upstairs and back to her room, careful not to disturb the pile of laundry in the middle of the floor. She walked over to the small desk and put the envelopes in the drawer.

TUBEALLOY

★ ★ ★ ★ ★

LEONA AND SUCCESS IN CHICAGO, DECEMBER 1942

"He sank a Japanese admiral," Leona said.

Laura Fermi's question had floored Leona Woods, and she couldn't think of anything else to say. Doublespeak. Metaphors. These were the tools of those bound by secrecy, even in the face of friends and family.

Why, Laura had asked, *was everyone congratulating her husband?*

It was a question the 23-year-old Leona had no permission to answer regardless of the fact that Laura had extended such kindness to Leona since she began working at the Metallurgical Lab at the University of Chicago not quite six months ago. Post-laboratory evenings spent at the 55th Street promontory swimming in Lake Michigan with Dr. Fermi often ended up at his home, where Leona had enjoyed many meals prepared by the beautiful Laura, listening eagerly to stories of their life in Italy before leaving the country to escape Fascist rule. The Fermis initially lived as enemy aliens in America, constantly in fear of how others perceived them, nervously stashing emergency getaway money in a pipe under their first house in Leonia, New Jersey, when Fermi was still working at Columbia. Leona did not want to lie to Laura. But the truth was not an option.

The truth was, earlier that day, Leona had watched as her Italian mentor orchestrated the proceedings on the former doubles squash courts under the west stands of Stagg Field at the University of Chicago. Chicago Pile 1 (CP-1) loomed in front of them, costing in the neighborhood of 2.7 million 1942 dollars. The pile was a 57-layer matrix made up of 380 tons of graphite, six tons of Tubealloy metal, and about another 50 tons of Tubealloy oxide. It stood roughly 20 feet high and was 25 feet wide. It was the Project's hope that this pile would create the world's first ever self-sustaining nuclear reaction.

His shirt removed, Fermi and the team of scientists waited as Tigger, Piglet, Kanga, and Roo sprung into action. Forty-one-year-old Fermi had been reading A. A. Milne's *Winnie the Pooh* in order to help him improve his English and had decided to nickname his instruments accordingly. This lent a playful air to a procedure risky enough to require a so-called "suicide squad," standing by to halt proceedings in case they got out of hand.

Leona's contribution to the pile was a boron trifluoride counter inserted after the fifteenth layer. Leona's counter measured neutron activity as each successive layer of the pile was added. These measurements would determine how large the pile would need to be in order to achieve "criticality," the point at which a chain reaction would be self-sustaining. In other words, the point at which enough neutrons would split enough atoms to trigger ongoing fission in their neighbors.

Fermi described a chain reaction as similar to a "burning of a rubbish pile from spontaneous combustion." A tiny portion of the pile would "burn" and soon ignite another portion and yet another until, "the entire heap bursts into flames." In the pile, neutrons, not sparks, are emitted from the fission of Tubealloy and bombard other nearby atoms. This would then "ignite" or result in other small fissions, which then, of course, resulted in even more neutrons and more fissions until the little pile of atomic leaves was sparked by enough neutrons to get a fire going.

But no one wanted it to burst into anything too big.

If the reaction needed to be stopped, an emergency bell would ring and rods covered in neutron-absorbing cadmium could be inserted into the matrix, stopping the reaction. One rod was controlled by hand. Others were automatic. There was an additional rod tied to the balcony on the courts and controlled by SCRAM—the Safety Control Rod Axe Man—and the suicide squad was ready to douse the entire pile with a cadmium solution if all else failed.

Fermi had calculated that the 57th layer would be the one to make the pile jump to criticality. On the morning of December 2, 1942, the measurements proved his estimation correct. He instructed everyone to return that afternoon ready to go. Leona, Fermi, and Herb Anderson, a nuclear physicist and one of Fermi's right-hand men, went to Leona's apartment near Stagg Field, where Leona served the anxious group plates of very lumpy pancakes.

When afternoon came, Leona put on her sooty, blackened-by-graphite lab coat and went to join the other freezing team members gathered on the spectator's platform of the old courts. She prepared to take notes during the procedure and monitor the various instruments as the reaction progressed. The suicide squad was in place. A few scientists present openly admitted to being scared, but Fermi appeared calm and collected, almost Pooh-like. At 2:30 in the afternoon, it began.

One by one, control rods were removed, allowing more neutrons to roam free within the pile. Physicist George Weil, who had also worked with Fermi at Columbia, controlled the last rod, pulling it out of the pile a bit at a time. The counter clicked away, percussively increasing with each increment of removal. Leona took the measurements, calling out the escalating readings to the anxious crowd, as Fermi directed George to continue removing the final rod.

"Another foot, George!" Fermi shouted.

Clickclickclick . . .

"Eight! Sixteen!" Leona called out.

"Another foot, George!"

Clickclickclickclick . . .

"Twenty-eight! Sixty-four!"

"Another foot, George!"

Voices and clicks and measurements and calls continued in an anticipatory cadence punching through the graphite-coated tension as each click became indistinguishable from the next. Finally, Fermi announced, "The pile has gone critical!"

A new era had begun, the theoretical made provable, a monumental if secret gain achieved in their own snowy hundred-acre wood.

Theoretical physicist Eugene Wigner opened up a bottle of Chianti he had brought from Princeton to Chicago. The wine was poured into paper cups, its straw-bottomed bottle signed by those in attendance. Laboratory head Arthur Compton called James Conant, then head of the National Defense Research Committee, and relayed the news in a manner reflecting both secrecy and a lack of secure phone lines:

"The Italian Navigator has just landed in the New World," Compton said. "The earth was not as large as he had estimated and he arrived sooner than expected."

"Were the natives friendly?" Conant asked.

"Yes. Everyone landed safe and happy."

Success. A sustained nuclear reaction was possible. What's more, the Project could now build a reactor that would use Tubealloy to produce another new and highly fissionable element, Element 94, also known in the Project as "49."

★   ★   ★

Some hours later, Leona and the Italian Navigator trudged through the snow, reeling from the day's events. It was bitterly cold, even by Chicago standards. Leona was bundled to the brim, black eyes peeking out over the collar of her overcoat. Hers was a captivating face, and the only female one in the crowd on the courts that day. She walked briskly alongside her small, fiery mentor, each of them quietly wondering if they really had been the first to pull this off, or if the Germans had already surpassed their achievements without any of them knowing.

They were headed to a gathering at the Fermi home that had been in the works for weeks. The date, when initially chosen, was random. However, in light of what had happened, the party took on an added level of celebration, at least for those guests privy to the day's events. Laura Fermi was not.

Laura had done her best to adjust to the new level of secrecy in her life. She hadn't always been out of the loop. She had spent many an evening surrounded by her husband's colleagues, discussing his work over wine and food. It was different now, but her curiosity would not be so easily dodged. With every coworker who walked through the door, a "Congratulations" was given to her husband. As the list of backslappers and well-wishers grew, Laura began asking what her husband had achieved that was so remarkable. She wasn't getting very far.

Ask your husband . . . Go talk to Enrico . . . You'll find out sometime . . .

Laura turned to Leona for an answer. Leona was younger, yes, but imposing in her own way. She was tall and attractive with a strong build, and Laura had heard that Leona possessed a stratospheric IQ. But when Leona started talking about sinking admirals, Laura had no idea how to react. For a time, Laura had felt as though Leona looked down on her. Now she felt her husband's protégée was ridiculing her.

. . . a Japanese admiral . . .

But Leona's creative metaphor was immediately and emphatically backed up by other scientists present and Laura let it pass.

Laura would later write that she thought it significant that so many of the project scientists were not from the United States, that many were recent immigrants like her own brood. Maybe others thought it commonplace that experts, no matter their citizenship, should be involved in ventures of such importance. But Laura read more into it. These scientists—Hungarians, Italians, Germans—knew the power and speed with which a dictatorial state could mobilize. Universities. Military. Research. Back in their war-ravaged homelands, these entities, each with their own expertise and power, were under a single direction, guided and controlled by one hand.

"A dictator decrees," she later wrote, "a president asks Congress for permission to organize."

The Project, it seemed, would make no such mistake.

Her husband had achieved the unbelievable before, Laura thought. Perhaps there was a way to sink a ship while buried under snowdrifts in Chicago. When she finally confronted her husband a few days later, the results were no less perplexing.

"Did you really sink a Japanese admiral?" she asked.

"Did I?" came the response.

"So, you didn't?" Laura volleyed.

"Didn't I?" her husband returned.

Doublespeak. Metaphors. Laura knew that continuing along this line of questioning was futile. She may not have known what her husband was working on in the University of Chicago's Metallurgical Lab, but she was sure their work had precious little to do with metallurgy.

Just four Decembers earlier, Lise Meitner had sat pondering the possibility of what the team in Chicago had now made a reality. She and Ida Noddack remained an ocean away and well outside the growing Project. Lise's nephew Otto Frisch would soon find himself with other Project scientists at Los Alamos, New Mexico. Leona and the Italian Navigator would eventually make their way to Site W, where the success of CP-1 would be applied on a massive scale. Lise, too, had been invited to join the Project but declined. She knew what they were developing. She wanted no part of it.

★　★　★　★　★

Only Temporary

Spring into Summer, 1944

We were indignant all over again when we got to Oak Ridge. Why couldn't we have been warned about what a raw place we were coming to?

—Vi Warren, *Oak Ridge Journal*

Colleen Rowan waited patiently for her turn. The effusively outgoing 18-year-old brunette was on line for the shower; business as usual in a trailer camp with communal baths that served thousands of shift workers. The showering took place in shifts, as well. Colleen had encountered lines at every turn since moving here. This was just one more.

She found herself staring at the embroidered peacock on the back of the blue chenille robe of the woman in front of her. Chenille was a big hit. And here in East Tennessee they were within striking distance of the tufted bedspread capital of the world, Dalton, Georgia. When Colleen's family first came to Oak Ridge, they had passed the vendors on the highway, selling chenille bedspreads. Other roadside entrepreneurs offered up squirrels to hungry travelers, tiny cooked carcasses hanging alongside soft, tufted strips of fabric in pastel pinks, mint greens, and blues. The roads were full of people selling what they had, trying to get by. The Rowan family from Nashville drove past them, heading to a bigger place with better jobs for everyone in the family who was of working age. They were moving on to what they believed would be a land of opportunity and of purpose.

At first, Colleen hadn't been sold on the idea of moving to CEW. The first thought that had sprung to mind a year earlier when her family came to visit relatives here was, *No way, no how.* And she told her mother as much.

"But this is where we need to be," Colleen's mother had explained. "We should do this, not just for us, but for Jimmy. For the war."

Bess Rowan's family were mostly plumbers: Spike, Robert, and Uncle Jack had come to CEW to work. One of Daddy's brothers, John, had moved here, too. The men had learned about the jobs via their plumber's union. Spike, Robert, and Jack all worked at the K-25 plant, where Colleen now worked.

Conditions at CEW took getting used to. Many of the construction workers were living in one-room hutments, each with three other men. And where were the sidewalks and proper streets?! Colleen stared in disbelief as she watched women in dresses walk barefoot through the gunk that covered everything within sight, their shoes hoisted high over their heads. She couldn't imagine why on earth her mother would want to leave Nashville for this.

But with nine children still at home and her brother Jimmy in the Philippines, Colleen knew better than to tangle with her mother. And Colleen wanted so badly for Jimmy to come home safe. If this would help—and they were told it would—she would do it.

"It'll be just like camping," Colleen's mom said, trying to convince her. "It's only temporary."

Colleen had survived the Depression. She had survived the nuns at Cathedral High School. She could survive this.

This was life in a place called Happy Valley.

★   ★   ★

Townsite was the section of CEW originally set aside for living and shopping and other quotidian comings and goings. It sat in the northeast corner of the Reservation, backing up against the Black Oak Ridge and bounded to the south by Old Tennessee 61. Happy Valley sprouted out of the dust in the shadow of K-25, housing its thousands of workers, just one of several necessary residential additions to CEW.

Initially, Stone & Webster (S&W), out of Boston, served as principal contractor for CEW's plants and other structures, and started work on the administration building—the "Castle on the Hill"—in November of 1942, while evicted locals were still packing up. Moving full steam ahead meant the gentle rise and fall of the verdant landscape had been reduced to dirt and clay. Barren tracts made easy targets for rains which transformed them into meandering rivers of mud.

S&W failed to impress the General with their plans for the residential Townsite area. So the Pierce Foundation and their associated architectural firm, Skidmore, Owings, and Merrill, came on board. Pierce had a knack for modular housing, with an eye for town design, and had dipped its toes into the prefab market during the Depression. It developed, with the Celotex Corporation, a cheap, versatile material called cemesto board.

Cemesto. Cement and asbestos, a pairing that in many ways made the town of Oak Ridge possible, was a potent mix of prefabulousness. Wall sections could be mass-produced, shipped, stored, and used to erect everything from homes to schools to shops. In early 1943, it was decided that the Pierce Foundation and Skidmore would design the Townsite. Stone & Webster would oversee construction and handle infrastructure services like telephone, sewage, etc.

But early on the Pierce-Skidmore team had some basic questions.

How large did the town need to be?

Where would the town be located?

Project reps were loathe to offer answers, as they might provide clues to enemy snoops as to what was going on at CEW. For location, the Project provided highly edited aerial photos that gave an idea of topography but little more—they could have been taken anywhere. The Project initially told Pierce-Skidmore to base their designs on a town of 13,000. When the time came for a site visit, the architects were instructed to go to New York City's Penn Station at a particular time and place. They were met by a representative of the Project, ushered onto a train, and then told their destination.

Soon CEW began to take shape: There were seven gates in all. The three plants—Y-12, K-25, and X-10—were kept separate from

Townsite for safety and security purposes. Y-12 and K-25 were roughly 17 miles apart themselves, so that if there were a disaster that destroyed one, the other would survive. Y-12 took up around 825 acres and was roughly five miles from Townsite. It sat on the far side of Pine Ridge in the Bear Creek Valley, with topography helping to deter damage in case of any accidents or explosions.

By the spring of 1943, roughly 55 miles of railroad and 300 miles of paved roads were already in place. The original plan for a town of 13,000 was already scrapped by the fall of 1943 when Celia and Toni first arrived and at this point the Project anticipated CEW might have as many as 42,000 residents.

There were a variety of single-family homes, apartments, and dormitories planned for Townsite. Homes sat upon the new streets in as equidistant a manner as possible. Though the homes varied in their number of bedrooms, the prefab nature of all the structures meant the bones beneath were essentially the same. When viewed from a distance, Townsite exhibited a uniformity, a visual reinforcement of shared circumstances and hardships, even if that was not strictly true.

But despite all this progress, this tribute to modern science and city planning, there were no sidewalks.

★   ★   ★

At least Colleen's family had their own trailer now. At first, only Colleen, her mom, and her brother Brien came to CEW. Her father stayed in Nashville with the rest of the kids, still waiting for his Statement of Availability.

The national "Statement of Availability" program was designed to prevent workers from job-hopping, which could hamper wartime industries dependent on a consistent labor force. If a worker left a job vital to the war effort, he or she had to obtain a document from their employer before being eligible to be hired elsewhere. If someone were laid off, there was no problem. But if a worker was fired or quit—say because they wanted a better-paying job—an employer could deny the Statement of Availability. This meant the worker had to wait *at least* 30 days before they would be able to be hired again, often longer.

The Project had gotten some help circumventing restrictive labor practices put in place to keep wartime industries humming along. Under Secretary of War Robert Patterson issued a directive stating anyone applying for a war industry job through the United States Employment Service had to be recruited by the Project first. If they were rejected—they didn't pass the security clearance, for example— only then would they be available for another position.

As construction began to pick up in 1943, workers were leaving at a rate of as much as 17 percent a month. By the end of 1943, the regional office of the War Powers Commission proclaimed, "the unknown demand at Clinton Engineer Works overshadows all known demand . . ." In early 1944, Union Carbide noted a 25 percent turnover rate for construction workers at K-25. Based on exit interviews, complaints ranged from work conditions to food and housing, which, for the construction workers, was generally trailers or tiny hutments. By mid-1944, continued plant construction and expansion were in full swing, and the need for workers was crucial. So the under secretary of war and the president of the International Brotherhood of Electrical Workers came to an agreement—the Brown-Patterson Agreement— enabling the Project to yank workers out of existing jobs, send them to CEW, and retain them for three months. Employers would receive official recognition from the War Department. Employees got a bit of a pay raise, overtime opportunities, and would retain any seniority they had back home. Travel was provided, and housing—in some form—was paramount.

Housing options ran the gamut, from three-bedroom houses for a family of four down to hutments like the ones Colleen's uncles and Kattie and Willie lived in. Though on-site housing was a recruiting perk, need continued to outstrip availability. Housing guidelines were strict and getting stricter. A childless couple could not live in a two-bedroom house, for instance. Proper single-family houses were generally reserved only for those earning $60 or more a week and were assigned depending on the number and gender of children. If you worked for an hourly wage below the position of foreman, you needed special approval for a house. If you lived within 40 miles of CEW, then you were out of luck altogether. You commuted. If you were single, there were dorms or barracks. Some civilian married couples found themselves destined for separate dorms with no in-room visitation for members of the opposite sex.

When the Rowans decided to move to CEW, Colleen's father left his job at the post office. But the Postal Service was vital to the war effort, so James Rowan had to wait for his Statement of Availability before he could be hired by another company. What Colleen's parents did not anticipate, however, was that her father's absence would complicate their search for housing. Only "heads of households" were eligible to apply for available on-site family housing. Women were not, no matter their circumstances, considered heads of household.

Despite the fact Colleen's mother was the primary family member at CEW, working to support her children while her husband took care of the kids back in Nashville, she was not regarded as a "head of household." So she was ineligible for a house, apartment, or trailer when she first arrived.

Women who made enough money or held the right positions— though the vast majority did not—*might* be able to get a house for their family, but it required additional approval from the District Engineer, an approval that Colleen's mother would never receive. In some cases, women were told they might—MIGHT—be considered for some sort of family housing if they could find another female employee to share the house with them.

Most of Colleen's extended family was at CEW. So when they arrived, Colleen lived with her aunt Nell and uncle Jack, and her mom lived with Uncle Spike. Colleen slept on a bed at the far end of the trailer that folded up during her waking hours to make a table. Cleaning was easy enough. As Aunt Nell would joke: just walk the length of the trailer and kick the drawers shut.

Finding room for household items like high chairs was another matter. When Uncle Jack had taken some metal pipe from the K-25 job site and crafted a high chair with it for one of his kids, he couldn't get the finished chair in the door. Instead, it stayed outside, sinking down into the mud, baking into place by the sun. At least Aunt Nell could keep the baby close by while she was hanging up clothes.

★   ★   ★

The Happy Valley encampment featured row after concentric row of identical trailers. Thousands had been hauled to the Reservation by train and dumped on the newly razed ground.

Everything's goin' in . . . Nothin's comin' out . . .

Once James Rowan received his Statement of Availability, he took a job with J. A. Jones Construction. The entire clan—Colleen, her parents, and eight brothers and sisters—moved into a double-wide trailer in the J. A. Jones Trailer Camp, near K-25, where Colleen and her mother worked. Colleen's family lived toward the back of the camp near the security barrier. Colleen's youngest sister, Jo, still in elementary school, was scared to approach the barbed wire, certain that the Germans were lurking in the woods on the other side of the fence. Thoughts of Jimmy and the specter of war were always with them. As soon as the Rowans moved in, Bess Rowan was quick to hang their service flag in the window, a reminder to everyone why they were here.

Some trailers had small, makeshift yards and some trailer sites were given street names, hoping to make residents feel a bit more at home in their temporary surroundings. Happy Valley also included H-shaped barracks with male and female wings and hutments for white single men. Trailer camps like Colleen's were hot and dusty in the summer when they weren't covered in mud from temperamental southern thunderstorms. Bright streetlights shone all night to support the 24-hour shifts, giving everyone a feeling of never quite being at rest. Blackout curtains—normally an air-raid go-to—were indispensable if you could get them.

The Rowan family's double trailer at times housed eleven people— though it was hardly designed to do that. There was a double bed at each end of the trailer and a kitchen in the middle. It was larger than Aunt Nell's single trailer, but small compared to their two-story house in Nashville. The trailer had electricity but no bathrooms. Water had to be hauled from a distribution center down the hill and stored under the sink, which drained into a bucket. Some families kept what they called slop jars for waste. Everything was emptied by crews with the daunting task of servicing the quickly multiplying structures dotting the landscape. A stove served double duty for heat and cooking. It often leaked oil onto the wooden floorboards below. If you weren't careful, one stray spark and the whole thing could ignite.

Taking advantage of shift work was key to making a snug, pressed-metal trailer fit large families. Family members slept in shifts, ate in shifts, cleaned in shifts. If there was a cot free, you slept on it. If a child needed to be picked up from school, you fetched her. If there was some food, you ate it. And you had better clean up after yourself, because everyone else was too busy to do it for you.

Happy Valley began in 1943 when J. A. Jones built about 450 hutments on the south side of Gallaher Ferry Road near K-25. The area was so raw that they had to have water trucked in. Just months later, Happy Valley was bursting its brand-new seams. Colleen's uncles told her that citizens of Clinton were renting out garages and smokehouses to CEW workers, sometimes on a shift basis. Have sheets will travel. Others stayed in common rooms in hotels, with workers coming in and out at all hours. Now new roads and housing appeared in the time it took Colleen to leave for work and return home again. Throughout CEW roving construction crews worked in tandem: One crew laid foundations, a second pass added chimneys standing alone above bulldozed ground, then finally the cemesto siding was slapped on. At the peak, it was estimated a house went up every 30 minutes.

Many people living in the camps at Happy Valley had never laid eyes on CEW's main Townsite, only 10 miles away. They knew only the trailer camps and the ever-growing plant. Though Colleen may have loved taking the bus to Townsite, Happy Valley had everything: Cafeterias (there were 11 scattered throughout CEW by now) operated virtually around the clock to account for the 24-hour work schedules. Snacks at 2 AM? Sure, why not.

There was the communal bathhouse, a post office. Most news arrived by mail. Calls for Colleen and others living in the camp were announced over loudspeakers posted to electric poles for all to hear. Indeed, personal phones were practically nonexistent. Only those who could demonstrate need or importance had a phone in their homes.

Laundry was another adventure altogether. Colleen soon learned it was better to do your own with a scrub board, though keeping clothes clean hanging on the line was a Sisyphean battle against the elements. Gusts of wind blew trailer site soot, and pounding rain sent muddy spatters flying. Better this than take your clothes to what many referred to as "the shredder." If you were lucky, you might get your clothes back from the drop-off service in four or five days. If you were unlucky, they might be lost or mangled. *Why risk it?* Under no circumstances would you gamble panties with elastic. Those were hard to come by in wartime, as rubber now served a purpose higher than a young lady's waistline.

There was shopping, too, though it was more akin to "waiting." Waiting in line for cigarettes. For soap. For meat before it ran out. For Jell-O. When available, Jell-O was a real score and guaranteed a wait. Sugar was rationed and Jell-O was a little something sweet. All you had to do was add a little hot water and you could have yourself a ruby-hued, cool, bouncy treat in the hot Tennessee summer.

Colleen soon realized the second she saw a line she had better get on it. Chances were there was something good at the other end.

Most services were managed by the Roane-Anderson Company, so named for the two counties in Tennessee that CEW straddled. Roane-Anderson, a shell company of Turner Construction, was created for the Project and operated as an agent of the government under the direction of the United States Engineering Department. Luckily, some services came to you. The library, for example, headed by the New York Public Library's Elizabeth Edwards, was in Townsite. Soon Edwards instituted the rolling library. There was a rolling grocery, too, that made the rounds through the trailer sites, propping open its shutters for a quick treat. Each Thursday it offered copies of the *Oak Ridge Journal.*

The front page read:

NOT TO BE TAKEN OR MAILED FROM THE AREA

Under no circumstances should pictures of the various installations or panoramic views be taken!

Colleen always wondered why you weren't allowed to take the *Oak Ridge Journal* off the "area." There was never any real news in it.

"Dog bites in Oak Ridge: 40 a month . . ."

But what *could* the paper print? If *Colleen* wasn't allowed to know what she was doing, how could they print what anybody else was doing? The *Journal* was useful for mass schedules and social events. It featured reports on "presenteeism" in the plants and a smattering of fashion news—always useful to the woman up to her knees in mud 24-7.

"It's just like camping. . . . It's only temporary. . . ."

So went Colleen's mother's mantra, one for all of those who have endured tough times. Oak Ridge was difficult, yes, but also exciting and different. Colleen knew she wanted to remember her time here. She began collecting bits and pieces of her life. Two fires during her childhood had robbed Colleen's family of so many personal memories. Those experiences had made her oddly sentimental. She began saving almost everything she got her hands on: important newspaper clippings, memorable photographs, sketches, and poems inspired by her new adventure. Each ticket stub glued into a scrapbook or stuffed in a keepsake box further cemented her spot in a place that she was certain would be only temporary.

Sakes alive, look at it! How could it be anything but?

★　　★　　★

A flashlight moved across Kattie's sleeping face. It was the guard again, coming into Kattie's hut. They were allowed, it seemed, to come in almost whenever they wanted.

"Ain't nobody here but you, but there are four beds," the guard barked at Kattie.

He left, flashlight waving, no doubt heading to the men's area to see if he could shake the women out of there.

Guards were a very regular presence in the black hutments and always stationed outside "the Pen"—the name that Kattie, her friend Katie Mahone, and the other women who lived in the black female hutment area had taken to calling their little corner of CEW. Kattie had noticed it when she first arrived, the barbed wire. High, tall fencing with barbed wire separated the women's hutment area from the men's, which was across a ditch and up a bit of a grade. That's where Willie was, and would stay, for the foreseeable future.

They didn't put men in a pen, though, Kattie noticed. Her hut was around back, right near the fence, wire in every direction. There was only one way into the Pen and the guards were there, night and day, making sure no men entered the women's area. She still saw Willie every day after work at his hut. But there was a curfew. Come 10 PM, flashlights waved and folks scattered. Were they FBI men? Kattie thought so. Oh, but the women hated those guards. Most of them, anyway. The head guard, the one who looked the oldest to Kattie's eyes, was quite nice.

It was authority, he explained to Kattie, that made the younger guards behave the way they did.

"Get your marriage license the next time you go home," he told her one day when she was being hassled by one of the younger guards. "Don't let them tell you who you can and can't visit."

He never ran her off from Willie's hut, not once. Of course Kattie always made sure she was back inside the Pen before curfew. Not all the women did, though. And then the flashlights came out.

There had been plans for an entire Negro Village, one that would have resembled the main Townsite with construction like the white homes, separate but essentially equal. But as housing became limited throughout CEW in 1943, it was decided that the Negro Village would become East Village—for whites. Lieutenant Colonel Crenshaw, who was in charge of the program, explained why. Negroes didn't want the nice houses, he wrote. His office had received virtually no applications for the village. The negroes felt more comfortable in the huts, that was what was familiar to them—or so went Crenshaw's rationale. Black and white construction workers and some GIs lived in hutments, but no white women lived there. The hutments remained, no matter one's marital status, earnings, or seniority, the only housing for black workers. Five grown men might live in the 256-square-foot space if the coal stove was removed in the summer to allow for one more cot. When the Negro Village became East Village, hutment areas for black residents were equipped with separate roads that took them to the nearest stores, fenced off from the white areas. Theft was a persistent problem, privacy practically nonexistent, and amenities few.

Treatment varied widely, and some black residents wrote letters of complaint stating they were not permitted to visit their spouses at all, no matter the time.

B. W. Ross, spokesman for the Colored Employees of Roane-Anderson Company, wrote:

And too, at the war man power board where we signed for employment on these jobs we were promised living facilities that would allow man and wife to live together. And now we colored married couples are here working on this Govt. Project. With our wives living in one house and we being their lawful married husbands are living in separate houses alone to our selves. We are not allowed to visit our wives home. And our wives are not allowed to visit our homes at no time day or night.

The black cafeteria was close—right near the huts—but Kattie could not, no matter how she tried, stomach the food. One resident penned a letter of complaint detailing food served in the black cafeteria—"rocks, glass or some dangerous piece of harmful trash in this food"—and sent it to Roosevelt himself. Kattie remembered the night of the dreadful turkey thigh—at least she *thought* it was a turkey thigh—her cramps kept getting worse and worse, so severe. Willie had to physically carry her to the bathroom.

It must have been a buzzard *thigh*, she thought in retrospect. Once they arrived at the communal bathroom, it was full. Apparently, she hadn't been the only one whose stomach had been torn up by the buzzard. So Kattie made Willie go into the men's bathroom to check and see if the coast was clear. It wasn't entirely—there was another man there and in obvious intestinal despair—but she had no choice.

Something had to change.

There may have been better pay here, but there was not better food. Kattie knew she had to figure out another way to get something decent to eat. There had to be a way to make this place feel a bit more like home. She was going to figure out a way to cook in her hut, out of sight of the guards, rules or no.

★　　★　　★

Celia had been getting ready to turn in when her dorm mother buzzed her room. Celia had a phone call.

Was it her family calling about her brothers?

It was late—already close to 10 o'clock. She went down to the lobby and picked up the phone. The voice on the other end was one she had been waiting to hear for some time. It belonged to Henry Klemski.

"Do you remember me?" Henry asked. "You picked me up at the train station."

Did she remember him? Celia stifled a laugh.

There was certainly no shortage of available men, but Celia had found herself thinking about Henry more and more. After that first meeting, Celia had begun to distance herself from Lew. She liked him, but he was talking marriage, and Celia wasn't ready for that.

She also knew that if Henry thought that she was still dating Lew, there was no way Henry would ask her out. So she let Lew down easy.

"I'm not going to get serious with anybody," she'd said. "I'm taking up your time. See if you can find another girl."

Time passed, and Celia had begun to wonder if she'd ever hear from Henry. And then, seemingly out of the blue, he rang.

"Meet me for coffee at the cafeteria," Henry said to her.

"I can't. It's too late," Celia said. "The dorm mother won't let me go."

Celia found her dorm mother to be strict, but not unreasonable. That said, she still didn't think that this idea would fly.

"Put her on the phone," Henry said.

Celia handed over the phone to the dorm mother and stood by watching as she spoke to Henry for a few moments and then hung up.

"He sounds like a nice guy," the dorm mother said. "You can go."

Celia freshened up and ran over to Jackson Square to meet Henry at the cafeteria. She had been given one half hour. And that was all the time she'd need. Now, a few months on, she and Henry were spending more and more time together. But one person she had been hearing less and less from was her brother Clem.

★ ★ ★

By the summer of 1944, the dorms were teeming with thousands of individuals. Single white women lived in dorms where they could be strictly monitored. Along with the no-cooking rule, there were rules against gambling and liquor. And, perhaps most challenging in a town with dorms chock full of single men and women in their late teens to mid-20s: No male visitors allowed. Sexual infractions meant eviction and were often punished most severely. Dorm mothers were relied upon to regulate comings and goings, and curfews. Some of these marms had been lured from places like Bryn Mawr and Smith and trained other dorm mothers about how best to handle the challenges of looking after so many single young girls living away from home for the first time.

There were violations and complaints. Some of the griping made it as far as the District Engineer, who found himself visited by a delegation of ministers. Some of their congregants—the "good girls"—had complained about "bad girls" breaking dorm rules, including those prohibiting male visitors. The ministers suggested that all the "bad girls be moved into their own separate dorm, so as not to disturb or, by association, damage the reputations of the rule-abiding women." The Engineer told them it was a fine idea. All the ministers needed to do was supply two lists: one of the good girls and another of the bad girls. The Engineer did not hear from them again.

Despite her initial panic and thoughts of turning tail and returning to Hornbeak, Dot began adjusting to life in the dorms. There were those living in the dorms who complained about laundry, or cafeteria food, or about having to share a bathroom. But Dot didn't think it was any worse than the "two-holer" outhouse she had grown up with. She had only brought one bag from home—mostly hand-me-downs from her life as the youngest of seven children—so she found her room to be big enough. The furniture was so new that some women had to unwrap the plastic from their dressers when they moved in.

One young woman reported moving into a dorm that was so new the windows weren't yet installed. She slept in an overcoat and found ice gripping the edges of her water glass the next morning.

Dot's adjustment was also thanks to Katie and Thelma, two women who lived down the hall. Though they were only a few years older than Dot, they seemed to have it all together and took Dot under their wing. Most importantly, the two women loaned Dot money when her cash ran out, as it always seemed to, and the arrival of a paycheck was still a few days off. If the rent was due or Dot needed an infusion of dollars for the cafeteria or a movie in town, Katie and Thelma always came through. Dot always paid them back. She may not have saved much, but she was having the time of her life. Learning to manage her finances was a tiny bump in the road. The nervousness and fear she first felt was soon replaced by a heady feeling of freedom. There was no farm and no chores to do. All she had to do was go to work.

For those who had gone to college, like Jane, the statistician, Virginia, the budding chemist, and Rosemary, the nurse, the dorms had a familiar feeling. Everyone was roughly the same age, all living together for ostensibly the same purpose. Friendships were cemented as fast as saddle shoes in wet clay in Oak Ridge during the war, and clubs sprouted quickly. Jane and Virginia eventually joined the College Women's Club, organized by a mutual friend. The members of the College Women's Club got together to socialize, sometimes putting on fashion shows or dances. But their primary activity was babysitting for local families—families living in real, honest-to-goodness houses—for 25 cents an hour. The idea was to raise money for a college scholarship fund for girls graduating from Oak Ridge's high school.

There were perks to babysitting, as well. The women enjoyed a night in a house with access to a real kitchen. If they could cobble together enough sugar ration coupons, they baked cookies and maybe brought a date along. Sometimes another couple would stop by and the young women could sit in a real living room and play a game of bridge or relax in mixed company without fear of running afoul of dorm regulations.

Celia's friend Rosemary babysat occasionally for the head of the hospital, Dr. Charles Rea. After a short stay in the dorm, Rosemary and the other nurses finally got their own living facilities, a housing complex right next to the hospital. Rosemary loved the convenience, and her new rooms were definitely a step up. Two rooms, rather than a whole hall, shared an ensuite bathroom. But she, too, liked to enjoy the comforts of what felt like a real home now and then. Dr. Rea and his wife had taken Rosemary in, in many ways. That first Christmas when she wasn't able to travel home to Holy Cross, Iowa, she spent the holidays with them. And if they got home late, she would often spend the night at their home rather than go back to the dorm.

Dorms and dating, babysitting and bridge. CEW was in many ways an outpost best suited to the young, those for whom enthusiasm trumped exhaustion and the sense of adventure outran hardship.

★   ★   ★

For some residents, however, life on the Reservation was *too* trying. Chief Psychiatrist Dr. Eric Kent Clarke, who had just arrived several months earlier in March 1944, found himself challenged by what he soon realized was a very unique community. Combine cramped quarters with isolation and secrecy and he discovered that a lot of people were in a perpetual state of edgy exhaustion. The kind of rehashing of a day's work with a spouse or roommate that most adults took for granted was not permitted. Relieving stress by talking about what was worrying you was not an option, since most worries were related to work, an off-limits topic.

Residents had left familiar traditions and support networks behind, and there was little to replace them. Clarke reported that it had for some time been suspected that there were many psychiatric problems plaguing the residents of Oak Ridge, but that these situations were neither recognized nor well defined. That's where he came in.

"By March, 1944, the need for specialized service to cope with the personality disturbance became apparent and the psychiatric service was established," Clarke wrote in one of his early reports.

From the beginning the residents have been subjected to many additional stresses absent in the usual community which have created tensions. Material necessities were still in embryo form, and it required a true pioneer spirit, that was often lacking, to make an easy transition to a community still in the making.

But how did one foster community from scratch amid nonstop deadlines, round-the-clock work schedules, and a high turnover of residents and laborers? The Project had little time or inclination to institute social change.

Despite all the planning the military did with regard to Townsites and homes and religious groups and softball leagues, there was no real plan for Oak Ridge beyond the timetable of the war itself.

CEW had a single goal: to enrich Tubealloy for the Gadget.

But whether the Project had intended it or not, CEW *was* a social experiment of sorts. A military-run Reservation handling the most top secret of assignments but inhabited by not only military men, but civilians, women, children. Native Americans from Oklahoma worked alongside construction workers from Mexico and good ol' boys from Virginia. Black employees who were segregated and forced to live without their children and apart from their spouses in small hutments, and construction workers packed like sardines into tin-can trailers lived mere miles from out-of-town PhDs, who enjoyed prefab yet roomy homes. Those PhDs themselves—some living under assumed names for security reasons—might be next door to a plumbing foreman and his family, neither knowing the other's job.

Women added a social dimension to this military installation that had not yet been taken fully into account. They were an essential part of the Project's success. Without them, there would be no Product, and without Product there would be no Gadget. But women brought a sense of permanence. Social connectivity. Home. Women seeking work or promotions were quizzed about whether they planned on having a family. Families—babies especially—were potentially disruptive to the production process. Women were powerful. And oh so necessary.

Women infused the job site with life, their presence effortlessly defying all attempts to control and plan and shape every aspect of day-to-day existence at Oak Ridge. The Project may not have known what was to become of the town after the war, but the women knew that while they were there, they would not only work as hard as the men, but they would make it home.

The Project probably never saw this coming. The government wasn't interested in social experiments, didn't give a second thought to the cultural-anthropological ramifications of the world they had set in motion. The Project had put all the pieces in place: single young men and women from all over the country. Wives. Mothers.

They lived in close quarters, surrounded by visual reminders of solidarity, camaraderie, and sometimes threat. Maybe it was the gates, or the common enemy. Maybe it was the tracts of identical housing, which served—at least for some, at least in their immediate surroundings—as reminders that no one was better than anyone else. A bond formed among them. For those who chose to stay, there was going to be community and family, *planned* or otherwise, like it or not.

The military may have been in charge, but the irrepressible life force that is woman—that was well beyond their control.

The only thing that would be temporary was the war.

TUBEALLOY

★ ★ ★ ★ ★

THE QUEST FOR PRODUCT

Tubealloy's journey started deep in the earth, much of it in Edgar Sengier's Belgian Congo mines, with a bit arriving from Canada and a smattering from vanadium mines out west. The first leg of Tubealloy's trip was often a long voyage across the sea to the New York metropolitan area in 55-gallon drums. There the Tubealloy might head to Eldorado Mining in Canada for processing and then perhaps take a trip to Westinghouse in New Jersey, Iowa State College in Ames, or maybe St. Louis, where it landed at Mallinckrodt, or to Cleveland, where it was welcomed at Harshaw. At different times during the Project, these companies transformed the Tubealloy into a variety of forms—oxides, fluorides, salts, metals—before it was piled on trains or trucks and bound for Project sites including the Clinton Engineer Works in that tiny corner of Tennessee.

Between there and Los Alamos, Tubealloy might be chloridized, oxidized, sublimized, fluorized, vaporized, bombarded, spun, separated, weighed, assessed, assayed, measured, and measured again, its very characteristic scrutinized at each stage of processing.

The challenge was not securing enough *raw* Tubealloy; it was transforming that raw Tubealloy into fuel for two different models of the Gadget. One version of the Gadget would use *enriched* Tubealloy: Tubealloy with a high concentration of isotope 235. The second version of the Gadget used 49 for fuel, an extremely powerful and toxic by-product of Tubealloy fission.

Three principal Project sites were engaged in around-the-clock work to tackle this task of creating and fueling the Gadget, with the help of other facilities and companies across the country. Gadget design and assembly took place at Site Y in Los Alamos, New Mexico, on the site of a former boys' school. Principal production of 49 went on at Site W in Washington State. Site X, Clinton Engineer Works in Tennessee, would eventually house four different plants dedicated to handling Tubealloy.

SCALING UP

In February 1943, construction of the plants code-named Y-12 and X-10 began at the Clinton Engineer Works. X-10 was a pilot reactor, but much bigger than the pile created by Fermi's team in Chicago. Using slugs of Tubealloy, canned by the Aluminum Company of America, X-10 produced 49 by means of a fission chain reaction. As Tubealloy gives up its neutrons, not only is energy released, but those free neutrons split neighboring atoms, which in turn release their neutrons, and so on. But some of those neutrons are *captured* by other atoms. When this happens, the eventual product is 49.

On November 4, 1943, X-10 went "critical": The chain reaction of neutrons splitting other atoms was self-sustaining. Enrico Fermi and Arthur Compton had traveled to CEW—under the names Henry Farmer and Arthur Holly—for the anticipated event and were yanked from their beds at the Guest House in time for the momentous occasion. The larger scale reactors at Site W in Washington were based on the success of X-10. The remaining three plants at CEW—Y-12, K-25, and S-50—were dedicated to *enriching* Tubealloy alone: separating the Tubealloy 235 from the Tubealloy 238.

The success of the Project hung on the three little neutrons that differentiated T-235 from T-238. Tubealloy 238 is more commonly found in nature. But it's not as fissionable as the less frequently found Tubealloy 235. In fact, only about seven out of every 1,000 *atoms* of Tubealloy are isotope 235. So for every 1,000 pounds of Tubealloy (T), only *seven* are T-235. Imagine having 1,000 grains of rice and only seven of those would cook the way you want.

The Gadget would only get cooking with those precious little grains of T-235. That was the sole purpose of these gargantuan plants: ferreting out those rare and valuable atoms that were needed to fuel the Gadget.

THREE PLANTS: THREE DIFFERENT METHODS

Separating T-235 from T-238 had to be done *physically*, exploiting the minuscule difference in mass between the two. Each plant at CEW used a different approach to—hopefully—achieve this: Y-12 via electromagnetic separation; K-25 via gaseous diffusion; and S-50 via liquid thermal diffusion.

By the summer of 1944, the Project's expenses were roughly $100 million a month and construction was about halfway done at the mammoth K-25 plant. Situated on a 5,000-acre site, site preparation for the K-25 plant had begun in June 1943, construction in late September. Construction continued at a breakneck pace at the half-mile-long structure, but the General still didn't know when he would be able to flip the "on" switch.

K-25

The plant's soaring cooling towers, rising like Appalachian skyscrapers above the secret site, recirculated a volume of water that could serve a city of five million. When finished, the plant would have four stories, more than 44 acres of floor space under a single roof (more than 44 football fields). This made it the largest building of its kind in the world—though precious few, including those who lived in the vicinity, knew it was there.

K-25 used gaseous diffusion to separate T-235 from T-238. Such a method had never been tried on this scale. Here's how it works:

Tubealloy is converted into a gas, TFL6, which is then pumped through a series of tubes comprised of what the Project called a "barrier." The barrier was a thin, porous sheet of metal, with identically sized, submicroscopic openings. These openings were incredibly small—numbering in the hundreds of millions per square *centimeter.* The barriers were rolled into tubes, which were sealed in another, larger airtight pipe. The idea was that as a high-pressure stream of Tubealloy gas was pumped through the barrier tubes, more of the lighter 235 would diffuse through the barrier while more of the chunkier 238 would not. As the Tubealloy traveled through a series of these tubes, the lighter 235 would head up the cascade of tubing to the next highest level.

One pass through this process would not be enough—closer to 3,000 stages were needed, accounting for K-25's gigantic U-shape. (It was as though the shape of the building itself announced to anyone flying overhead what was being processed inside.) Tubealloy would pump through stage after stage, snaking its way around the giant U on a mile-long trip, becoming more highly enriched as it did. That was the idea, anyway.

There was a problem: Design of the barrier still eluded the Project's scientists. The first barrier tested in a lab had been about the size of a silver dollar, but K-25 would need *acres* of barrier material. So while scientists labored frantically for a solution, workers kept building K-25. Pipes and other structural elements arrived, were inspected and put in place where possible. A company called Midwest Piping had produced three million feet of nickel-plated pipe, and all of it had to be both leakproof and able to resist the corrosive effects of the Tubealloy gas. Standard welding would not suffice—new techniques were developed; a school was set up to train employees. Every detail was crucial, right down to every last spot weld on every single pipe.

Y-12

Meanwhile, in another area of CEW, the Y-12 plant remained the only fully operational option for enriching Tubealloy, ground zero for the electromagnetic separation process that Ernest Lawrence had developed at Berkeley's Rad Lab. This process centered on calutrons—*Uni*versity of *Cali*fornia Cyclo*trons.* If Tubealloy was the lifeblood of the Project, then Y-12's calutrons were CEW's beating heart and soul.

There were Alpha and Beta calutrons, which differed primarily in their size and the material fed into them. Alpha calutron tanks were the larger of the two, and were often arranged in oval groupings called racetracks. Ninety-six tanks, alternating with giant electromagnets, stretched 122 feet in length, 77 feet wide, and stood around 15 feet high.

Tubealloy entered the calutrons as a salt, TC14: unremarkable brownish-greenish crystals. A heater cranked up the temperature until that Tubealloy salt vaporized. An electron filament producing highly charged electrons zapped the vaporized Tubealloy, ionizing the atoms. Now, the Tubealloy had a positive "charge."

Pump a charged ion through a magnetic field and its path will bend, with the radius of that path dependent on its *mass.* So charged Tubealloy ions traveling through a magnetic field traveled along a semicircular path, with the heavier T-238 traveling on a radius larger than that of its lighter counterpart, T-235. At the end of this magnetized trip was a collector with two delivery slots, targets for the slightly different paths of the 238 and the 235. The Tubealloy ions slammed into a metal plate, looking like tiny metal flakes. The 238 was captured in one receiver—the Q slot—and the precious 235 was collected in another— the R slot. The distance between the slots at the end of the Tubealloy's magnetically charged journey was roughly ³⁄₁₀ inch.

Calutrons were not called as such by the vast majority of workers at CEW, but were more commonly referred to as D units because when viewed individually they looked like giant letter Ds. Cubicle operators sat in front of giant stations working knobs and levers that controlled source heating, voltage, and ionization by visually monitoring their panels.

Beta calutrons were roughly half the size of the Alphas and were arranged in a rectangular configuration. T-235 collected from the Alpha calutrons was fed into the Beta calutrons for a second stage of enrichment. After a run through the Alpha calutrons, a batch of Tubealloy was enriched to about 12 or 15 percent 235—not a high enough percentage of 235 for the Gadget. After a Beta run, the enrichment level reached around 90 percent T-235, which *was* good enough for the Gadget.

The gist was the same for both Alpha and Beta runs: Tubealloy went into the calutrons as a salt, was ionized and accelerated through a magnetic field, and finally came out of the calutrons separated into two different isotopes: T-235 and T-238.

Workers removed Tubealloy from the collection boxes and scrubbed out the rest of the unit where possible with nitric acid. Everything was processed, to retrieve as much of the Tubealloy as possible. Workers' clothing was often processed as well, to retrieve even the smallest bit of usable material. Before, after, and between Alpha and Beta runs, Tubealloy passed through hands and beakers and spectrometers and centrifuges and dry boxes. As it assumed its different forms, it was given a variety of code names: 723 for TO3, a yellowish powder, 745 for TCL5, greencake, yellowcake, and so on. A slew of chemists worked with the Tubealloy, like chefs hovering over a secret ingredient of a recipe they were not permitted to know. And at every turn, in every department, individuals accounted for the Tubealloy, from building to building, lab to calutron. Any time even a dusting of Tubealloy was transferred, someone filled out a waybill. How much. Assay. Analysis. Code number. Clerks hand-cranked calculators, couriers ferried sealed envelopes from building to building.

When completed, K-25 would be the largest building in the world, but the scale of Y-12's operation was equally astounding. Magnets, for example, commonly require copper. And Y-12's magnets were massive— the Alpha magnets were more than eight feet tall. But the rest of the war—the not-so-secret parts of the war—needed copper, too, for things like shell casings. So the Project used silver to construct its magnets. Who had a few tons of spare silver lying around? The US Treasury.

When Y-12 was being built, the District Engineer met with Under Secretary of the Treasury Daniel Bell to discreetly request around 6,000 tons of silver. This baffled a man normally accustomed to speaking of silver in troy ounces. A more official request followed, from the secretary of war to the secretary of the treasury: They agreed not to discuss specific details about how the silver would be used, only that it would, at some point, be returned to the federal government. Eventually, about 13,540 short tons of silver (395 million troy ounces) were borrowed from the US Treasury, taken from government vaults at West

Point, and used to construct the calutron magnets. Price tag: more than $300 million.

While K-25 was still being constructed, Y-12 was already a complex of structures: Alpha and Beta calutron buildings, cooling towers, chemical processing, change houses, pump houses, steam plants, cafeterias, and much more. Buildings sometimes had various designations. Several of the buildings, despite the secrecy surrounding the Project, began with the number 92: Tubealloy's atomic number. When the General first learned of this numbering trend, he did not find the choice particularly amusing or wise. He would later say the plant names were essentially random: the X in X-10 probably came from Site X. Y-12's moniker was meaningless. The K in K-25 was for Kellex or Kellogg, the company responsible for that plant's design and development, and 25 was used "throughout the Project," according to the General, to refer to T-235.

HOW BIG IS BIG ENOUGH?

Tennessee Eastman, a division of Eastman Kodak, oversaw operations at Y-12, and though the company was vigorously recruiting for Y-12, there never seemed to be enough workers.

At first, the General and his team estimated that 2,500 people should be able to operate Y-12, but as early as the fall of 1943, nearly 5,000 workers had been hired. On September 9, 1943, the General had ordered the size of Y-12 to be doubled, in response to yet another revised estimate regarding the amount of T-235 needed for the Gadget. *More! Much more!*—had become an unfortunately familiar and unwelcome refrain. At that point, not even a year had passed since breaking ground at CEW when the Scientist and his Los Alamos team said they needed *three times* the amount of T-235 stated in their most recent estimate.

Three times as much.

It wasn't the first such revision. Shortly after taking over the Project, the General had asked the scientists to estimate how much Tubealloy would be needed for testing and building the Gadget, and he wanted a degree of accuracy to go along with it.

Answer: The numbers were good within a factor of 10.

The General was flabbergasted. He was demanding, yes. Difficult, sure. Odd, perhaps. (An FBI investigation into his life revealed a habit of stashing chocolate in his safe.) But wanting a more accurate estimate was hardly unreasonable.

The size of the plants depended on the accuracy of these estimates. Equipment purchases depended on the accuracy of these estimates.

The number of people needed to work in the plants depended on the accuracy of these estimates.

So for, say, 100 pounds of Product, wiggle room of a factor of 10 meant they might need 10 pounds or they might need 1,000. The General felt like a "caterer" told to "plan for between 10 and 1,000 guests." The Y-12 plant alone originally required more than 38 million board feet of lumber. That was akin to building the catering hall without knowing how many guests were coming for dinner.

The first of the three Alpha buildings initially planned for Y-12 was up and running in September 1943, but that Christmas, the first in CEW's existence, the General had traveled to CEW to shut it down for repairs. The magnets caused enough shimmying to pull the several tanks out of line. Unlike X-10, which was a much smaller version of the larger nuclear reactors being built at Site W, Y-12 was *the* plant. There was no pilot plant upon which to work out kinks. It was the only electromagnetic separation *plant* in the country—the world, for that matter. (Or so the Project hoped.)

A second Alpha racetrack was ready to go in the beginning of 1944, and by that March a Beta track was completed. The four Alpha tracks had finally begun operating together in April, four months later than planned. As estimates of the amount of Product increased, so did the number of calutrons. Despite challenges, the chips were still down on the electromagnetic separation process, though there was a growing hope that the K-25 plant, once up and running, would provide a more efficient and cost-effective mode for enriching Tubealloy. The idea was that eventually enriched material from K-25 would be fed into Y-12. But that wouldn't happen without a working barrier.

So, the Project continued to explore other viable options. That's where the fourth plant, S-50, came in.

MRS. H.K. RISES TO AN UNUSUAL OCCASION

Evelyn Ferguson (née Handcock) had been widowed just six months when she first met with the General. Her late husband, Harold Kingsley Ferguson, had been head of the H. K. Ferguson Company of Cleveland, Ohio, one of the most reputable constructors of war plants in the country. H.K. had had a go-get-'em attitude and a knack for getting factories done on time. Eve, an attractive and energetic woman, had often traveled with him on business. Now she traveled alone, a heart attack having taken her 60-year-old husband from her. She may still have been "Mrs. H.K." to everyone who met her, but now the H. K. Ferguson Company—her husband's legacy—was in her charge.

Eve's meeting with the General was inspired by some compelling news he had received from the Scientist in Los Alamos. At the Philadelphia Navy Yard, Nobel Prize–winning physicist and codiscoverer of neptunium, Phil Abelson, had been working on enriching Tubealloy using a process called *liquid thermal diffusion.* He was, according to the Scientist, making excellent progress.

Liquid thermal diffusion employed concentric vertical pipes, cooled on the outside by water and heated on the inside by high-pressure steam. The different isotopes of Tubealloy—235 and 238—would rise up through the columns at a different rate, with the 235 adhering more closely to the heated surface and rising more rapidly than the 238, which preferred the cooler surface. A 100-column pilot plant was being built at the Navy Yard and would likely be finished midsummer, 1944. Couldn't that slightly enriched Tubealloy also be fed into the insatiable monster that was Y-12?

It was not the first time that the Project had considered the thermal diffusion process. Abelson had successfully enriched a small amount of Tubealloy in 1941. The verdict was, at the time, that the process would take too long, cost too much—even by the Project's spendthrift standards—and wouldn't produce enough highly enriched Product for the Gadget. But advances had been made. Maybe now whatever enrichment liquid thermal diffusion could achieve might help move things along in the other plants.

The General sent a team to Philadelphia and liked their report. He decided a plant *could* be built at Site X, one that would be operational by 1945.

Enter Eve Ferguson. H. K. Ferguson Company's motto was "We design, build, and equip your plant—one contract, one responsibility, one profit," and it fit the Project's modus operandi to a T. Simplicity. Delegation. Compartmentalization. A subsidiary company, Fercleve, was created to handle operation once the construction was complete. But things had to move fast. The General wanted the plant operational in 120 days and its features had to be, as he put it, a "Chinese copy" of the Abelson's pilot plant. But much bigger.

Bigger! More! Now!

This was precisely the kind of challenge H.K. would have loved. "Stop worrying" he was once quoted as telling an under-the-gun manufacturer. "Leave the worrying to Hitler and Hirohito." The new plant, code-named S-50, wouldn't have a paltry 100 separation columns, but instead would boast 2,142: each 48 feet long, comprised of nickel pipes surrounded by copper pipes, then swathed in a cool jacket of water, and then wrapped snugly again in galvanized iron. The columns were gathered into racks, or groups, of 102 columns. The location would be near K-25, which would provide the much-needed steam for the process.

"You can't win a modern war at thirty-five miles an hour," H.K. once said, referring to his lead-foot tendencies on the road and in business. The General would likely have agreed. And a mere thirteen days after the General handed Eve Ferguson her company's assignment, site clearing began. It was July 9, 1944: Eve's 47th birthday and almost seven months to the day since she'd lost her husband. He couldn't have done it better himself.

Perhaps father of the calutron Ernest Lawrence was right when he said the General's reputation depended on the Project's success. But the success of the Project depended not solely on the General nor the brilliance of the men in New Mexico.

The most ambitious war project in military history rested squarely on the shoulders of tens of thousands of ordinary people, many of them young women.

CHAPTER 6

★   ★   ★   ★   ★

To Work

Then we started stewing about the furnace and the laundry
and the mud and the sitter problem—and forgot all about the
project.

—Vi Warren, *Oak Ridge Journal*

The contest had been the Engineer's idea, though it was unclear if
the young women even knew they were competing.

One of the Project's more enthusiastic, ambitious, optimistic, and
inspirational characters, Ernest Lawrence found it impossible to believe what the District Engineer was saying: Those high school girls
they had pulled from rural Tennessee to operate his calutrons in Y-12
were doing it better than his own team of scientists.

In Berkeley, only PhDs had been allowed to operate the panels
controlling the electromagnetic separation units. When Tennessee Eastman suggested turning over the operation of Lawrence's
calutrons to a bunch of young women fresh off the farm with nothing more than a public school education, the Nobel Prize winner
was skeptical. But it was decided Lawrence's team would work out
the kinks for the calutron units and then pass control to the female
operators.

Then the District Engineer gave Lawrence some surprising news:
the "hillbilly" girls were generating more enriched Tubealloy per run
than the PhDs had. And Product was all that mattered.

A gauntlet had been thrown down.

The two men agreed to a production race. Whichever group generated the most enriched Tubealloy over a specified amount of time

would win—though "winning" only meant bragging rights for the Engineer or Lawrence.

By the end of the designated contest period, Lawrence and his PhDs had lost handily.

They just couldn't stop fiddling with things, Lawrence thought, trying to make things run smoother, faster, harder. Still, he was surprised.

The District Engineer understood perfectly. Those girls, "hillbilly" or no, had been trained like soldiers. Do what you're told. Don't ask why.

He and the General knew that was how you got results.

★   ★   ★

Women occupied every corner of every workplace at CEW, from the personnel processing down to chemical processing. They were janitors, saleswomen, chemists, operators, and administrators. Those women who worked in personnel processing were considered a lucky bunch, as they often got first look at newly arrived men. News of a group of incoming GIs would spread rapidly through any affected offices. Oh-so-fortunate was the girl who filled out personnel security questionnaires (PSQs) for incoming men. Everything you wanted to know was there: age, marital status, education, where they were from. You name it. The PSQ had it all. In triplicate.

CEW was a social limbo in many ways, neither here nor there, where transplants felt at once rootless and immediately grounded. New place, no history, instant community. A fresh start for some. Most GIs were sent to CEW without their wives, and not all of the married men working on the Project—GI or not—were quick to share details of their marital status at a dance or the bowling alley. Some advertised their status, some did not. It made more than a few women a little leery about falling hard for anyone, and made those women who worked in personnel processing at any of the plants or administrative offices particularly valuable as friends, and they were routinely quizzed by friends about potential new suitors.

Is there a wife in the picture? Could you check . . .

Knowing something might mean bearing bad news. (Yes, there was a wife. Children, too.) Other times, the woman in the know could wave a friend on toward romantic bliss. Green light, all systems go. A quick, highly forbidden glance at a file was enough to send a potential girlfriend to the rafters with joy or sulking away in disappointment. In a world of secrecy, where infractions—including the unauthorized accessing of personnel files—could be punished with firing and eviction from your home, this kind of delving was nonetheless seen as a necessary risk.

★   ★   ★

Celia's work in the Castle was happily predictable: she typed memos, took the transcription, completed insurance forms. She did not have to type or file any coded materials—words, numbers, strange names, and other gibberish—though some other secretaries did. "G.G." visited now and then, and everyone continued to scurry like mice when he arrived. Celia still didn't know why. It was a year later, and they had yet to be properly introduced.

Being on a day schedule meant no graveyard shift. This made it much easier to find time to spend with Henry, which she did, often meeting him for dinner. Lew had taken it all quite well. The friends continued to socialize together. In a town as small as Oak Ridge, if you lost a date you moved on to whoever had room on their dance card. No one knew how long they would even be living here— certainly not once the war was over.

Elsewhere in the Castle, Toni found herself on yet another coffee run. There were a number of secretaries in the pool who could have gotten coffee for the group visiting Mr. Diamond, but Toni had always been an antsy sort. Here was another opportunity to get up, move around, socialize.

Across the hall from Toni's office was a room full of members of the Women's Air Corps. As far as Toni could tell, all the WACs did was read newspapers. She struggled to remember a time when she saw them doing anything else. All day they sat, periodicals in their hands, intently scanning each page. Toni wasn't the only one who had noticed; some of the other secretaries had, too, and a theory about what they were doing had developed. (No one would dare ask the WACs directly.)

Word around the pool was that the WACs were looking for secret words in the papers, words the government didn't want mentioned. What were the words that were off-limits? Neither Toni nor any of the other secretaries had the slightest. But when one of the WACs spotted an offending word, that newspaper got a visit from . . . well . . . Toni didn't know that part, either. FBI, maybe? FBI had become a knee-jerk response to many questions without obvious answers.

Who was back home asking about me? I don't know, FBI?

Whom did he get in trouble with? I think FBI.

Toni's work was routine, but the contracts she was always typing up for her immediate bosses in Lieutenant Colonel Vanden Bulck's section, Sgt. Glen Wiltrout and Sgt. Ed Whitehead, were a bit strange. Despite her inauspicious interview, Toni took a lot of dictation. It still didn't make much sense, but often it was because of the words rather than Mr. Diamond's accent.

To her mind, it sounded nonsensical, like repetitive, wordy say-nothingness:

The subcontractor is hired and is given the responsibility to do the work prescribed to get the assigned task done . . .

She thought the goal was to say as little as possible but to wrap that lack of information in as many sentences as you could. Each day, scads passed her eyes and ears, but as far as she could tell, they made no sense.

Today's latest trip to serve coffee to Mr. Diamond and his out-of-town visitors was followed by a visit from Sergeant Wiltrout.

"Toni," he began, "do you know why Mr. Diamond always asks you to get coffee when he has guests?"

"No," Toni answered. She hadn't given it a second thought.

"Well," Glen continued. "He asks you to bring it in because he said he wants his guests to hear how the natives speak."

★   ★   ★

On a typical day, women who worked as cubicle operators arrived by bus at Y-12 and passed through yet another set of armed gates. There was an around-the-clock bus system on the Reservation. Bus trips to the plants were free, otherwise you could buy bus tokens to travel to places like Knoxville for shopping or a movie. Commuters living off the Reservation might have caught a bus at 4 AM to arrive in time for a 7 AM shift.

CEW may not have officially existed, but it had a bus system the size of which rivaled some of the largest cities in the entire United States. Buses were packed, reminding cramped riders of the origin of the term "cattle car." Some were retrofitted flattop trailers. Part of the transport fleet had originally been used in the World's Fair in Chicago. Many buses had benches running down either side of the car and a wood-fired stove right smack in the middle. This was good, if crowded, in winter. In summer, sweltering, sweaty bodies swayed and jostled along roads that were dusty or muddy, depending on the weather.

Guards checked badges at every turn. There were fences within fences here, with individuals monitored almost as closely as the Tube-alloy they were processing. In addition to a resident's pass that let workers roam freely about the nonworking areas of the Reservation, workers had badges dictating which plants or buildings they were allowed to enter. Coded by number or color depending on where you worked, badges announced to anyone looking—and someone was always looking—where you could work, which bus you could ride, and even which bathroom you could use. Near the entrance to the plants, guards would stop and board buses, shining their flashlights up and down the aisles if it was nighttime. Once through the plant entrance, a stop at the change house was first for some women, including Helen, an Alpha-3 cubicle operator. There she changed into zippy blue pants and a top. Calutron cubicle operators reported to their assigned buildings, depending upon which units, Alpha or Beta, they were operating.

Cubicle control rooms were immense. Rooms were long, ceilings high, and the noise, at times, quite jarring. Piercing light, sparking sound. Cavernous. The soaring ceiling heights and concrete and metal surroundings of the vast rooms generated a cacophony of sound—work boots pounding concrete mixed with the chattering of voices, and was occasionally accompanied by an electrical short or the scrape of grounding hooks against metal.

These women had never seen, let alone laid hands on, contraptions of such complexity and enormity. It may have been a day's bus ride from a farm in western Tennessee to the guarded gates of the Y-12, but it was a world away in scientific development from just about anywhere in the world, no matter where you hailed from.

Panels lined both sides of the room, creating a gauntlet of technology in which the women sat throughout their shift. There they monitored the instruments that controlled, as most of the workers called them, D units. They knew also that the units they monitored were arranged in something called the racetrack, which was located nearby, in an even larger room. The women were not supposed to venture there, though some did. Shifts were eight hours, but often seemed longer when you were perched on a stool the entire time. Operators usually minded at least two panels, each covered in knobs, dials, gauges and meters, all of which had to be carefully watched.

Dot, Helen, and the other young women monitoring panels had been trained to keep their needles and gauges within a certain visual range. The basic operations explained to the women in training had been fairly straightforward: If your needle veered a bit too far to the right or left, a knob was adjusted until the needle fell back within the acceptable range. Most of the work was done by sight alone, though disruptive crackles might indicate a unit needed adjusting. Each young woman had four or five gauges or "needles" to monitor. And each control room had a supervisor who watched panels of their own at the back of the long room and monitored the women's performance, troubleshooting when necessary. The supervisors weren't completely in the know, either. No one in the cubicle control room had all the pieces of the puzzle of which they were an integral part.

When needles started going haywire, sparking could start. For some women, this took getting used to. It sounded as though a breaker were blowing and if the correct adjustments couldn't remedy the issue immediately, the unit itself might stop working completely.

Each unit operated on a charge that would last for only a specified amount of time. Once the unit shut down, operators would pick up the phone next to their panel and call the men to come and empty what they called E boxes.

They didn't know what was in those E boxes, but it needed to be emptied regularly.

Dot and Helen heard other letters thrown around as well, including Js, Ms, Qs, and Rs. When a needle on one of the gauges veered too far from center, the corresponding knob was adjusted. Helen didn't know what the letters stood for, but she knew the idea was to get as much R as possible so that when the men came to empty the E boxes of the D units there would be a nice amount in there.

But it could be tricky. The cubicle flew into what she started calling a "flurry"—the voltage kicking on and off, sometimes accompanied by what sounded like electrical charges—and the supervisor would have to leave and come to check and see what was happening.

What's in the E boxes?

What does Q stand for?

Smart girls didn't bother asking. Those who asked too many questions or hazarded answers or theories were soon gone.

But little bits of information did trickle about, words and phrases passed around.

You wanted your R high. That was better than Q. There was a charge near the bottom of the D unit. Something was vaporized. There was a Z. The E box caught everything. Open the shutters. Maximize the beam. Supervisors spoke of striking a J. M voltage. G voltage. K voltage. And if you got your M voltage up and your G voltage up, then Product would hit the birdcage in the E box at the top of the unit and if that happened, you'd get the Q and R you wanted.

It was that simple.

There were always men milling about, fixing this or that, trying to talk to the roomful of fetching operators. Dot was adapting quite well to the social life in her new home. Dating, completely forbidden her by her stricter-than-usual father back on the farm, was now an option. When you weren't allowed to date, stealing a kiss in the middle of the road or the back of the bus on the way to football games was your only option. Not here.

Here, her life and possibilities were wide open. Shift work didn't just apply to her own individual schedule at the plant, it applied to her social schedule as well. Three shifts meant three times the dating opportunities, she liked to joke. But amid all the available men, the one that caught Dot's attention was a young supervisor named Paul Wilkinson.

When the machines started sparking or making noises, Dot would think to herself, *What's wrong with me? Why can't I get this thing to keep quiet?* Then one day Paul walked the length of the room and sat on the stool next to her. Dot introduced herself and watched as he took over her panel. He had the nicest hands she had ever seen, almost like a surgeon's. And his fingernails—so clean! Boys back home in Hornbeak never kept their nails groomed like that—they always harbored a week's worth of dirt from farms and cars.

From then on, whenever Dot had a problem, Paul would sit next to her and massage the knobs and dials until the machine subsided, purring like a kitten. Dot did not believe she had the same magic touch. It seemed to her that no sooner had she taken over than the machine would go berserk. However, it was nice to know that any problems she was having, Paul would come fix. Maybe the machine going haywire had its benefits. Paul had gone to college. He was well mannered. Dot took one look at him and thought he might have some real potential.

Helen never told anyone she met that she was a cubicle operator. After her experience with the two men who recruited her to spy, she knew better than most that people were always listening, people you might never suspect. She noticed things, though. Helen had been told not to go back on the racetrack, but she occasionally walked back there anyway to fiddle with the units that her panels were controlling. Normally, you could pick up the phone at your panel or even yell back to one of the men who monitored the racetrack. But they weren't always there. She knew she was not supposed to do this, but if there was no one back there to help out, what was her choice?

Above the racetrack was a catwalk. She always tread carefully and was sure never to wear any metal. Much may have been secret about those units, but the magnets were common knowledge and terrifyingly strong.

DANGER! KEEP WATCHES AND IRON OUTSIDE RED LINE!

She and others had been warned about the magnets during training. They would pull bobby pins right out of your curls, unhinge the workings inside your watch, and pin you against the wall if you were forgetful enough to have worn a belt buckle. Woe betide the maintenance man with a nail or two stuck in his shoe—he could find himself rooted to the spot.

Helen peeked, too, when men came to pull trays out of the units and scrape what looked to her like some sort of dust out of them. The E boxes. Sometimes the maintenance men who worked back on the racetrack would add what some of the women heard called 714 to the unit. They carried it around in a bucket, smoky fumes rising from it. (Over at the K-25 plant, Colleen noticed that they used 714 too . . . Only where she worked they called the substance by a different code: L28.)

The eight-hour shifts, if everything went smoothly, ran from 7 AM to 3 PM, 3 PM to 11 PM, and 11 PM to 7 AM. The watching and twisting and turning and staring kept going shift after shift until the charge for a calutron unit ran out. Throughout the day and at the end of their shifts, Helen and Dot wrote down readings from their various dials and gauges in a notebook that sat next to their stations. At the end of a shift, a courier came to collect them and whisk them away. The cubicle operators did not know the significance of the data or where it was being taken; they just knew that whatever they were writing down in those books was important to someone, somewhere.

Though the importance of secrecy was drilled into everyone at CEW, people couldn't help guessing what might be going on. Helen remained remarkably immune to this spirit of inquiry: The two men who had approached her at her dorm wanted her to report back to them about just such conversations. Helen cared about earning a steady paycheck, playing ball, and helping end the war. But for others, it was a natural curiosity, a course of amusement to hazard guesses at what might be going on.

Some of the young women joked that—judging from the color scheme that surrounded them on the Reservation—CEW was manufacturing drab green paint. After all: such a huge factory, so much activity and maintenance and they never saw anything leave the Y-12 plant. As for Dot, she was sure that the twisting and turning of the knobs and dials must have had something to do with making those informational war films they played at the movie theater before the main feature. After all, she thought, the plant was being run by Tennessee Eastman. They made film, didn't they?

It seemed only logical.

★   ★   ★

After the Tubealloy was cleaned out of the E boxes, a slew of chemists sized it in its various incarnations, assessing the percentage of all Tubealloy present and *assaying* samples to determine what percentage was the desired T-235. Virginia, who had finally landed in a lab at Y-12, was one of those chemists.

Virginia had left personnel when it came to her attention that she was being held back for promotion. It was odd: After consecutive A evaluations, she received a D. Shocked, she tried to figure out what went wrong. Word around the office was that in order to avoid giving raises and promotions, supervisors tried not to give too many glowing evaluations. To keep things in check, a bad one would be thrown into the mix. This pattern continued until they were willing to offer a raise. Then Virginia learned she would not be eligible for a promotion because she was not working in her designated field. So she asked for a transfer to a lab—any lab—so that she could finally do the work she had expected to do all along.

Virginia's life at Y-12 had nothing to do with voltage or E boxes or Qs or Rs. Her world was one of dry boxes and cakes. Virginia called the product she worked with yellowcake. No matter what name she or anyone else in her lab called it, Virginia, like some other scientists, knew precisely what the Tubealloy/yellowcake/Product was. She did not know where it had been before it landed on her lab bench or where it was going once her analysis was complete. Some daring chemists made the trek over to the University of Tennessee to page through *Mellor's Handbook of Inorganic Chemistry*, where one could read all about Tubealloy (listed, of course, under its real name). None of the chemists lingered there too long—you never knew who was watching—but ink smudges on the page and a well-creased spine would later tell the story of that volume's popularity.

Even those who managed to work with Tubealloy and knew what it was were instructed, and agreed, never to use its name. So even if you had figured out part of THE BIG SECRET—or thought you had—there was no reason to use transparent language in public, since you would never get confirmation about whether you had, truly, determined why CEW and all its plants existed. Loose lips!

So workers used codes for even the most innocuous of materials, and designations might switch from plant to plant, lab to lab. In Y-12's chemistry department, you might find these:

704: hydrogen peroxide.

728: liquid nitrogen.

703: nitric acid. (This made mincemeat of cotton work clothes.)

720.724 was TO4, Tubealloy oxide.

723 reacted with 753 to make 745 (TC15) which was transformed by sublimation (think dry ice in a Halloween punch) into TC14—feed for the calutrons.

Of course, across the ocean, the Germans had their own way of doing things. They called Tubealloy oxide "preparation 38."

★   ★   ★

In another building of the Y-12 complex—which would eventually contain 268 permanent structures—clerks raced to arrive at work earlier than their coworkers, and for good reason: The Marchant and Monroe adding machines. Early birds dove on the newfangled automatic models to avoid the slower hand-cranking machines. The extra effort to lock down a model that worked a little more smoothly was worth the minuscule loss of sleep when you took into consideration the long shift ahead.

Jane Greer spent most of her days—and sometimes nights—in that room, monitoring the workers as they sat punching a slew of numbers into their adding machines. Like the cubicle operators in another building in Y-12, a room that these women never saw, clerks worked around the clock, each woman performing a single function. Each day, the couriers arrived and brought Jane the numbers that she needed. The numbers were passed to the group of young women she supervised, who put them through the series of calculations Jane had painstakingly explained to them.

They seem so young, Jane often thought. But in truth, most of the women were only a few years her junior.

Instructing and supervising was old hat for Jane by now. She had worked part-time during college teaching physics to Army Air Corps cadets at the University of Tennessee, so she had developed her own knack for explaining mathematical processes and calculations to those who had not used them that often or, in some cases, ever.

She had started out in building 9731 of Y-12 as a production records clerk, making thirty-five dollars per week. Within a couple of months she was given a raise to thirty-eight dollars. By Christmas of 1943, she had already been made chief clerk, and had helped establish the plant's statistical office, checking the reports that were arriving from, as she was told, various production departments. With the most recent promotion came yet another raise, this time up to thirty-nine dollars per week, and soon a move to the production manager's staff. In addition to her supervisory role, Jane prepared summaries of operating data that were submitted daily, weekly, and monthly. She checked every calculation the women made and then compiled all their information into one, larger report that would tell her superiors something about how production was going.

But despite her constant advancement, it hadn't taken Jane long to learn that men working beneath her were making more money than she was. Other women throughout the Reservation had observed the same. This came as little surprise to Jane, in particular, a young woman who had been denied entry into engineering school because of her gender. But it was no less disheartening.

Jane chose to focus instead on the importance of her job. Her purpose. She couldn't imagine the other job opportunities she had passed up turning out any better than this one had. At Oak Ridge she felt needed and was grateful she could remain close to home and her widower father. She also felt valued by the young women who worked with her, and that camaraderie meant a lot and suited her nature. Flighty Jane was a social bird, no doubt. She was a Greer from Paris, Tennessee, after all, a true Southern Parisian in every respect. Boyfriends, parties, impromptu performances in her parents' parlor—Jane was up for anything. But once at work, the magna cum laude graduate got serious.

Her own training had been quite intense. The "technical knowledge of the production process" had been explained to her in great detail along with the chemistry and production calculations involved. Everything was presented in an exhaustive manner that was at once specific and yet still vague. Jane was given much more information than many at CEW—men or women—but never, of course, the whole picture. Her meticulous notes detailed the material, the T, as it worked its way through the Y-12 plant.

Here's what Jane learned, in a large, coded nutshell:

There were two processes, Alpha followed by Beta, during which the feed material went through D units. Jane had painstakingly sketched the semicircle production unit at the heart of these processes and when necessary referred to her notes. Across the top of her sketch, she had written simply, THE D. She drew a detailed flow chart, marking E boxes and Alphas and Betas. She labeled D units, Q readings and R readings, and T material.

Then came the mathematical equations. Now *here* was where Jane could shine. Jane may not have been *told* what T stood for or the real name of the D, and she certainly had never laid eyes on them in person. But as a statistician she knew how to calculate just about anything. Just give her the numbers and get out of her way.

How the production process related to the production reports—that's where the rubber met the road for Jane. She collected tallies from her flock of Marchant and Monroe mistresses and checked and compiled them, computing the final data that she herself had to submit. Her final reports were picked up by two security guards and delivered to her department head. The work must have been important: Someone stopped by her desk during her training session and stamped her personal, handwritten notes in a bright red SECRET.

Jane loved it.

★　　★　　★

Pipes came in and pipes went out. Men welded and pounded and split beam upon beam. Kattie looked up at the construction workers overhead, sparks flying as they welded a constant flow of two-by-fours together. The fire and flares popped and flew and finally fell, fading as they approached the ground. She looked again and thought the answer to her prayers might be found among the glints and flashes raining down from above.

Kattie was on the swing shift, sometimes working from 8 AM until 4 PM, sometimes from 4 PM 'til midnight. She entered the massive K-25 plant through the Clock Alley (so called because that was where all the workers clocked in). Once in, she was sweeping and scrubbing every inch of space in her section of what was, though she did not know it, the largest building in the world.

There were enormous tanks to shine, too. Work was fine, she thought. She was meeting other women. They'd talk and gossip as they worked from one end of the floor to the other and back again. Willie was working on the railroad tracks, one of many men sweating and singing, day and night.

> *Hey boys, can't you line,*
> *Hey boys, just a hair,*
> *Ho boys, line them over,*
> *Hey boys just a hair . . .*

The tracks they maintained routed train cars and their cargo straight into K-25. Perhaps nowhere else was the perplexing absence of tangible product more evident than where the train tracks crossed into CEW. At this juncture, workers from Louisville & Nashville railroads transferred control of railcars to crews working for the Project. Those L&N workers watched as thousands of packed train cars made their way onto the Reservation while only empty ones ever exited.

Everything's goin' in and nothin's comin' out . . .

Willie earned a good bit more than she did—and goodness knows she was working just as hard as he was—but the amount she earned was nearly *twice* as much money as she'd made cleaning the library back at Auburn University in Alabama.

The night she received her first check, she hurried home to her hut. She carefully took the cash out of the envelope she'd gotten from the bank and laid all the crisp, new bills out over the top of her cot. She just stood there, looking at it all. So much in one place at one time. After relishing the moment, she gathered it up in her hands and began to divide it up as she always had with every bit of money that had ever crossed her palm: One pile for expenses, one for savings, and the biggest chunk to be sent home via Western Union to her mama and the babies she missed so much. *Babies.* They were getting bigger all the time, whether or not she was there to see it with her own eyes.

But good pay alone was not enough to solve her more immediate problem. She wanted to cook at home, badly. And she knew that to do this she would need a pan. Today, she thought she might have found an answer.

Kattie looked closely at the construction workers. When they cut off the end of a beam, they tossed it aside. It looked to Kattie like there was plenty of material that the men weren't using. They were treating it like trash! There was no reason for any of that good material to go to waste, not if she could use it.

She waved to one of the workingmen overhead, getting his attention.

"Make me a biscuit pan!" she yelled up, straining to make her voice heard over the incessant grinding and pounding and yelling of the construction crew.

Kattie didn't know who on earth this worker was. She had no idea if—or why, for that matter—he would do as she asked. He had no reason to. Everyone certainly had enough work to do in this place. But sure enough, the next morning when she showed up for work, there was not one but three pans waiting there for her before she started her shift. They were far from perfect—a little rumpled and crinkled at one end or the other, far from flat and a far few angles short of being rectangular. But they were done and they were hers.

She carried them home at the end of her shift, careful not to attract too much attention from the guards. She left them in Willie's hut and began gathering ingredients so that she could bake her first batch of biscuits, wondering how she was going to keep her cooking under wraps and out of sight.

How about that: A mere construction afterthought. Trash.

But those slabs of metal, scraps that would never be missed by the soaring girders of K-25, would serve to make her and Willie and the rest of her hutment friends some fine biscuits.

★　　★　　★

Colleen Rowan had never seen pipes so big, and she came from a family with more than its share of plumbers.

After the training at the Old Wheat School—a repurposed remnant of one of the evicted communities—she had spent the first few months of her new job working upstairs in the conditioning building. There she spent her days among a maze of pipes while working as a leak tester.

Her new position and life were awash in acronyms and numbers: She worked in building 1401 for FB & D at the K-25 plant on the CEW and had earned a Q clearance. Her boss was a GI with the SED who had been recruited from the ASTP. She rode the AIT bus and, being the good Catholic girl that she was, attended CYO at Father Siener's B house.

Ford, Bacon & Davis operated the conditioning building, which was located back and to the right of what most called the big U building (though most knew not what that letter might represent). When Colleen first began working in 1401 she was out on "the floor," an enormous, open, airplane-hangar-sized room. A wall of square-paned windows ran the length of one side and the whole space was full of people and pipes and vats and cranes. And *clean*. There may have been mud outside, but inside was spit-shine, inspection-ready spot-less.

There were pipes of every size and shape imaginable. The multi-story ceiling height and hard surfaces amplified the clinks and clanks of jostling metal, the squeaking and rustling of chains of pulleys and gears, the low grunts and high shouts of workingmen and working-women.

Colleen stood at her station alongside other leak pipe testers, all of them women. She looked up: Overhead, tiny open-air cars piloted by a single man shuttled back and forth along a ceiling track that ran the entire length of the room. One at a time, these tiny ceiling trol-leys would hoist pipes at one end of the room and ferry them to the awaiting leak pipe testers at the other. The millwrights—the pilots—lowered the pipes in front of Colleen and the others. On the floor, the pipes were open and not connected to each other. The millwrights connected one end of the pipe to a vacuum pump and sealed the other using a red, sticky resin called "glyptal." As their promotional materials would later trumpet:

> Glyptal! From General Electric. The Paint Industry at War! When the complete story of the formation of protective finishes developed for specific war needs is known, it will be as important to a Nation at Peace as it now is to a Nation at War.

With one end sealed and the other connected to a vacuum pump, all the air was sucked out of the pipe and it was Colleen's turn to go to work. She used a probe that was connected to a tank which most workers referred to simply as a leak detector. She would slowly run the gas-emitting probe along every centimeter of every weld on every pipe, making sure never to miss a spot.

As she worked, she kept one eye on the gauge of the machine con-nected to the pump. She watched the needle. She kept moving the probe, nice and slow, looking to see if the needle jumped. If it stayed put, the pipe was okay and was taken away. If the needle moved, then she had a leak. When that happened, she moved the probe over the suspected area one more time, working to locate the trouble spot. As she finished with each pipe, Colleen would take a piece of chalk and mark it as "OK" or designate any spots that had caused her needle to wiggle. After she finished each, an inspector checked her work.

Most times it was a GI. Sometimes it was Bess Rowan, Colleen's mother, another supervisor.

Once all was done, Colleen signaled the millwrights, who took the pipe away and brought in the next one. There was no end to these pipes. Where did they come from? That door over there. Where were they going? That other door right there. What was on the other side of those doors? Probably more pipes.

Then Colleen was then offered a new assignment. One of the GI trainers, Clifford Black—Blackie, they called him—came to her section looking for a handful of women to work in another part of the building.

Colleen was always up for a change of scenery and happily volunteered. The group made their way down into the basement of the conditioning building. Colleen's new assignment was explained in the usual fashion: a lot of information about *how* to do what you were doing, but precious little about *what* you were doing. An important distinction. As Colleen understood it, she would be working on converters. At first glance, the work appeared to be similar to what she had been doing upstairs. The main difference, as far as she could tell, was that all of the pipes here appeared to be fixed in place—no millwrights ferrying back and forth overhead—just one seemingly endless labyrinth of metal.

She would still be testing pipes for leaks, but there was a difference: These pipes were giant. For some of the largest ones, she had to get a ladder and physically climb up on top of the pipes in order to be able to run her probe along all of the various welds. At times, she had to maneuver substantial heights. Though she had already started getting used to wearing pants, this new assignment got her fully broken in in a jiffy.

Dressing like men was still a bit of an adjustment for some women, but Colleen kind of liked it. She remembered the first time her little sister Jo saw their mother in pants and a kerchief. Jo just started sobbing and wouldn't stop. She wanted to know where her mother had gone. Colleen used to think the only women who wore pants were Katharine Hepburn and Marlene Dietrich. (And only fast women wore bobby socks.) Images of Hepburn and Dietrich sporting two-legged fashions in *Modern Screen* captivated many a young woman in the 1940s. And now here Colleen was, scaling pipes all day in mixed company. She had little choice when it came to apparel.

Welds, probes, and gauges. Colleen did not know what those pipes carried and she never asked. One day, while she was working, one of the GI supervisors approached her with some friendly advice.

"If you smell something . . . anything funny," he warned her, "you be sure to get out of here."

"Okay," Colleen said, and went about her business.

The GI walked off.

Huh, Colleen thought to herself. *Whatever's going through these pipes must smell real bad . . .*

★　　★　　★

Rosemary, perhaps more than the other women, interacted at work with just about every walk of life at CEW. But early in the morning on July 7, 1944, work and tragedy brought her in close contact with those outside the fence, as well.

Rosemary had spent the night at Dr. Rea's home, having babysat for the couple's children. Dr. Rea had been called to the hospital in the middle of the night, and when he returned early the next morning, he told Rosemary she needed to go back there with him. There had been a terrible accident.

Many of the soldiers had been lying in their berths when it happened. Others were headed there, having just come from the chow car. The train's passengers, just over 1,000 of them, were all new inductees into the Army.

It was around 9 PM, and the train was moving along at a good clip, already jostling some of the boys as they crawled into the tiny beds, or maneuvered the Lilliputian sinks and bowls in preparation for rack time. This section of the L&N line on the Louisville-Nashville leg boasted more than its fair share of hairpin turns as it twisted its way through the Cumberland Mountains that straddled the Kentucky–Tennessee line, just south of Jellico, Tennessee. One quick turn had tossed a few privates from their bunks, alarming some, barely rousing others. But then the impact came, and with it, gasps and cries as steel wheels departed the iron rails and hit rock and earth. Then 6 of the 14 cars sailed downward, careening 50 feet to the bottom of the Clear Fork River Gorge at the Jellico Narrows.

Tons of buckled steel from the derailed cars stacked one atop the other in the bottom of the ravine. Some of the soldiers were pinned and trapped beneath debris and wreckage, others had been thrown clear or had stumbled away, dazed, into the night. The crushing sound of metal brought local men and women down from their mountain homes. They fashioned block and tackle pulleys to retrieve the injured from the wreckage. No small feat, hoisting the battered bodies up the steep incline of the overgrown bank, where they would lie until more help arrived.

Ambulances, medics, and officials were soon on the scene, but as much as 12 hours after the initial crash, soldiers were still stranded. One private lay helplessly pinned down beneath the weight of four dead soldiers. He had been in the Army 13 days.

CEW was the best first option for the soldiers before plans could be made to move them to a larger facility. When Rosemary walked through the door of the hospital, injured soldiers lined the halls. As head of emergency she worked her way down the corridor, making sure soldiers were comfortable, medicating those who needed it. Of the 34 soldiers who died, Oak Ridge's hospital issued 31 of the death certificates and cared for dozens more. Just two months later, in September 1944, Dr. Rea would write a memo entitled, "Number of Deaths at the Oak Ridge Hospital." In ten months, he noted, the average number of deaths per month—not counting those from the Jellico wreck—was 8.8. This statistic raised the question as to "whether it is desirous to have a funeral home on the Area," which would also likely require a cemetery. Rea's recommendation was, for the time being, to continue using embalming facilities in the surrounding areas. This was perhaps another reminder that no matter the Project's initial plans for Site X, Oak Ridge was fast becoming less of a temporary military outpost and more of a permanent home. Fences could not isolate them from neighbors in need when disaster struck, and though Oak Ridge had been born of youth and vigor and determination, it would eventually need to care for the elderly, the infirm, and those who were gone.

★　　★　　★

Mr. Diamond called Toni into his office, as he had so many times before. But this time he had an unexpected proposition, almost as unexpected as the day he decided to hire her.

"Would you like a promotion?" he asked Toni.

Toni thought. A promotion would sure be nice. The extra pay, the new title, maybe even better benefits.

But then she remembered the constant trips to fetch coffee just so Mr. Diamond could trot her out in front of his Yankee friends and get her to talk like a "native" for his amusement. But now, for once, the decision was hers.

She looked Mr. Diamond square in the eye and gave her answer.

"No."

"You *don't* want a promotion?"

"No."

"You do realize that it would mean a pay raise," he asked, bewildered.

"Yes, sir, I do," Toni answered.

Mr. Diamond's round face appeared puzzled and annoyed. Toni knew the poor man had no earthly idea what to make of her— probably never had—but she did not care one bit. Deep in her bones, her Clinton, Tennessee, bones, she felt good, proud, and satisfied.

She would work, yes. She would work hard. But in whatever way she could, she would do so on her own terms, no matter how it looked or sounded to anybody.

Mr. Diamond had nothing else to say. He was not happy.

Toni was.

She walked out of the room, a native strolling with her head held high, her East Tennessee twang carried on the dusty Oak Ridge breeze, never to be muffled.

TUBEALLOY

THE COURIERS

Two couriers boarded the train. First stop: Chicago. The containers they carried were composed of nickel and lined with gold, but the couriers weren't privy to those specs, nor the container's contents.

At the end of the Beta production process, Y-12's Product, enriched Tubealloy, was combined with fluorine for a clandestine coffee-container trek by courier to Site Y in New Mexico. In this form—Tubealloy tetrafluoride—it waited to depart CEW. The pretty teal crystals of TF4, called green salt by some, sat in a bunker nestled into the ground near one of the remaining farmhouses still standing on the grounds of CEW. Cows grazed, a silo loomed, but machine guns and guards also hovered, safeguarding the Tubealloy until couriers came to collect it.

The first shipment of Product from Site X to Site Y had been sent via courier in early March 1944: roughly 200 grams of all that Y-12 could belt out, about 40 teaspoons. Y-12's first successful production run had been January 27, 1944. The concentration of the Product wasn't what they were hoping for—only about 12 percent T-235—but it had been a start. It had been enough to keep the experimental beast of Los Alamos temporarily sated with some T-235 left over to feed Y-12's first Beta track, which came on line in March. Since then, production had improved. There had been two shipments of Tubealloy, enriched to about 60 or 65 percent T-235, sent to New Mexico in June.

Clad in suits, the couriers could have been mistaken for salesmen, which was, of course, the idea. The containers were placed in small briefcases and handcuffed to the arm of one of the men. If the couriers could manage to sleep, they did so on top of the briefcase. Most stayed awake. From Chicago it was on to the Santa Fe Chief for the second leg of the trip. *"Extra Fast-Extra Fine-Extra Fare,"* was the Chief's slogan. The maroon-and-gold Pullman train emblazoned with a headdress streamed along the passenger cars as it barreled west toward the coast through mountain and desert. The Chief had been known for carrying its share of starlets and other Hollywood types from Los Angeles to points east and back again. Native Americans had first followed these trails, conquistadors after that, then mules gave way to stagecoaches and the gold rush blew the Santa Fe trail wide open, iron and steel and steam linking Hollywood glitz to the plains of the Midwest. A lot of history had transpired along this route. This trip was no different.

Site Y had no train station. The couriers descended at Lamy, New Mexico, where they were met by a car. The calutron-enriched Tubealloy was handed off and sent up the desert highway into nothingness, until it reached the hands of the waiting scientists. There, they would extract the Tubealloy from the TF4 and transform it into a metal as they continued to design the Tubealloy's ultimate container: the Gadget.

CHAPTER 7

★ ★ ★ ★ ★

Rhythms of Life

[W]e learned to confine the conversation with men to the lighter
topics, and we did appreciate how nice they were about finding
one a chair or lighting a cigarette.

—Vi Warren, *Oak Ridge Journal*

Thunderstorms were a blessing and a curse in the summer of 1944, as
they had been the summer before. The downpours came, eradicating
dust and replacing it with sludgy yellowish muck, bursting the swol-
len seams of a humid-heavy sky. The release of tension would only
build up and rain down again the next day. This weather cycle offered
both frustration at the muddy conditions and temporary respite from
the stifling heat. Predictably violent outbursts in the afternoons, a
cool breeze in the evening if you were lucky, followed by quietly growing swelters again the next day.

Life on the Reservation had its own rhythm as well, cycles of work
and lines and food and work and then more lines again. The war
overseas was present in every moment, yet strangely distant, oceans
away with news arriving in fits and starts. If you were lucky enough to
have a radio, you could keep up with the latest developments. If not,
you were left to ferret out nuggets of information from newsprint and
word of mouth, perhaps the occasional piece of mail arriving at last
from far away. Any details offered within those precious letters was
already weeks or months out of date by the time its intended reader
gazed upon the words. Or worse, the reader found nonsensical sentences, the words having been blacked out by censors.

June 1944 brought the liberation of Rome and the storming of the beaches at Normandy. The situation in the Pacific continued to escalate. For some at Site X, concern for family or friends fighting was augmented by the stress of a life of secrecy. Americans were making due everywhere. Everyone was rationing, volunteering at the USO, waiting for sweethearts and sons to come home. But not every American was enduring those hardships while managing round-the-clock work schedules and living behind armed gates amid legions of rumored informants.

The result made for a potent mix of anxiety and inspiration for some: the anxiety of not knowing, of being watched, of worrying you might say something out of turn, and the inspiration to stay on the job and do it well, because whatever you were working on was going to help end the war. That much you knew, that much you had been promised.

But drive and goals were not enough to keep some spirits buoyed. Morale, though often boosted by patriotic duty, remained vulnerable to the strain of daily life. Those in charge knew that there needed to be more diversion, or people would be more vulnerable to stress and, worse, lose their motivation.

★　　★　　★

As early as December of 1943, roughly one year into Oak Ridge's existence, a pervasive "discontent" was reported in the documents of the Recreation and Welfare Association. Project representatives and Roane-Anderson took notice at the urging of a Mrs. Brown, special assistant to the District Engineer, that the people at CEW—especially single young women in the dormitories—needed something to occupy their time.

"Anyone not living that way can't realize how drab existence is there," she told the group of nine assembled. "You just get through work, freshen up, eat, and go back there."

What do they want to do? How can we help? were the questions from the others at the meeting. A lengthy discussion followed.

"Here there are no organizations to start with," Mrs. Brown continued. "In an ordinary town you have paid commercial recreation, you would have various school clubs, college alumni, church groups,

YWCA, and YMCA . . . Dormitory life, for everyone except the very young, is very abnormal and difficult . . ."

This sentiment was echoed later by psychiatrist Dr. Clarke when he arrived in spring. Bringing together people from all walks of life with a common purpose but, in most cases, no familial or societal ties certainly encouraged individuals to get to know one another rather quickly. But the rate of adjustment varied. It took more than houses to make homes, more than cafeterias and bowling alleys to build community. Dr. Clarke noted upon arriving that homesickness, especially among the young women, remained a concern, as did morale and depression.

For many women, Oak Ridge was in some ways similar to the colleges they had attended; for others, it was how they imagined college might be, had they had the chance to go—minus the gates, guards, and guns, of course. Rosemary, the nurse from Iowa, was finding life at the Clinton Engineer Works to be a real pip—young, single, and with good money to boot. But she, too, had noted the depression cases that made their way to Dr. Clarke's office, just around the corner from her own. When she observed women with children, and others who had never left home before, she realized it could be quite jarring for the less adventurous, and especially tough for housewives and young mothers.

But in a town where groups of folks chatting in the streets might be broken up by plainclothes informants, Mrs. Brown and others knew there would be challenges.

"I presume the feeling would be that Military Intelligence wouldn't want to bring in various organized groups," Mrs. Brown stated.

"You will never get permission of security to let organized personnel come in," a Captain Teeter later added, "for the same reason for disallowing information to leave here about the size of the town . . ."

Recreational groups should, like everything else, be organized and controlled from the top down as much as possible. A controlled system of recreation would keep everyone, at the very least, distracted.

A lot had happened in the six months since this December meeting. The Project knew activities were not going to sprout up out of the mud without a little fertilizer. So at first they had helped get things started by instituting groups and game nights and dances in the existing rec halls.

Everything will be taken care of . . .

But soon, the enterprising, hardworking, and optimistic among residents began creating their own activities to fill the void, and through Roane-Anderson, the Project provided facilities wherever possible. Individuals were actively encouraged to form their own clubs. If they did, space and sometimes a little bit of money might be available.

The results were stunning. Activities at CEW had grown from Monday "quiz night" and dancing at the far end of the Townsite's only cafeteria to beer taverns, a drive-in, miniature golf, roller skating, and trampoline tumbling. The newspaper pleaded for residents to suggest activities. This eventually resulted in groups that served every interest imaginable: music appreciation, jazz records, Boy Scouts, Girls Scouts, chorus, and drama. Virginia's favorites were hiking and photography. Bridge was a huge hit, as was bowling, with leagues forming at all the plants. Gardening—don't forget those Victory gardens!—volleyball, softball, baseball, basketball, horseshoes, tennis, badminton, archery, men's glee club, arts and crafts, an ornithological group, the Rabbit Breeders Association, and the Red Cross, which also sponsored a sewing room in the Townsite recreation center. There was the Civil Air Patrol, concert band, American Legion, Masons, DAR, VFW, and the symphony, founded by Waldo Cohn and John Ramsey and conducted by Cohn himself, a biochemist who had arrived in 1943 with his cello in tow. And of course, the Miss Oak Ridge contest was not to be missed.

The problem of what to do and where to go on Saturday night has been solved for Oak Ridge citizens . . . dances will be held for the public every Saturday night on the Townsite tennis courts. The first dance will be held this Saturday, July 22, [1944] at 8:30 PM. . . . (*Oak Ridge Journal*)

This was great news coming on the heels of the very popular Fourth of July dance. Tennis court dances were a hit. There was even the added promise that upcoming dances might feature local talent. At the inaugural July 22 fete, the Oak Ridge Orchestra played and the entry fee was 50 cents for men. *(Psst! Wring out those stockings, ladies—just 25 cents for you.)*

Dances were already popular around the Reservation, and there were several held each and every week at various recreation halls. Sunday nights, for example, were for the Ridge rec hall. Dances on the tennis courts were welcome because the outdoor locale allowed you to enjoy swinging and swaying in the cool night breeze—if nature decided to cooperate—rather than indoors where the day's heat still lingered. Glenn Miller and Johnny Mercer filled the air as all the twentysomethings gathered, ready to "Begin the Beguine" until it was time to go home.

With so many bodies jostling and jitterbugging, dances could render some makeup a sweaty, goopy mess. Heat and humidity were especially challenging for those women who went the extra yard and wore leg makeup. Some young women even drew seams up the back of their legs to simulate stockings or hose, much of which had gone to war, where their fabric was needed for parachutes. If you were a woman handy with a needle and thread, you might get that fabric back in another incarnation: Many young brides had taken to fashioning wedding dresses from the very parachutes that had brought their loves safely back down to earth. Fashion's contribution to the war effort, come full romantic circle.

Some women wore boots to wade through the mud, then changed into more fetching shoes upon arrival at the dance. Any pairs of stockings that women did have were safely guarded, not to be sacrificed too freely for a mere dance. Stockings were just one of the fashion casualties of war. Zippers took a hike overseas as well—nimble buttoning fingers prevailed. And lipstick was now carefully removed from cardboard or plastic containers and applied gingerly with fingers, since many of the factories that had manufactured the makeup's metal cases had shifted to constructing shell casings or other munitions. And some of the ingredients needed to make the lipstick itself, including petroleum and castor oil, were also in short supply. Sacrifices had to be made—big and small. And *maquillage* crisis or not, young women did what they could with what they had when it came time to primping for an evening out.

Colleen had held on to one or two of her old metal lipstick cases long after the lipstick had disappeared from them. Wielding a paper clip, she would fastidiously dig out the remaining bits of pigmented oils and wax from any remaining tubes—or from a newly purchased cardboard tube—and carefully melt it down on a stovetop before pouring the emulsified liquid back into the precious metal case. Women pulled their hair up, perhaps in a chignon, or curled it using whatever was available, bobby pins if you had them for a pin curl, or otherwise a night's sleep with your tresses twisted around some old rags would do the wavy trick as well.

Any effort was worth it: The average age at CEW was 27. It was a heady mix of backgrounds and personalities: GIs and chemists, construction workers and truck drivers, college girls from big cities far away and high school graduates from farms down the road. Meeting new people was at once easy and a tad complicated. While most everyone was open and anxious to meet new friends, conversations were as restricted as the property itself, usually limited to talk of family and home, safe topics that had nothing to do with your work.

What do you do?

This simple phrase, a standard opening line in many a social situation, was not to be uttered within or without the fences of the Clinton Engineer Works by anyone who worked there if they wanted to keep their jobs.

Where are you from?

This, however, was an entirely acceptable inquiry and one that echoed throughout the dances, cafeterias, and newly constructed recreation halls throughout the Townsite. The emcees of the dances themselves helped make temporary partners of potential wallflowers by filling the nights with dance contests and games orchestrated to coax strangers into one another's arms—but not too tightly.

Colleen loved the dances and tried never to miss a one. It didn't matter whether she went with Blackie or with a gang of girls from the dorm where she now lived. After a week clambering over pipe after pipe, she was more than happy to stay on her feet a little while longer if it meant music and friends. Everyone needed this break from routine. It wasn't like the outside world, where you left work and went "home." Work was everywhere you looked on the Reservation. But if they had to work hard, they were going to play hard, too.

Now that Colleen had finally moved out of her family's trailer and into the dorms, dating was a lot easier. She had moved into her cousin Patricia's single room. Roane-Anderson would have converted it to a double soon enough, anyway. The two did what girlfriends and family did: share clothes. They had each arrived at Oak Ridge with only one small cardboard suitcase, so having a similarly sized roommate meant doubling your wardrobe. But Patricia kept bringing Colleen's blouses back with various small holes burnt into them. It had happened at work, Patricia said. Colleen didn't ask how. She didn't know what Patricia did. It wasn't her business.

Once Blackie had come around to asking Colleen out, she was happy to oblige, but she certainly wasn't ready to give up her other beaux. No sensible woman would. She had no idea how long she would even be here. After the war was over, she and her family would likely go home. Blackie was in the military, and he would probably be assigned somewhere else. Everything about the CEW looked so temporary—even as every day it began to feel to Colleen to be more and more permanent.

Despite the plethora of available men in Oak Ridge, dating a GI did have its perks, including access to the PX, which was otherwise off-limits to civilians. Colleen's understanding of what SED meant was that Blackie had initially enlisted in the Army, but because he had studied engineering they had rerouted him to CEW. The SED hadn't existed before the Project, so there wasn't much history to know. But then again, she didn't need to know much more about him than she already did. He was a Yankee—from Michigan—and an only child to boot. Colleen struggled to imagine a house that wasn't spilling over with kids. He wasn't Catholic, but hey—nobody's perfect. Blackie shared her longing to travel, but for the time being, dates on the Reservation were often a visit to the cafeteria, convenient and affordable. For the ever-sociable Colleen, sitting up late with Blackie and friends in the cafeteria was one of her favorite things to do, and she loved catching an earful of an unfamiliar accent and learning about faraway places. There, a sing-along was always ready to break through the clink of utensils and the rumbling hubbub of shift changes, and Johnny Mercer's 1944 tune could have been the theme song for the entire Reservation. For the entire war.

"You've got to Ac-Cen . . . Chu-Ate the positive and E-Lim . . . Uh-Nate the negative . . . Latch on, to the affirmative and Don't mess with Mr. In-be-Tween . . ." Most importantly, as far as Colleen was concerned, Blackie knew how to impress a girl.

Case in point: On one of their first dates, he brought her a box of Ivory Flakes soap.

Who needs flowers? Roses fade, but flaky soap available from the PX lasted *months*. Having Ivory Flakes was a rarity in itself, and also saved her valuable time—one less line to stand in, only to find that the grocer was out. Again.

That was romance, as far as Colleen was concerned. Maybe this guy was a keeper after all.

★　　★　　★

Romance was not first and foremost in Helen Hall's mind. What little spare time she had between shift work was dedicated to basketball or softball. Oh, how her brother Harold would love the ball courts in her new town! Helen went weak-kneed at the site of those gymnasiums with gleaming new courts and plenty of regulation balls. No more laboring to cut down trees, burying them deep in the Tennessee clay, and then climbing up to nail old privy buckets to them.

She remembered Harold fashioning balls out of hog bladders after the Thanksgiving Day slaughter, and watching them pop and shrivel the minute they bounced out of bounds and into the brush on their small family farm. Helen would have to spend hours in the woods surrounding their farm looking for the most perfectly round rock she could find and painstakingly wrap it in twine that she snuck from the barn. Daddy didn't like that, no sir. But he did always come to her games at school. Not like her mother, who found basketball shorts a bit revealing for her taste.

I won't go see you play naked! was the gist.

But passing and shooting five-pound rocks with her brothers had developed her game in a way few fancy courts could. She was a decent height, with shoulder-length locks in chestnut waves, and those workouts had given her long legs muscle and shape, her lungs endurance, her arms reach and definition, and her shooting accuracy. She could play with the best of them. Yes, Harold sure would love these ball courts. She wanted him to come home safe so maybe he'd get a chance to see them himself.

That was the recruiting Helen wanted to do! She wanted more girls for the Y-12 basketball team, the Robins. She wanted to talk to her coworkers about teams and sewing uniforms and maneuvering practice schedules around the constantly changing 24-hour shift work, not eavesdrop on their private conversations in the cafeteria or goad them into disclosing information they probably didn't even mean to share in the first place.

★　　★　　★

Religious services were a major concern of the Project from the very beginning, as officials appreciated the extra weight that spiritual communities might bear in a brand-new town with no preexisting social connections.

The Chapel on the Hill was the center of much religious activity. That single space would eventually serve 29 different religious groups. Catholics claimed the lion's share of parishioners, edging out the Baptists at number two with Methodists pulling in at third—a clear indication of just how many out-of-towners had moved into this Bible-belt region.

The Chapel boasted a packed schedule. Catholics started arriving at 5:30 AM Sunday, Jewish services were at eight o'clock Friday night, and in between was an array of denominations and activities. (Colleen, Celia, and Rosemary still had the option of attending mass in

Father Siener's living room, as the priest continued to set up an altar in his own abode on Geneva Street.) The Chapel also played host to Episcopal vespers and youth group meetings. The Baptists also met at the high school, as did the newly organized Christian Scientist group. Services continued to be held in various rec halls throughout the Reservation, though early morning services in these sometimes meant kicking a bottle or two out of the way and erasing reminders of the previous night's diversions to make way for the present day's devotions. It was not unusual for the marquee above the movie theater in Townsite to proclaim: *NOW SHOWING: Methodist Church.*

Every area of what was now a bustling "factory-tropolis" with several distinct town centers had its own recreational activities. The Grove Center had its own rec hall, and a very popular skating rink that ran throughout the night. Happy Valley had its own amusement fairway called Coney Island, full of skeet ball and darts, where "Sugar Blues" blasted through the loudspeakers well into the wee hours of the morning in a part of the Reservation that knew no night—thanks to 24-hour floodlights.

Coney Island Workers, in their late teens to early 20s (some even younger, if they could squeak by without questions), awarded oh-so-precious cigarettes as prizes for winners of darts, air rifles, and coin tosses. It was an oddly magical setting, the playful suspension of responsibility in the shadows of the most massive industrial war plants ever constructed. It was a land of music and distraction for characters as diverse as the young pinboy on the duckpin lanes named Edgar Allan Poe (really) and a young college girl on break who relished every time she got the opportunity to page him over the loudspeaker. She and others like her closed up shop at 2 AM and went out to drink homemade wine, or got a ride to the Plantation Club near the town of Rockwood to dance all night.

★ ★ ★

Venturing off-site was popular, as buses provided transportation to places like Norris Dam or Big Ridge Park. Couples packed picnic lunches, folded up a few blankets, and hopped on a bus or crammed in a car.

As housing continued to be tight, some singles were assigned to group houses, which were ideal spots for quick and informal roll-up-the-rug dances. A house full of chemists might host a group of cubicle operators, perhaps none of them aware of what the others did day-in and day-out, though they might even work in the same plant. It didn't matter: Beer tallies were kept on the fridge so that everyone paid their fair share, and romance blossomed on the small porches that some of the C and D homes in Townsite offered.

For any and all activities, finding some alcohol to imbibe posed a bit of a challenge—but not too much for such an industrious collection of young people. Yes, there were one or two small taverns on-site, but none was anyone's first choice. They were crowded and offered only 3.2 percent beer, a staple of military life and Army posts during wartime, which some considered a deterrent to bootleg booze.

"The sale of 3.2 beer in the post exchanges in training camps is a positive factor in Army sobriety," the Office of War Information stated in a report cited by the Brewing Industry Foundation in the April 19, 1943, issue of *Life* magazine. ". . . In dry states and in states where there is local option, the military faces the problem of bootleg liquor. Bootleggers cannot be regulated; legal dispenses can be regulated."

Off-site outings could be made to places like the Ritz Club in nearby Clinton, where the occasional visit from CEW guards sent drinks scattering to the floor and sometimes resulted in a quick wink and offer of cash from the proprietor. Clinton Engineer Works and this part of Tennessee were technically dry. Ah, but this kind of prohibition had long served to bolster one of the state's most significant, if illegal, industries: moonshine.

Hooch was available, if not entirely healthy, from a variety of sources. Drop a few bucks in a basket on a back porch and snag a bottle of homemade innards-stripper from a stash in the washing machine. Taxi cab drivers from nearby towns like Clinton and Harriman made a pretty penny escorting folks to off-site spots where some "splo," a local and potent moonshine, could be bought. The more industrious families made wine and beer beneath their small, rickety, mass-constructed porches: A little canned grape juice, some rationed sugar, and the magic of fermentation were all you needed to get the party started.

If obtained off-area, there was the matter of getting your booze through the gates and past the guards, who themselves enjoyed a serious cache of confiscated rotgut in the guardhouse. Inspection was expected, the passengers of any car knew that. As you approached the gate and slowed to a stop, passengers prepared to have their car and bags opened. The guards were on to most of the tricks by now: the bottles in the wheel well, a container carefully positioned on the floor between the long-skirted legs of a female companion. The more hilariously duplicitous buried purchases in the bottom of bags of odiferous diapers. (Sleeping babies in bassinets weren't enough of a deterrent.)

That was the key: Put it somewhere the guards didn't want to go. One surefire trick when returning to the Reservation after a quick trip to secure a fifth or two of Tennessee's finest? Bury the bottle inside of a box of Kotex, carefully shielded by at least one or two pads.

★　　★　　★

August in East Tennessee is a sweaty panting mutt, breathing down a dust-caked neck that has been baked by the southern sun. And just when it seemed as though fall would never break through the swelter, it happened: On August 3, 1944, the US Army Corp of Engineers, those kings of colossal construction, outdid themselves. They opened the swimming pool, one that was believed to be the largest in the country. It was fed by a spring that had been dammed up to form a lake, and now the sides and bottoms were covered in concrete. Residents could dip into 1.5 acres of wet, wonderful swimming surface area, a cool 2.1 million gallons of water. Yet even cooling off on the Reservation wasn't mud-free—swimmers could feel their toes sink into bits of muck at the bottom of the massive pool, but they didn't care. Their hot, tired bodies bobbed in the fresh, brisk springwater, replenishing temperatures and restoring spirits, albeit temporarily.

Segregation forbade black Oak Ridgers from swimming in the pool and infiltrated most forms of recreation on the Reservation.

Black and white pin boys couldn't work in the same bowling alleys, for example, if there were not separate bathroom facilities available. There was a recreation hall near the hutment area, where Kattie occasionally ventured. She liked getting dressed for a dance now and then, sure, but overall there wasn't too much to do there beyond boxing matches and playing cards. Black residents could not attend the movie theaters, either, though there were now several throughout the Reservation. Occasionally at the rec hall near the black hutment area 16 mm "race" films were shown. For 35 cents, viewers could sit on crates and watch stories—produced predominantly by white movie studios—about poor southern blacks making their way to the north for a new life. In the theaters in Townsite or Grove Center, it cost only 5 cents more to see first-run films, cartoons, and newsreels.

Church served as one of Kattie's primary social activities, when it was an option. Black workers strove to find time and space to worship, some holding prayer band meetings in their huts, others reaching out to pastors in Knoxville, who came to preach in the rec hall, the cafeteria, or wherever there was room. Kattie eventually attended the "church on the side of the road" as her small congregation came to call it. It was a small, but adequate building that wasn't being used for any other purpose. It was a gift, an oasis of peace and community.

But there were movements afoot to try and change the living conditions for black workers at CEW. Numerous contributions to the war effort had been made by the black workforce here in Oak Ridge as well as overseas in battle, and from the earliest of the Reservation's days. Hal Williams, a black construction worker, helped to lay the first concrete slab at K-25.

One of the first actions of the Colored Camp Council was to pen a letter of complaint to the Army and Roane-Anderson. The earlier decision to forego construction of a Negro Village did not go unmentioned, but the primary focus of the letter was the current inequity between black and white housing for those with families. Family homes separate from labor camps and similar in amenities to the white family homes was requested, and the appeal made note of the patriotism and sacrifices of the black community.

"We feel that you, as a high official in the American Army in which so many Negro Youth are fighting and dying for democracy and the preservation of America, will sympathize with the requests of those of us who are laboring on the home front to supply the battle front . . . ," read one July 1944 letter.

Those who signed the letter found themselves on the receiving end of a robust background check, but no new homes.

★　　★　　★

Celia got the mud off of her shoes as best she could, scraping here, knocking there. She didn't want anyone in Knoxville to be able to tell that she had come over from behind the fence.

Trips to Knoxville were a treat. A nice dinner might be followed by a stroll up and down Gay Street for some window-shopping or a visit to one of the bigger department stores to seek out stockings or soaps and, if you were splurging, a nice outfit. The Miller's in Knoxville far outshone the one in Townsite. It was all worth the drive, worth cramming everyone into a single car. If you had a car and gas ration coupons, you had five passengers. You could bet on that.

But many who lived at CEW had begun to notice a trend. The Knoxville shopkeepers, many of whom stayed open late on Monday nights *specifically* to serve those individuals coming from CEW, were often unfriendly.

The relationship between the Clinton Engineer Works and their immediate neighbors was a testy one. Things hadn't exactly gotten off on the right foot, with nearly 60,000 acres of land being taken from people whose families had lived there for ages. Though many people from surrounding areas worked at CEW, the suspicious and condescending "you're one of *those* people from *that* place" strained the fabric that tenuously held this hodgepodge of communities together. Socializing did occur, professionally and personally, as the communities forged a reluctant yet unavoidable partnership. Still, locals complained about the outsiders who lived and worked at CEW. Some were sure that the CEW was getting more than their fair share of rationed goods, for example. What else could all those trains be carrying in there all the time?

Everything's goin' in . . . Nothin's comin' out . . .

Others had very specific issues with their strange new neighbors, openly accusing people from the Reservation of stealing vegetables out of their gardens or snatching eggs or even entire chickens from their yards. There were foxes behind those fences and now they were coming into the henhouses.

Local companies, too, were angered by the Project, as workers were drawn away by greater pay. As early as 1943, the Project was offering as much as 57.5 cents per hour for laborers, far exceeding the normal rates in Anderson County, and draining factories like the Bacon Hosiery Mills, in Loudon, dry of workers. Textile mills needed laborers by the thousands, but there were none left to be found. Farm equipment had been bought by the military, the best schoolteachers, too, had been lured to CEW. Employers on the outside wanted to know what was going on behind the barbed wire. It couldn't be a mere war project, but more likely some New Deal socialist experiment, and they let their representatives, like Senator McKellar, know that they deserved to know the truth. They did not hear the truth. No one would until the job was done.

To many in the surrounding areas, including Knoxville, those who lived on the inside had wallets bursting with money and ration coupons, and stores filled to the rafters with rationed goods to be purchased with ease.

And Knoxville salespeople had learned to spot Oak Ridgers a mile away by a telltale sign: mud.

Celia would often walk into stores like Miller's or George's and stand at the counter, waiting to be helped. She grew more and more annoyed as she watched other customers stroll up after her only to be served first. The first time it happened, she didn't think too much of it. Just a fluke, she thought. But now it seemed to be turning into a pattern. When she finally mentioned it to her friends, other women complained of being turned down for service entirely when requesting a particular item, especially one that was rationed.

"Do you have . . . ?" they'd ask.

"We're saving them for civilians," the shopkeeper might say.

No matter the pains Celia took to wash the mud off her shoes—her *civilian* shoes—she never surmounted this obstacle. Maybe it was her accent. Maybe it was her friends. Somehow the shopkeepers always knew she was one of those people from that government place.

★   ★   ★

Celia was finding her financial independence tricky at times. She had begun insisting that she and Henry go dutch when they ate together. He had refused to give in at first, always reaching for his wallet to pay as they made their way to the end of the cafeteria line or when the check came at a Knoxville restaurant. He was not accustomed to letting any woman, especially a girlfriend, pay her own way. The X-10 worker was charming and forthright, traditional and generous. Broad-shouldered and built low to the ground, Henry *adored* the new pool—he had as formidable a personality as he did a broadstroke. But Celia was no pushover. She had been a workingwoman for several years now. Celia was, as she had explained to Henry time and time again, earning her own money, thank you very much. She was able to pay her own way. If they were going to continue eating together as often as they were—which they did most every night now—he should let her pay her fair share at least some of the time. Henry was stubborn, but then again, so was Celia.

Her social life had changed a little now that she was seeing more of Henry. But she still saw friends she had met at the dorm, like Rosemary, and others who were part of the CYO group that met every week at Father Siener's house for potlucks, Colleen among them. The potluck spirit. Everyone bring your own, everyone pay your own way. That was an idea Celia could get behind, even if the men were still playing catch-up.

★   ★   ★

Toni was sure that Sherry was the one to ask. Lieutenant Colonel Vanden Bulck's secretary was tall, blond, always well-put together, and rarely seen wearing the same thing twice.

A friend from Clinton had invited Toni to an ROTC dance at the University of Tennessee and even arranged for Toni's date. Toni needed a dress and some transportation. (She was lucky when it came to nylons; her daddy now worked at Magnet Mills, the hosiery mill in Clinton.) Toni didn't have time to go to Gay Street in Knoxville to find just the right frock.

She had celebrated her first paycheck on Gay Street, shopping there for her baby sister, "Dopey." Toni remembered Dopey's birth. She watched the doctor arrive with his bag—where she believed the baby was hiding—and waited on the porch until she was allowed inside. Toni had wanted no part of that baby, until, that is, her mother said this child was Toni's. Toni liked that idea. Her parents directed Dopey to Toni for permission to play with her friends, or go for a soda. And though Toni could not remember ever owning a new thing in her life of hand-me-downs and homemades, she wanted her Dopey to have *proper* clothes.

But Toni herself was short one party dress. Sherry obliged, but would need the dress back. Another hand-me-down, but so be it. Toni stood at the gate and hitched a ride to the UT campus with a man leaving CEW, placing the dress on the backseat. When she got to campus, she looked for a bathroom so she could change.

That's when it hit her.

Oh no . . . she thought. *Sherry's dress!* She had left it on the backseat of the stranger's car, and he was long gone.

Not one to miss a party, Toni attended the dance in the clothes she'd worked in all day. But she still had to track down Sherry's dress.

She knew which entrance the man used to enter the Reservation, so the next morning, at 4 AM, Toni stood at the gate, desperately scanning cars. She wondered how to explain to Sherry she'd lost a dress that was supposed to be on her body the entire evening.

Then she spotted him. She waved furiously, and he pulled over and popped the trunk. He'd hidden the dress there for fear his wife might see it, leaving him to explain why another woman's dress was on the backseat of his car.

When Toni got to work, she stopped by Sherry's desk.

"Thanks," Toni said. "It's in excellent condition. I never took it out of the box."

★   ★   ★

Toni considered herself the world's luckiest scatterbrain.

Her badge . . . goodness, how many times she'd forgotten that. Her usual technique for avoiding trouble was to just keep talking. She would jabber on, chatting up the guards and trying to make them laugh, hoping they wouldn't notice that she wasn't wearing her badge while they were inspecting a car at the gate. More often than not, all her charm won her was a trip back to the dorm with an armed escort.

She had taken to wearing the badge on her jacket, *under* her lapel. It was easy that way, walking past the guards up to the Castle—she casually flipped over the strip of fabric to reveal the badge and kept moving. Then one day, as she walked with her boss, Sergeant Wiltrout, she mindlessly flipped over her lapel as she walked past the guards unaware of the fact that there was no badge underneath.

Shouts from the guards—"Stop! Don't move! Where's your badge!"—snapped her back to reality.

But unfortunately her instinct that day was not to stop and sweet-talk, but to break out instead into a full-on run.

She escaped, no worse for wear. But the next day when she arrived at work, Wiltrout read her the riot act.

"Toni," he said, "they're going to shoot you one of these days."

TUBEALLOY

★　★　★　★　★

SECURITY, CENSORSHIP, AND THE PRESS

In August of 1944, the Allies were on the move toward Paris, hoping to wrest the City of Light from the dark cloud of Nazi occupation.

Scientists were mired in their own battles—one for the present (how to accelerate the timeline for the Gadget) and one for the future (what was the future of this science *beyond* the Gadget).

In mid-July, Dr. Zay Jeffries, a consultant with General Electric at the Met Lab in Chicago, had written Arthur Compton, the director of the lab, with an idea. There were going to be some questions that might arise, he believed, some issues regarding how to employ this new energy. Wouldn't it be best to meet these head-on?

> Obviously, no one can now foresee the future, but your group is in as good position as any to speculate—and intelligent speculation is all that can be done now. The speculation of men knowing the fundamentals of atomic energy as now disclosed should be far superior to the wild guesses of laymen . . .

Compton wanted Jeffries to head up a committee of scientists—Fermi the Italian Navigator and James Franck among them—to look into the field that Jeffries had termed "nucleonics" and to formulate ideas about what might lie ahead with this new energy in the postwar world. Comments were solicited and began to roll in within a week. They included a missive dated August 8, 1944, from M. C. Leverett, director of the engineering division of the Met Lab:

> There is no intent to disparage the opinion that atomic power is a wonderful thing and has a revolutionary future. . . . Until we get it, we should not talk like magazine ads for postwar plastics . . . The possibilities should be viewed with the greatest optimism, but any commitments as to one's ability actually to put atomic power to useful work should be made very conservatively . . .

★   ★   ★

Keeping the lid on this burgeoning science and its applications was one of the General's biggest concerns, and one that grew more difficult the longer the Project existed and the bigger it grew. The General knew as early as 1943 that the Project would have to set up its own security staff to take over from the War Department's Counterintelligence. Each facility had its own security officer and assistants. The General continued to believe that compartmentalization—compartmentalization of knowledge, of responsibility, of information—was the "heart of security."

Germany was his primary concern. No other nation would be able to readily use any information they might be able to gather. Not Italy, not Japan. The General remembered his first week on the job when he'd learned that the Russians were using American Communist sympathizers to get info on the lab at Berkeley. And there were workers on the Project who had not, as far as he was concerned, been properly cleared. He decided that in addition to keeping the Germans from learning about the Project, they had to focus on keeping the Russians in the dark as well.

Every security protocol he put in play was guided by a simple rule: "Each man should know everything he needed to know to do his job and nothing else." People weren't here to grow and learn, they were here to do a job. Period. Visually, living was separate from factories, factories were separate from each other, and ridges and valleys served to help further geographically detach it all. At work, floors might separate access as well as buildings, numbers, hierarchy. Top down, to each his own. There was no need to talk to anyone except those directly above or below you. None of the cogs needed to understand the size, shape, and purpose of the machine of which they were a vital part. In other words, the General felt, just "stick to your knitting."

Employees would be screened for a variety of infractions, not all obvious. "We had to know if they were in trouble, or if they had bad companions," Col. Stafford Warren, chief of the medical section, would later say. "Were they crooks, drug addicts, homosexuals, or things like that? We were not so worried about those particular items, per se, but by the fact that they would be vulnerable to pressure which might make them likely to say things that they shouldn't if they were black-mailed." Workers from other countries were trickier, but security did the best it could. The General knew there were those within the Project who considered his techniques too "Gestapo"—that was the term he'd heard. But he felt he was doing what was necessary considering the circumstances. When he first took over the Project, he was alarmed at how many people working for the Project hadn't been cleared. The General also knew if they let someone with details about the Project go, that person was a major risk if he or she felt there wasn't cause for dismissal.

Security measures also meant unions would not organize at CEW. Throughout the country, unions had limited rights within military or-ganizations. Despite these restrictions, when the war was over, unions that had played nice with the Project would be in the perfect position to organize the existing labor force—thousands of workers deep—that was present in the monstrous new plants.

But there was no way to get extensive background on every con-struction worker or employee. The thoroughness of investigations var-ied according to what kind of job that individual was going to perform. Background checks might be as simple as fingerprints and a check for an arrest record for a truck driver to a full examination of a person's life, if that person was a physicist with access to top secret informa-tion. Prints went to the FBI. Anyone guilty of such crimes as arson, narcotics, or rape was not hired. Public drunkenness? Well, they might be interviewed. There was a labor crisis, after all, and the Project had booze locked down on the Reservation—or at least they tried.

Dealing with the press was something else altogether.

On December 19, 1941, less than two weeks after the attack on Pearl Harbor, President Roosevelt issued Executive Order 8985, establishing the Office of Censorship, which issued the Code of Wartime Practices for American Broadcasters and encouraged what was called "voluntary" censorship. The Project worked with the Office of Censorship and also individual editors. The situation was delicate, but the message was quite clear: No publishing anything that would disclose vital information or draw unnecessary attention to the Project.

Where information was published also made a difference. Big-city newspaper stories were riskier because of readership size and visibility. The Project also did not want papers blindly reprinting articles from abroad. Good foreign intelligence agents would know how to take a tidbit from one source, add it to a smidgen from another, put it all together, and come up with enough of a theory for their governments to run with.

All papers and magazines were asked not to use certain phrases that might disclose what the Project was about, as seen in this June 28, 1943, memo, which went out to 20,000 news outlets:

> . . . You are asked not to publish or broadcast any information whatever regarding war experiments involving: Production or utilization of atom smashing, atomic energy, atomic fission, atom splitting, or any of their equivalents. The use for military purpose of radium or radioactive materials, heavy water, high voltage discharge equipment, cyclotrons. The following elements or any of their compounds: Polonium, [tubealloy], ytterbium, hafnium, protactinium, radium, rhenium, thorium, deuterium.

And, of course, mentioning the location of the Project's sites or the General's name was completely off-limits. Job advertisements, sports league results, or a war bond drive might make their way into the Knoxville paper, but rarely more.

The WACs that worked in the Castle with Toni and Celia did their part, scouring every publication, making sure periodicals stayed in line. Infractions might result in a call or visit from a Project representative.

Policing this policy had not been without oversights, ranging from local violations to wire stories. Enforcement was a challenge, and there were infractions: the Mutual Broadcasting Company mentioned Columbia University, atomic energy, and explosives in a broadcast. A newspaper in Atlanta wrote of the "hush-hush" Reservation outside Knoxville and referred to workers as "orderly, well-paid ghosts" who "pledged to unnecessary secrecy for the simple reason they do not know what they are working on." Seeking to avoid a showdown between the Project and the press, heavy hands were replaced with those outstretched in patriotic cooperation. The press would be a reluctant partner rather than an adversary. As it was explained to them, everyone had the same goal in mind: Victory. Safety.

CHAPTER 8

★ ★ ★ ★ ★

The One about the Fireflies . . .

Q: What are they making in those plants?
A: About 80 cents an hour.

Frances Smith Gates found the restrictions a bit trickier to maneuver than most. She was editor in chief of the *Oak Ridge Journal* now, a widow of a West Point graduate and officer who had been killed in the war, and not unfamiliar with Army life and the need-to-know approach to information exchange that went along with it all. There was other news to cover. There was no shortage of pictures, most of which were courtesy of Ed Westcott, the man with access to everything. Dances and Boy Scout clothing drives, cigarette lines, and war bond rallies; if you saw a picture of Oak Ridge or the Project, it was likely first glimpsed via the lens of the Photographer's Speed Graphic camera.

The policy of the paper was explained to the residents of the CEW as follows:

Editorial policy under this regime has been, and continues to be determined by the United States Engineering Department in any controversial issue. However, the editorial staff is allowed a maximum of freedom in reporting the news as they see it. The content of the news has always been limited to Oak Ridge events and personalities. No effort is made to cover outside events and news except in so far as it affects the Oak Ridge community. An effort is made to concentrate on future events, rather than to report past ones.

Every week, Gates took her copy to Army officers for review, a requirement she found relatively painless, even if it seemed antithetical to the essence of journalism. There were still hiccups, some harder to anticipate than others. It wasn't long before she learned that even the most innocuous of stories could be viewed as a security threat.

Not even the Man of Steel could escape the power of the censors. When the McClure Newspaper Syndicate ran the first comic strip of a new Superman series titled "Atom Smasher," in which our hero battles a cyclotron, the Office of Censorship was effectively kryptonite for the story line. McClure replaced the series with a safer, All-American alternative in which Superman single-handedly plays a baseball game.

Within the fences, a story about local kids selling homemade comic strips featuring a character called Atom Man earned Gates a talking-to. On another occasion, Gates assigned a series on dorm life that mentioned 17 PhDs were living in one single dorm. The problem? Enemy agents might now view that dorm as an ideal target for infiltration. Another incident involved a story about the additions being made to the hospital to accommodate the growing population.

Why so many more rooms? the enemy might ask. *Is this top secret project dangerous? Are there a lot of injuries? Can we estimate how many people are living there if we combine this new hospital information with what we've been able to glean about the cafeterias and bus system?*

This particular editorial snafu made its way all the way up the chain of command and finally landed on the desk of the General, who had not approved the piece before it was printed at the Chandler printing press in Knoxville. Win some, lose some.

Classifieds? Okay. Coupon updates? Sure. But no important names. Steer clear of births and deaths, especially the unfortunate suicide of an officer's wife. But not all news was so easily dismissed. In early 1944, the *Oak Ridge Journal* reported that a welder who worked on the Reservation tried to get around a guard and drove his car into a restricted area. The guard tried to arrest him and a "scuffle" ensued. The man was shot. Twenty plasma injections, three blood transfusions, and one operation later, the man was pronounced dead.

That made the paper, too.

"Remember always," the article continued, "that we are in a military area established for a vital war job."

★   ★   ★

Helen worked her fit frame up and down the basketball court, working off the day's stresses. She had noticed the men in the dark suits sitting in the bleachers earlier during practice. They had been sitting there for a while, just watching.

Helen wasn't paying them much mind. They were probably coaches for the next team scheduled to practice. Schedules were packed for the available courts at CEW. With so many players on shift work, practice schedules took some coordinating.

Once her session finished, Helen gathered her things and headed off the court with the rest of her teammates. Sweating and exhausted, the group of women walked toward the door, chatting and rehashing practice, ready to hit the dorms and rest up for another day's work in the plants.

As they reached the exit, one of Helen's teammates approached her.

"That man over there wants to talk to you," she whispered.

Helen turned.

She eyed the man. He was standing now, waiting. One of the men in the suits. Helen guessed the two men weren't there waiting to coach the next team after all.

"Well, I don't know him," Helen said and kept right on walking.

Another man in a suit wanting to talk to her alone.

Not again, she thought. *What do they want me for this time?*

Helen continued on her way, gear in tow. But she could feel the man behind her. He was following her.

Who was it? Were they angry she hadn't been mailing in her "informant" envelopes? She had in fact never touched them, and never intended to.

"Helen Hall?" he said.

Helen whirled around.

"Yes," she said.

"I coach a basketball team out of Knoxville. How would you like to come play for us?"

Helen was surprised. Flattered. *Relieved.*

"You don't want me," Helen said. "I work shift work. Besides, I don't have any transportation to get to Knoxville for practice."

"That's not a problem," he continued. "We'll come get you."

I love ball, Helen thought. Another opportunity to play, *and* with a team in the city.

"Okay," she said. "You come get me then and I'll play ball with you."

That was how it so often began: A Very Important Man in a suit wanting to talk.

A knock on a door, a seemingly chance encounter. An important man approaches a young woman to speak with her about something of the utmost significance and secrecy.

Helen recalled the man whose words had brought her to the Secret City in the first place. He had come to the soda fountain on the main square in Murfreesboro, Tennessee, several times, often for coffee and a doughnut. Helen had served him at the counter or rung him up when she'd been working the register in the druggist's. He was friendly but never talked about what he did or why he was in town. She had, however, noticed him going into the municipal building across the square a few times.

When he asked Helen to step outside one morning, she was a bit nervous. When he suggested she go to work for Tennessee Eastman about 20 miles outside Knoxville, she was curious. But when he finally told her the pay—65 cents an hour, almost twice what she was earning—she was sold. She knew her parents wouldn't approve, so she didn't tell them. She got word to her sister Mary in Nashville—*65 cents an hour!*—where she was training as a beautician. Then Helen cashed her last paycheck and a war bond. She bought two one-way bus tickets—one for herself and one for Maude, an old friend from school who couldn't afford the fare and who needed a good job. The two girls were gone the next day.

Helen had been an ideal recruit—smart, independent, a high school graduate—and the pay scale overrode any uneasiness about the lack of details regarding the wheres, whens, and hows of the job itself. A job was a job.

For Helen, gates, guards, inspections, and badges were off-putting at first, but they soon faded into the background and became a part of the everyday scenery that she passed on her way to and from dorm to cafeteria, from Y-12 to basketball practice. The folks who worked in the basement at Y-12 on the vacuum pumps, for example, had a 1 on their badges and couldn't come upstairs where Helen worked as a cubicle operator. Guards stood on stairwell landings to make sure no one accidentally wandered onto the wrong floor. There were very few 4s seen on badges. You might never see a 5, but you heard about them. The 5s were the ones who knew what was going on here.

Helen learned early and often that someone was always watching, whether innocuously as you played basketball or more carefully as you worked. She knew what she herself had been asked to do for the cause, evidenced by the still-unused envelopes that sat gathering dust in her dorm room.

She had no doubt that other people who had been asked to perform the same task had agreed to do so, because she herself had seen what she believed to be the consequences. Twice, she had seen girls escorted from her workplace. One of them had been a bit drunk. That made sense to Helen. You couldn't have that kind of behavior on the job.

As for the other young woman, well, Helen was never sure why she had been whisked away in the middle of the shift, never to be seen again. Helen didn't talk about it with any of her coworkers, and she certainly never asked her supervisor. The experiences made an impression, though, made her think before she said anything to anyone, before she answered unexpected questions. She kept her head down and did her job, coming up to play ball when the opportunity arose.

★   ★   ★

Q: What do you do out there?
A: As little as possible.

Celia used the phone in the lobby to call home whenever she could, to see how her mother and father were faring and to hear if there was any news from her brothers overseas. She occasionally got letters from her brothers, but Clem's had stopped coming. He had landed in Salerno, Italy, shortly after Celia arrived in Oak Ridge. His letters soon became less frequent, then stopped altogether. Then came word: Clem was missing in action. There had been no telegram confirming the worst, but with Clem officially MIA, Celia's mother wanted her daughter to come home. Celia, however, wanted to stay with the Project. Celia worked in the headquarters of CEW after all, and had been told that their work there would bring a quick end to the war. She believed that was Clem's best hope.

Then one day, Celia's mother called with an unexpected request: Stop writing home. This from the woman who never wanted her to move away in the first place.

"I just can't understand your letters!" her mother complained. "Stop writing them."

"What do you mean, you can't understand them?" Celia asked when she got her mother on the phone. "Everything's all blacked out," Celia's mother finally explained.

Blacked out? Celia wondered.

"There are these big, black bars covering all these words in your letters," her mother continued. "I can't make any sense out of them!"

Every letter she received, her mother told her, was the same: Words and phrases struck through with black ink, leaving her to try to make sense of what remained.

At least Celia's mother's letters had managed to get through.

On occasion, people who tried to write family members living at Site X by addressing the letters to "Oak Ridge" got those letters returned to sender with a note reading simply: "There is no such place as Oak Ridge, Tennessee."

When Celia finally grasped that her letters were being censored, all she could think was, *What have I ever written about that I wasn't supposed to?*

She turned past correspondence over in her mind. It all seemed so bland and uninformative. She wondered if some sort of reprimand was in the offing. She had been with the Project longer than most and knew as well as anyone that she wasn't supposed to write about work. She could not, for the life of her, imagine what her transgression might have been.

But it must have been something. They wouldn't censor her for no reason. Would they?

I must have done something wrong, she thought.

She just didn't know what.

★ ★ ★

And therein lay the magic.

Not knowing what you were working on, what was important or irrelevant, meant *anything* you might do or say *could* pertain to the larger Project about which you knew nothing and, therefore, *would* be out of line. Possibly dangerous. So if you had even the slightest doubt, it was best not to say anything at all.

What happened to loose-lipped folks? Where did they go when, one day, they ceased to appear? Interviews, security briefings, and the pervasive zip-your-lip reminders rarely spelled out specific consequences for security transgressions. The great unsaid left plenty of room for dramatic interpretation, vague allusions to damning consequences. The longer people stayed at CEW, the more their imaginations fed the already active rumor mill. Public information officers purposely fueled stories that subversives or dismissed workers could not only be fired, but then be immediately drafted and dropped in the South Pacific. Official warnings given at hiring were compounded over time by rumors that could neither be confirmed nor denied, fodder for increasingly nerve-rattling scenarios.

The Project wanted it clear that valuable and dangerous details could be gleaned from the most seemingly innocuous of sources—even the trash bin. One of the rumors circulating throughout CEW was that illiterate individuals were hired to empty the garbage as an added security measure. One young woman was instructed never to speak to the workers on the shift before hers. Last names of children were kept out of printed materials as they might indicate who their parents were and therefore what kind of expertise that parent had, which could conceivably allow someone to deduce what type of work might be going on there.

Sure, there were a lot of high school football teams that didn't wear names on their jerseys—that was an expense many rural schools couldn't afford—but the Oak Ridge High School team never gave rosters to their opponents.

Most residents learned to take these limits in stride. Questions from family, friends, or even total strangers they ran into in a Knoxville department store were often greeted with whimsical replies. The heightened restrictions also offered a sense of security. Many residents did not bother to lock their doors. For some there was a sense that someone might not just be watching you, but watching *out* for you, as well.

★   ★   ★

Q: How many people are working in Oak Ridge?
A: About half of them.

"Are you all right, Dot?"

Dot jumped at the sound of a voice she did not recognize emanating from someone she could not clearly see in the dark.

The man asked again, this time leaning in through the car window. She could see him now, but still did not know who he was. He clearly wanted their attention—Dot's and her date's.

For a first date it had started out pretty nice. She stopped by his tiny, cramped trailer—he was a construction worker—and they had a little something to drink. She thought it tasted awful, local and illegal, but it was wet enough and par for the course considering their theoretically dry county. They had gone out to eat—his treat—and, finally ended up here, sitting in the car on a quiet country road. This was a far-from-unusual pastime for dates on the Reservation, since there was little privacy available anywhere and men were forbidden in the dorms. The stranger hadn't interrupted anything too personal, but still, an unexpected visitor peering in from the darkness was incredibly unnerving. Dot managed to regain her composure.

How on earth does he know my name?

Dot assured the man that she was fine, but the experience brought a quick end to the date and sent Dot scampering back to her dorm.

It wasn't the first time, after all, that she had felt eyes on her in unexpected places. Once, while waiting in line at the movies with a group of friends, a woman had suddenly appeared.

"Spread it out!" she barked. "One behind the other."

And they did. Discouraging large groups kept things orderly, sure, but Dot had also heard that the powers-that-be didn't want people congregating in large groups and *talking*. As house lights went down and the newsreel started, monitors—creeps, as they were called—might walk the aisles shining flashlights down the rows of patrons, checking to see who might be whispering in the dark.

Dot took her place in front of her cubicle the next day, and got to work as usual. Men milled about in the vast space: delivering this, picking up that, speeding away with logbooks, tweaking the giant panels, or pretending to do any of the above when their only real intention was to flirt.

A man approached Dot as she was minding her dials. Another maintenance man trying to get a date? Didn't seem to be.

"Are you Dot?" he asked her.

"Yes," she answered. Again, she didn't recognize him. He appeared to be a little older. He introduced himself as the boss of her date from the night before.

"I don't want you to see him anymore," he explained.

So, they did follow us, she thought.

Whoever had approached the car last night had reported back to her date's boss.

She agreed. The man left. Dot never learned his name.

★   ★   ★

Loose lips might not only sink a ship but also endanger the top secret Project. Should you forget this, there was propaganda plastered on every available surface, positioned in every line of sight, to quickly remind you.

Billboards, posters, pamphlets, notes in the newspaper. Blackboards throughout CEW offices and labs were stamped with reminders that users should erase all work at the end of their shift. Propaganda ranged from inspirational, up-by-the-bootstraps images designed to inspire patriotism and responsibility to ominous images depicting death by enemy hands, or losses on the battle front resulting from a moment's indiscretion. These reminded anyone who wasn't doing their part that they were aiding the enemy. Oak Ridge was inundated with the Message.

Ride sharing and bond buying were popular themes. *When you drive alone, you drive with Hitler!* Other posters found throughout the United States were absolutely foreboding. Images of graves and injured soldiers. A lonesome dog or child alone at home holding a service flag embroidered with the single golden star of a now-gone brother. Drowning men and bodies impaled on barbed wire. Messages were crafted to keep individuals quiet and working hard. If you spoke out of turn, you were not only un-American, you were responsible for the senseless murder of troops. If you dared inquire too closely about your job, you were endangering the lives of innocent children, damning democracy, and joining the ranks of Hitler and Hirohito.

There were messages of support and encouragement as well. Advertisements in magazines showed mothers and daughters standing side by side, canning food. Cookbooks like *War Time Meat Recipes* and Armour's *69 Ration Recipes for Meat* helped women maneuver the world of rations and coupons. They taught the value of all forms of protein and how to reproduce juicy, meaty flavors with the clever use of easier-to-come-by staples like potatoes and oatmeal, lessons modern-day vegans still use today. Advice columns and friendly tips were echoed in the *Oak Ridge Journal*, and were the refrain of many a man or woman who had grown up during the Depression:

Use it up!
Wear it out!
Make it do!
Or do without!

Contests for good work attendance were routinely held at various plants. The importance of a plant's work rate and production at the 24-hour Reservation were drummed into the workers' minds. But reminders to keep quiet were perhaps the most prevalent.

Who Me? Yes You . . . Keep Mum About This Job
Think! Are You Authorized to Tell It?

One large billboard on the Reservation featured a large looming eye, its black iris surrounding a large swastika-embedded pupil. It read:

The Enemy is Looking for Information. Guard your Talk.

Mandates greeted workers at every gate. Patriotism and secrecy went hand-in-hand. One of the most memorable Oak Ridge billboards featured a virile Uncle Sam, hat off, sleeves up, forearms thick with muscle. Three monkeys sat before him, one covering his eyes, another his ears, and the third his mouth:

What you see here,
What you do here,
What you hear here,
When you leave here,
Let it stay here.

Such propaganda was not exclusive to the Project, but arguably made for a disquieting backdrop to a nascent town striving to grow into a community. But many Oak Ridgers didn't see it that way. These disparate residents had come together to work, to love, to get married, and plant Victory Gardens behind makeshift trailers and cemesto prefab homes. They fought to smile through the lines and the mud and the long hours, dancing under the stars and under the watchful eyes of their government, an Orwellian backdrop for a Rockwellian world.

★　　★　　★

Q: What are you making over there?
A: Babies.

Guns and badges and checkpoints and propaganda were only part of the force that kept the lid on the Project. The Intelligence and Security Division had around 500 plainclothes agents in addition to its uniformed personnel. And the more informal creeps played a key role in maintaining the aura of secrecy that pervaded life and work in Oak Ridge and the other Project sites. The actual number of creeps on the Project would be difficult to estimate, but what many residents did know was that anyone—*anyone*—could be a creep.

They came in all shapes and sizes, from official-looking, suit-wearing types to the workers next door. They could be anywhere: across the table from you in the cafeteria, down the hall in the dorm, in a dining car on a train, or even lying in bed next to you. They could be men or women. The real power of this unseen force moving in and among the population was not that these monitors were all-knowing, well-heeled government types, with some sort of high-ranking role within the Project. It was that the informants themselves were just like the people they were observing and writing reports about. For a young woman of 18 years like Helen Hall, whose experience beyond the family farm had been limited to the sleepy diner of a nearby town, being approached by dapper men and asked to inform on fellow workers, friends, and roommates likely felt like more of a directive than a request.

What this meant for everyone living and working in Oak Ridge was that anyone you met, anyone you passed on the street, anyone you befriended could be reporting your conversations and activities. Anyone at all could be deciding whether your actions or discussions were endangering the Project. Anyone might pass judgment on your encounters and associations. When coworkers suddenly stopped showing up for work, no one dared ask why—because no one could be sure that the person to whom they were speaking was not a creep, too. That lack of details about what had happened to the individual in question amped up existing suspicions, leaving others to imagine anything from a simple firing to relocation to a remote island in the Philippines. Since mail was censored going in and out of Oak Ridge—albeit in a rather haphazard and unsystemized fashion—the possibility of word arriving from that recently departed coworker describing the details of their dismissal was slim.

★　　★　　★

The work of the creeps dovetailed nicely with the Statement of Availability. It meant that once the Project got their hands on a worker, it was easier to keep them on and provided an added incentive to help keep workers focused and tight-lipped. If you lost your job as a result of subversive talk or *seditious* activity, it meant no Statement of Availability and no new job without a 30- or 60-day wait, sometimes longer. "Seditious talk" was loosely defined. To merely be accused by an informant was enough to cause a worker to be let go *with* cause. No SOA.

From a memo dated June 14, 1944:

". . . personnel discharged for cause will not be permitted to work for any other organization on the area unless investigation reveals that discharge for cause was improper. . . ." Suggestions were made in an effort "to obtain maximum labor efficiency," emphasis was to be put on "continuing urgency of the program," "appealing to the sense of patriotism" and making it clear that "we now can afford to weed out inefficient personnel and that it is intended that such action will be taken . . ."

So, if a creep dropped an anonymous letter about your seditious activity into any one of the cloaked drop-off points throughout Oak Ridge and that missive arrived at the offices of the fictional ACME Insurance Company, within 24 hours, you, your family, and all of your belongings might be plopped down outside the gates. If the worker in question had initially relied on CEW or one of its construction contractors, for example, to provide for transportation to the site, he or she had to foot the bill for their return to outside civilization. Or worse, in some cases the dismissed workers were required to pay back the money that had been spent to transport them to the site in the first place, money that would often wipe out the precious last pay-check that they had received.

★ ★ ★

Q: What are you all doing over there?
A: Pinning diapers onto fireflies.

"What kinda bread y'all want today?" Kattie called out to the small crowd gathered around Willie's hut.

"Cornbread!" was more often than not the answer she got back. Cornbread or biscuits. Kattie quickly found that her brand-new, re-purposed K-25 biscuit pans were coming in handy and in ways that she had never anticipated.

Not only had she begun to solve her "what to eat" crisis, but she had discovered an entirely new use for her hut-baked treats: bribery.

Cooking and eating was done at Willie's hut. The couple was lucky that they could manage to work the same shift often enough. When they did, the two of them would head back to the huts right after work to get ready for dinner. Kattie had three pans in all and, thanks to some trial and error in the standing-room only hut, she had per-fected her system for cooking with them.

Her method worked equally well for biscuits and other breads. The key to it all was the potbelly stove in the middle of the tiny hutment.

When it was cranked up, the stove got red-hot. So hot, in fact, that Kattie couldn't set the pans right on top of it or the biscuits would burn on the outside before they were cooked on the inside. So instead, she carefully leaned the blackened pan at an angle against the stove's potbelly. She kept them from slipping and sliding with a brick she'd found lying on the ground near Willie's hut. She took her special bis-cuit mix, formed dollops of the sticky, southern staple, and put them on the pan near the bottom, closest to the floor. Once the first side was nice and brown, separating effortlessly from the metal, she carefully flipped the biscuits over to the other side.

The savory smell filled the small hut, wafting out doors and windows and hanging in the air with the dust. Dinners became the highlight of their day, and she made an effort to make each of them as good as they had been back home. Kattie always left the pans at Willie's hut, since she was allowed to go to visit him, but he was never permitted to visit her (although he did try scaling the barbed-wire fence once). Her friend Gerdy—lovingly called "Small" because she was—occasionally made a trip all the way to Knoxville to find affordable stew beef. Kattie adored Small. She came from Tupelo, Mississippi, and worked with Kattie at K-25. Kattie cut the meat up nice as was possible and the group might cook it in a little orange juice that one of them bought at the grocer or from one of the trucks that made the rounds near their hutment area. There were usually some greens to be had, perhaps some snap peas, bought from nearby farmers who sold their produce and chickens outside the gates. This meat was often available without coupons, which was an even bigger boon. Kattie would boil those together with the little bit of stew beef and serve it with the fresh-baked, brown-bottomed biscuits. It was as near a feast as you could get.

There was always a little harassment from that young guard, the one with the attitude. Others had it far worse, as is evidenced by complaint letters from other residents detailing some of the harassment found in the hutment area:

"Police guard can be found in these colored women hutments any time day or night and oftime when these Police Guards go to these colored women hutments the Police Guards never knock on the door," one such letter read, ". . . and oftime our women are partly dressed when the police guards enter. . . ."

Everyone had their own way of coping with the hardships and ill treatment. Kattie baked. Now, when a guard came by Kattie's hut, there was a biscuit or two waiting. Cooking in the huts was off-limits. But once that guard had gotten a taste of those contraband biscuits, he didn't ask about the misshapen biscuit pans or anything else. He just let Kattie keep on cooking. There were rules, but Kattie knew that she could not only learn them but work them, too.

From the warped, discarded metal of a top secret war plant to her hands came a simple pan and some fresh biscuits. She gave them to that guard, kept him happy, kept him quiet, and kept herself at Willie's hut a little longer, relatively free of hassle, blissfully free of stomach cramps.

TUBEALLOY

★　★　★　★　★

PUMPKINS, SPIES, AND CHICKEN SOUP,
FALL 1944

This was a new one for the coroner.

Philadelphia had had its fair share of mysterious deaths, but to have the causes of death of two men kept from the coroner's office itself pushed the boundaries of credulity.

In this case, the General stepped in personally and made sure that word did not get out about the three men working in the transfer room of the Philadelphia Navy Yard's liquid thermal diffusion works.

A simple clogged tube had been the culprit. But it was the Tubealloy—in liquid hexafluoride form—and high-pressure steam coursing through the concentric pipes that posed the real danger.

The thermal diffusion process was still being perfected at the Philadelphia Navy Yard as the H. K. Ferguson Company neared completion of the S-50 plant at CEW. On September 2, 1944, physicist Arnold Kramish, then an SED soldier on loan from Oak Ridge, was working with Peter Bragg Jr. and Douglas Meigs. Bragg and Meigs were unclogging the tube when an explosion reduced it to nothing, spewing Tubealloy, steam, and hydrofluoric acid all over the men, their lungs filling with Tubealloy compounds.

Bragg and Meigs died shortly thereafter. Kramish was badly burned and not expected to survive. A Navy chaplain, Father McDonough, arrived to administer last rites. As he approached Kramish, the Jewish soldier was strong enough to refuse the blessing before losing consciousness.

He hung on, and several days later got an unexpected and unauthorized visitor. The stranger made short work of the guards posted at his hospital room door, got inside, quietly lifted up Kramish's oxygen tent, and poured something down his throat.

Warm liquid soothed Kramish's gullet.

Chicken soup.

His mother, Sarah, had carried her soup in a jar for three days on her long trip from Denver. A cousin and newscaster had seen news of Kramish's death come over the wire, and contacted Kramish's parents. When Sarah learned her son was dead, she fainted on the spot. When she came to and was informed by station KLZ in Denver that her son was in fact alive and in a hospital, she was on a mission. She was going to get chicken soup into her son and no one was going to stop her. No one did.

Information about the cause of the blast was not disclosed, nor was the fact that a large amount of radioactive materials had been released into the atmosphere.

Kramish survived, his mother's chicken soup in his belly, Tubealloy lurking in his bones.

★   ★   ★

The same month of the Philadelphia tragedy, the General had decided to invite an Army Air Corpsman into the ranks of an elite group: those who knew of the Gadget.

Twenty-nine-year-old Lt. Col. Paul Tibbets had returned to the United States from bombing missions in North Africa and Europe. He was a pilot, testing the new B-29 bomber, and the General thought he had found his man: someone with the experience—the big-plane experience—who knew the Army's newest bomber as well or better than anyone else in the world. This was the man the General needed to oversee his cadre of deliverymen. Wendover Army Air Field in Utah would be the perfect place for them to start training. There they would eventually commence dropping their "pumpkins," placeholders for the Gadget, until the General had something more for them to ferry.

★   ★   ★

No one was immune to a little surveillance. Even top scientists, no matter how indispensable, were monitored by the Project. Many of them had left their lives in Europe behind. They worked throughout the Project—at the Met Lab, Los Alamos, Oak Ridge, Hanford—and often traveled where they were needed, and under assumed names. Enrico Fermi was Henry Farmer, Niels Bohr was Nicholas Baker. It was a stellar group of minds: Hans Bethe, Leo Szilard, Edward Teller, Ernest Lawrence, Richard Feynman, Eugene Wigner, James Franck, Emilio Segrè, George Kistiakowsky, and more.

Scientists arriving from academic institutions were a particular security challenge. They had all been exposed to more than the usual amount of Communist literature on their campuses, when compared to the average American, which was a flag for the Project. Oppenheimer had close friends and associates who were associated with the movement, including a girlfriend who wrote for the Communist periodical *Western Worker* and a wife who had been a party member. The FBI opened a file on the scientist in 1941, before he became the Project's "Coordinator of Rapid Rupture." The General wasn't crazy about anyone with what appeared to be ties to Communism. But all the Project could do was pay close attention to how strongly any one person in question appeared to follow the party line.

The Americans and British each had their own means of investigating scientists who worked on the Project, and the General occasionally had his top scientists tailed. He considered this to be as much for their safety as for the good of the Project. Niels Bohr had proved an interesting subject for the General's agents. One report of "Nicholas Baker" strolling with his son, Aage ("Jim Baker"), hardly made the Nobel Prize–winning physicist sound like a member of the brain trust behind the biggest wartime military project in history:

Both the father and son appear to be extremely absentminded individuals . . . On one occasion, subjects proceeded across a busy intersection against the red light in a diagonal fashion, taking the longest route possible and one of greatest danger. . . . If the opportunity should present itself, I would appreciate a tactful suggestion from you to them that they should be more careful in traffic.

★   ★   ★

Despite elaborate and far-reaching efforts, security was far from foolproof. Problems—and people—slipped through carefully watched cracks.

The General was likely unaware of two SED recruits who had made their way to Oak Ridge in the summer of 1944. One had studied with Arnold Kramish at the City University of New York, and was a health physics officer at CEW. The General—and indeed the world—would not know for decades that this man had close and curious friends far away. The other recruit, an Army machinist, had left an Army base in Jackson, Mississippi, and been assigned to the Clinton Engineer Works in July. The General probably did not pay particular attention when this man was transferred to Site Y at Los Alamos in August. Nor did the General know that this man had a brother-in-law who was very interested in the work taking place at Site Y, and that this brother-in-law had contacts overseas equally interested in the Project. These contacts may have been citizens of a country that was, technically, an ally, but nonetheless the General did not want that country informed about the Gadget. Not yet.

But those interested parties overseas did know about the young machinist and where he was headed. They had given him a code name, "Kalibr." They also had their own name for the Project: "Enormoz."

Maybe the General would not have been surprised at all, had he known any of this at the time.

Maybe he would have simply said, "See? I told you so."

CHAPTER 9

★ ★ ★ ★ ★

The Unspoken

Sweethearts and Secrets

It is a terrible shock to a woman when a usually companionable husband suddenly stops telling her things. At first she is hurt, then indignant, then determined to find out for herself. Fortunately, for security purposes, most of the women of Oak Ridge had passed through these preliminary stages before they arrived at the gates.

—Vi Warren, *Oak Ridge Journal*

Jane turned the box over in her hands and gently tugged at the makeshift tab.

> *Process Statistics Office*
> *9201-2 Y-12,*
> *T. E. C.*
> *Oak Ridge*
> *Where Ever That Is.*
> *Today.*

There was more to the message. "SECRET" was stamped in bright red on the adding tape which was painstakingly rolled and concealed within an empty and innocent-looking box of Monarch Standard-Width Staples. A slit had been carefully cut into the box, and a small strip of the long roll of paper—topped off with a strip of cellophane tape—peeked out, forming a pull tab.

"Pull out gently and read other side," the instructions read.

Jane began tugging and reading. On the reverse of the paper was an endless stream of tiny handwritten messages. Each little pull of the paper revealed more notes.

What have those girls gotten up to while I've been gone? Jane wondered.

She was enjoying a brief visit with her sister Kat and brother-in-law Maurice, in Staten Island, New York. But here in her hands was a reminder of the strange place from whence she traveled, a memento from behind the fence.

How did they get this past the mail censors? was one of Jane's initial thoughts. Jane smiled and kept unfurling the adding machine tape, revealing message after message, all scribbled diligently on the tiny width of paper usually reserved for elaborate computations of Product percentages.

Dear comrade in arms . . . (Whose?)

You wanted us to rite to U sew hear wee hour, all reddy to go!

There must have been a note from almost every one of the nearly 100 clerks that she supervised on one shift or another. Her eyes moved down the ever-lengthening roll, reading the well-wishes, inside jokes, office gossip, and updates on the weather.

> *A lady statistician named Jane,*
> *Said addition would drive her insane.*
> *Screaming with rage,*
> *She'd tear up a page,*
> *And start adding over again.*

Jane laughed. The dateline: *Oak Ridge. Wherever that is. . . .* That's how they all coped with the heightened security, with winks and nudges and nods to the mystery. Some found the watchful eye of the Project unnerving, but Jane never let it get to her. On at least one occasion, the Scientist—a gangly man in a big hat visiting from an unnamed place—had entered her small Marchant-and-Monroe domain. He was intently interested in the numbers Jane was running. Those percentages clearly *meant* something to him. There was an entourage of management types tagging along behind him, hanging on his every word, hoping he was pleased with what he saw as he peered over Jane's shoulders.

Jane was never properly introduced. She didn't mind. She knew she was being watched.

Humor in the face of watchfulness remained common, as was occasional hypothesizing about the Project's purpose. Theories ranged from inspired to ludicrous: They were making flamethrowers. They were making fourth-term buttons for Roosevelt.

No, it was a special kind of blue paint that would be spread across the top of the ocean so that when submarines broke through the surface, it would appear to the enemy that the vessel was still submerged.

One woman was convinced she knew what the Secret was. She confided in a friend:

"It has something to do with urine!" she said.

The woman worked in processing, where potential employees were given physicals. Not coincidentally, she asked for urine samples day in and day out.

Stories weren't just for nosy outsiders or curious adults, either. They were for kids, too. Ask a child walking through the streets of Townsite, "What's going on around here?" and they might answer, as if it were the most obvious thing in the world, "They're making molasses!"

★   ★   ★

October 7, 1944, was a cool Saturday evening, the kind that made the tennis court dances all the more pleasurable, a brisk breeze comforting bodies warmed by sweat and heat of jitterbugs and Lindy hops. Fall had arrived and dulled the edge of the summer's heat. Outdoor dances were even more of a treat, and less of a swelter. Bill Pollock was making a name for himself as the master of ceremonies at the dances. He provided recorded music from his own specially designed sound system—the Pollock Wired Music System—and kept the evening humming along with matchmaking dance games perfect for a dance floor full of relative strangers. Every few tunes that he spun,

Pollock would give the crowd a "Paul Jones," a mixer dance that was always a hit and was designed to pluck wallflowers who were rooted to their solitary spots.

Paul Jones took some of its moves from traditional square dancing. Men and women formed two concentric circles, men on the outside. When the music began, men performed the Grand Left as the women standing before them moved Grand Right, easy and familiar dance moves that placed the young dancers in front of a slew of potential new partners. Skirts swayed, trousers strutted, smiles and nods swirled by in anticipation of . . .

"Paul Jones!" Pollock would call, or give a blow to his whistle.

When the signal sounded, the music stopped and so did the dancers. The men and women stood facing their new partners. Pollock would load up another tune and the new couples would hit the floor together. When the music came to a stop that lovely autumn evening, Toni was pleased to find herself face-to-face with a handsome young soldier who, for at least the next song, would be her dance partner.

Toni had always liked a man in uniform. This one was quite tall, easily six feet two, she thought, with close-cropped blond hair and strikingly clear blue eyes. He wore a khaki uniform; neat and pressed and tucked and spit-shined from head to toe. What was more surprising was that he managed to speak first, before Toni, champion chatterbox, ever got a chance.

"I'm happy I stopped in front of a tall girl," the young man said. "That way my knee won't hit you in the stomach when we dance."

Toni laughed, wondering what he would say next.

"So," he continued, "are you a Democrat or a Republican?"

What an odd get-to-know-you question, Toni thought. But all she could do was answer, "I'm a Republican."

This appeared to make the young man quite happy. He smiled and nodded.

"I'm Chuck Schmitt," he said.

"I'm Toni Peters," she responded, wondering what kind of reception she would have received from Chuck if her answer to his opening inquiry had been "Democrat."

No matter. She and the blond-haired-blue-eyed soldier danced not only that dance, but many others that evening. Between turns around the floor they talked. No talk of work, of course. The standard Oak Ridge salutation would have to do:

Where are you from?

Chuck, Toni learned, was from Queens. Toni also learned that Queens was in New York City. That bit of information actually explained a lot, as she had been wondering why all of these Rs kept on finding their way into syllables where she never knew they belonged. Rs seemed to appear and disappear at will, with these northerners, depending on which corner of the Northeast they called home. Despite a year at the beck and call of Mr. Diamond, she had yet to become fluent in any flavor of "Yankee." But unlike Mr. Diamond, Chuck made Toni want to make a little more effort.

Chuck's story was as interesting as any she had yet to hear. He hadn't been in Oak Ridge long and had only recently completed basic training at Camp Reynolds in Mercer County, Pennsylvania. He was about to be shipped out with the rest of his unit when he, his buddy Fred, and another soldier were taken aside by someone they hadn't met before. This man told them that they had been reassigned. They would not be shipping out. Instead, they would be leaving on a train that night.

Chuck was handed a piece of paper with a phone number on it.

"You're going to take the train to Knoxville, Tennessee," the man instructed them. "When you get to the station, call this number. You are not to speak to anyone along the way. The only thing you are to say to any person who asks who you are or where you're going is the sky is blue and the grass is green."

With that, Chuck and Fred boarded a train bound for Knoxville, a place where, Chuck believed, everyone ran barefoot, lived in shacks, and still had outhouses. And here he was, talking and dancing with one of those very hillbillies, shoes and all.

Toni was becoming more smitten with the New Yorker with every incomprehensible word he uttered. She thought of Ken York, whom she had been dating back home in Clinton. Ken was away with the

Navy now, and Toni was never in love with him. But she felt a little bad taking up with another fellow. Her mother had always told her that no matter who Toni might meet in Oak Ridge, she had to be good to Ken.

"You have to date Ken when he comes back to town 'cause he's fighting for our country," she told Toni. "He's counting on you."

Toni agreed. But she thought maybe she could date Chuck while Ken was away. When Ken came back to town, well . . . she would figure out how to cross that particular bridge when she got to it. She'd always been one for thinking on the run.

Soon the sounds of "Sleepy Time Gal" wafted over the crowd of bodies on the tennis courts, letting everyone know the evening's swinging and swaying was coming to an end. *Sleepy time gal, you're turning night into days . . . Sleepy time gal, you've danced the evening away.* Toni danced with Chuck, his knees nowhere near her butterfly-ridden stomach, knowing it wouldn't be their last ballad.

★　　★　　★

As a nurse, Rosemary met all walks of Oak Ridge life. Most made their way through the clinic doors at some point, from kids with runny noses—separate primary-care physicians' offices didn't exist— to on-the-job injuries and train wrecks. She had even treated the General early one morning. His shoulder was bothering him again and the physical therapist hadn't arrived yet. She wasn't told why he was in Oak Ridge, and set him up as best she could and then went about her business. It wasn't the first time the General had visited the clinic. Rumor had it that he liked disappearing into the maternity ward to sneak naps.

Rosemary "stuck to her knitting," to borrow a favorite phrase of the General's. Nevertheless, she still had an encounter or two that piqued her curiosity. One night when attending a dance with a group she soon found herself out on the floor with an attractive, clean-cut young man. He had come with several of his own friends, and the two groups of singles found themselves mingling and making plans to get together.

The men shared one of the larger houses in Townsite. (Rosemary wasn't sure which type—all that alphabetical housing began to blur after a while.) Houses were perfect for impromptu parties. Soon Rosemary and the man began seeing each other, and there were things she noticed about him. He was around one week and gone the next, on no particular schedule that she could discern. She had never seen him wearing any sort of uniform, but he and his friends did have that close-cropped, military-looking hair. Physically, they were very fit. She could not imagine any of them being 4-F (unfit for military service). Sometimes Rosemary and he would make plans and then, with little notice, he would have to leave town. He didn't say where he was going and often didn't know for how long.

It was difficult at times, forming opinions about people with so little to go on. Rosemary had already found herself the unsuspecting date of a married man. At least he was nice enough to confess his status on their second—and last—date. But Rosemary was fairly sure *this* fellow wasn't married. She and her girlfriends had theories. FBI? Very possibly. Or maybe he was one of those high-level intelligence agents. None of it bothered her. She was well aware of the Project's secrecy mandate and in a sense felt more liberated than others. She never felt she couldn't say she was a nurse, for example. She treated everyone, from plumbers to generals.

But in this man's case, she knew there was no asking. She never felt uncomfortable about it. He and his friends were perfect gentlemen and a lot of fun, to boot. The curiosity was there, but it was quelled easily enough. Their dating was casual and without any looming commitment, especially considering his odd schedule and frequent out-of-town travel. She wasn't in any hurry to settle down. If she had been, she would have stayed at home in Holy Cross.

★   ★   ★

While young singles packed their days and nights with working and socializing, many young and not-quite-as-young, stay-at-home wives were prone to go a bit more stir-crazy. For couples accustomed to sharing in each other's lives, Oak Ridge was a challenge, one perhaps felt more strongly by married women than those merely enjoying a dip in the dating pool.

Trips to crowded stores could take hours with babies in tow. And mud, always mud. Carriage wheels—or wagons, for those who couldn't afford a proper carriage—sunk deep into sludge and bumped endlessly over unfinished surfaces, rousing even the soundest of sleepers. Evenings, when they saw their husbands, there was precious little to talk about.

"How was your day?"

This simple phrase, uttered by countless spouses since the dawn of the workaday week, took on an entirely different meaning here: *I know you can't really tell me how your day was in even the vaguest of terms, but I feel like I should ask you anyway.*

Even a woman of Vi Warren's stature had had to adjust. She was the wife of Stafford Warren, head of the medical section for the entire Project. His position meant he had more secrets to keep than most. Vi had gotten a taste of the classified life before arriving in Tennessee. When they were still living in Rochester, New York, her husband's out-of-town trips had become more frequent, while details about them grew scarcer. After one such trip, her two sons decided to play detective. They gathered all the evidence they could find about their father's travels—mostly matchbooks—and used it to compile what they believed to be an itinerary. After dinner, the young men presented their findings. Stafford Warren rose, took the matchbooks and, without uttering a word, threw them into the fireplace.

No clues of any kind were ever found in his pockets again.

Vi was well educated and socially active. When she moved to Oak Ridge with her children—her oldest, Jane, was already living there with her new husband—she channeled her healthy curiosity into writing. She shared her views about life at CEW in a column for the *Oak Ridge Journal*, titled "As You Remember . . ." The column was part commentary, part trip down a short but odd memory lane. But the prescient Vi had a feeling that—though the town had only been in existence for two years—theirs was a journey that people would want to know more about in the years to come.

Being suddenly shut out of a significant chunk of your partner's life was a struggle. Sometimes spouses might be gone seven days a week, with no explanation as to why. And woe betide the hardworking, unsuspecting man whose wife found a stack of envelopes suspiciously addressed to "ACME Insurance Company" in Knoxville secreted away in a closet for safekeeping. Who was he *really* writing? Another woman? Marriages had been threatened by less. Secrecy took its toll on relationships that once enjoyed open and frank communication, and were now stifled by duty. Secrecy became the norm. "Silence," as one Project poster read, "Means Security."

Writing and volunteering were perhaps Vi's way of coping. Solidarity helped immensely, knowing you weren't the only one being kept in the dark, like a lifeboat in a sea of not-knowing, even if that boat was filled with some gossiping and complaining.

For women left to wash mud out of their houses and off their clothes, or battle finicky furnaces and the soot that went along with them, an afternoon spent darning socks or sharing favorite recipes was something to look forward to. A sympathetic ear was always close by, and the latest news rippled down the plastic-coated laundry lines that ran the length of streets in neighborhoods and trailer camps, forming a spinal cord of communication that supported life in the small outpost. All a woman needed in order to tap into the information it carried was a clothespin.

But you were still being watched: In one case, it wasn't long before security agents took notice of one of these regular "meetings" that took place behind closed doors.

Agents approached a group of recipe-swapping, sock-darning housewives one afternoon and demanded to know the topic of their conversations. What were they talking about in there, with their needles and thread? Why, they demanded, were these women meeting on such a regular basis, and so *secretively*? The situation blew over when the women explained theirs was a run-of-the-mill coffee klatsch.

Darn those socks, ladies. But maybe try not to be so subversive about it.

★   ★   ★

Dr. Clarke, on-site head of psychiatric services for the Project for seven months now, submitted a "Report on Existing Psychiatric

Facilities and Suggested Necessary Additions" on Halloween, 1944. He had, over the last half year or so, begun to familiarize himself with the unique challenges faced by those who lived in Oak Ridge, which were at times perplexing. Considering the times in which they lived—coming out of the Depression, in a World War—it would have seemed believable that Oak Ridge and the other Project sites would have *less* than their fair share of issues.

After all: If everyone had steady work, a place to live, and a good wage, what kind of problems could they possibly have?

Judging from the people he'd seen seeking counsel, attitudes about Oak Ridge were as varied as the people themselves. There were those who thought the Reservation was an absolute "hellhole" with no redeeming qualities. There were those who could take it or leave it. But that was okay—it was only temporary. Few believed the site would exist beyond the war, including those operating further up the Project ladder. And finally, there were those who thought that this odd new place they had come to know as Oak Ridge was the best thing that had ever happened to them.

"The difficulties of housekeeping and the inability of mothers to get away from the constant care of children is beginning to exact its toll . . . ," Clarke wrote, as if channeling the frustrations and anguish of every woman in the country, let alone those on the Reservation. It was compounded by what Clarke described as an ongoing case of "never enough." There never seemed to be *enough* of the kind of food you wanted, there were still never *enough* roads, not *enough* housing, *enough* places to shop, *enough* hours in the day to wait for what was already limited.

"Confusing public relief with social welfare" was how Clarke described the Project's approach to residential mental well-being intentional or not. No number of bowling leagues, dances, or drama clubs could completely alleviate the uneasiness that resulted from working so hard, for so long, under such secretive conditions.

"The pressure of work upon the executives of major and minor divisions has become so great that neurotic reactions due to fatigue are appearing frequently," he wrote in the confidential report. He felt the community "differs from other communities in that as yet there is no centralized organization charged with the responsibility for integration of community life to help solve personal problems of its residents. The need for this seems to have arrived."

Dissatisfaction with housing was by far the biggest complaint and the root of many difficulties. Dr. Clarke had also seen acute anxiety neurosis, which he viewed as similar to battle fatigue overseas. He later wrote in a journal article of "fatigue reactions with associated tension states [which] have been most prevalent and are easy to understand, particularly in the executive group. Long hours, continued strain, a driving sense of pressure, no relaxation and a situation that was never stable exacted their combined toll. . . . One source of frustration to many of the minor scientific group, who were not aware of the total picture, was that they were required to spend months of repetition of a single chemical analysis without knowing what had gone before or what happened afterwards." He also noticed there were many workers who were aware that they were dealing with toxic materials that were generally unknown to them.

He believed a small psychiatric ward had to be added to the existing outpatient service. He found it challenging, to be sure, treating the variety of patients that he did, individuals that he characterized as ranging from Nobel Prize winners down to "hill folk." But professionally, it was a unique and exceptional experience, and the population he served continued to grow like mountain mint—creeping, then leaping all along the Black Oak Ridge.

He suggested the psychiatric service could benefit from two additional social case workers—one for those living in the trailers and one for those in permanent housing—a full-time probation officer, children's recreational services, and a children's psychiatric worker.

Of one thing Clarke was sure: Attitude made a huge difference in how someone managed life within the fences. He was still routinely inspired by the spirit and resilience of many of the residents, especially the "democratic spirit in trailer camps and demountable houses." Life on the Reservation, he observed, was "particularly hard on those who lack a sense of humor."

Who among them had ever been involved in building a city from scratch? When had Americans ever built a city whose sole purpose had to be kept secret, not only from the outside world but from the vast majority of its own inhabitants?

In the face of not only war, but of lack, of not-knowing, of creeps and security checks, these people—the hill folk, the scientists, everyone in between—continued to endure despite everything he had laid out in his 10-page report, and so much more that was yet to come.

★   ★   ★

Chemist Virginia Spivey recoiled at what she had heard. She was having lunch with her colleagues when another lab worker—a man recently arrived from Nevada—casually and assertively said he didn't think women needed to go to college. He said this right in front of her, and in front of her colleague and friend Emily. Then he resumed eating.

Aside from this episode, Virginia had been enjoying her lab job. She had gone to college—no matter the lunchtime consensus was about women in higher education—to work in chemistry. And now sitting here, surrounded by workbenches dotted with beakers and microscopes, she knew that this was where she belonged.

The bus dropped many Y-12 workers like Virginia at the plant complex's North Portal and from there it was a brief stroll down the hill to 9202, which housed chemical processing and bulk treatment. It was a serious atmosphere, but the group of about 10 of them talked throughout the day, their noses down, microscopes extended from them like an extra appendage. And more often than not, the group ate lunch together.

Her supervisor, Al Ryan, was easygoing and friendly. Emily Leyshon had become a good friend and was the only other woman with a science degree in the lab. There was another young girl who worked in the lab doing cleanup, and Virginia found her delightful. She was from nearby Rockwood, if Virginia was not mistaken. Virginia was from the south, too, but even she was learning some new language now that she had left eastern North Carolina for southern Appalachia. For example, a paper bag, she soon learned, was a "poke."

Even the coworker who had infuriated her was likable. But the comment—after all her hard work—got the soft-spoken Virginia riled. She did something she didn't often do: She spoke up and let him know that she did not agree.

How could she? Her parents had lived life with eighth-grade educations and worked too hard to make college a possibility for her. After her father's sudden death in a car accident when she was just twelve, Virginia watched her mother, a talented seamstress, raise six children alone off a buck-a-dress income. Word spread around their small town of Louisburg, North Carolina, and customers would come by the house with an armful of material and patterns, from places like Sears, Roebuck and Co. Virginia's mother would whip out her measuring tape and fit them in a flash. College had never been an option for Virginia's mother, but she never let Virginia or any of her other siblings worry that they wouldn't be able to pursue higher education. After two years as a day student at the local junior college, Virginia earned a scholarship to Chapel Hill. Her sister Sophia, four years Virginia's senior, had already gotten a bachelor's from UNC and was there working on her master's. Four years' difference meant Virginia and her sister graduated the same year, but her sister always did so with the higher degree and seemingly a greater share of attention. But that was of little consequence. Virginia enjoyed sharing an interest in science with her sister.

She had grown up very poor, but now she was here working, earning good money, and had a degree from a good university to her name. She rarely felt her background was an issue, let alone her gender. Outside of work, she never knew what the other people milling around Y-12 were doing, so she never sensed any large social distinctions. She moved from the dorm to the plant and back to the dorm again, interacting with women and men, excelling at work, making new friends, without much acknowledgment of class differences in her day-to-day existence.

A few years before coming to Oak Ridge, Virginia and her sister discussed the strange new paucity of information in magazines, newspapers, and journals about developments in their field. After such an active period, it seemed as if news of chemistry and physics had disappeared completely from popular literature for a couple years now. They wondered why.

But now, Virginia was in the middle of the same sorts of advancements she had once read about, awash in precious cakes of yellow and green, made from ingredients rarer and harder to come by than any wartime ration. She analyzed the cakes for their Tubealloy composition. How much had been chlorinated? What was the percentage? What was the analysis? The assay?

Meanwhile, not too far away, Virginia's friend Jane was plugging answers like those into complex calculations, while young women like Dot and Helen guided the Tubealloy through the calutrons and Colleen tested seal after seal of massive pipes at K-25, its acres of floors and towers of tanks scrubbed clean and shined by Kattie. The injured were cared for by women like Rosemary and recruits and contracts and generals came and went through the Castle on the Hill, helped along by Toni and Celia.

War had brought them together, in dorms and at dances, at work and on buses. But another, elusive and unspoken link—Tubealloy—brought together their efforts, and was completely dependent upon their abilities.

Virginia knew that this lab, this life, was uniquely hers. She had earned it.

★   ★   ★

Colleen and her mother had gotten a jump on Christmas. They had to, if the package was going to reach Jimmy in time. Colleen didn't know where her brother would be spending the holiday—or even where he was, for that matter. All she had was his APO address.

Soldiers had to travel light, so she and her mother had baked some Christmas cookies and a fruitcake (a treat designed for long-distance travel) and had bought a leather wallet, which they packed full of recent family pictures.

Once the presents and treats were wrapped tight, they began popping the popcorn. The stovetop-prepared, farm-grown packing material would help cushion the presents and ensure Jimmy didn't open a box of fruitcake crumbs Christmas morning. They carried the package down to the post office and shipped it off, hoping the kernels would hold up during the trip overseas.

Here at home, her little brother Harry wanted a trumpet, just like bandleader Harry James, whose hit with his big band "You Made Me Love You" rocketed up the charts the week that Pearl Harbor had been bombed. But Colleen and her mother had doubts they could find one. Certainly not in Oak Ridge. Pickings were slim at the Reservation stores and only marginally better in Knoxville, which would have required a trip on the bus or hitching a ride with someone who had a car. Guitars were easier to get your hands on, so a guitar it was. Harry would not be entirely happy, but what could they do? They made the best of it. They had no Christmas decorations, so they made paper chains and Colleen's sister Sara painted ornaments with red fingernail polish. Colleen worked all day on Christmas, scaling pipes. Neither the Project nor the war stopped, no matter the season.

TUBEALLOY

★ ★ ★ ★ ★

COMBINING EFFORTS IN THE NEW YEAR

The end of 1943 had been marked by sputtering and electrical failures at the Y-12 electromagnetic plant. The end of 1944 was shaping up to be much better, if unpredictable. At this point, Y-12 was just over 95 percent complete, while the construction and development of K-25 and its gaseous diffusion process kept plugging along, the barrier still an issue.

For the Project, the outcome of the November elections was a good one. There had been little doubt this time around about Roosevelt's intentions to run for reelection, and perhaps even less doubt about his ability to win the Oval Office again, despite the fact that he had occupied it longer than any other president of the United States in the 155 years since George Washington had first been sworn in. Roosevelt took on Missouri's Harry S. Truman as his running mate, a man who had not actively sought the nomination and who as senator had sought to curb reckless wartime spending. For the time being, the outcome of the presidential election meant one less new person for the General to brief.

Autumn had Project heads from both the science and military camps thinking hard about the feasibility of employing the three main plants—Y-12, K-25, and S-50—together, in some sort of tandem. This was no easy task. S-50 would be able to take the Product from 0.7

enriched up to 0.9 percent. After that, the electromagnetic process at Y-12, with Alpha and Beta stages operational, should be able to achieve a percentage good enough for the Gadget. That was the initial thought at least.

And the day before Halloween, the first Product had been taken from the S-50 thermal diffusion plant. Lt. Col. Mark Fox, unit chief for the thermal diffusion section, had overseen the breakneck pace of S-50's construction. The Engineer had been advised to "Put a good administrative man on the job to clean up the paperwork," after he was done. Joints were leaky, but steam was moving through them.

At K-25, the Project hoped to start operating individual sections as they were ready. The Engineer put a team together to examine every possible production combination, as different sections of the plants became operational. The team decided that any enriched material from S-50 should go into K-25 first, not Y-12. Initially, the estimate was that K-25 should be able to produce Product enriched to 1 percent or so to feed Y-12's Alphas. Then, once enough sections of K-25 were completed, it could produce Product enriched to 20 percent to feed directly into the Y-12 Beta tracks.

The question remained whether K-25's top stages should be completed. The charts that the team produced told the story. K-25, with all stages operating, wouldn't yet produce as much as the base plant alone feeding the Y-12 Betas. Nor would Y-12 alone, with more Alphas added, be substantially more productive. Taking all into account, the thinking was to build additional gaseous diffusion base units at K-25 and another Beta track at Y-12. The new gaseous diffusion facility would be called K-27. The plan would add $100 million to the budget and would, hopefully, be done by 1946. The Engineer briefed the General while enjoying a postdinner stroll past Pennsylvania Station in New York City. The General had had two predinner drinks, which might have smoothed the approval process, and he gave the plant the green light.

The Engineer and the General felt that by August of 1945, at least one version of the Gadget would be ready. Possibly two.

CHAPTER 10

★ ★ ★ ★ ★

Curiosity and Silence

A three-year concentration of curiosity should be quite a potent brew for the average woman.

—Vi Warren, *Oak Ridge Journal*

"Henry won't be coming home tonight," the voice said. "We need to keep him here."

Another call from work, another cryptic message. Celia wondered if this would be the last time she would get a call like this about her new husband.

Sometimes Henry turned up the next day, sometimes it was two. When he did arrive, it was not with much of an explanation. Celia knew—and Henry had told her as much—that he himself didn't completely understand why he had to stay and couldn't tell her what went on while he was there. All Celia knew was that sometimes he had to stay over. Celia never got used to it, never stopped wondering if Henry was okay. It would be years before she would learn the stories behind his workplace sleepovers.

They had just gotten married in January 1945, sooner than Celia had anticipated. At her mother's request, Celia had gone to visit her family in late 1944. Celia's mother and father had moved closer to Celia's grandmother in New Jersey, as her father's silicosis had only gotten worse and there was nothing left for him in the mines. Still struggling with English, he had taken a job as an elevator operator in a silk factory in Paterson. Always the charmer, and despite his linguistic challenges, he still managed an innocent flirt with his fairer female passengers. It had all been hard on her mother, especially with two sons fighting—one of whom was missing in action—and Celia doing whatever it was that she was doing. A visit wasn't enough. Couldn't Celia find a way to work in New York again? her mother wondered. No matter how old Celia was, she found it hard to deny her mother. At least Henry had promised to come visit.

She had had another request for a visit while she was in the north, this one from the Project. Celia had, on occasion, made trips to Washington and New York for the General and Mr. Smitz. They booked her in a private train compartment with instructions to deliver documents. This time Project officials wanted her to come in and discuss her work in Tennessee. *What could they possibly want to know about my filing, dictation, and memo writing?* Celia wondered. She took the train into Manhattan and, after a familiar walk through the city, arrived at the offices and was brought before an Army colonel.

He asked her to take a seat.

"I would like to talk to you about your work," he said.

Before he asked her a word, he began hooking her up to some sort of machine. Celia had never seen anything like it. A cloth band was wrapped around her arm; it looked a bit like the kind that doctors used to take your blood pressure. Celia sat, patiently. Nervous. There was little explanation. Then the questions began.

What kind of work have you been doing since arriving at the Clinton Engineer Works?

Have you told anyone about where you're working?

What about where you live? Do you talk about where you live with others?

Celia said no.

What about friends back home? What did you tell them about your new job?

What about when you write your family?

Celia assured them that she didn't tell anyone anything about what she did or where she lived.

What did you write them? he demanded.

The bizarre interrogation continued. Celia was scared, but honest. She didn't think she had done anything wrong. When the ordeal was over, she returned home, relieved.

Celia was delighted to see Henry when he came to visit, and he began charming her family immediately. Celia could tell Henry was making a fantastic impression.

Then Henry announced the real reason for his visit: He wanted to get married. Celia, on the other hand, wanted to wait.

Why not wait until June? she thought. *What's the rush?*

But Henry was insistent. Celia couldn't think of any real reasons *not* to marry him. He had a good job. He was from a nice Polish Catholic family out of Hockessin, Delaware. He'd won over her very demanding, no-nonsense mother. He worked to speak a little Polish with Celia's father. And he was a good dancer, to boot.

But Henry's proposal was not the only news at the Szapka household: While she was visiting her parents, they learned that her brother Clem was coming home.

He had turned up in an Army hospital in Germany. He had lost his memory for a spell but would soon be on his way home. Everything seemed to be falling into place. If Celia got married, Clem could be there to see it.

But where to do it? If the two of them got married in Tennessee there would be the issue of securing visitor passes and finding a place for them to stay. And though she liked Father Siener, she wanted her darling brother Ed to do the honors. If it hadn't been for him standing up to their mother, she wouldn't be here, with someone like Henry. Father Ed had to be a part of this day. He had helped make it happen.

So Celia had taken the train back into New York City, this time to pick out her wedding dress. She found a wonderful gown, a real beauty: long sleeves, tapered to a delicate point at the wrists, slightly fuller around her shoulders, but not too puffy. The bodice was sheer around her décolletage, but solid around the waist and gathered down the front and over the hips. The train was just long enough and the material smooth, not too fussy.

She wore her brunette waves down around her blue eyes, with a flower in her hair and more on a veil that arrived at her knees. She had bought her flowers and bouquet from a florist who had discouraged Celia from ordering her favorite, gardenias, for the big day.

"They're not going to hold up," the florist had warned. Celia bought them anyway. Then on January 27, 1945, she strolled down the aisle of St. Stephen's Church in Paterson, New Jersey, her brother Ed presiding, her brother Clem home safe, clutching bunches of gardenias that looked as though their bloom would never fade.

That was a few months ago now. Since then, she and Henry—now Mr. and Mrs. Klemski—had returned to CEW, moved out of the dorms and into a little E-1 apartment on Tennessee Avenue, quite close to the hospital and her old friend Rosemary in the nurse's dorm. (They had arrived at the gates at 3 AM with a backseat full of wedding presents which conveniently camouflaged a load of booze left over from the wedding reception.)

At first, Celia had gone back to work at the Castle, happy she still had a job after the inquisition in New York. Lt. Col. Vanden Bulck assuaged any remaining fears about how she had conducted herself during her interview. The New York office probably just wanted to better understand how things were in Oak Ridge in the early days when Celia first arrived, the lieutenant colonel said. But that was all water under the bridge now. She wasn't working anymore. Henry was against it. Henry wanted a family and he wanted one soon. That meant no more work for Celia.

It also meant more time on her hands. More time to think about phone calls that did or didn't come at night when he was late for dinner. Whatever was going on at Henry's job at X-10, she trusted that when she was allowed to know the truth, Henry or someone else would tell her.

★   ★   ★

Stark. Bare. That's how the apartment looked now.

Rosemary barely recognized the place, though she had lived in it for several months. Naked, unadorned walls, no curtains to punch up the bland palette. Stripped floors, rugs that had lain there only recently now gone. Bars on the windows.

It hadn't been that long since Rosemary had moved out, but the space had been completely transformed—depersonalized—in preparation for its new purpose.

Rosemary had been very happy in the nurse's dorm, but when it was announced that some E apartments near the hospital were going to be made available for senior nurses in order to free up dorm space, Rosemary had jumped at the opportunity. Even better was the location: right next to the hospital. So she and Helen Madden, the hospital's chief dietician, had decided to put their names into the hat and soon found themselves in their very own E-1 apartment on Tennessee Avenue in Townsite. There was one bedroom with two beds and a real kitchen, so they could cook their own meals, bake if they felt inspired, eat breakfast at home instead of waiting on line. It was a welcome switch from dorm life. Even though it was slightly more expensive than the nurse's dorm, it was still affordable and the upgrade in lifestyle was absolutely worth it. The two women settled in quickly. They bought a rug, hung some curtains. It was turning into a real home.

But it wasn't meant to last.

Rosemary could tell by the look on Dr. Rea's face when she saw him in the hospital hallway that day that she did not want to hear whatever it was he had to say.

"Rosemary, I hate to tell you this," Dr. Rea began when he stopped her in the corridor. "But we are going to have to use your apartment for a mentally ill patient that is going to have to be contained."

Rosemary was disappointed but could never begrudge Dr. Rea for almost any request. Since she'd arrived, he and his wife had been incredibly kind and welcoming to her. Rosemary was happy to help him out, but nonetheless disappointed. Dr. Rea assured Rosemary that he had little choice in the matter. The hospital was short on space. Rosemary remembered when she'd first arrived in 1943 that the plan for the hospital was 50 beds. *Fifty beds!* But even now, with 337 beds, a new wing and constantly expanding facilities, there wasn't proper space to treat such a specialized case. This particular patient could not be kept with the general population.

So there it was. No more kitchen. No more living room. No more curtains and cooking. Luckily, the women hadn't spent too much money. The apartment was already furnished with the usual military-issue, wrapped-in-plastic, wooden furniture. She had hoped that there would still be room for her back at the nurse's dorm.

Rosemary had never laid eyes on the mysterious patient. But she had known that he was on the premises. The young naval ensign's arrival at the hospital got tongues wagging even beyond the hospital. Nurses on emergency-room duty had seen the young man brought in, but he was quickly shuffled away behind closed doors. In the day or two that followed, some hospital employees noticed that a trailer had appeared behind the hospital. Rosemary hadn't seen it herself but had heard that someone highly agitated had been admitted, someone rambling about his job, talking about things he shouldn't have been talking about.

The doctors determined that keeping the man among the other patients was not going to work, especially if he kept going on about his work at Y-12. Bringing in the trailer was the first step. But it was soon decided that the trailer would not suffice. This patient needed a private, secure space of his own where he could be treated away from as many prying eyes and ears as possible.

Dr. Rea explained the best place to keep such a patient was in an apartment near the hospital. Rosemary knew that her apartment made good sense. It was a small, one-bedroom end unit, easily accessible. The route from the hospital's west side entrance to the apartment's entrance was direct, following a short pathway and making it an easy trip for doctors and nurses to leave the hospital, administer treatment, and return without spending too much time traveling.

Dr. Clarke, head of psychiatry, would be in charge of treatment. He had seen almost everything during his short tenure here and had developed a knack for creative problem-solving.

There was little to go by, no other town quite like Site X to look to for guidance. During his first year, many of the issues he had dealt with as chief psychiatrist were the same types of problems that a psychiatrist would find in any community: illegitimate pregnancies, alcoholism, and, as he later put in his writings, the "occasional homosexual gang."

But what Dr. Clarke found surprising in his day-to-day observations of the population at the Clinton Engineer Works was a "lack of curiosity as to what was going on." He felt this was indicative of the behavior of many individuals living here at Site X.

"Those with basic paranoid tendencies found much to accentuate suspicions," he wrote. "No one knew who belonged to the intelligence force or when one was under surveillance."

However, lack of curiosity was not the case with this latest patient.

There were "noncritical" patients who, if they were not exposed to, or generally aware of, the more classified aspects of life at Oak Ridge, could be transferred to another hospital or treatment center if their needs could not be adequately handled on-site. Of course, hospitals in nearby Knoxville and elsewhere in Tennessee had their own space issues. The hospital staff at Oak Ridge had to make it work as best they could with the facilities that were available. But for those patients who did have some sort of classified knowledge—whether they knew how their piece fit into the whole puzzle or not—loose lips meant arranging for some sort of closed treatment. Even if the patient were to be transferred to another medical facility, even a military hospital, elsewhere in the country, it would present too much of a security risk, too much of a potential leak of secure information. Clarke knew that releasing the young Navy man from Y-12 to another facility was never going to be an option, not while the war was going on, and not while this man was spouting information about what he was doing at work.

Not only was he talking out of turn, he also wanted to travel to Japan and warn the emperor about what was going on here at CEW.

Once Rosemary and her roommate had been notified to vacate the apartment, it hadn't taken long to get the place in shape and ready to receive its new resident. Dr. Rea got the news on February 9, 1945, from his associate psychiatrist, Carl Whitaker, that all was good to go:

> At your request the apartment at 207 Tennessee has been converted into an isolation ward with grille covered windows, soundproofing between it and the next apartment, doors which open from the outside so that emergency help can get in, but are locked from the inside, and an emergency bell connected with the emergency room for calling aid.

Guards would work three 8-hour shifts at the apartment and the psychiatrist would make rounds at 8:30 in the morning and at 6:30 at night.

The shock machine was reported as leaving Chicago the evening of February 6 . . . Patient himself is still in much the same state he has been with periods of assaultive behavior in which he might be dangerous to those about him and to himself.

So here Rosemary now stood, inside her onetime apartment. If she had been led there blindfolded, there was no way she would have recognized it. There was an MP outside, guards to look after the patient. The bars on all the windows were the biggest shock. She had moved out in such a hurry that she had left a good bit of the decoration behind. Maybe Helen had taken the curtains? Now the main living area appeared stark and austere with just a single table and chair. There were nurses living in the apartment next door, and someone residing with the patient around the clock.

When she first saw him, Rosemary didn't think the man appeared dangerous. He seemed calm, not agitated at all. He was young, perhaps in his twenties, maybe thirties. During the time that Rosemary spent in the apartment, the patient didn't do or say very much. Rosemary was left to assume that he must have been on medication to calm his anxiety. But the apartment remained locked down just the same.

Rosemary was part of the small team of nurses who were assisting Dr. Clarke during the procedure. The machine had just arrived and regular treatments would now begin. She watched as the electrodes were placed on the patient's head. Rosemary had seen this sort of treatment during her nurse's training back in Chicago. There was a technician who physically operated the automatic controls on the machine and controlled the voltage, but Dr. Clarke oversaw everything. The patient was compliant and not hostile before or during the procedure. Rosemary didn't think this was his first treatment.

Though electroshock treatment had just been introduced in the United States in 1940, it was gaining in popularity among physicians and was a part of training for doctors in the military during World War II. Ads for electroshock machines soon began to appear in the *American Journal of Psychiatry*. Newer models boasted such advances as the ability to predict a patient's resistance to certain currents. But one of the main concerns remained patient injury.

One of the nurses placed a rubber block in the patient's mouth. Rosemary's role was a minor but important one. She and another nurse present carefully braced the patient's legs and arms so that the treatment didn't cause him to break any of his own bones or harm anyone else.

The technician turned the dial. As the current coursed through the man's body, his hands clenched and his muscles thrashed as he reacted to the voltage. It was akin to a grand mal seizure. Watching the patient's reaction to the jolt, Rosemary was in fact reminded of seizures she'd seen. After his muscles contracted and went rigid, twitching followed. How long that lasted depended on the patient and the shock administered: maybe 10 seconds, maybe a minute. Eyelids and extremities, the seizure now past, quivered in the aftermath. The treatment was often used for depression. Depending on each patient's situation, it might take a series of treatments to get results. In some cases, it took only a few treatments.

Rosemary didn't know how long the patient's course of treatment would be or how many sessions he had already had. She hoped he would get better. But she doubted he would be able to go anywhere beyond the barred windows of her old apartment until the war was over, and Oak Ridge's secrets revealed to everyone, including the Japanese emperor the man so badly wished to warn.

★　　★　　★

The first time she heard it, Kattie found the noise deafening. It scared her to death at first, like someone had flipped a single switch and started the entire monstrous building running all at once. If she had been outside, even a town over, she would have seen the steam rising as it had been for months. Steam from K-25 could be seen miles away. But this was different. Something in her section of the plant was stirring.

Inside, where she stood, she wondered if everything would be all right. Louder and louder, the din grew, bouncing off the towering walls, filling the vast, gaping yaw of a workspace. Now, she and her friend Small and the others had to holler just to hear each other. *Where was it coming from? Had something gone wrong?* The truth was, she had spent months cleaning in a factory that wasn't fully operational. Now, as far as she could tell, the whole plant was kicking on at once. Work on the floor had never been quiet up to that point—far from it. But something in the concrete cavern she cleaned every day had come alive.

It was spring 1945, and winter was winding down. Not a minute too soon, as far as Kattie was concerned. The winters here in southern Appalachia were something she never thought she would get used to. She had never seen so much snow. People would talk about how it wasn't as cold as it was up north, in places like New York or Massachusetts, but she wasn't from up there so it didn't matter to her. She had seen a few flurries in Alabama. Dainty and harmless on their own, they seemed to magically appear out of a heavy gray sky but never got together with enough of their brethren to cause any real trouble. A little cold, a little slick, a little excitement for the children, and a little rush to the grocer and woodshed for the adults.

Winters here were longer and colder and snowier. Kattie was sure it was the worst place she had ever seen in her life. The ground was hard, and it was cold when she tucked herself into her cot at night. When she arose early the next morning—she prided herself on being the first to clock in, so she could be among the first to clock out—it was even worse. She would look outside the door of her hutment (there were no proper windows) and all she could see in every direction was snow. Much worse than any amount of shoe-sucking mud, as far as she was concerned. Spears of ice hung from the edges of the hutment, a little bit of sun and they would be sent spiraling downward, points glimmering, sharp, freezing and deadly. Seeing the white melt and sink into the brown beneath brought color and hope back into her days, her spirits rising with the temperature.

Kattie worked cleaning the tanks and the floors, but was more than happy to clean the bathrooms when the opportunity presented itself. She couldn't understand why some people didn't want to do it. She got more privacy while she was working in the bathrooms, and there was less walking. If she cleaned it with a friend, the two could actually talk face-to-face. The tanks she cleaned were so massive that she couldn't see Small working on the other side. Cloth in hand, Kattie scrubbed and cleaned the tanks each day until they gleamed above the floors that were her other primary responsibility.

When they worked on the floors, there were always a few women in front, walking slowly, throwing damp sawdust on the concrete as they moved along. Then Kattie and other women followed in behind, sweeping it all up. They had a wheelbarrow to carry the spent sawdust away, making sure none was left on the floor. The sawdust did its job, absorbing grease, oil, and other sludge left on the floor from the prior construction, while the friction of the powdery wood remnants rubbed against the concrete and worked the surface into a shine like glass by the time Kattie and the others were done with it. There was a long row of workers walking to and fro, about 30 janitors in all, working their way down the length of what appeared to be a long lane in the K-25 plant. One appeared to Kattie to be as wide as some of the larger houses she had set foot in. It took them about an hour to get from one end to the other, sweeping and scooping as the sawdust piled up.

Chatting had always been the way to pass the time. Now, though, she had to scream and yell at the top of her lungs just to be heard by coworkers who were standing on the other side of the huge steel tanks that populated the floor. Spread, sweep, pile it up, cart it away, do it again. From one end to the other then back again, each and every day, until it was time to punch out and go to Willie's hut and get cooking. There she would leave the deafening rumble of mysterious and invisible progress behind. She and her coworkers would continue to wait in the shadow of steamy Appalachian skyscrapers for the war's end, which they were all working to speed.

★   ★   ★

Over at Y-12, work and progress hung firmly on the percentages of Tubealloy—or Product or alloy or greencake, depending on your role in the process—coming out of the calutrons.

Virginia continued analyzing the material that came in the lab door—from where, she did not know. Dr. Larson oversaw her lab's activities, and Virginia quite liked him. She found him intelligent but easygoing, despite the pressures they were all under. As their supervisor, he would occasionally stop by the lab to say hello and to check on progress and the all-important percentages.

"How was the last sample?" he'd ask Virginia. She'd tell him, and offer to write the information down. But almost every time, Dr. Larson refused, offering to call later to get it again. Some time later, Virginia's phone would ring. Dr. Larson would ask the same question and Virginia would give the same answer. Only this time, Larson's response was much more effusive.

"Oh *MY!*" he would begin, his volume cranked up to 11. "Ninety-eight-point-nine percent? That is *wonderful!*"

This happened more than once, and Virginia began to understand: Dr. Larson was waiting until he had a group of bigwigs in his office to make that call. Saying it out loud must have had more impact than passing around a number on a scrap of paper. *Smart man*, she thought. Whoever he was trying to impress and whatever those percentages meant to them, one thing was becoming clear to people like Dr. Larson: The percentages were, compared to a year earlier, much better.

TUBEALLOY

★ ★ ★ ★ ★

THE PROJECT'S CRUCIAL SPRING

The longer the Project went on, the bigger it got, the more people in the surrounding areas began to wonder if this city behind the fences wasn't anything more than a massive failure—or worse, some sort of intricate swindle at the expense of taxpaying Americans. The "everything's going in and nothing's coming out" joke hadn't died down. It had only become less amusing.

For the Project, however, progress could finally be seen: Although in the very early months of 1945 they were not getting the enrichment levels they hoped for, there were clear signs of improvement. The Alpha and Beta tracks at Y-12, though still plagued by some maintenance issues, were humming along more smoothly than a year earlier. At long last, K-25 and its seemingly elusive barrier were coming under control. By March 1945, the largest building in the world—with a price tag of roughly $512 million—was beginning to send its first (barely) enriched supplies of Tubealloy to the calutrons of Y-12. Mrs. Evelyn Handcock Ferguson, the H. K. Ferguson Company, and its subsidiary, Fercleve, had all come through in spectacular fashion in the fall, completing and even starting operation of S-50 within just 69 days of the start of construction. At the beginning of the year, early operational troubles ironed themselves out. By March, all 2,142 columns were up and running, and S-50, too, was sending slightly enriched Tubealloy to K-25 and Y-12.

Y-12 was still carrying the bulk of the Tubealloy enrichment load. What had originally been budgeted as a $30 million plant came in with a price tag closer to $478 million. At least winter was past. During the dark, colder months, if snow sent a bus skidding off the road, delaying the arrival of the next shift of workers, whoever was perched on a stool stayed there until relief arrived. This could sometimes mean a 16-hour shift.

Rapid pace combined with exhaustion sometimes made for safety and health issues. The electricity alone coursing through the plants and factories could be dangerous for anyone exercising even a momentary lapse of judgment. Some of the cubicle operators of Y-12 were unfortunate enough to witness a maintenance man enter the cubicle control room and forget to hang his grounding hook on the unit before beginning work. He was electrocuted instantly.

There was now a fairly regular stream of Product heading to the scientists at Site Y in the New Mexico desert, some of it with a percentage potent enough for the Gadget. Armed, plainclothes couriers continued to travel by train, occasionally by air, transporting the precious cargo across the country. Medical personnel routinely met the couriers in Oak Ridge to see how they were feeling after their journey. They were taken to the hospital, given a massage and a bath and a big, juicy steak—quite a perk in rationed times. Then, for dessert, a sedative, giving them a solid day's sleep and recuperation.

Billions of dollars were on their way to being spent. Tens of thousands of acres cleared and hundreds of thousands of people working around the clock. All of the financial and intellectual and physical sacrifice and commitment and collaboration and man-hours boiled down to this: one small suitcase with an even smaller, gold-lined container inside, grams of results from the most comprehensive and expensive military program ever.

The health and safety of the couriers themselves was addressed by Dr. Hymer Friedell, a doctor with the Project who worked closely with the chief of the Project's medical section, Stafford Warren. In a

November 1944 memo sent to one of the Project's intelligence officers, Friedell had written:

The conditions under which couriers transport radioactive material have been discussed . . . and it has been definitely established that only under extreme circumstances would it be possible for an agent to receive more than the tolerance dose. The radioactive material is carefully measured and proper shielding provided. Measurements are made with the shield and container in various positions to establish the adequacy of protection. It may be feasible for couriers to carry radiation monitoring devices (film badge) which are available through the Manhattan District Medical Section, but a regular program of blood analyses should be introduced only in the case of a courier who transports such material more frequently than twice per month.

In Los Alamos, the design for the gun model of the Gadget using enriched Tubealloy coming out of CEW was set. A test of the implosion model of the Gadget, using 49 being produced at Site W, was planned for July. But this new element had other considerations as well. It was feisty, very active, and posed potential health problems, the extent of which were still being determined.

On January 5, 1944, scientist Glenn Seaborg, a codiscoverer of 49, had written to one of the Project's health directors that "the physiological hazards of working with [49] and its compounds may be very great. Due to its alpha radiation and long life it may be that the permanent location in the body of even very small amounts, say one milligram or less, may be very harmful."

Shortly thereafter, Stafford Warren, in turn, wrote:

"Information on the biological effects of these materials is urgently needed and these materials are now available in suitable quantity for experimental work."

The maximum permissible body burden for 49 remained unclear. Was it as hazardous as radium? More hazardous?

In August of 1944, the Scientist had authorized programs designed to develop ways of detecting 49 in the body. But he didn't want those experiments to be handled at Los Alamos. After meeting with members of the medical section, the group decided a research program was in order, one using both animal and human subjects.

By March 1945, doctors at Los Alamos were not happy with the urine samples of some of the workers there. Dr. Louis Hempelmann, health director at Los Alamos, recommended "a human tracer experiment to determine the percentage of [49] excreted daily in the urine and feces."

But starting the program had been delayed. Doctors were "awaiting the development of a more satisfactory method of administration of product [49] than is now available."

CHAPTER 11

★　★　★　★　★

Innocence Lost

Quite often, at first, when we were talking to some man, we would suddenly see a blank expression come over his face—an "I really wouldn't know" look that warned us we were on dangerous ground.

—Vi Warren, *The Oak Ridge Journal*

It was early, just past 6:30 in the morning, as the vehicle motored along the road carrying six people to work. Ebb Cade, his two brothers, and their friend Jesse Smith had left nearby Harriman, where the four of them shared a home, and picked up two other workers along the way. It was a Saturday, March 24, and the rising sun had just crested the horizon, making itself barely visible over the Black Oak Ridge that ran along the western boundary of the Reservation. The car headed due east toward Blair Gate near the southwest corner of the Clinton Engineer Works. The gate sat near Poplar Creek and just north of the K-25 plant, their final destination.

Cade had been working construction for the Project, mixing cement for the J. A. Jones Construction company, and his days either started early, lasted late, or maybe both, depending on which end of the 24-hour shift he found himself. He had been born in Macon, Georgia, and then moved to North Carolina along with his brothers—the Hickory-Greensboro area—before the group came west to Oak Ridge to find work.

Roads were uneven and overused, tires were easily taxed and rarely replaced, whether for rations or lack of funds. As the vehicle approached the gate, a guard approached and stopped the group, inspecting everyone for their badges and then sending them on their way, a long day ahead of them.

It wasn't too far from the gate to the plant itself. The group might not have been even a mile and a half from K-25 when they saw something up ahead of them. It appeared to be a large government vehicle and it was stopped on the side of the road, its rear wheels jacked up. As Cade and the others drove past, they had to maneuver around the oversized vehicle.

As Cade's vehicle swerved around the vehicle, a dump truck appeared directly ahead. The sun was a good five minutes into its day, now. Could that have blinded the drivers, or caused enough of a squint or glare so as to dull their reflexes? A moment longer delayed by security at the guardhouse might have made a difference in the end. But now there was no more time. The two vehicles drove directly into each other's paths. They collided head-on, metal crumpling under the force of the crash, bodies buckling beneath the impact.

All six of the passengers in Cade's car were taken to the Oak Ridge Hospital, where they were examined and treated. Besides Cade, at least one was hospitalized. Cade looked as though he had lost some blood, but there was no mention of a life-threatening condition in the initial report.

Cade's presence in the hospital drew additional attention.

The short report began:

This patient, a fifty-three-year-old colored male, was hospitalized on March 25, 1945, following an automobile accident in which he sustained comminuted fractures of the left femur and right patella and a transverse fracture of the right radius and ulna. Physical findings of note included a left lenticular cataract and marked hypertrophic and atrophic arthritic changes in both knees, together with osteochondromatosis of the left knee . . .

Timing probably played a role in what happened next.

The recommendation for the injections arrived March 26, just two days after the crash itself. Then just a few days after that, the samples of 49 were shipped by Dr. Wright Langham in Los Alamos to Dr. Friedell in Oak Ridge so that he could, if the opportunity presented itself, try them out on the subject. As Friedell related the circumstances, the "colored male" was "well-developed" and "well-nourished," though he had sustained fractures in his arms and legs. But he was communicative enough to let the doctors attending to his needs know that he had always been in good health.

The patient stayed hospitalized and was treated with the exception of his legs. They were not set immediately. They would not be. Not just yet. Not until the doctors knew how they were going to proceed.

And from this moment forward, the black construction worker and accident victim admitted into the Oak Ridge Hospital as Ebb Cade became known as HP-12.

★　　★　　★

Spring turned to summer in 1945 and the Clinton Engineer Works was in its toddlerhood. Still, new people continued arriving. Another expansion had gotten under way in early 1945. Small two-family Victory cottages—very basic, temporary dwellings made of plywood and roll roofing—sprouted up from the dusty ground as if seeds just watered by the Appalachian rains. They offered residents one bedroom, with a combined living room and kitchen, and were believed to have a life span of three years. There were approximately 28,834 people living in family units and apartments. There were roughly 1,053 people still living in farmhouses that had been left over after the initial phase of construction of the Project, minimally renovated. The dorms themselves had 13,786 men and women, and a staggering 31,257 individuals were living in barracks, trailers, and hutments.

This third phase of expansion estimated a population of 66,000. But that was low. The resident population was now at its peak: 75,000. This was a remarkable increase over the initial 13,000-some estimate made in the very early stages of development of Site X itself. Employment peaked at 82,000 in May 1945, so more than 100,000 people were on-site each day, if you combined residents and commuters. The bus system was one of the 10 largest in the United States, ferrying passengers into and around Site X. In 1944, a fare was instituted and rides that were once free cost a nickel. The 800-bus fleet carried an average of 120,000 passengers per day at its peak. There were 163 miles of wooden "sidewalks" and 300 miles of roads, and the cafeterias—17 of them now—served roughly 40,000 meals per day. So populous, so secret. Oak Ridge boasted an electricity bill that made New York City look like the Dogpatch that this neck of Tennessee was mocked for resembling. Yet there was still not yet a hint of Oak Ridge's existence on any maps.

Women continued to make up a large portion of the new arrivals. At Oak Ridge, women found both job opportunities *and* a lively social life, with one sometimes unexpectedly affecting the other. Virginia the chemist now found herself gravitating more and more toward conversations with men at social gatherings. It wasn't that Virginia hadn't had the opportunity to meet other women like herself—college-educated and single. But every now and again, when she found herself at a party, she noticed she had little in common with married women. She would wander into conversations, seeking to meet new female friends, but soon noticed that many of them spent their time talking nonstop about diapers, shopping, and home life.

Virginia had two older brothers and was always comfortable chatting with the opposite sex. One brother, denied admission into the US Air Force, joined the Canadian Air Force. Virginia remembered him coming home for a visit when she was still at home. He was six years older than she but still so young. Virginia watched as he stood in their yard, leaning against a tree, talking about what he'd seen. He looked so devastated, so sick of war. For Virginia it was one of those memories that stayed with her, one that reminded her why she wanted to make a difference. Few Oak Ridgers cared whether they were let in on the Secret, so long as the war ended, and brothers would come home again, the images of war dulled if never erased, soothed by family, by the familiar.

Virginia never felt bothered by the restrictions, was never fazed by the secrecy. Though she had heard that informants and spies walked among them, she never worried about who might be listening or think she knew enough to be particularly informative. But sometimes she was reminded that perhaps she did know more than she realized.

She once went on a hike with another scientist whom she was dating, and fell into one of the more brazen discussions she had ever had about the purpose of CEW. Virginia loved hiking. Getting away from the concrete and the cold, antiseptic feel of the lab and out into the surrounding ridges, where trees and underbrush still held on dearly to the clay and soil beneath them, was restorative and invigorating. The forest of nearby Big Ridge was popular with many of the town's residents. Perhaps it was the seclusion, being physically removed from the factories and the mud and the activity of the Reservation that made people feel more comfortable chatting about life's secrets. There, it seemed no one was listening, save the ever-present cardinals and occasional red-bellied woodpecker and whomever you had chosen as company. No eyes staring down from billboards, no ears leaning in to your conversation from across a table or a few seats over on the crowded bus.

As Virginia and her date walked, he rambled on, speculating about CEW's purpose. He had no incontrovertible proof, so to speak, but Virginia listened, enjoying the young man's company and the stimulating conversation.

"You're a scientist," he had said to her as they climbed among the pines and sugar maples. "You must know what's going on here . . ."

Her date proceeded to tell Virginia his theory. Hadn't she noticed how coverage of advancements in nuclear physics and things like fission had disappeared from the press? Indeed, this is precisely what Virginia and her sister had noticed a couple of years ago. Virginia's friend believed such a raw, previously unleashed power was being harnessed in Oak Ridge and was going to be used to end the war.

He had no specifics, had not been told anything definitive by anyone with any kind of authority. He had arrived at his own theory the way so many scientists on the Reservation had. Not being allowed to know or discuss something does not turn off a mind conditioned by a lifetime of inquiry, and does not cause one to stop thinking, devising, deducing.

His words made complete sense to Virginia, the components of his logic snapping together in her scientific brain. She knew after that illuminating walk in the woods not to discuss the conversation with others. She wasn't unnerved, but she didn't go looking for opportunities to talk about work outside the lab, either, even if others couldn't help themselves.

But when those discussions found her, she found them much more scintillating than talks of a domestic life she had yet to experience, one which did not yet hold as much intrigue or appeal.

★　　★　　★

Intrepid leak tester Colleen Rowan also loved climbing over felled trees and forest floor as a break from scaling pipes. She was getting serious with Blackie, though they had not explicitly stated their exclusivity. But neither was actively dating anyone else. Colleen had even taken to wearing an old pair of Blackie's fatigues to work at the plant. She had sewn new bars on them and rolled up the oversized sleeves. They came in handy, considering her constant climbing up and along giant pipes and walking back and forth to work through the mud. It took its toll on clothes. Shopping at the PX and borrowing fatigues were two unexpected-yet-welcome perks of dating a soldier.

Colleen's change in wardrobe hadn't gone over well with everyone at the plant however. One morning she arrived at the conditioning building and headed downstairs to begin her day. She went to her station, took hold of her probe, and began carefully inspecting welds. She was immersed in her work when she looked up and saw a sergeant approaching. Colleen had never seen him before. He strutted straight up to Colleen, reached over, and ripped the stripes off the sleeves of Blackie's fatigues.

"You have no right to be wearing these," he said. "It's disrespectful."

Colleen stayed silent. The man stalked off.

She knew she wasn't a soldier, but she would never do anything to intentionally disrespect anyone in the military. Her brother was a soldier. Her boyfriend was a soldier. She felt proud of what they were doing. She thought she was showing her support. She began to understand her mistake—how a military uniform should be respected and worn only by someone in the service—but wished the man had explained her transgression to her instead of humiliating her.

She let it roll off her back. She rolled up her unadorned sleeves, loose threads now sprouting from the fabric, and got back to work.

This episode was hardly the most serious wardrobe faux pas for a member of Colleen's family. Her brother Brien—one of the family working at CEW and possessing the irrepressible Rowan wit—thought it would be funny to fashion a hat with small wings attached to either side, *à la* fleet-of-foot Roman god Mercury. It would be a kind of millinery nod to the materials Brien believed he was working with. It would be an "I know more than you think I do" fashion statement, best appreciated by those as well versed in their mythology as they were in their chemistry. He knew they were working with mercury—maybe he didn't know why, but he knew they were. He wore his hat with pride to work one day, and that day was one of the last days Brien ever worked.

Such were the lessons learned while working for the first time on a military Reservation. There was a code of behavior beyond "keeping to your knitting," but it wasn't always clearly stated. Colleen had had training in leak pipe testing, a baptism by fire into the deep and endless waters of acronyms, and lecture after lecture not to talk about what she saw or what she did or where she worked to anyone. But there had been no "don't wear your boyfriend's fatigues" lecture.

Most just rolled with the punches, making mental notes of what they could and couldn't do.

Joking about work was *okay* . . . up to a point.

Showing your patriotism was *encouraged* . . . if done in the right way and under the right circumstances.

Making fun of the cloak-and-dagger nature of life in Oak Ridge was sometimes celebrated with laughs onstage at the theater in Jackson Square . . . until you took the humor too far.

Colleen and so many like her were young civilians adjusting to life in a community that was part science and part industry, part civilian and part Army base, socially stimulating like a college campus, but locked down and patrolled like the military Reservation it was.

Out here in the woods, acronyms and regulations had no place. Colleen relished her time off-Reservation with Blackie, and their outings to Big Ridge were some of her favorite dates. So it should have seemed only natural that Blackie took advantage of the privacy of Big Ridge to ask Colleen something that had been on his mind: Did she want to get married?

Married?! Colleen thought.

She knew she shouldn't have been surprised, but she wasn't expecting the question, either, not so soon. Maybe that's how proposals were supposed to be: a surprise, but not *complete* surprise.

Colleen adored Blackie. Her family had taken to him, too, and he seemed to return the kindness, though a family as big as hers could have sent many an unsuspecting suitor running. Still . . . *marriage.* What was the rush? Everything felt so temporary here.

So she gave Blackie, her boyfriend, her sweetheart, an only child from a Yankee background who had taken with such ease and patience to the football squad–sized southern Rowan clan, the man who shared her desire to travel, her longing for adventure, the only answer she could in good conscience:

"No."

★　　★　　★

For Dot and Celia, life in 1945 was very different than it had been just months earlier. What Colleen continued to resist, these two had already embraced.

Both were married now, and their lives in Oak Ridge as young, single working girls were coming to an end. The transition was an abrupt one for Celia. Henry had wanted to start a family immediately, and they were off and running: Celia got pregnant almost immediately. She was now realizing that what she initially believed would be a brief bout of first-trimester nausea was turning into a permanent condition. Her morning sickness showed no sign of abating and was almost intolerable. Every day, without fail, she was as sick as could be. And alone. She might have a cup of coffee with a neighbor if she felt up to it, but the days of work and commuting and chitchat in the secretarial pool at the Castle or in the cafeteria were gone. Spring was rapidly turning to summer, eastern redbuds and dogwoods had long yielded to flame azaleas, and oxeye daisies would soon fight their way up through the clay. With this came the heat and humidity, compounding her already debilitating symptoms. She was miserable.

Dot, in her new life as wife to Paul Wilkinson, her former supervisor, had discovered the ceaseless wonders of canned ham.

Thank goodness for Spam, she thought at first as she struggled to learn her way around the small kitchen she and Paul now shared. The spiced canned meat was a favorite for shipping overseas—no refrigeration necessary. Massive six-pound cans had been specially devised for the military. In many ways, it was the meat of the times. As journalist Edward R. Murrow had said just two years earlier, while reporting from London over the holidays, "Although the Christmas table will not be lavish, there will be Spam luncheon meat for everyone."

Dot and Paul had married during a lovely early spring wedding at the Chapel on the Hill. The chapel still served countless denominations, and it wasn't unusual to see menorahs and a Star of David swapped out for chalices and crucifixes, as one group departed after service and another arrived to begin their worship.

The chapel's setting was lovely: It sat up on a hill behind Jackson Square, a large expanse of land in front of it, a quaint white steeple with a clapboard finish. From a certain angle, at the right time of day—if you squinted a little—the chapel atop its hill could have been a small, mud-covered town square in New England.

Dot's first instincts about Paul eventually played out: He was smart—if an occasional know-it-all—who was well-mannered and from a good family. She knew he would always take care of her, be a good father. That mattered to her. Dot had gone shopping in Knoxville for her dress and found a lovely pink crepe gown at Miller's department store. The ceremony was very small, attended only by family. Dot's mom and sister Margaret came for the service as did Paul's mother, sister, and father. It was nice to have everyone there, but since they were getting married on the Reservation, Dot and Paul had to arrange ahead of time to get everyone security passes. They didn't have a lot of money to spend but did host a small reception at the Guest House, by far the nicest option within the gates. There was dinner and cake in the small banquet room on the main floor of the hotel—but no alcohol. Afterward, the newly married couple took a trip to nearby Gatlinburg, Tennessee, for their honeymoon.

Back on the Reservation, Dot noticed her social life was changing. She had loved the dorms—the freedom, the friends. She was usually tired after work, just enough time to go home, wash out some undergarments in the bathroom, string them up in your dorm room, and then head to bed. But on those occasions that she felt like being social, but not necessarily going out, she could visit with girls down the hall. There was always an open door, someone to gossip with or have a flip through a magazine.

Now, it was just her. Nights were hardest. Paul sometimes worked the overnight shifts at Y-12 and Dot found herself lying in bed at night, scared, kept wide-awake by a cacophony of noises—buses, voices, bugs, breezes that rattled the shaky walls of homes destined to last only a handful of years—the nighttime soundtrack of a nonstop factory town on a mission.

She had worked for the first couple of months of marriage, but now she was feeling a little sick. Pregnancy had arrived almost instantly for her as well, which was fine, but she finally told Paul she was going to quit her job. He didn't give too much argument, although he did like the extra money Dot was bringing in. Keeping house in the little one-bedroom flattop—essentially a plywood box on stilts—on Altoona Lane took up more time than she initially imagined it would, even though the prefab structure occupied just under 600 square feet of space.

There was no car for her to use, so she walked to and from the market. She shopped more now, since her days didn't revolve around the cafeteria and snack bars. The house came furnished with the basics—beds, dresser, table—but she did have to buy dishes, pots, and pans. She experimented in the kitchen and had to learn to cook. Despite her best efforts, it wasn't long before Paul's stomach told him that it was time to take over meal prep from his new wife. At least as far as his meat was concerned. Paul liked his meat rare. Dot was used to cooking the precious rationed entrée into a grayish slab devoid of any visual reminder of from whence it came. Spam had been an early lifesaver—just crank open the can, scrape off the jellied fat if you liked, heat it in a pan, and you were good to go.

But after too many nights of relying on canned ham, Dot found herself making a vow: If this war was ever over, and rationing somehow became a thing of the past, and they could buy and eat whatever and however much they wanted, she would never, ever, eat Spam again.

★   ★   ★

Benchmarks for progress were often difficult to assess at CEW. While workers in other areas of the war-at-home machine could point to tanks or tires or bombers as achievements, many, if not most, workers in Oak Ridge did not have those kinds of touchstones of accomplishment. A quick end to the war was a motivator, certainly. The safe return of troops, absolutely. But something tangible to hang your pride on—that would be nice.

So workers often created tangible goals of their own. Kattie, Colleen, and other workers at the K-25 plant had donated two weeks' worth of overtime pay to help build a brand-new plane called *Sunday Punch*. The bomber had been delivered to its pilot just several weeks earlier on March 18, 1945. Kattie and others could point to its existence as something they had helped make a reality.

Two Sundays were easy enough for Kattie to budget. She had always been smart about managing what little money came her way, whether stretching it through rations and between paychecks or making sure enough made its way back home to Auburn. Sending funds was much easier now than it had been in the early days. When she and Willie had first arrived, their options had been limited. Usually Willie would fill one of his small tobacco bags with the dollars designated for those at home and pin the precious cargo to the inside of Kattie's blouse. Then she endured a long, nerve-racking bus ride back to Alabama, their savings strapped close to her bosom, on her way to visit her mother and children.

She certainly managed their money better than her boss, who routinely borrowed money from her. He was nice enough, a little older, white, and with a penchant for chewing tobacco, rivulets of juice dripping their way south along the time-worn creases of his mouth.

"Kattie . . . ," he'd say with a sheepish smile.

One look and Kattie knew what was coming next. It was always the same.

"Give me ten dollars."

Kattie knew good and well that he went down the road to entertain some of those Chattanooga women with Kattie's 10 hard-earned dollars fattening up his wallet.

She always gave him the cash and her boss had always paid her back quickly. Kattie had built good relationships with all her supervisors, something she felt was important. It made for less hassle.

She never missed work and she was never late, which was a point of pride for her. Each and every day she clocked in trying to be as near to first as she could for her shift. "Four five five six!" she'd call out to the one-armed man who worked the alley. She had never in her life seen a man with one arm work so fast. *Man works like he has three arms*, she thought. She went to work when she probably shouldn't have, too. Passed clean out one day and hit the floor. It was the kind of day that most would have clocked out and gone home to recuperate, but not Kattie. No. She was going to wring every cent she could out of her job. After all the sacrifice, she couldn't imagine any other way. That day she took a few minutes to lay down in the room they kept for women who were feeling under the weather during their time of the month. But that's not what had caused her to collapse. Exhaustion was the culprit, plain and simple. As soon as she could, she was back on her feet. She did not want to go to the hospital, despite a coworker's request. Kattie wanted to work and proudly donated some overtime to the *Punch*.

The phrase *Sunday Punch* meant a knockout hit—and a film bearing that name had been a hit at the box office just three years earlier. Now a very lucky 1st Lt. Tom Evans of Knoxville, Tennessee, would soon take the keys, so to speak, of the brand-new B-25J plane, which had been christened at the Knoxville Municipal Airport. When 22-year-old Evans heard that the bomber recently arrived at his base near Karachi, India, had been bought and paid for by the hourly workers toiling away behind the fence down the road from his hometown, he knew he had to get into that pilot's seat. The *Punch* was a stunner, her name in all caps emblazoned on the side of the plane beneath the cockpit. The total cost of the bomber rang in at approximately $250,000, a price tag that the thousands of K-25 workers had calculated could be covered by just two Sundays' worth of work.

The bomber was now bound for the Chinese-Burma-India theater, with the 81st Bomb Squadron (the Battering Rams) of the 12th Bomb Group (the Earthquakers), in the 10th Army Air Force. How long Evans and *Sunday Punch* would be flying missions in the Far East depended not only on Evans's skill and fortune or on the endurance of the Japanese. It depended, too, on the success or failure of the employees who had helped make *Sunday Punch* a reality.

★   ★   ★

Over in the hospital, care had taken a disturbing turn for the automobile-crash patient HP-12, formerly known as Ebb Cade. He had been set on a new course of treatment not related to his immediate injuries: The injections had begun April 10, 1945. The first dose that was administered to HP-12 was 4.7 micrograms of 49: plutonium.

Years later, a Dr. Howland would state that he had initially objected to the instructions he'd received to inject HP-12 with plutonium. There was no consent given from the patient to proceed with the injections. But he stated he performed them in any case, because he said he was given a direct order from his superior, Dr. Friedell. This was an order that Dr. Friedell, for his part, later claimed never to have given. Indeed, Dr. Friedell said HP-12's injections were administered by a Dr. Dwight Clark. This has never been resolved.

The doctors made plans to collect biological samples—tissues, urine, feces—all of which would be tested for the presence of plutonium, to see how it would travel, how much of it would remain in the body, and what effect it might have on HP-12. The day after the injection, Dr. Friedell sent news to Los Alamos. "I think we will have access to considerable clinical material here and we hope to do a number of subjects," he wrote.

As for HP-12's broken bones, they were not set until April 15, 20 days after the crash. The doctors felt it would be easier that way, considering the tests that needed to be done. Bone tissue was sampled 96 hours after the initial injections. The bones could be set after the biopsy was performed. So on April 15, surgery was performed to retrieve the samples and HP-12's bones finally ended up in a cast. The doctors had previously noticed tooth decay and inflammation of the gums in the patient. So the doctor—Clark or Howland, depending on who later was relating the story—decided that in addition to the bone samples, they would remove 15 of HP-12's teeth. The teeth were removed and shipped off to New Mexico, where they would be thoroughly examined to determine whether or not there were any signs that plutonium had made its way from HP-12's bloodstream to a smile now missing 15 of its original members.

TUBEALLOY

★ ★ ★ ★ ★

HOPE AND THE HABERDASHER,
APRIL–MAY 1945

"Next time I see Franklin," the ever-so-pleased secretary of war said to the District Engineer, referring to President Roosevelt, "I'll tell him that the Army has been able to do more for Tennessee while fighting a war than the TVA (Tennessee Valley Authority) accomplished with all its dams."

Secretary of War Henry Stimson was speaking to the District Engineer after completing this, his first-ever tour of the Clinton Engineer Works. He'd arrived April 11, 1945, along with his aide and the General. The Secretary, still handsome and mustachioed at 77 years of age, was in need of some assistance getting around the roughshod, sidewalk-free outpost. Mud, stairs, boardwalks. The Engineer had made sure that ramps were built at all the key locations the Secretary would be touring, cane in hand and fedora atop his head. The result of the sudden appearance of ramps outside Oak Ridge's buildings fueled the Reservation's already active gossip pump: *President Roosevelt is coming to town!*

The size of the operation impressed the Secretary, and few, if any, of the workers recognized him as he was led on his tour. Retiring to the Guest House after his first full day in town, he wrote in his diary that he had just seen "the most wonderful and unique operation that probably has ever existed in the world."

The tour continued the next day. When the Secretary returned to Washington, he continued the rapturous account of his visit, penning in his diary he'd seen the "largest and most extraordinary scientific experiment in history," that he had been "the first outsider to pierce the secrecy of its barricades" and described Oak Ridge as an "orderly and well-governed city."

He added that although the Project had proceeded as planned, and that he was 99 percent sure of success, the only real measure of success was yet to come. The value and efficacy of the Gadget would be judged by its first war trial.

★   ★   ★

The General found out from a fellow officer who, in turn, had heard the news on the radio.

On April 12, 1945, President Roosevelt had died in the "Little White House," Warm Springs, Georgia, of a massive cerebral hemorrhage.

A nation fell into tremendous sadness for the loss of their longtime leader. The people had elected President Roosevelt to not one, not two, but to *four* consecutive terms in the Oval Office. There were young adults who did not remember ever having any other White House occupant.

For the Project, the timing was not ideal. There could be no stopping, no slowing down, no pausing to regroup. The timetable did not allow for it. The majority of members of Congress had no idea the Project existed, and it was often extremely difficult to obtain additional funding without raising some fiscal eyebrows. With each additional financial request, the General and the Secretary encountered at least minimal difficulties. Each time they had to trot out vague explanations for how each fresh infusion was going to be spent—something beyond the standard explanation that the appropriation was destined for "the war effort." They needed the president on board.

The tricky business of divulging Project information *without* divulging any Project information was usually achieved by focusing on the purchase price of lands, housing costs, construction, and infrastructure. But the Secretary and General were careful not to give too much information about the costs and size of the actual plants themselves.

Everything was described in the broadest believable terms. Yet earlier in the year, it was becoming clear that some members of Congress might need to be brought into the loop. If House leadership were on board, several key members could be invited to Clinton Engineer Works where an idea of the size and scope of the Project might be more easily grasped, even if details were withheld.

With Roosevelt's approval, the General and Secretary had been planning to meet with leading members of the House on April 13. In light of the unfortunate events of April 12, that meeting was now canceled.

Now former Vice President Truman was inheriting not only the helm of a country at war. He was inheriting the Project.

He knew precious little about what was taking place in the mountains of Tennessee, the desert of New Mexico, the flats of Washington State, and elsewhere. Truman would have to be briefed and soon. The Missourian had been vice president just 82 days now. Besides not knowing of the Gadget, there were growing tensions with the Russians, who were now moving on Berlin.

The Secretary had mentioned to President Truman that there were some important items that needed to be discussed. But the responsibilities of a new president were legion. There were schedules and meetings to be juggled. There were administrative transitions to manage and moving his family into the White House and the list of tasks went on and on, compounded by the ongoing war.

So the Secretary made it clear that this particular meeting could not wait:

April 24, 1945

Dear Mr. President:

I think it is very important that I should have a talk with you as soon as possible on a highly secret matter.

I mentioned it to you shortly after you took office but have not urged it since on account of the pressure (sic) you have been under. It, however, has such a bearing on our present foreign

relations and has such an important effect upon all much thinking in this field that I think you ought to know about it without
much further delay.

Truman immediately sent a reply, handwritten on the very same
letter. His appointment secretary, Matthew Connelly, put the secretary of war on his appointment list for the very next day, Wednesday,
April 25.

The former haberdasher from Independence, Missouri, could not
have fathomed the information about to be dropped into his lap. This
man had once served as so notable a head of the Senate Special Committee that the body soon became better known as the Truman Committee, a group determined to make sure that the American public
was getting its money's worth as far as national defense spending was
concerned.

Welcome to the Oval Office, Mr. President. You're about to get an earful.

Truman listened as the largest expenditure in the history of the
American military was laid out before him in full detail. As he listened,
he worked to understand the enormity of the long-term effects of this
Project on not only the conflict at hand but foreign policy in years to
come. He worked to wrap his mind around the decision that likely
stood before him, a decision that was fast approaching.

The brand-new president felt, as he later wrote, "like the moon, the
stars, and all the planets had fallen on me."

Both the General and the Secretary were on hand to drop the cosmos on the newly burdened head of President Truman. They brought
him up to speed, from the earliest days of research through the development of the Manhattan Engineer District and up to their current
projections for delivery of the Gadget. The Secretary's trip to CEW
turned out to be well timed—the information was now as fresh in his
mind as it was in the General's.

They explained that a version of the Gadget—the implosion version,
using 49 as fuel—would be ready for a test in July, just three months
away. A second version of the Gadget—the gun version, using enriched

Tubealloy from CEW—would likely be ready for deployment by roughly August 1.

Truman listened. He was on board.

It was suggested that five congressmen—one of whom had already raised questions about this cloaked and horrendously expensive project—be given a tour of the CEW so that they, too, might understand the scale and necessity of this unprecedented military venture.

Truman was hardly green when it came to knowledge of military spending, having investigated a number of items on the defense agenda that he believed to be evidence of overspending. He had on more than one occasion, while heading the committee named for him, pushed the Secretary to fully explain this Project and why it was costing so much and just where on earth all the money requested could ever possibly be going. The Secretary had not said a peep. And now President Truman had his answers. All of them. The moon and stars and planets had landed, and Truman could now see the breaking dawn of a new, untold universe.

★　　★　　★

"THE WAR IN EUROPE IS ENDED! SURRENDER IS UNCONDITIONAL; V-E WILL BE PROCLAIMED TODAY; OUR TROOPS ON OKINAWA GAIN," announced *The New York Times* in a banner headline covering the front page on May 8, 1945.

Germany had officially remained in the war just over a week after Adolf Hitler's death on April 30. Not that the writing hadn't already been on the wall before Hitler and his new bride, Eva Braun, walked into the *Führerbunker* 50 feet beneath the city streets of Berlin. Above them, the once-gleaming European capital was succumbing helplessly to hordes of Russian troops. The pair would never see sunlight again.

VE Day came mere weeks after the deaths of Benito Mussolini and President Roosevelt and shortly after President Truman learned the full truth about the Project. Within 24 hours of the official end of the war in Europe, a group of Project representatives, chaired by the Secretary, gathered for the first informal meeting of the Interim Committee, a group tasked with discussing and assessing not just how the

Gadget itself would be used, but also the role of the Gadget and the science that had made it possible in the postwar world. How would information be shared among nations that differed in political ideology? How would the science be controlled internationally and what kind of legislation would be put in place to regulate it all?

Wartime information control and publicity were more immediate concerns. At the second informal meeting of the Interim Committee, on May 14, the General attended. A scientific panel was agreed upon that would include Fermi, Compton, Lawrence, and Oppenheimer, and the committee discussed how best to disperse information to the public.

"William L. Laurence, a science editor of *The New York Times*, now under contract with the Manhattan District, should work up drafts of public statements . . ."

The committee knew that all their many years of private toil on the Project would soon be very, very public, and they needed guidelines about how to share information about the Gadget with the world.

★　　★　　★

As post-Hitler Europe began to take shape, Allied forces tracked down ten German scientists—Lise Meitner's former colleague Otto Hahn among them—and detained them at Farm Hall, a country estate in Godmanchester, England, just outside Cambridge. There they would be kept under wraps and out of sight until the war was over and until the Allies had determined, once and for all, just how close Germany had come to creating a Gadget of its own.

The German scientists sat at Farm Hall, with nothing to do but debate the reason they were being held there and how long their detainment might last. As they did, the Allies listened. This was Operation Epsilon.

". . . I wonder whether there are microphones installed here?" Kurt Diebner, physicist and head of Germany's research into Tubealloy, asked his colleagues.

"Microphones installed?" answered Werner Heisenberg, the man who brought the world the uncertainty principle of quantum theory. He was laughing. "Oh no, they're not as cute as all that. I don't think they know the real Gestapo methods; they're a bit old-fashioned in that respect."

★ ★ ★

Victory in Europe brought joy and relief to those with family or loved ones stationed overseas and meant, they hoped, soldiers might soon be headed home. Meanwhile, work at the Clinton Engineer Works didn't skip a beat.

No sooner had news of Germany's surrender hit the papers than brand-new messages were slapped up on CEW's billboards, reminders that it was business as usual. There was no slowing down now. If anything, the pace needed to pick up.

One billboard that sprung up seemingly overnight featured a buff Uncle Sam pulling up his shirtsleeves. His gaze was fixed on a map of Japan, while behind him a white flag flew over the land of Germany. It proclaimed:

One down, One to go now,
Give it all we've got. Stay on the job, finish the job.

Another, more emotionally jarring reminder that "it's not over until it's over" was captured in an image depicting soldiers under heavy enemy fire. Two lay on the ground, as a third looked up at a dark sky peppered by mortar and artillery spray. The caption read: *Whose son will die in the last minute of war? Minutes Count!*

Sixteen days after victory in Europe was declared, Tokyo was hit hard again. The bombing runs back in early March—Operation Meetinghouse—had made a terrifying impression. Before the sun rose in the east on the morning of March 10, 1945, the skies over Tokyo had filled with 279 B-29s. By the time the incendiary attack had finished, more than 267,000 buildings had been destroyed, roughly equal to about one-fourth of the entire city. The bombing left more than 83,000 people dead, many more according to some estimates, and scores were homeless and injured. The attack had resulted in the single highest death total of any individual day of action thus far in the war. Now, in May, the B-29 payloads skirted the urban and industrial areas near the Imperial Palace.

A massive modern marvel, the B-29 Superfortress was the flying powerhouse of World War II and the Pacific Campaign. Remote-controlled gun turrets. A pressurized cabin. More than half a million dollars, each traveling 350 mph at 40,000 feet. With the Mariana Islands now in United States control, the small spits of land in the Pacific served as an ideal air base to launch repeated attacks on Japan, and the Project had begun work of its own on the island of Tinian in February. The B-29 had already expanded beyond its originally intended purpose to conduct daylight bombings at high altitudes to include low-altitude runs at night. This go-to bomber of the war would now be adapted for yet another unique mission.

For the Project, VE Day raised new questions. The General listened intently to Under Secretary of War Patterson's inquiry. How far off was the end of the war? Did the victory in Europe mean that plans for using the Gadget on Japan might change?

Why should it? the General thought.

Had Germany's surrender caused Japan to retrench, to lighten her attacks on Americans? No, it had not. He remembered the Secretary saying that the reason for the Project was to end the war, and to do so "more quickly than otherwise would be the case and thus to save American lives." As far as the General was concerned, the Gadget was to be used against enemies, and Japan was still conducting herself as one.

A report from the Interim Committee's May 31 meeting made its way to Truman a week later containing recommended uses of the Gadget, the power it relied upon, and future exchange of the research that made it tick. This was followed by the formation of another committee at the Met Lab, among its members Leo Szilard, Glenn Seaborg, and its chairman and namesake, James Franck. The Franck report disagreed with the Interim Committee regarding use of the Gadget—it suggested a demonstration of the Gadget's power first—but the Scientific Panel of the Interim Committee overrode them, stating they saw "no acceptable alternative to direct military use."

For himself, the General had no doubts about what was to be done with the Gadget. A decision was coming, true, and not one that would be made solely by the General and the Secretary. High-level briefings and meetings would be conducted among themselves, within their offices in Washington and with colleagues across the country and across the pond.

But as for the final call, the buck stopped—as the sign on his desk in the Oval Office read—with President Truman.

CHAPTER 12

★　★　★　★　★

Sand Jumps in the Desert, July 1945

> She packed the husband's suitcase and told him goodbye without
> knowing where he was going. She expected to be asked to leave
> the room after dinner so that her husband and his guest could
> talk about their secret. She got used to the left-out feeling but
> sometimes she wondered sadly whether she would ever be in her
> husband [sic] confidence again.
>
> —Vi Warren, *Oak Ridge Journal*

July 17, 1945: On his way back to Washington, the General sat next
to several scientists. They had been in each other's company for several days now. He looked at them. They appeared exhausted and still
markedly upset by what they had witnessed in the last 24 hours.

The General arrived in the capital around noon, his work far
from over. He had more reports to both write and code before sending them to the Secretary and President Truman, both of whom
needed more detail about what had just happened in the desert
beyond the cryptic and brief summation that he had sent off immediately following the event. The General also had an appointment
to keep with photographer Ed Westcott, who was already seated
outside the General's office, waiting patiently, as he had been for
many hours.

Ed Westcott's journey had been an unexpected one. The instructions were simple but vague: *Take a train to Washington.*

Details were stranger than usual. The train would come late at
night. He should wait at the Elza Gate railroad overpass, a place where,
to his extensive knowledge of CEW, no passenger trains traveled.

232 ★

There was no indication beyond the tracks themselves that a train might pass. But the Photographer did as he was instructed.

Midnight approached. Westcott stood waiting alone in the dark, cameras and gear in tow. Sure enough, the slightest tremors began quaking the ground beneath his feet. Out of the darkness a glimmer appeared, growing larger as the locomotive's headlamp came into full view. The train slowed and came to a full stop for him and him alone. A door flew open and a set of stairs dropped from the car. Westcott boarded and the train pulled away into the night.

After arriving early the next morning in Washington, DC, Westcott was taken to the General's office in what was then the War Department Building (now the State Department building). Rooms 5120 and 5121 were the General's original offices there, though he had taken over some more space as the Project had grown. When Westcott arrived, he learned the General was not available and was given no other information. So the Photographer sat down and waited.

And waited.

Hours passed, lunch came and went. Finally, late in the afternoon, the General arrived. This was not the first time Westcott had seen him. For nearly three years now, Westcott had documented the life of the Clinton Engineer Works, from plants to dorms, strident searchlights shining from the watchtowers to twinkly lights hanging over the tennis court dances. The General had made plenty of appearances at CEW. But the normally buttoned-down, well-groomed General did not look like his usual spit-shined self. He looked tired more than anything, and badly in need of a shave. The General greeted the Photographer politely but immediately excused himself.

Westcott waited again, assuming the General wanted to freshen up before taking photos. This would be no run-of-the-mill portrait session, not after what had just transpired in the blinding dark morning of the New Mexico desert.

★　　★　　★

The morning of July 16, after roughly 25 miles of jostling around on the back of her friend's motorbike, Joan had finally arrived at the crest of the small hill. Others had had the same idea, but whispers and darkness concealed those who had successfully eluded the guards at checkpoints surrounding the test site. At least for the time being.

Young graduate students like 22-year-old Joan Hinton had not been invited to the secretive test, but they knew it was happening. Site Y was small, the confines of the labs smaller still. Word spread quickly and easily.

The athletic and attractive blond woman had been working in Los Alamos, New Mexico, since the previous year, fresh from her doctorate work at the University of Wisconsin. She worked with Fermi's group on reactors, control rods, and more. There weren't many women in the labs, but Joan found enough camaraderie among the scientists. She played in a quartet with Hungarian theoretical physicist Edward Teller and Lise Meitner's nephew, Otto Frisch. The Italian Navigator was always organizing outings, sometimes hiking and, her personal favorite, skiing. (The shop where they fashioned their reactor components was also handy for sharpening skis.) Joan had qualified for the 1940 Olympics, but they were canceled due to the war. Now here she was in the desolate New Mexican desert 250 miles south of Los Alamos. And, along with the other uninvited spectators who had evaded security and snuck out to witness the test, she anticipated a countdown she could not necessarily hear but knew was coming.

★   ★   ★

Elizabeth Graves was with her husband, Al, in Cabin 4 of the less-than-swanky Miller's Tourist Court in Carrizozo, New Mexico. Their instruments were laid out on the bed. Seismograph. Shortwave radio. Generator. Everything was at the ready. The Geiger counter sat in the window, as if it, too, were waiting for a signal from the desert.

Both Graveses worked at Site Y. Elizabeth—Diz, as she was better known—had worked at the Met Lab in Chicago. Before accepting a position at Site Y, Al had demanded that Diz be hired on as well. She had been working, among other things, on neutron-reflecting surfaces that would surround the core of the Gadget, swaddling it in material that wouldn't absorb neutrons but rather keep them in motion, help the reactions along.

Celia (Szapka) Klemski   Colleen (Rowan) Black

Jane (Greer) Puckett

Housing options included dorms and prefab homes, but also hutments and trailers, like those pictured here.

A view into a prefab home.

Mud was an unavoidable consequence of Oak Ridge's rapid construction.

New homes dot Oak Ridge's young landscape. At the height of construction, new homes were erected as quickly as one per every thirty minutes.

Women working in an administration office. In addition to making sure the plants were up and running, creating a town of Oak Ridge's size and scope meant managing the daily lives and needs of thousands of workers and their families.

Oak Ridge residents waiting at the post office.

A booming population meant Oak Ridge's residents encountered lines everywhere, whether for books, groceries, or cigarettes.

Many groups and organizations, for both adults and children, sprung up throughout Oak Ridge. Here, Girl Scouts explore their very unique surroundings.

The offices of the *Oak Ridge Journal*. Here, photographer Ed Westcott takes a turn on the other side of the lens, second from the right.

Recreation facilities ranged from skating and dances to rabbit breeding and organized sports.

Access to Oak Ridge was through one of seven guarded gates. Resident badges and searches were the norm, and no one got a free pass—not even Santa.

Billboards and posters extolling patriotism and discretion were found throughout the United States during World War II. Images throughout Oak Ridge reminded residents to work hard and keep quiet about what went on inside their fences.

Left: A close look at a cubicle control panel in the Y-12 plant. *Right:* Keeping Oak Ridge running meant keeping one of the largest bus systems in the country running. *Below:* Shift change at the Y-12 plant, which boasted roughly 22,000 workers in the spring of 1945, many of them young women.

A massive Alpha "racetrack" in the Y-12 plant is shown here.

Young female cubicle operators monitor the activity of the calutrons, the heart of the uranium electromagnetic separation process at Y-12.

Cleanup was a highly important part of the work at Oak Ridge. Worker uniforms were often washed and processed in an effort to retrieve any infinitesimal amount of the Product.

The gargantuan, U-shaped K-25 plant contained approximately 44 acres of floor space. It housed a maze of pipes that had to be specially conditioned to ensure they were absolutely airtight.

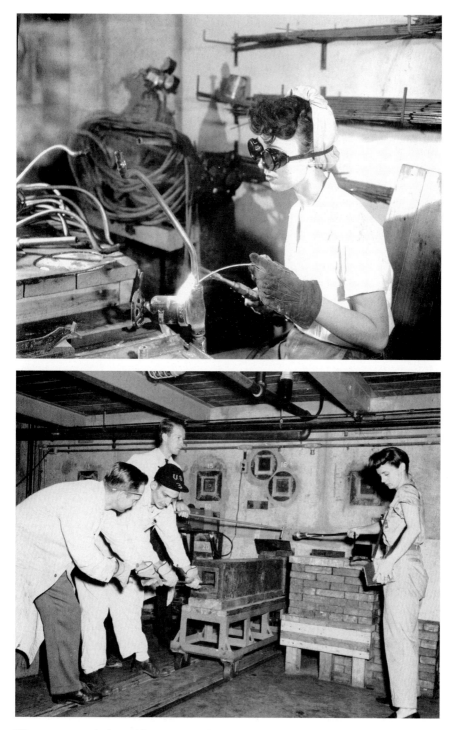

Women occupied a wide variety of roles at Oak Ridge, wielding everything from blowtorches to Geiger counters.

Gen. Leslie Groves, scientist J. Robert Oppenheimer, and others examine ground zero of the Trinity Test at Alamogordo, New Mexico.

A fireball resulting from the Trinity test of July 16, 1945, rises above the New Mexico horizon as the world enters the nuclear age.

On August 14, 1945, Oak Ridgers and people everywhere celebrated the end of World War II.

Celia (Szapka) Klemski

Colleen (Rowan) Black

Jane (Greer) Puckett

Diz knew her husband was worried, as much about her condition as the test that was about to happen. Seven-months pregnant was far enough along for them to be concerned about any number of things, among them radiation. They opted to measure the fallout 40 miles away from the test site. But Diz was not one to be easily rattled. In mere months, she would be seen standing in her lab, intently focused on her neutron scattering, all the while timing her contractions.

Now, along with everyone else, they waited.

★   ★   ★

The original idea had been to place the Test Gadget inside a specially constructed, 10-foot-by-25-foot steel container nicknamed Jumbo. The General and the team believed it would be best not to scatter the remnants of the test, in order to prevent later health hazards in the area. They also hoped to be able to recapture some or all of the 49 that was serving as fuel for this, the implosion version of the Gadget.

But that was last year, when they first began planning the test. Now the team of scientists at Site Y and the General were optimistic the test would produce a substantial outcome. Jumbo would likely cause more problems, possibly sending shards of steel airborne for miles. Instead, the Test Gadget was suspended from a tower 100 feet high. The test site, Alamogordo, had been selected for its size—about 432 square miles—and its remoteness, as well as its existing designation as a military base, which made securing the area all the easier.

The Scientist was concerned about the weather. The night of the General's arrival, there was gusty wind and some rain. Not ideal. Rain would cause the majority of the fallout to drop in a concentrated area, rather than dissipate. Heavy rainfall might affect electrical components. Wind direction needed to head away from populated areas. The observation planes needed to be able to see. This test was their only chance to visually assess the size and reach of the implosion Gadget.

For everyone, excitement was tinged with a bit of trepidation and a touch of dark humor. Dollar bets had been placed as to the resulting size of the blast, and Fermi took side bets as to whether or not the test would wipe New Mexico off the map. The General spoke with the

236 ★ The GIRLS of ATOMIC CITY

Scientist. A delay would cause problems, especially with President Truman at the Potsdam Conference in Berlin that very moment. What happened here would impact his discussions with British prime minister Winston Churchill and Soviet premier Joseph Stalin.

The goal was to perform the test at 4 AM the morning of July 16: early enough so that most people in the surrounding areas would still be sleeping and dark enough for the photographic needs. The exceptionally well-read Scientist later said he supposed he named the test Trinity because at the time he was thinking about a poem by John Donne entitled, "Batter my heart, three-person'd God," from the sixteenth-century British metaphysical poet's *Holy Sonnets*, in which the narrator entreats God to dominate him. The "three-person'd God" represents the Trinity, but later biographers would point out that the Scientist's study of Hinduism may have also played a part, as the Hindu trinity is comprised of Brahma the creator, Vishnu the preserver, and Shiva the destroyer.

Everyone knew the drill: Lie down, feet toward the blast, head away, and cover your eyes. There were three observation camps, each roughly 10,000 yards from the tower. The officially invited crowd included scientists and other special guests—Monsanto's Charles Thomas was there, as was a man named Klaus Fuchs, a physicist then known by the name "Rest" to the Soviets. In 1950, he would be revealed as a Soviet agent and atomic spy.

No one was supposed to look directly at the flash. Once it had passed, you could watch, but only through the special welder's-style glasses supplied. The test was postponed briefly because weather wasn't cooperating. Then, at 5:10 AM the countdown began.

The Project was using the same frequency as radio station KCBA out of Delano, California. At that moment, the station was broadcasting melodious strains of "The Star-Spangled Banner," which intermingled with the voice of physicist Sam Allison as he counted down the final moments to the test.

The General got in position and waited. What would he do, he wondered, if once the countdown ended, *nothing happened*?

"*. . . by the dawn's early light . . .*"

Years of preparation. The money. The manpower.

"*. . . at the twilight's last gleaming . . .*"

Then at 5:29:45, Mountain War Time, it happened.

"*. . . And the rocket's red glare . . . the bombs bursting in air . . .*"

★   ★   ★

Up on the hill 25 miles away, Joan Hinton felt the heat first. She would later say that it "looked like a sea of light" that was "gradually sucked into an awful purple glow that went up and up into a mushroom cloud. It looked beautiful as it lit up the morning sun." Then came the rumbling.

In Carrizozo, Cabin 4 shook. But it wasn't until 3 PM that afternoon that Diz noticed the Geiger counter revving up. That was when the wave of radiation—a swath approximately 100 by 30 miles—reached Carrizozo. By 4:20, one click was indecipherable from the other as the counter kicked into high gear. She and Al phoned the base camp. The General thought about evacuating the area, but the Geiger readings soon died down. The people of Carrizozo were none the wiser. Thanks to the Office of Censorship and a well-placed officer at the Associated Press office in Albuquerque, the average citizen heard a cover story:

"*A remotely located ammunition magazine containing a considerable amount of high explosives and pyrotechnics exploded . . .*"

More than 100 miles away, the *Socorro Chieftain* newspaper also reported of the "explosives magazine" mishap:

"*The flash was intensely white and seemed to fill the entire world. It was followed by a large crimson glow . . .*"

David Greenglass, the spy known to his handlers as Kalibr, was on his way to a bus stop in Albuquerque to head into work at the lab when he saw a flash over the horizon. He had been working at Site Y for almost a year now. He knew it must have been the test. He would now have more to report.

Trinity was a blinding success. The Test Gadget annihilated the steel tower and carved a crater six feet deep and 1,200 feet in diameter. The temperature at the center of the mass of fire was four times the temperature at the center of the sun. The resulting pressure, more than 100 billion atmospheres, was the greatest ever to exist on the surface of the earth. It knocked men down who were standing 10,000 yards away and the resulting flash was visible for more than 200 miles and audible for at least 40. And 150 miles away, a drowsy-eyed woman in Arizona told the local paper she wondered why she "saw the sun come up and go down again." For days following, residents from miles around noticed an odd white powdery substance settling on surfaces, as if a mid-July frost had unexpectedly set in.

The General had instructed his personal secretary, Jean O'Leary, to be in his office back in Washington, DC, at 6:30 AM the next day to receive any message he had to send. Her code sheet at the ready, O'Leary waited for the communiqué to come so that she could then interpret it and pass it along. O'Leary took the message then went, in person, to the Pentagon to speak to a Mr. George L. Harrison who, in turn, communicated the General's information to the secretary of war, who was in Potsdam, Germany.

The message the Secretary received was brief and coded:

"The baby is born."

★   ★   ★

Truman was in Potsdam, just outside the capital city of Berlin, for a two-week meeting with Stalin and Churchill and was about to be faced with the most monumental decision ever pondered by any American president in perhaps the nation's history.

The three leaders were meeting in Potsdam to tackle questions including: What would the world look like after the war? Politically, geographically? How would Germany be divided once the war was finished? What of the creation of a council of foreign ministers to orchestrate and supervise the new occupied zones? Other matters were more contentious. How real was the growth of Communism? How would the victorious allies meld their respective political systems—democracy and Communism—as they moved forward?

The war in the Pacific was a priority, and crucial June victories in Okinawa and Iwo Jima meant that Japan was within striking distance of American troops.

The day before the conference began, the plainspoken Truman, still preoccupied with the Trinity test, wrote in his diary:

"I hope for some sort of peace—but I fear that machines are ahead of morals by some centuries and when morals catch up perhaps there'll be no reason for any of it. I hope not. But we are only termites on a planet and maybe when we forge too deeply into the planet there will be a reckoning—who knows?"

As talks in Potsdam began, Truman kept his cards close, especially with Stalin, whose country planned to declare war on Japan in mid-August.

"I can deal with Stalin," he wrote. "He is honest—but smart as hell." When Stalin began talking during their meeting, he made it known that he had some questions that perhaps weren't on the agenda. When Truman told him to "fire away," the response, the president shared, was "dynamite."

"But I have some dynamite too which I'm not exploding right now," Truman wrote in his diary later that evening.

The day after Trinity was decidedly different. Even though he had not yet received the full report, the news out of New Mexico had inspired confidence in Truman. He would share news of Trinity's success with Churchill first, but wanted to wait for the right time before informing Stalin. He knew Stalin believed that cooperation between their nations would be more difficult in peacetime than it had been during the war. Stalin shared information with Churchill and Truman about a telegram from the Japanese emperor "asking for peace." Truman wrote of this on July 18. Each had their own ideas of how the war should end and what would happen afterward. For Truman, Japan's unconditional surrender remained a key issue.

"Believe Japs will fold up before Russia comes in," Truman wrote. "I am sure they will when Manhattan appears over their homeland. I shall inform Stalin about it at an opportune time."

★　　★　　★

The Photographer looked up and finally saw the General emerge, appearing much neater and put together. The General said nothing of his recent trip. The two got down to business.

The government needed photos for an important upcoming press release which was already in the works—though the event it described had yet to take place.

Westcott was a pro and the Project was his reluctant muse. He had set foot on the disrupted East Tennessee soil earlier than most as the 29th employee of the Project. The Chattanooga-born, Nashville-raised man had documented the goings-on at Site X, from the building of the plants, right through the growth of the unexpected community.

He had been there, Speed Graphic or Deardorff View in hand, at the Castle on the Hill, the first building ever finished at Site X. He was there for the groundbreaking of Y-12, and K-25, and X-10 and S-50. He was there for comic-book sales and Girl Scout meetings, war bond drives, and VIP visits. The tired yet smiling faces of housewives at the grocer, kids at school, workers at dances, segregated privies— all passed before his lens. He'd been there for the town's quotidian joys and hardships: the butcher shop, the commissary, dates at the movie theater, first loves, and jitterbugs, slogging through mud and smiles on fresh young faces as they strolled through security gates at the end of a long shift. He had taken countless pictures of men and women and children living a new life in a new place that hadn't existed just three years prior, working on a Project that was unlike any other ever attempted. He took pictures for the general population that graced the scant pages of the *Oak Ridge Journal* and he took pictures for a select few blessed with the proper clearance that no one else would see for a very, very long time.

Today, he took a number of pictures of the freshly scrubbed General. He had learned over the years how to work with men of power, how to gently push them. You had to let them know you were the boss; they respected that, especially if it was going to result in a better image. He was particularly proud of the results of one snapshot in particular: The General stood in profile before a wall map of the world. The General looked and pointed to the map in front of him. The Photographer pointed his camera. It was a picture tailor-made for the press packets for the event that had not yet occurred.

July 31.

That would be the earliest date that the Gadget could be used, the General thought. The Photographer's camera clicked away as the General stood in his office, beside the map, his gaze and index finger fixed on the island in the Pacific that marked the war's final showdown, the site of the event that had yet to occur: Japan.

★   ★   ★

As the General began work on his more detailed Trinity report, a group of project scientists drafted a letter of their own: a petition addressed to President Truman.

"Discoveries of which the people of the United States are not aware may affect the welfare of this nation in the near future," the one-page missive began.

As the communiqué continued, it discussed the new discoveries revealed throughout the Project and unleashed at Site Y, the innovative technologies that would be developed from them, and the potential uses of this humbling new power. The commander in chief was facing what the group of men called "the fateful decision": whether or not to use the Gadget, the result of the Project to which they had committed years of their lives, the test of which had proved startlingly successful.

Their original fear, the petition explained, was that the United States might be attacked by the very kind of Gadget they had just tested, and that a counterattack would be "her only defense." But now, "with the defeat of Germany, this danger is averted, and we feel impelled to say what follows . . ."

The July 17 letter from scientists at the Met Lab pleaded with President Truman to use the Gadget only if "the terms which will be imposed upon Japan have been made public in detail and Japan, knowing these terms, has refused to surrender." They urged him to consider the "moral responsibilities" involved in using the Gadget. This was but the beginning of a new age.

"[T]here is almost no limit to the destructive power which will become available in the course of their future development," the scientists wrote. "Thus a nation which sets the precedent of using these newly liberated forces of nature for purposes of destruction may have to bear the responsibility of opening the door to an era of devastation on an unimaginable scale."

An initial, more direct version of the petition had been drafted July 3. Hungarian physicist Leo Szilard was the main force behind the letter, as he had, years before, been one of the main forces behind Einstein's letter to Roosevelt and the creation of the Project. He knew that his views and the views of those who signed the petition—59 for the first version, 70 for the second—were "by no means shared by all scientists."

More petitions and counterpetitions from Project scientists followed. One read in part:

"Are not they, who are risking their lives for the nation, entitled to the weapons which have been designed? In short, are we to go on shedding American blood when we have available a means to speedy victory?"

★   ★   ★

Even before the General sent his full Trinity report across the Atlantic on July 21, Prime Minister Churchill had already noticed a change in Truman's demeanor during their meetings with Premier Stalin. Churchill had no idea what could have caused such an infusion of confidence in the Midwesterner, who was now palpably more direct with Stalin. However, once Truman informed Churchill about Trinity, Churchill better understood Truman's more assured manner.

Meanwhile, on July 23 in Oak Ridge, Holly Compton met with the Engineer to discuss a recent poll of scientists at the Met Lab. The Engineer had approached Holly directly wanting to know who was in favor of using the Gadget and who wasn't.

The 150 scientists polled were given five choices, ranging from not using the Gadget at all to using it in the manner "most effective in bringing about prompt Japanese surrender." Small percentages of scientists voted at both ends of this spectrum. Twenty-six percent wanted a demonstration in the United States with Japanese representatives present. The majority, Holly told the Engineer, 46 percent, favored "giving a military demonstration against one of the Japanese cities to be followed by a renewed opportunity for surrender before full use of the weapon was employed."

And what do you think? the Engineer asked.

Holly paused. "What a question to answer!" he later wrote, thinking of his "pacifist Mennonite ancestors."

"My vote is with the majority," he told the Engineer. "It seems to me that as the war stands the bomb should be used, but no more drastically than needed to bring surrender."

★   ★   ★

The same day the Engineer met with Holly, a young courier, Lt. Nick Del Genio, left CEW with briefcase in hand, and boarded a train. His coffee-cup cargo contained the last bit of Product the Gadget would need.

For the last year, roughly 22,000 people had been working at Y-12 day in and day out, 24 hours a day, as 1,152 calutrons managed to enrich 50 kilograms, or just over 100 pounds, of enriched Tubealloy.

The General prepared the orders for the operation and sent a memo to the Secretary in Potsdam that included a map of Japan he'd snipped from a recent issue of *National Geographic*. He included a description of the four potential targets.

The doubts of the scientists made little sense to the General. What was the point of all the security measures if the intent was not to strike targets with an element of surprise? He admired Truman for the decision he now faced, for undertaking it knowing full well that he would ultimately be viewed as responsible. No matter how many scientists or generals weighed in with their two cents, Truman would be viewed as the one who made the final call. It was on him and he knew it. The General respected him for that.

Truman finally informed Stalin about the United States' "new weapon of unusual destructive force." Stalin did not appear overly surprised at the revelation. Russian stoicism? A masterful poker face? Or did Stalin already know more than Truman and the Secretary realized, as if he had been briefed on the progress of the Project all along?

It would later be revealed that thanks to David Greenglass, Klaus Fuchs, George Koral, and others, Stalin had been more informed about the Project than anyone knew.

On July 25, Truman gave the go-ahead to issue orders that the Gadget be used as soon after August 3 as would be possible. The next day those orders were passed along to General Spaatz, commander of the US Army Strategic Air Forces. Wheels were in motion. Also that day, the Engineer packaged the survey, a letter from Holly Compton, Szilard's petition, and other documents with a cover letter stating, "It is recommended that these papers be forwarded to the President of the United States with the proper comments . . ." He sent it to the General.

The evening of July 25, still in Potsdam, Truman wrote in his diary that the Gadget "may be the fire distruction [*sic*] prophesied in the Euphrates Valley era, after Noah and his fabulous ark. . . . An experiment in the New Mexican desert was startling—to put it mildly." He wrote that he had told the Secretary to "use it so that military objectives and soldiers are the target and not women and children."

Regardless of how they felt about their enemy, Truman did not want the Gadget used on "the old Capitol or the new." He added: "The target will be a purely military one and we will issue a warning statement asking the Japs to surrender and save lives. I'm sure they will not do that, but we will have given them the chance . . . It seems to be the most terrible thing ever discovered, but it can be made the most useful."

Terrible but useful. Just a week had passed since the General, scientists, and other guests had watched the terrible, useful display in the desert. Bill Laurence of *The New York Times,* the only journalist present for Trinity, was there taking notes that would later be disseminated to news outlets across the country. The Gadget had been a stunning, overwhelming success, its strange iridescent purple, pink, and orange beauty forever seared on memories of those first witnesses.

Moments after the Trinity, once they'd regained their footing, Kenneth Bainbridge, the test director, had turned to face the Scientist.

"Now we are all sons of bitches," he said.

The Scientist later said he recalled a line from the Hindu text the *Bhagavad-Gita*: "Now I am become Death, the destroyer of worlds."

★   ★   ★

The young courier would not be immediately returning to Tennessee.

When Lieutenant Del Genio opened his return orders, he learned he was to depart July 26, 1945, for a small island in the Pacific called Tinian, in the Northern Mariana Islands. This time his cargo was a canister about two feet high, and maybe another foot or so wide. Whatever it contained, he had to keep it within sight until he landed at Tinian, well on the other side of the International Date Line. Clocking in at just roughly 39 square miles of land area, the tiny island just south of Saipan boasted little beyond its six massive 8,500-square-foot runways.

As Del Genio made his way out over the Pacific on July 26, Britain and China joined the United States in issuing the Potsdam Proclamation, which called for the unconditional surrender of the Japanese. If the emperor refused, the Japanese would face "prompt and utter destruction."

At a secluded Farm Hall in England, July 26 brought more speculation among the captured German scientists interned there. The large three-story brick estate home was comfortable, but the men were unable to send or receive news from their families. Otto Hahn, Lise Meitner's former colleague, was recorded as saying:

> They will not let us go until they are absolutely certain that no harm can be done or that we will not fall into Russian hands or anything like that. . . . I have told the Major: "If my American and English friends knew how I am being repaid for all my work since 1933, that I am not even allowed to write to my wife, they would be very surprised . . ." The outlook for the future is dark for all of us. I have not got a long future to look forward to. . . . Men are not idealists and everyone will not agree not to work on such a dangerous thing. Every country will work on it in secret. Especially as they will assume that it can be used as a weapon of war.

★   ★   ★

Over the past two years, Ed Westcott had taken, developed, and sorted through thousands of photos. From these, photos were selected by Project heads to help tell CEW's story—at least the version of the story the Project was ready to share. Soon everyone would know, in broad mighty strokes, what had been going on in Tennessee and elsewhere.

On July 27, 33 photos were packaged with 14 different press releases that had been carefully crafted with the help of William Laurence. Some were flown under the guard and protection of the Air Force to Site Y, Site W, and Washington, DC, while intelligence agents transported other packets to major southern cities. There they waited. The information in these packets was not to be reviewed or released to news outlets until further instructions were received.

Meanwhile, the 27th brought the Secretary to Frankfurt for a lunch and a meeting with General Dwight D. Eisenhower, Supreme Commander of the Allied Forces in Europe. The two men discussed the Project, and General Eisenhower shared his misgivings about use of the Gadget. He told the Secretary he hoped "we would never have to use such a thing against an enemy," because, as he wrote three years later, he "disliked seeing the United States take the lead in introducing into war something as horrible and destructive as this new weapon was described to me."

Several days later, on August 1, the General delivered the Engineer's package of petitions and other documents to the Secretary's office. As far as the Engineer was eventually able to surmise, the package was then filed away and never delivered to the president, who was still in Potsdam. The Engineer understood. The scientific panel had made their opinion known and the decision, after all, had already been made.

★   ★   ★

Early August 1945 and it was business as usual at CEW: There was an insatiable need to keep enriching Tubealloy. No stopping, no slowing.

One day, a nurse had entered patient HP-12's room only to find he wasn't in it. His leg had finally been set and his teeth removed, but now no one seemed to know where he was. All that was left of Ebb Cade in the hospital were some biological samples. No more would be taken. Ebb Cade had gone missing, a pernicious payload of plutonium still coursing through his veins.

Had he checked himself out? Did he even bother? Did someone mention they saw his wife? All they did know was that he was gone.

Unaware of this development in the hospital, Rosemary remained occupied with staffing and supplies. The administrative post suited her, and she was one of the top nurses at the booming medical facility. For a small-town girl from Iowa, the responsibility and opportunity had turned out to be more than she likely ever would have been able to find back home, or even in Chicago where she'd gone to school.

Helen was headed to New Orleans to visit friends from back home now working there, a trip she'd planned for a while. She had taken a plane from Knoxville and was anxious for a break from her day-to-day routine, a change of scenery, and quality time with some good friends.

The married girls, Celia and Dot, were busy at their homes, navigating both their nausea and their new roles as nonworking housewives. Jane's team of number crunchers continued examining the figures that landed on tables dwarfed by massive Marchand and Monroe calculators, before passing their results along to Jane, who, in turn, sent them up an invisible chain of command.

Y-12 was still bearing the brunt of production. K-25, still not fully producing at the level that the Project had hoped, was nevertheless providing an enrichment boost. Kattie kept her floors and tanks clean. Colleen navigated her pipes and hunted down leaks. But one thing had changed and was causing her a bit of concern: Blackie hadn't proposed lately.

Work at all the plants, in other words, continued at a breakneck pace. There was no reason to think anything would change.

★ ★ ★

Virginia's mind was on a long-awaited vacation to Washington, DC. She was heading off with her friend Barbara Smedley, a Lexington, Kentucky, woman who worked in Y-12. Virginia was looking forward to a little time away. They were planning to take the overnight train and had arranged for a sleeper car. The two were going to do all the things that tourists were supposed to do: walk along the mall, go to the museums. And there were plans to take a boat down to Norfolk so Virginia could visit her sister.

But as Virginia's departure approached, she had an interesting encounter with some of her colleagues. They took her aside, out of earshot.

"You might not want to go anywhere right now," they said.

What on earth are they talking about? she wondered. Some of these men worked more closely with Dr. Larson, and they always seemed to have their ears tuned in to what was going on. More than Virginia felt she did, in any case.

"Whatever it is," they continued, "it's about to happen."

CHAPTER 13

★ ★ ★ ★ ★

The Gadget Revealed

The men themselves were strangely quiet at first. It seemed as if the strain of keeping certain things secret had stopped their flow of conversation completely. . . . And then the radio began to talk! It came like a physical blow to all of us.

—Vi Warren, *Oak Ridge Journal*

The very first thing Toni wanted to do was call Chuck at work. She had always assumed he would know before her, but no matter. She *did* know and she needed to hear what he thought. Everything would change now, wouldn't it?

Toni was beside herself. Phones rang, women gabbed uncontrollably, giving not a thought to what they were allowed to say, and no one even tried to stop them. Not once. The merest of details gleaned from paper, radio, or flapping gums were making their way down the halls, into corner offices, and throughout the secretarial pool. Slowly the entire Reservation was igniting, ripples of information expanding outward via word and wire. For every voice that uttered the News, at least two more spread it from there forward, faster this time, exponentially increasing the radius of those now in the know.

"It's a bomb!" Toni blurted when Chuck finally picked up the phone.

She heard nothing in response.

"Chuck! Chuck! Did you hear me? It's a BOMB!!!"

All Toni heard was a click at the other end of the line. Chuck hung up without saying a word.

★   ★   ★

Rosemary Maiers entered Dr. Rea's office and looked around at the others already gathered. No one knew why they had been summoned.

The day had started off unremarkably until Dr. Rea blustered in, excited, but serious.

"There's a meeting in my office at eleven o'clock," he told her. "There is going to be a very important public announcement from the president of the United States."

Now here she stood, along with a handful of other hospital staff, crowded around Dr. Rea's radio. Waiting.

Rosemary assumed—as did most others—that an important gathering around a radio must have something to do with the war. But how was it Dr. Rea seemed to know about the report ahead of time? Why did he know it was important enough to drag people away from their duties to listen?

Dr. Rea walked over to the radio and turned it on. As he turned the dial, the alternating sounds of static and bursts of clear channel broadcasts filled the room. The station locked. Anticipation peaked. And an address that would shock the world began.

Sixteen hours ago an American airplane dropped one bomb on Hiroshima, an important Japanese Army base. That bomb had more power than 20,000 tons of T.N.T. It had more than two thousand times the blast power of the British "Grand Slam" which is the largest bomb ever yet used in the history of warfare.

The Japanese began the war from the air at Pearl Harbor. They have been repaid many fold. And the end is not yet. With this bomb we have now added a new and revolutionary increase in destruction to supplement the growing power of our armed forces. In their present form these bombs are now in production and even more powerful forms are in development.

It is an atomic bomb. It is a harnessing of the basic power of the universe. The force from which the sun draws its power has been loosed against those who brought war to the Far East.

President Truman sat aboard the USS *Augusta* en route back to the United States having issued this, the most important address of his tenure, from the middle of the Atlantic.

Hiroshima was one of four potential targets chosen by the Target Committee. The General knew it to be an embarkation point for the Japanese Army and home to a local Army headquarters, storage, and industrial sites. The General had also favored Kyoto as a target due to its size, believing it to be a significant military target and ideal for determining the impact of the bomb. But the Secretary objected to bombing the cultural and ancient capital, as did the president.

The overseas journey of most of the Gadget had begun July 16, the same day of the Trinity test. The USS *Indianapolis* carried the Gadget to Tinian, in the Northern Mariana Islands, where it arrived on July 26, the same day that the final bits of Product and the remaining parts of the Gadget left on a C-54 aircraft from New Mexico, under the watchful eye of Lieutenant Del Genio.

The *Indianapolis* survived only four days after delivering its cargo to Tinian. It went down on July 30 along with roughly 900 crew members after an attack by a Japanese submarine. The ship, it was later learned, was extremely vulnerable to torpedoes and could be sunk by a single one.

The General's orders of July 23 had stated:

"The 509 Composite Group, 20th Air Force, will deliver its first special bomb as soon as weather will permit visual bombing after about 3 August 1945, on one of the targets: Hiroshima, Kokura, Niigata and Nagasaki," and that "additional bombs will be delivered on the above targets as soon as made ready by the project staff."

No test of this, the gun model of the Gadget, using Product from CEW, had ever been conducted. The enriched Tubealloy was too scarce. The scientists were fairly confident that this model would work, however. Isometric drawings of the gun model were sketched by Miriam White Campbell, an architecture student who had joined the Army in 1943 and was eventually sent to Los Alamos, where her skills were put to use creating intricate drawings of the internal workings of the bomb.

The first few days of August featured uncooperative weather. Hiroshima, with its 25,000 or so troops and a castle housing an army headquarters, was the primary target. There would be other "non-Gadget" attacks coming from the air the same day. The B-29 *Enola Gay*, piloted by Colonel Paul Tibbets and named for his mother, would carry the atomic bomb, nicknamed Little Boy. There were two observation planes for the *Enola Gay* and a spare plane headed to Iwo Jima as a backup in case the *Enola Gay* suffered mechanical difficulties. Additionally, planes flew to Kokura Arsenal and Kokura, the secondary targets, and Nagasaki, a tertiary one, to provide eyewitness reports on weather in those locations.

Atmospheric reports on August 5 looked more favorable. A midnight briefing led to a pre-flight breakfast and religious services before the *Enola Gay* and its payload took to the air on August 6, 2:45 AM Tinian time. The bomb dropped at 9:15 AM. The weaponeer of the *Enola Gay*, Captain Parsons, reported two "slaps" hitting the plane after the flash. At 10:00 AM he could still see the cloud, which he estimated to be 40,000 feet high. He and the others who observed the blast thought the Japanese might believe they were struck by a meteor.

The General had initially believed another Gadget like the implosion model tested at Alamogordo in New Mexico would arrive at Tinian on August 6:

Before 1939, it was the accepted belief of scientists that it was theoretically possible to release atomic energy. But no one knew any practical method of doing it. By 1942, however, we knew that the Germans were working feverishly to find a way to add atomic energy to the other engines of war with which they hoped to enslave the world. But they failed. We may be grateful to Providence that the Germans got the V-1's and the V-2's late and in limited quantities and even more grateful that they did not get the atomic bomb at all.

The battle of the laboratories held fateful risks for us as well as the battles of the air, land, and sea, and we have now won the battle of the laboratories as we have won the other battles.

Beginning in 1940, before Pearl Harbor, scientific knowledge useful in war was pooled between the United States and Great Britain, and many priceless helps to our victories have come from that arrangement. Under that general policy the research on the atomic bomb was begun. With American and British scientists working together we entered the race of discovery against the Germans.

A cloud hung over Hiroshima. The estimated damaged area was 1.7 square miles, with initial calculations indicating approximately 70,000 people were killed instantly—nearly the population of Oak Ridge—with roughly the same number of people injured. Those reports would soon be revised up, with closer to 140,000 people dead, though precise numbers are impossible to know. News about the bombing began to spread quickly across the world as well as the Reservation. Wives with access to radios and phones called husbands at work. Whispers became shouts; gossip morphed into fact. At K-25, Colleen Rowan heard the news after a coworker's wife had called. She went out to buy a copy of the Knoxville newspaper. It usually sold for a nickel, but today "extras" were going for $1—and everyone had sold out.

The United States had available the large number of scientists of distinction in the many needed areas of knowledge. It had the tremendous industrial and financial resources necessary for the project and they could be devoted to it without undue impairment of other vital war work. In the United States the laboratory work and the production plants, on which a substantial start had already been made, would be out of reach of enemy bombing, while at that time Britain was exposed to constant air attack and was still threatened with the possibility of invasion. For these reasons Prime Minister Churchill and President Roosevelt agreed that it was wise to carry on the project here. We now have two great plants and many lesser works devoted to the production of atomic power. Employment during peak construction numbered 125,000 and over 65,000 individuals are even now engaged in operating the plants. Many have worked there for two and a half years. Few know what they have been producing. They see great quantities of material going in and they see nothing coming out of those plants, for the physical size of the explosive charge is exceedingly small. We have spent two billion dollars on the greatest scientific gamble in history—and won.

But the greatest marvel is not the size of the enterprise, its secrecy, nor its cost, but the achievement of scientific brains in putting together infinitely complex pieces of knowledge held by many men in different fields of science into a workable plan. And hardly less marvelous has been the capacity of industry to design, and of labor to operate, the machines and methods to do things never done before so that the brain child of many minds came forth in physical shape and performed as it was supposed to do. Both science and industry worked under the direction of the United States Army, which achieved a unique success in managing so diverse a problem in the advancement of knowledge in an amazingly short time. It is doubtful if such another combination could be got together in the world. What has been done is the greatest achievement of organized science in history. It was done under high pressure and without failure.

Jane Greer stood up, walked away from the numbers she had been crunching, and strolled to the window, unable to ignore the growing ruckus. Nothing had changed since Germany's surrender. But now shouts and cheers rose up to her second-story window in building 9731. She looked down and saw something unexpected, especially during a workday.

A large crowd was gathered on an expanse of muddy ground outside the building. People were ecstatic. They hugged each other and yelled excitedly to any other curious passersby.

Whatever's going on must be big, Jane thought. As she opened the window, the volume of the throng increased. She leaned out over the mayhem, trying to get someone's attention so that she could find out what had happened. Surely, it had something to do with the war.

Or did it have something to do with them?

We are now prepared to obliterate more rapidly and completely every productive enterprise the Japanese have above ground in any city. We shall destroy their docks, their factories, and their communications. Let there be no mistake; we shall completely destroy Japan's power to make war.

It was to spare the Japanese people from utter destruction that the ultimatum of July 26 was issued at Potsdam. Their leaders promptly rejected that ultimatum. If they do not now accept our terms they may expect a rain of ruin from the air, the like of which has never been seen on this earth. Behind this air attack will follow sea and land forces in such numbers and power as they have not yet seen and with the fighting skill of which they are already well aware.

Leaflets to this very effect were dropped on Japanese cities following the bombing, stating that this bomb had been used because of the rejection of the declaration to surrender issued from Potsdam.

ATTENTION JAPANESE PEOPLE. EVACUATE YOUR CITIES.

Because your military leaders have rejected the thirteen part surrender declaration, two momentous events have occurred in the last few days.

The Soviet Union, because of this rejection on the part of the military has notified your Ambassador Sato that it has declared war on your nation. Thus, all powerful countries of the world are now at war with you.

Also, because of your leaders' refusal to accept the surrender declaration that would enable Japan to honorably end this useless war, we have employed our atomic bomb.

A single one of our newly developed atomic bombs is actually the equivalent in explosive power to what 2000 of our giant B-29s could have carried on a single mission. Radio Tokyo has told you that with the first use of this weapon of total destruction, Hiroshima was virtually destroyed.

Before we use this bomb again and again to destroy every resource of the military by which they are prolonging this useless war, petition the emperor now to end the war. Our president has outlined for you the thirteen consequences of an honorable surrender. We urge that you accept these consequences and begin the work of building a new, better, and peace-loving Japan.

Act at once or we shall resolutely employ this bomb and all our other superior weapons to promptly and forcefully end the war.

EVACUATE YOUR CITIES.

Pamphlets floated down from a troubled sky, as the Japanese season of the Obon was about to begin, a time of communing with the spirits of one's ancestors, a time when the living honor their dead. The papers landed on grass and rubble, warning of distant fires, smoky remains, and more destruction to come.

In the United States, the president's statement continued:

The Secretary of War, who has kept in personal touch with all phases of the project, will immediately make public a statement giving further details. His statement will give facts concerning the sites at Oak Ridge near Knoxville, Tennessee, and at Richland near Pasco, Washington, and an installation near Santa Fe, New Mexico. Although the workers at the sites have been making materials to be used in producing the greatest destructive force in history they have not themselves been in danger beyond that of many other occupations, for the utmost care has been taken of their safety.

Oak Ridge?
Ears in Dr. Rea's office and across the Reservation perked up.
OAK RIDGE! Those with access to phones yanked receivers from cradles and began dialing furiously. Others found themselves rooted to their spots in front of the radio, lest any more information about Oak Ridge be divulged.
This was different.
This announcement wasn't just about a bomb.
It was about what had been going on here the whole time.
Oak Ridge's secret was out.

The fact that we can release atomic energy ushers in a new era in man's understanding of nature's forces. Atomic energy may in the future supplement the power that now comes from coal, oil, and falling water, but at present it cannot be produced on a basis to compete with them commercially. Before that comes there must be a long period of intensive research.

It has never been the habit of the scientists of this country or the policy of this Government to withhold from the world scientific knowledge. Normally, therefore, everything about the work with atomic energy would be made public.

But under present circumstances it is not intended to divulge the technical processes of production or all the military applications, pending further examination of possible methods of protecting us and the rest of the world from the danger of sudden destruction.

I shall recommend that the Congress of the United States consider promptly the establishment of an appropriate commission to control the production and use of atomic power within the United States. I shall give further consideration and make further recommendations to the Congress as to how atomic power can become a powerful and forceful influence towards the maintenance of world peace.

★　　★　　★

"Now you know what we've been doing all this time."

Rosemary looked at Dr. Rea as he spoke to the small crowd still gathered in his office. The address was finished, but for Oak Ridgers, the news was just beginning to sink in.

Bombing Hiroshima with this new and powerful weapon was enough of a development to digest. But Oak Ridgers now scrambled to learn more about their roles in what had happened.

It all made sense now: the gates and the guards and the plants and the schedule and the secrecy. Of all the words the president had uttered, that single mention of "Oak Ridge" had caused perhaps the greatest shock of all.

Rosemary found the entire experience—finally learning what had been going on around her for the past two years—unnerving, exciting, a bit skin-crawling. Definitely shocking.

And now there was an ultimatum for Japan to surrender.

But would they? If they did, it would mean the end of the war. This was the conversation on the lips of many Americans, but at CEW, Oak Ridgers struggled to process not only the event itself, but the fact that they had all, in some way, played a part.

★   ★   ★

"It was evident when the war began that the development of atomic energy for war purposes would occur in the near future and it was a question of which nations would control the discovery . . ."

So stated Secretary of War Henry L. Stimson in his own "Statement on the Bombing of Japan" released August 6. He went into limited detail about the atomic bomb, describing the new weapon as perhaps the "greatest achievement of the combined efforts of science industry, labor, and the military in all history."

"Improvement" would be made, increasing effectiveness and possibly the "scale of magnitude." Little Boy's impact would pale in comparison to what might be developed down the line.

"The possession of this weapon by the United States even in its present form should prove a tremendous aid in the shortening of the war against Japan," he said.

Exact methods would not be revealed, obviously, but "in accord with its policy of keeping the people of the nation as completely informed as is consistent with national security, the War Department wishes to make known at this time, at least in broad dimension, the story behind this tremendous weapon which has been developed so effectively to hasten the end of the war."

Stimson started in 1939, with the discovery of fission, and emphasized that the "fundamental scientific knowledge" that was the basis for the development of the atomic bomb was known in a number of countries. Japan, he felt, would not be using an atomic bomb in this war—which was not yet over—and any efforts by Germany to develop her own weapon ended with her defeat.

He described the close work between the United States and the United Kingdom, how the Project had started first in the Office of Scientific Research and Development, under Dr. Vannevar Bush before control of the project was transferred to the War Department and the command of now Maj. Gen. Leslie R. Groves.

This man—General Groves—had officially taken over the Manhattan Project just under three years ago. By sheer force of will and roughly $2 billion, he'd bulldozed his way to a successful Gadget with the help of a team of scientists led by J. Robert Oppenheimer and hundreds of thousands of workers across the country.

> A Government-owned and operated city, named Oak Ridge, was established within the reservation to accommodate the people working on the project. They live under normal conditions in modest houses, dormitories, hutments, and trailers, and have for their use all the religious, recreational, educational, medical, and other facilities of a modern small city. The total population of Oak Ridge is approximately 78,000 and consists of construction workers and plant operators and their immediate families; others live in immediately surrounding communities.

Stimson continued: "The large size and isolated location of this site was made necessary by the need for security and for safety against possible, but then unknown, hazards."

He detailed the plants in Hanford, Washington, and the labs in New Mexico, identifying Dr. J. Robert Oppenheimer—the "genius," in Stimson's words—largely responsible for the development of the bomb. Stimson also acknowledged the many "smaller" sites and universities—Columbia, University of Chicago, Iowa State, and more—and countries and governments, including Canada. He thanked the many companies involved—M. W. Kellogg, Union Carbide, Tennessee Eastman, DuPont, and more—but did not mention the specific names of the plants they helped construct and manage: Y-12, K-25, S-50, and X-10.

Stimson thanked the press as well for complying with the requests of the Office of Censorship. Across the country, news editors had finally run their fingers under the gummed flaps of the envelopes they had been instructed not to open until further notice. As they did, official statements and photos poured out, many of which had been taken by the Photographer, Ed Westcott. There was talk of patent control and the need to maintain adequate supplies of the element known to thousands of Project employees by the name "tubealloy." As for the ultratight security and the remarkable ability for so many thousands of people to keep such a big secret as well as they had, Stimson admitted:

> The work has been completely compartmentalized so that while many thousands of people have been associated with the program in one way or another, no one has been given more information concerning it than was absolutely necessary to do his particular job. As a result only a few highly placed persons in Government and science know the entire story.

There was an inherent promise to atomic fission in peacetime, he said, and a question of how to employ this science going forward, since its most visible use thus far was as a devastating weapon. He predicted it would take many years of research "for the conversion of atomic energy into useful power. . . . We are at the threshold of a new industrial art . . ."

★　　★　　★

What had for so long been a drought of information came now as a flood. But people who worked in the plants at CEW still wondered what, *exactly*, they might have been doing all this time. The specific details of their roles in the Oak Ridge story did not always trickle down. The complete story would, for many of them, remain beyond their grasp for decades to come.

No one took Helen and Dot aside to explain what happened when they turned their knobs this way or that, or told them they were helping operate calutrons. Colleen was not then told what the pipes she continued to inspect carried. Kattie did not know what the plant she cleaned had done. Yes, chemists like Virginia Spivey and statisticians like Jane Greer could assemble the informational pieces a little more easily for themselves, but the full picture from start to finish was not made public.

Everyone at CEW found themselves recasting discussions and experiences in light of the new information. Oak Ridge's precise role was not entirely clear to many. Some assumed they had built the bomb itself. That they had actually been helping create the atomic bomb's fuel source was too abstruse for many to comprehend. And most details remained top secret.

But that was no matter.

Oak Ridgers finally knew *something*. There was something to pin their efforts and their work on. They had played a part in what appeared to be a key turning point in the war, one that might end it for good.

Elizabeth Edwards, Oak Ridge's librarian transplant from the New York Public Library, went to the shelf containing the encyclopedias. She looked over the spines and stopped at the volume containing the letter *U*. As she picked up the book, it fell open as if on command, the spine already worn and bent and broken from more than a year of being opened to the same page over and over by chemistry-savvy people trying to make sense of what they thought might possibly be going on.

On that well-worn page was a long streak of black ink, smudged by fingers of sweaty, overworked hands, leading to a word, the element that gave the Clinton Engineer Works its reason for existence.

★　　★　　★

In the ensuing celebration that day and into the night, words that previously had gone unmentioned, whether unknown or forbidden, passed everyone's lips, ricocheting off walls and the hushed spaces of plants, and cafeterias and buses.

Uranium!
Atomic!
Bombs!
Radiation!
Plutonium!

There were 235s and 238s ringing in people's ears, even though most of them had never heard of either. Children were in a tizzy jabbering on about the "automatic bomb." "Stay on the job" still remained the message at work. The war was not yet over, still many workers took to the streets. Cubicle operators abandoned their panels, chemists walked away from their benches. As the celebration and the release of so much pent-up curiosity continued, some recoiled at the sound of words they had been explicitly forbidden to utter. Scientists who had banished certain terms from their vocabularies found it hard to hear the language bandied about so freely.

In Y-12, one young chemist, Bill Wilcox, reached for his daily calendar. He was a smiling, bow-tie-clad man from Pennsylvania, a Yankee who had fallen for a Tennessee redhead named Jeannie on the dance floor, a traveler to Dogpatch who had now seen everything from backwoods "splo" (moonshine) stills to the unleashing of the power of the atoms he had studied at university. Listed in some documents as "Chemist #40," Wilcox took a red pen and circled the date at the top of the page. Monday, August 6. He still felt odd, somehow, writing the *U* word. Instead, on his calendar page he wrote, quite simply and in large letters, "T Day."

Other scientists felt as though a gag order had been lifted. Among them was Waldo Cohn, biochemist and cofounder of the Oak Ridge Symphony. He was seen driving through town, yelling out the window of his car, without a care or fear in the world, for all to hear:

"Uranium! Uranium! URANIUM!!!"

★   ★   ★

Physicist Lise Meitner was on holiday, in the small lakeside village of Leksand, Norway. Her hosts brought her the news. She sat, shocked. Tears came. She went quiet. Soon a local reporter arrived. What could she say about her work on the bomb?

She had *never* worked on any atomic bomb, she said. Still, she was followed by cameras and questions, and stories were concocted of Lise fleeing Germany with valuable information about the bomb that she then gave to the Allies. Her picture—including one of her with a goat—accompanied the exaggerated and often-fabricated tales, images of the exiled physicist on holiday the day the bomb was dropped.

★   ★   ★

At the holding facility in Farm Hall, England, the detained German scientists were processing the news.

Otto Hahn felt personally responsible. He drank, heavily, until the alcohol began to dull his nerves. The other scientists were reluctant to believe word of the bombing at first, thinking it some sort of elaborate ruse by their captors. Once it sunk in, the news consumed their conversation, for hours, then days.

> **WEIZSÄCKER:** I don't think it has anything to do with uranium. . . .
>
> **HAHN:** At any rate, Heisenberg, you're just second-raters and you may as well pack up.
>
> **HEISENBERG:** I quite agree.
>
> **HAHN:** They are fifty years further advanced than we.
>
> **HEISENBERG:** I don't believe a word of the whole thing. They must have spent the whole of their 500,000,000 pounds in separating isotopes; and then it's possible.
>
> **HAHN:** I didn't think it would be possible for another twenty years . . .
>
> **WEIZSÄCKER:** I think it's dreadful of the Americans to have done it. I think it is madness on their part.
>
> **HEISENBERG:** One can't say that. One could equally well say "That's the quickest way of ending the war."
>
> **HAHN:** That's what consoles me.

Two days later, the scientists at Farm Hall prepared a memo to clarify their work in Germany "on the uranium problem." In it, they hoped to clarify the research conducted, as they felt Germany had been misrepresented in the press. Of the discovery of fission, they wrote:

> The fission of the atomic nucleus in uranium was discovered by Hahn and Strassmann in the Kaiser Wilhelm Institute for Chemistry in Berlin. . . . Various research workers, Meitner and Frisch were probably

the first, pointed out the enormous energies which were released by the fission of uranium. On the other hand, Meitner had left Berlin six months before the discovery and was not concerned herself in the discovery.

★　　★　　★

Col. Kenneth Nichols, the District Engineer, tried to let his wife, Jacqueline, know before everyone else. Nichols had sent everything he could get his hands on regarding the bomb over to their house, so that Jacqueline would not have to wait for the radio address like everyone else. It was a gesture he wanted to make after all the secrecy and silence she had endured.

But when the envelope arrived at their home, Jacqueline was entertaining Vi Warren. Jacqueline, ever discreet, and knowing that Vi, of all people, would understand—decided to leave the envelope unopened until she was alone.

Then the phone rang. It was Jacqueline's sister-in-law asking what Jacqueline thought of the news. Jacqueline immediately turned on the radio and opened the envelope, absorbing it all. She was, as she later told her husband, "terribly disappointed that the bomb had been dropped on civilians," but was glad to know that the Project that had taken so much of her family's time was a success, and that her husband had played a key role. More than anything, she was glad it looked like it was all going to be over now.

★　　★　　★

In many cases, stay-at-home women found out about the bomb before their working counterparts. Currents of information trickled speedily among the cemesto prefabs and trailers that had spread like kudzu across the Reservation over the last three years, disrupting the usual conversations that sprung up between loads of muddy socks and chemical-stained shirts.

News began to fly from kitchen windows, down those laundry lines and out into the streets. Celia wanted to celebrate along with everyone else but she couldn't. She was at home, waiting for the next wave of nausea. She heard the crowds and the honking and the growing chorus of joyful, boisterous noises. But she just felt too sick to participate. So she stayed put, alone at home, far from the Castle and even farther from Manhattan, where she and the Project had begun.

★　★　★

Apparently while Helen Hall was traveling from Tennessee down to Louisiana, the entire world had changed.

She couldn't believe that now, after waiting for her vacation, she was actually heading *back* to Tennessee without having spent so much as a night in New Orleans.

Her friend Pee Wee had been living there with her husband, who was working at some sort of government job that Helen didn't really know much about. Pee Wee had grown up in Eagleville, just one grade behind Helen. As children, they had been thick as thieves, and as young adults they were still a tight-knit pair despite the distance between them.

Helen had been looking forward to spending some time relaxing with her old friend. But no sooner had she stepped foot on the cobbled streets of New Orleans than Pee Wee announced that she and her husband were heading to Tennessee. They were excited about news of the bombing, as everyone in the country was, but the news about Oak Ridge's involvement was inspiring their change of plans. They were from Tennessee, and Tennessee, they had now learned, had played an important role in something big.

For Helen, it was as if she had stepped through some sort of time warp. She had boarded a plane in one world and gotten off in another; it wasn't location alone that had shifted beneath her.

Helen understood Pee Wee's reaction to the news and made the only decision that seemed sensible to her at the time.

"Well, I'm going with you, then."

She didn't unpack, just piled into the car with Pee Wee and her husband, and drove back toward her new vacation destination: Oak Ridge.

★　★　★

Toni had yet to hear back from Chuck. *Maybe he doesn't know yet*, she thought. If he still had his nose to the grindstone, in that parallel universe of Oak Ridge where words like "uranium" and "bomb" were not to be uttered, even in whispers, he must have thought Toni was out of her mind, about to get him—or more likely, herself—into some serious hot water.

Toni remembered a conversation she had heard just two days earlier when she and her friend Betty Coobs had run into Mr. Diamond outside the Castle. Toni now cast that exchange in a brand-new light.

"I figured out what they're doing here . . . ," Betty had said. Naturally, Mr. Diamond was all ears. Toni had stood stock-still, frozen in horror.

"They're gonna split the atom, harness the energy, and make a bomb."

It had all sounded like gibberish to Toni, who had laughed it off. She remembered that Mr. Diamond, however, was not as amused.

How on earth had she known that? Toni now wondered. Betty had always been smart, but splitting atoms? Of course what Betty did not know two days ago when she brazenly shared her theory—and what they had just found out today, as the atomic cat was out of the bag— was that Mr. Diamond had reported the incident to security.

"Betty, I had a talk scheduled for you for today," Mr. Diamond said.

But history had intervened and Betty had narrowly escaped a severe reprimand, if not the loss of her job.

Toni still didn't understand the bigger picture, but she had more pressing issues on her mind and a trip to plan. She would soon be traveling with Chuck to New York City, to visit his family in Queens. She wondered if they'd like her. They had gotten along fine with her brother Ben when he was sent from his Air Force base in Florida to New York to take a two-week communications course. Chuck's parents had invited Ben—a.k.a. Silver Buckles—to their home and he charmed them the way that only a nice southern boy from Tennessee could. But Toni knew it would be different for her. Chuck's parents hadn't even wanted their son to get a job or leave home and here Toni was, a woman, taking up a significant chunk of his emotional real estate. So much felt beyond her control.

What's next? Toni wondered. *Do I still have a job?*

Would Chuck go back to New York for good? Maybe the war would even be over by the time they visited his parents. Gosh, if that happened, maybe Silver Buckles would be home safe. Wouldn't that be something. Over. Finally.

★   ★   ★

It was a clear, sunny day as Virginia and her friend Barbara boarded the ferry on the banks of the Potomac that would take them down the Chesapeake Bay to Norfolk, Virginia, where Virginia's sister lived. After a little trouble sleeping on the train, the remainder of the trip had been fantastic. The two young women walked through L'Enfant's city, visiting museums and listening to bands playing on the mall near the Washington Monument. When she had left Tennessee with Barbara, Virginia had little idea how much the world was going to change during her short time away from Oak Ridge. Now in retrospect, the cryptic comments made to her in the lab before she left work made more sense.

"It's about to happen . . ."

She now knew what "it" was.

Other things started to make sense: the absence of articles from the scientific journals, her work in the lab, the percentages, her hike with her physicist beau who theorized they were building some sort of bomb, the mutterings of dates from Yale and Harvard, the hints dropped by her coworkers days before she left. As she and Barb stood on the deck of the ferry enjoying the late summer weather, the topic of conversation among the guests inevitably turned to the bombing of Hiroshima.

Virginia listened as people discussed the top secret Project gracing the front pages of the nation's papers. Soon someone mentioned that none of the people working in the plants had any idea what was going on.

Without thinking much about it, Virginia instinctively said, "Well, I did."

The curious, chatty mood suddenly turned accusatory.

"Nobody knew!" someone hissed. "All the papers said no one there knew. How would *you* know?"

Virginia withdrew as the small crowd pounced on her words, implying that she was lying, pretending to be something she was not.

A person in the know? This young girl?

Virginia only wanted to join in, add an interesting perspective. She wasn't intending to brag. *I never would have figured things out on my own,* she thought, though she knew the secret had to be chemical in nature, something to do with atomic energy. But she needed help putting the pieces together.

This had been perhaps the first time that she had said out loud—and to people who lived off the Reservation—what she believed. Their reaction made her feel as though it would likely be her last.

Virginia could finally *talk* about what she'd been doing all this time and no one wanted to listen.

Conversation ceased, the subject dropped, and Virginia kept any remaining thoughts to herself. But she found the whole revelation remarkable, that there were people at CEW who knew much more than she did, and still no one had really talked about it.

The more she thought about it, the more she realized: Oak Ridgers had kept the most amazing secret ever.

CHAPTER 14

★ ★ ★ ★ ★

Dawn of a Thousand Suns

I heard one man break out fiercely and instinctively with a loud "Sh-sh-shush!" Secrets that he had guarded with his life for over two years were being shouted out for all the world to hear. Data that had only been recorded in code and labeled "Top Secret" were being flung into the air. Facts that he had withheld from his wife as if she were an enemy were being exposed in full detail to everybody.

—Vi Warren, *Oak Ridge Journal*

Toni stood atop the Empire State Building, five blocks north—and more than 1,200 feet skyward—from one of the spots where the Project all began. There, shielded among the skyscrapers and office buildings, was the Madison Square Area Engineers Office, which had once been the center for securing raw materials for the bomb. What had begun on this small island had been brought to completion, in part, back in Tennessee, a scant few miles down the road from where she had grown up, all coming to fruition not far from where she'd picked peaches, gone on joy rides in "borrowed" cars, and known the unwavering love of two unique parents. She stood silently beside Chuck and considered her future, one full of more choices than she had ever imagined her little life would have, more than she wanted.

It was a different world in the days following the revelation. While everyone wondered if the war would soon be over, the people of CEW had additional concerns:

Would Oak Ridge continue to exist?

Retrofitted factories that had served wartime needs could well return to fashioning lipstick tubes or kitchen appliances. But Oak Ridge was not just a plant or a collection of plants. It was now a city, such as it was, sidewalks or not. Would everyone pull up stakes, leaving the monstrous edifices, temporary trailers, and prefab homes behind? Would it become a full-time military base? Would there still be a place for the thousands who had come to consider this just-add-water outpost their home?

★　　★　　★

After her trip to Washington, DC, Virginia returned to the lab. Work had not stopped. One of her immediate supervisors walked up to her in the lab, eager—as many were—to talk about the Big News.

"Virginia!" he said. "Did you know what was going on here?!"

What struck Virginia as odd was that he sounded as if he himself had had no idea. *How could he be so surprised?* she wondered. She would have thought someone in his position might have put a few things together during his time here. He was her supervisor, after all, and likely had access to more information than she did. But maybe not. She had no way of knowing without asking him directly, and she decided not to. Completely transparent discussions still weren't happening, even after the big reveal.

New rules were evolving. Going forward, what could and could not be said out loud in Oak Ridge would continue to change; details about the intricacies of the bomb would be parceled out according to what the Project believed appropriate. For workers, there was still so much about the big picture left unsaid.

Everything and nothing had changed. Reminders came that it was to be business as usual at CEW, though some workers were already making plans to move on, assuming the existence of their jobs and the town were as temporary as they hoped the war would now be. The War Department issued the following letter to all workers:

7 August 1945

To the Men and Women of Clinton Engineer Works:

Today the whole world knows the secret which you have helped us keep for many months. I am pleased to be able to add that the war-lords of Japan now know its effects better even than we ourselves. The atomic bomb which you have helped to develop with high devotion to patriotic duty is the most devastating military weapon that any country has ever been able to turn against its enemy. No one of you has worked on the entire project or known the whole story. Each of you has done his own job and kept his own secret, and so today I speak for a grateful nation when I say congratulations and thank you all. I hope you will continue to keep the secrets you have kept so well. The need for security and for continued effort is fully as great now as it ever was. We are proud of every one of you.

> Robert R. Patterson,
> Under Secretary of War,
> Washington, D.C.

Jane Greer opened the letter from her sister Kathryn, written the night of August 6, the day of the Hiroshima bombing. Jane began reading.

"Well, this has been quite an exciting day—more for you all than for us, I'm sure . . . ," the letter began.

Jane was always interested in what people on the "outside" had to say about her world, though she wasn't permitted to indulge their curiosity. She relished reading news of her father, the family home in Paris, Tennessee, her siblings' travels, and plans for the coming month. Jane herself was looking forward to visiting with Kathryn and the baby that was due to be born any day.

Their father was worried about Jane, "being so up there close to anything so powerful." Kathryn instructed Jane to write him about all the precautions Jane was taking at work in an effort to calm his fears.

"Goodness!" Kathryn wrote. "It's kinda scary the thing is so horribly powerful. I can't even imagine such a thing and when you think what destruction it can cause it really does scare you. If the wrong person gets hold of it, there we are or at least where are we? But I'm sure it will have many unbelievable and wonderful peacetime uses and let's hope that's what it will be used entirely for. It should shorten the present war—in fact, it seems as though they would be ready to quit tonight. I know I would. Let's hope and pray it does that one good thing and then is never used again for destruction."

★　　★　　★

It was used again, August 9: "Fat Man," an implosion bomb using plutonium—49—like the model tested at Trinity, fell on Nagasaki. Roughly another 40,000 people died instantly. If this second attack, coupled with the Soviet Union's declaration of war on Japan a day earlier, did not convince Hirohito to surrender, there was yet another bomb almost ready to go.

"The next bomb of the implosion type had been scheduled to be ready for delivery on the target on the first good weather after 24 August 1945," General Groves told Army Chief of Staff General George Marshall in a memo dated August 10.

"We have gained 4 days in manufacture and expect to ship from New Mexico on 12 or 13 August the final components. . . . the bomb should be ready for delivery on the first suitable weather after 17 or 18 August."

Before a third bomb was dropped, Japan's surrender arrived: August 14, five days after the Nagasaki bombing.

World War II left no life untouched. An estimated 16 million American men had gone off to fight. More than 400,000 lost their lives. Military and civilian deaths worldwide were estimated to be as high as 80 million.

Women—well over a million by 1942—had gone into factories and offices, and countless others rationed, collected scrap metal, bought war bonds, and danced with soldiers at the USO. While the entire country erupted, Oak Ridge was in a particular state of exuberance. Relief and pride mixed with shock and pensive consideration at the news of a second bombing. This new atomic bomb had brought an end to the war, and the people of Clinton Engineer Works had been a part of that One Thing that appeared responsible for victory. For many, knowing they had been a part of helping end the war was enough. For others, knowing was too much. One young K-25 worker left the singing and celebrating and retired to her dorm room. She sat there, thinking about the small role she had played in the bombings, and cried.

★   ★   ★

VJ Day. Ed Westcott, the Photographer, worked his way across the Reservation capturing reactions to Japan's surrender, from the plants—still working around the clock—to the dorms and trailer camps. The celebration raged. Jackson Square, the heart of town, was crawling with young men and women.

Sprawled across the front page of the *Knoxville Journal*, a banner headline proclaimed the news the world had waited six years to hear:

PEACE.

Westcott's shutter was on fire. The same shutter that had captured the birth of Site X now captured images of a dummy of Hideki ToJo, the prime minister of Japan who had authorized the bombing of Pearl Harbor, burning in effigy. Cars cruised muddy streets. Children ransacked kitchens and garden sheds and took to the streets banging on old buckets, pots, and pans, clanging lids, and thumping wheelbarrows. Anything that could make a noise did. Anyone who could raise a glass—whether beer or local moonshine "splo" or homemade wine— raised it high. Horns honked, people sang, couples danced. Chests across the country heaved a collective exhale at the long-awaited news. The war was over.

★   ★   ★

Bill Wilcox, the spiffy young chemist, and others like him who had missed fighting overseas, had, on more than one occasion, found themselves on the receiving end of cynical glances and suspicious inquiries.

Why weren't they doing their duty?

For years they had endured veiled—and sometimes direct— criticism without any kind of recourse, without being permitted to respond. Now, they had an answer for those who had doubted their patriotism, who had accused them of taking the easy way out.

Wilcox sat relaxing with friends at the Norris Dam, sitting along- side the water, enjoying the sun and company, processing recent events and his role in them. He began writing:

"At last, thank God, it's all over," he wrote his parents in Pennsyl- vania in a letter dated August 15, 1945. "After the din of battle dies for the last time, and after the first exuberant moments of rejoicing, one cannot but be sobered by the feeling that an end of another era has come . . . Never before has the knowledge of so vital a nature been entrusted to so many with so great success . . ."

For the first time, he poured out details of the life he had kept from his parents for more than two years. The writing was cathartic, taking pages out of him.

"You can pent up a hell of a lot of emotion in two years with people saying 'Why are you not in uniform and calling you a draft dodger . . . ,'" he wrote. He described the mind-boggling size and scope of the operation, the 16-hour days, the living conditions, and the strain. There were, in his words, love and admiration for the men and women with whom he had served and lived.

> Never before in the history of the world has so much responsibility been placed on the shoulders of such young people . . . no place for old men . . .
>
> Oak Ridge is not a town, city, or name alone, it symbolizes a great and unique philosophy which is felt only by those who have stormed, sweated, and cussed here for two years.

★   ★   ★

The *Oak Ridge Journal* had suffered the scoop of all scoops.

The biggest story of the war had been right under their noses and they were not permitted to know it, let alone report it. They were a weekly publication to boot, so by the time they got the information, they couldn't cover the story in their own pages until days later, after every major media organization on the planet had offered its take.

"Oak Ridge Attacks Japanese!" was the headline that finally appeared in the *Oak Ridge Journal*.

The feast of information fed from the War Department to the hungry media was, at first, enough to sate editors and reporters nationwide. But soon the public was hungry for *more*. More about the science. More about how the government kept this Project under wraps. More about the damage in Japan. And most important, more about what was next on the atomic frontier. But more was not available, except in discrete, periodically declassified batches.

"More has been written about Oak Ridge in the newspapers and magazines of the nation this week than the *Oak Ridge Journal* has been able to print during the almost two years of its existence," the August 16 edition of the paper quipped.

In the Letters section, someone suggested a new name for the paper—*The Atomizer*. The Oak Leaves section of the paper related the tale of a newsboy in nearby Knoxville, home of Oak Ridge's oft reluctant neighbors, howling on a street corner, extolling the region's change of heart toward the shadowy Reservation:

"Extra! Extra! Oak Ridge Makes Atomic Bomb! We used to hate 'em and now we love 'em!"

Hordes of reporters and news agencies descended on the town.

Press releases were primarily crafted by William "Atomic Bill" Laurence, the Pulitzer Prize–winning reporter from *The New York Times*, who had been at Trinity and aboard an observation plane during the bombing of Nagasaki. Releases included the first bit of insight into the Army Counter Intelligence Corps, one of the forces responsible for keeping the story locked down.

The first issue of the *Oak Ridge Journal* after the Hiroshima bombing featured a profile of public relations officer George O. "Gus" Robinson in the "You're in the News" section. Robinson had been responsible for helping keep the news about Oak Ridge and the Project under wraps across the country. He had met with editors and newspaper reporters for more than two years and finally, in the past week, was able to host them at CEW, his muzzle loosened—if not removed.

"He always manages to give the impression that he knows more than he is telling—which is usually the case," the paper wrote of their colleague Robinson.

Elsewhere in the paper were signs that life in Oak Ridge was humming along. Knight's store in Grove Center was expanding on August 17: *"We Are Not Whispering . . . We are Shouting About Our New Millinery Department."* A carnival was running through August 25 at Elza Gate—*Special Dare-Devil Act! Tilt Whirl! National Velvet* was playing at the Middletown Theatre and James Cagney was starring in *The Frisco Kid* at the Skyway Drive-In. Special VJ Day services were being held at the Chapel on the Hill. In other news, the dorms would move to a cash-only basis at the end of the month. Everywhere you looked, people were already packing up and leaving.

The message around the Reservation remained "Stay on the Job." It was on the billboards, it was printed in the upper-left-hand corner of the newspaper. A letter on the front page from Colonel Nichols, the District Engineer, drove the point home.

"We must become sufficiently equipped with our new and stupendous weapon so that no aggressor will ever dare attack us again."

★   ★   ★

Kattie watched as a coworker welcomed her boyfriend—just returned from the war—through the gates. Kattie was happy for her. But while everyone kept talking about how the world had changed, as far as Kattie was concerned, much was still the same. She was still living far away from her children. She was still sending home money to her family in Alabama. The community of black Oak Ridgers she had met over the past few years was divided. Maybe half of them wanted to go now that the war was over, half wanted to stay. But no one would want to stay without somewhere to raise their children and a place to send them to school. This place would never be home if she could not have her children with her. She and Willie had celebrated the end of the war along with everyone else, but they could not stop wondering if and when they would be able to bring their children to live with them, or if their time in Oak Ridge was finally coming to an end, the snows of East Tennessee melting into memory.

★　　★　　★

For Helen, the end of the war meant her brother Harold was coming home. She had never really gotten over the fact that he had shipped out right after training, without being given the opportunity to come home to say good-bye. He had been gone three years now, with not one leave. The letters she had received from him had been routinely cut to frustrating ribbons by censors. Helen assumed the same was true of the letters she had mailed him. It took at least a month for letters to get to her, and she just knew that her mama must have had an even worse time of it: the lack of contact, the silence, the not-knowing.

Helen finally got word. After arriving back in the States, Harold had been debriefed and flown to Nashville. Once there, he was dropped off on a country road, left to his own devices to travel the rest of the 25 miles to the family home in Eagleville. Once Harold was spotted by a neighbor, Helen's father hopped in the car and started driving down the road toward Nashville to find him. There was Harold, hiking home with all his gear, his father's car a welcome sight.

Helen didn't think that was any way for a returning soldier to be treated, but she was glad he was home safe and couldn't wait to see him again. But it wouldn't be for good. She had decided she wanted to stay in Oak Ridge. She had a job, softball, basketball, and a good place to live. Well, she *thought* she had a job. Right after the first bomb dropped, before Japan surrendered, word had begun to spread that the plants were closing. Some women at Y-12 were already making plans to move to Kingston, where Tennessee Eastman's main operations were based. Sections of the Y-12 plant were shutting down and reducing shifts. She would have to find a new job. *Could she? Would the whole town pack up?* Some people said it was just a matter of time. She, for one, hoped they were wrong.

★　　★　　★

Rosemary had a new offer of work. She didn't want to take it, but Dr. Rea kept hounding her. She felt flattered, but was not sold and had a decision to make, like most everyone in Oak Ridge. About half of the doctors in the hospital were heading home to their practices or the facilities they had left behind. Others were placing bets on the future of Oak Ridge, setting up their own local offices for the town's first private practices. The clinic she had come to know and shape was changing rapidly.

The bombings themselves were still hard for her to fathom, and she knew others who felt the same way. Anybody who had been working in Oak Ridge and had contributed to the development of something so tragic, so devastating, had to ask themselves the question whether it was the right thing to do. She felt incredibly relieved the war was over. She knew there were people who wondered if the death of so many thousands, so many civilians, was too big a price to pay, but she didn't think most people who worked in Oak Ridge felt that it was. The devastation after the bomb was hard to yet get a handle on; it was so unclear. She could not imagine being in President Truman's shoes, having to make that kind of decision. What a horrible responsibility, she thought.

Rosemary's first instinct was to go back to Chicago, back to the last place she had worked before coming to Tennessee. She did not necessarily want to work in a hospital setting and thought she might go back to school and study public health. A couple of the doctors in Oak Ridge had asked her if she wanted to come to work for them in their new offices, but that didn't feel like the right fit.

Dr. Rea's offer was on behalf of his friend Gene Felton, head of the medical facility at the X-10 plant. Felton was looking for a nursing supervisor for the plant's on-site facility.

Rosemary wasn't interested, but Dr. Rea went so far as to arrange for a car to pick her up at the hospital and drive her out to the X-10 plant to talk with Felton directly. Rosemary felt obligated to make the trip. If for no other reason, she was curious. It would be the very first time in her now two years at Oak Ridge that she had ever laid eyes on *any* one of the plants that stood within the confines of the Clinton Engineer Works. She had known they were there, but had only seen the residential parts of the Reservation. The big plants that occupied so many of the lives that came through the doors at the hospital had remained unknowable to her. Off-limits. But not today.

Rosemary liked Gene Felton immediately. She knew the plants had clinics of their own, at which they could deal with on-the-job injuries, ranging from falls from ladders to exposures to various chemicals. In some ways the position would be very similar to the job she had had in Chicago at the munitions plant, before she took the job in Oak Ridge. She decided to give the new job a try. If it didn't work out, she could always go back to Chicago.

In her new position, she would learn a lot more about radiation. She had of course heard about it when she was working in the hospital in Chicago, primarily associated with precautionary measures taken during the administration of X-rays. The long-term effects of radiation on a large scale were not yet clearly understood. There were precautions that CEW workers could take, film badges to measure exposure, blood tests. And X-10, home of the pilot plutonium plant, had already had its own share of exposures that needed to be dealt with.

Workers who found themselves exposed—either to plutonium or other damaging chemicals—would come to the clinic at the plant, where they were showered and scrubbed down intensely. Sometimes they had to stay overnight, as Henry Klemski had, often leaving their spouses to wonder what had happened, and with little more than a phone call from a supervisor letting them know that their husbands wouldn't be home that night.

★   ★   ★

Celia decided to make Saint Theresa the object of her nine-day daily devotion. The patron saint of headache sufferers seemed appropriate considering the discomfort that had plagued Celia throughout her entire pregnancy, not to mention the new headache that Henry's pending relocation was inflicting.

DuPont was transferring their workers to other sites now that the war was over. For Henry, that meant Charles Town, West Virginia. Henry may not have wanted to move, but he did want to stay with the company, the same one that he'd worked for back in Alabama and in Wilmington before that. But Celia could not face a move, not now.

"I *can't* go," Celia had said to Henry when he first broke the news. Celia was three months shy of her December due date. Flustered,

Celia weighed her options. They seemed few, and none that appealing. The thought of packing up their home and moving to another town sounded like a nightmare, especially in her condition. There was only one solution that she could think of.

"You go on to West Virginia," she told Henry, "and I'll go back home to have the baby, and I'll join you later."

It was not ideal, but at the time it seemed the best choice. Still, Celia didn't want to give up hope on another solution, one she hadn't thought of. But she needed time and some outside guidance.

Enter Saint Theresa.

Celia did not want to be separated from Henry. And their friend Lew Parker had told Henry and Celia that West Virginia was even worse than Oak Ridge had been in the early days. Celia just wanted to stay where she was. It was home now.

On the ninth and final day of Celia's novena, Henry burst in the door, having just come from work.

"I got another job!" Henry exclaimed.

"Where?" Celia asked, wondering what this now meant about West Virginia.

"Here in Oak Ridge," Henry said. "Monsanto came in and said I could stay here and offered me a hundred-dollar-a-month raise."

Celia thanked Saint Theresa and began preparing the house—not to pack it up and move it, but to bring their first child into what looked like would be their home for at least a little while longer.

★　　★　　★

"Remember that thing you asked me a while back?" Colleen said.

"Yes, I do," Blackie answered.

That was a relief. *But,* Colleen wondered, *is it too late to say yes?*

Since the very first time Blackie popped the question, while hiking at Big Ridge, he had repeated it on a fairly regular basis. And on just as regular a basis came Colleen's response: No.

Colleen liked Blackie. Her dad liked Blackie. Colleen's mother was fond of him for all the reasons mothers usually like potential son-in-laws: He was nice, he was polite, and he seemed to smile all the time. Colleen thought his smile was one of his best assets, wide and effortless. True. Blackie liked Mrs. Rowan as well, though there were some cultural differences to move past.

"Your mother's real nice," Blackie had once said to Colleen, "but I can't understand a word she says."

Colleen's mom always smiled right back at him, grins making up for any linguistic hurdles the two had to clear. Over time he had developed more of an ear for the Rowans' Tennessee accent and had come a long way from his first trip to the S&W cafeteria on Gay Street.

Colleen had discussed Blackie with Father Siener, wondering what her priest thought.

"This is a wartime situation," Father Siener had said. "When it's over, you'll be going back to Nashville with your family."

The young woman had originally taken the message to heart: Don't get serious. Father Siener had turned out to be right. Colleen's family and many others were moving out. The residential population was taking a nosedive. It would soon be at half its wartime peak of 75,000. Friends at the dorm were leaving and Colleen was feeling more certain with each passing day that she would be let go at the plant. But this feeling was in direct contrast to the message and billboards around town: "Stay on the job," and people began talking about "winning the peace." Bess Rowan was among those preparing to leave, ready to get back to Nashville so that they could all be there when Jimmy came walking through the door. From the beginning, the Rowan family's avowed purpose for coming to Oak Ridge was better jobs and a chance to help bring her brother Jimmy home. Goal achieved. But for Colleen, heading home meant leaving Blackie.

Staying without her family didn't seem to be an option, and leaving Blackie didn't feel right. Father Siener had another argument against the marriage as well: Blackie wasn't Catholic. Father Siener went so far as to say that if she persisted in the relationship he would not marry them, though Blackie had started going to church with Colleen. But now, with her family packing for Nashville and the possibility that Blackie might be shipping out somewhere else with the Army—maybe even overseas—Colleen was ready to change the answer to the question he had asked so many times.

Problem was, she hadn't been asked recently.

How about that! Colleen had thought at first. But she knew a man could take only so many no's. She was relieved to hear that Blackie at least remembered asking her. But it was clear he wasn't going to ask her again. So after reminding him, she gave a belated and revised response.

"Well," Colleen said. "Okay."

Blackie was over the moon. The pair soon took the train to Monroe, Michigan, to meet his parents, making sure to stop off in Cincinnati along the way in order to attend mass. Monroe was a little paper mill town between Toledo and Detroit. The visit was a short one. Colleen liked Blackie's mother and father, and the feeling appeared to be reciprocated. The couple returned to Oak Ridge and entered wait-and-see mode, as so many had, hoping for a job that would keep them there. In the meantime, they began taking their instructions in preparation for a fall wedding that, Blackie agreed, would be a Catholic one. Colleen was going to stay with Blackie, this much was clear. Whether they were going to stay in Oak Ridge, she hadn't a clue.

★   ★   ★

"Here's a bottle for your nightcap," Mrs. Schmitt said, offering Toni the bottle.

The knock had come at the guest-room door of the house in Queens, where she and Chuck were visiting his parents. Toni had retired to her room for the evening. So far, she did not like how the trip was going. And this late-night visit from Chuck's mother was no different.

"Oh, no, thank you, I don't drink," Toni answered.

But Mrs. Schmitt insisted. "Just take it in there with you, anyway."

Toni tried once more to refuse, trying so hard to be polite to her husband's mother, who, up to this point in their short visit, had been less than hospitable.

"No, ma'am, no, thank you, I don't drink."

Mrs. Schmitt physically leaned inside the doorway and placed the bottle on top of the dresser near the door. Then she disappeared down the hall. Not wanting to appear disrespectful, Toni didn't argue. She closed the door to her room and left the bottle on the dresser, unopened and untouched.

"My family is a little strange," Chuck had said to Toni before their trip. His parents did not like bright lights, for example, and had painted the lightbulbs in the house red. They didn't like the idea of Chuck, their only child, getting serious with anyone, especially a non-Lutheran. Chuck was still served first at every meal while everyone else, including Toni, waited.

Toni's own upbringing had not been perfect, but it had been full of love and joy. She lived every day knowing she was the light of her father's life, and was raised by a mother who periodically exploded into her room, exclaiming, "You're radiant with joy! There never has been, there never will be, there won't, nor there can't, nor there couldn't be anyone more wonderful than you!" Toni found Chuck's family perplexing and this visit to be uncomfortable, but she consoled herself knowing it would be a short one.

Even worse than the odd treatment she received from Chuck's mother was the rapid disintegration of Chuck's mood. Toni was exhausted from having spent the last several days doing her best to be what she considered to be a proper Tennessee girl with good manners. All sweetness and light, as her mother liked to say. All the while, Chuck only became more brooding and puzzling. Finally, he had asked her if she wanted to go into Manhattan. *Yes!* came Toni's answer. They had taken the train that morning, and from the moment they stepped out of Pennsylvania Station and out into Midtown, Toni had loved it.

But the change of scenery had done nothing to alter Chuck's disposition. He was still grim, silent, avoiding Toni's gaze. So there she stood, looking down 102 stories at tiny, bright yellow taxicabs. There were rows of them—four rows—all lined up, with passengers streaming in and out. She was fascinated by the perspective, the hum, the skyscraping quiet in the middle of metropolitan chaos. She broke away from her meditative moment and turned suddenly toward her beau.

"Chuck, I want you to tell me what's wrong with you," she said.

"Nothing," he said, lifeless.

"That's not true," she continued. "Something is wrong and I want to hear what it is."

No response, only the occasional chatting of other tourists fumbling for change for the viewfinder. *Is it the lipstick?* she wondered. Yes, she'd worn some. She wanted to be herself. These strange people had adored her brother Ben; how could they have taken so badly to her?

"Chuck, please . . . ," she begged him. She stood, waiting, the hot summer wind blowing. Then Chuck finally began to speak.

Oh dear, Toni realized as Chuck started relating what his mother had said to him, *it's not the lipstick.*

"First, I was shocked you asked my mother for a bottle," he began. "Number two, you exposed yourself indecently to my uncle Freddy. And number three, you insulted my mother by leaving a menstrual pad in the bathroom for her to clean up."

Toni was flabbergasted at the lies Chuck's mother had told him. But she was now beginning to realize the depths to which she would sink to destroy her son's relationship. Toni remained silent until Chuck had finished. She had started counting cabs now, trying to see how many she could find from her perch above Fifth Avenue. It was oddly calming. She knew one thing: She had no intention of defending herself against these ridiculous lies. She looked up at Chuck, into eyes that had gazed down at her since that night long ago on the tennis courts, and asked him a simple question:

"Do you believe your mother?" she asked, fire flashing in her eyes.

"No. No, I don't."

Toni looked down at her ring finger and the engagement ring she was already wearing.

"Chuck," she said. "I will not marry you unless you promise me that I will never have to live in a town that is within three hundred miles of your parents."

Toni stood at the top of the world's tallest building, battered but not beaten, and told Chuck that if he wanted to spend his life with her, this was the one condition to which he would have to adhere, the one issue on which she would never bend. She had sprung from a family steeped in love even when they lacked for niceties. She had lived two years in a world steeped in secrets and mysteries. She had known devotion and dedication, sacrifice for the sake of her community and her country. A marriage based on limits and criticisms, one borne of lies and manipulation, could never be in the cards.

The world may have changed, but she wasn't about to.

CHAPTER 15

★ ★ ★ ★ ★

Life in the New Age

Good morning friends. The housewives of Oak Ridge are speaking to the outside world from behind the barbed-wire fence. Yes,
we're still here. Did you forget about us? We just wondered, because we didn't find ourselves mentioned in the Smyth Report.
We are the ones who do the chores for the men who make atomic
bombs, and we bring up their children, bomb or no bomb. The
kids are two years older now, and we are at least ten. That's the
way you grow old—fast, when the going is tough.

—Vi Warren, radio address

The shuttle boat pulled away from the dock and began its short trip
across the harbor. It was clear and sunny as passengers awaited to arrive at the nearby destination, many of them quiet, pensive. Dot held
the lei in her hand. You could buy them onshore in any one of the
countless refrigerated stands she had seen since arriving in Hawaii—
in hotel lobbies, baggage claim areas, gift shops.

Her journey was almost complete. She had traveled more than
4,000 miles to do a single thing.

During the ride she must have thought of Shorty. She had lived a
big life in the years since that news had arrived, and had made her
own contribution to his war: the knobs and dials and gauges that,
unbeknownst to her, helped unleash the power of the smallest known
part of the cosmos, a power that helped to end the conflict that had
taken her brother's life.

She had entered the conflict herself as a teenager, soon became a
wife and mother, a member of a tight-knit community that was never

supposed to exist. The prospect of learning the answer to the question "What are we doing?" had been thrilling at first, but the reality snuck up on her, like it did most people she knew. What a strange mix of feelings it was after the bomb dropped. That was what was so hard for her and so many others to explain to those who hadn't lived through it—how she could feel both good and bad about something at the same time, pride and guilt and joy and relief and shame. She wasn't alone; so many of them now lived a life of jobs and husbands and babies, still saddened by memories of those who were lost forever, no matter how hard they had worked to bring them home.

★　　★　　★

General Groves addressed workers at Clinton Engineer Works at the end of August 30, 1945. If he had picked up a copy of the *Oak Ridge Journal* that day and perused the "As They See Us" column, he would have read the following editorial, reprinted in part from the *Washington News.*

> Oak Ridge is a new town in a new world, a world born the instant its maiden product destroyed Hiroshima . . . Utterly out of date are all the philosophies that gave Oak Ridge its birth . . . If the existing Oak Ridge and the potential Oak Ridgers are continued in the original spirit of aggression, their success can lead to nothing but extermination . . .
>
> The people of Oak Ridge, Tenn., indicate they are willing to go along with their baffling chores. They are content in their town of modern gadgets. In the beginning they asked only to help defeat the Nazis and Japs. They realize now that their assistance was stunning. With all that accomplished, they ask for jobs for today and for their tomorrows, there in the Cumberland hills.
>
> Oak Ridgers have not yet mastered twenty-first-century thinking, no more than have the rest of us. But instinctively they express what we all hope. In their own fashion they are saying: "We'd like to see all this new work turned into helpful things" . . . Men and women, wherever they are, must insist that Oak Ridgers be allowed to strive with atomics in the constructive measures of peace.

Stafford Warren, head of the Manhattan Project's medical section, traveled to Japan to assess the aftermath. Meanwhile, research into the effects of radiation continued in Oak Ridge and elsewhere. A radiology professor at the University of Rochester medical school before joining the Project, Warren was on the road in Japan from August 7 through October 15.

Warren—and the rest of the Manhattan Project—relied almost exclusively on Geiger counter tubes made by one woman at Chicago's Met Lab, Nancy Farley Wood. Nancy had the touch. She had worked on designs of several radiation detectors and when she tried to train others to make the tubes, no one, Warren thought, was as good as Nancy. She later went on to start her own company, the N. Wood Counter Laboratory. The "N." was so that no one would know she, a woman, owned it. It had been an odd trip, Warren remembered, following the trail of the fallout with their Geiger counters as random kamikazes ran up, swords in the air, trying to surrender.

Heading into central Hiroshima, "it stunk terribly, and there were flies everywhere," Warren later said. "The flies were so bad that we had to close up the windows of the car to keep them out. You would see a man or a woman with what looked like a polka-dot shirt on, but when you got up close, there was just a mass of flies crawling over a formerly white shirt."

And in Nagasaki:

We had descriptions from the Japanese of the trains backing down into Nagasaki about ten o'clock in the morning, two hours or so after the detonation, and thousands of people packing themselves on the trains. Then the trains would stop ten or fifteen miles out from the city, wherever there was a school or a flat. A lot of the more seriously wounded or burned would get off there. An awful lot of them would be found dead. They had been squeezed in the train all standing upright like sardines. These deaths I'm sure were due to a combination of shock and a high dose of gamma radiation. And then there were those who had lethal doses of a less amount, which had produced bloody diarrhea and the small intestine then fell apart. Four to six weeks later the bone marrow was destroyed and bleeding and the pallor were evident. It was about that time when we arrived.

Weeks into his trip, Warren traveled to the Tokyo home of Admiral Masao Tsuzuki, a Japanese doctor and the country's top radiation authority. After six weeks together, despite the circumstances, the two men had grown to like each other. Tsuzuki lived in a part of Tokyo that had escaped burning during the spring bombings. Warren didn't think he needed to tell his security detail where he was going. He entered the admiral's home, removed his shoes, and the sliding door shut behind him.

The admiral introduced his wife and son, but his daughter remained in the back of the house. Major Motohashi, who worked with Tsuzuki, sat across from Warren as they shared a pot of hot tea. Warren thought the major looked almost like a caricature, with his thick-framed glasses, dark hair, and squat build. He had been a broadsword fencing champion of Japan. Warren, a fencing buff himself at Berkeley, shared his passion for swords, and a sword presentation ceremony commenced after tea.

Motohashi unsheathed a samurai sword from its scabbard, presenting the edge to Warren. "More than three hundred years old," he said, showcasing the blade's balance. Warren, accompanied by a single aide and his whereabouts unknown to his security detail, thought about how this sword would have been used for decapitation. He felt sweat beginning to coat his skin. He looked at his aide; he, too, was exhibiting an unhealthy color.

Swords came and went, one a cavalry sword from the Russo-Japanese War that had belonged to Tsuzuki's father, and his father before him.

Warren admired it, sweating as the serrated edge hung within inches of his face.

"On behalf of Dr. Tsuzuki, I have great pleasure in giving you this," Motohashi said.

It was exceedingly generous—these men had nothing else to give. They had lost everything. Warren tried to refuse the family heirloom, but there was no way around it. Samurai swords were offered for General Groves, General Farrell, and (soon-to-be-General) Nichols, too. Though all had gone well, Warren was ready to extricate himself from a small room chock full of so much weaponry.

In exchange, Warren left a battery for Major Motohashi's electrocardiogram machine. There was bowing and pleasantries. And though Warren respected the men he'd come to know, he didn't even bother to lace up his boots before getting in the jeep and punching the accelerator.

Years later, Stafford Warren would return to the country with his wife, Vi, on a vacation with a mission. They would track down Tsuzuki's family—the man himself would be already deceased—and return one of the swords to them.

★　　★　　★

In the first several weeks after the Hiroshima bombing, the only readily available information had been prepared under the auspices of the War Department and under the close watch of General Groves himself. Japan sought to control the story as well. An intrepid journalist named Nakamura—one of three men who paid a boatman to ferry them down a delta clogged with dead bodies to get the real story about what had happened to their homeland—described his trip in concise, harrowing detail:

Suddenly a burnt arm stuck up out of the water and the hand grabbed onto the side of the boat. We couldn't ignore it and tried to pull it up. But the skin came off in sheets . . .

While Nakamura did manage to get word of what he witnessed to his editors in Tokyo, his story alarmed the censors. The news in the next day's *Asahi Shimbun* stated that "two B-29s had caused 'a little' damage to the city."

In September, a month after Little Boy was dropped and Warren's arrival in Japan, the first Western journalist, Australian Wilfred Burchett, entered Hiroshima. He documented what he called "an atomic plague" that continued to kill people. His story was published in London's *Daily Express* on September 5, 1945. General MacArthur tried to get the journalist removed from Japan and declared that no civilian journalists would be allowed in Hiroshima.

Early reports that the atomic bomb could keep killing long after its blast had subsided were dismissed by the US military as propaganda. The Allied occupation of Japan, from the end of the war through April 1952, made it easier to censor news reports. For this reason, both the Japanese and American public were slow to learn of the longer-lasting consequences of this new weapon.

Bernard Hoffman, renowned photographer with *Life* magazine, who had already documented the concentration camps in Germany, was the first American photojournalist to document the destruction in Hiroshima and Nagasaki. His pictures were featured in the October 15, 1945, issue of *Life*, the day Stafford Warren returned from his examination of the sites. The devastation was evident, but the mysterious ongoing deaths remained in the background, easily masked by the dust and ash that covered what remained of Hiroshima and Nagasaki.

★ ★ ★

On October 25, 1945, lead Manhattan Project scientist J. Robert Oppenheimer visited President Truman.

No one else in the world yet had the bomb and Truman wanted to do everything he could to keep it that way, to continue to keep the bomb and its technology secret.

What was commonly referred to as the Smyth Report had been prepared at the behest of General Groves and under the supervision of the War Department by Henry DeWolf Smyth. Smyth was the chairman of Princeton's physics department and worked as a consultant with the Manhattan Project and the Army Corps of Engineers. His report told the story of the Project from 1940 through 1945. Copies were available for purchase, and Oak Ridgers snapped them up.

Some higher-ups in the military worried the report gave too much away. However, as Vi Warren pointed out, residents would find little about their contributions within the pages. The veil of secrecy surrounding the Manhattan Project had hardly been fully lifted. As the preface explained:

"Secrecy requirements have affected both the detailed content and general emphasis so that many interesting developments have been omitted."

But Oppenheimer and others did not believe it was possible to keep the details about atomic power secret: The majority of the scientists that helped develop the bomb didn't feel that hoarding the information was the route to take as the world moved into an uncertain nuclear future.

That fall day, just two and a half months after the bombings, Oppenheimer told Truman he felt he had "blood on my hands."

Truman didn't like what he was hearing from the scientist who'd helped make the bomb a reality. *Blood on* his *hands?!* Truman didn't have any patience for a "cry-baby scientist" or, as he and the Appalachians would have said, "bellyachin'." Truman told Oppenheimer that if anyone had blood on his hands, it was Truman himself. Then he made it clear to his staff that he never wanted to see Oppenheimer again.

★　　★　　★

In September, the teeth that had been removed from Ebb Cade's mouth (patient HP-12) in March were sent to Los Alamos.

Dated September 19, 1945, the following memo was addressed to Mr. Wright Langham, part of the analytical chemistry group at Los Alamos, where he developed a method for assaying trace amounts of plutonium in urine. The memo was sent to Langham in Santa Fe, New Mexico. It read:

> Inclosed *[sic]* is a brief resume of E.C.'s medical history, and a graphic record of the patient's hospital course is forwarded under separate cover. The jaundice which this patient developed was apparently an infectious jaundice from which he recovered before his discharge from the hospital. At the time of discharge the patient was ambulatory and in good condition. Approximately 15 teeth have been extracted by Captain Peter Dale, and the rate of healing of the extraction sites was within the limits of normal. More bone specimens and extracted teeth will be shipped to you very soon for analysis. We would appreciate

receiving your records of the complete analyses on the urines *[sic]*, feces, bone samples, and teeth at your earliest convenience.

For the District Engineer: Very truly yours, David Goldright, Captain, Medical Corps, Assistant.

Conflicting language in memos such as this from the Atomic Energy Commission's archives and later oral histories conducted by the Department of Energy tell two different stories: One, that Ebb Cade had been discharged, and another, that he had, one day, just up and disappeared. What is known for certain is that within eight years of this memo, Ebb Cade died and was buried in Greensboro, North Carolina. The cause of his death was listed as heart failure. He was about 61 years old.

Ebb Cade was not the only test subject. It turned out that between 1945 and 1947, 18 people were injected with plutonium, specifically: 11 at Rochester, New York, 3 at the University of Chicago, 3 at UC San Francisco, and 1, Ebb Cade, at Oak Ridge. Several thousand human radiation experiments were conducted between 1944 and 1974. In 1994, President Clinton appointed the Advisory Committee on Human Radiation Experiments (ACHRE) to investigate these and other experiments funded by the United States government. Their final report was published in 1996.

★   ★   ★

In November 1945, just three months after the bombings of Hiroshima and Nagasaki, the Royal Swedish Academy of Sciences announced that the 1945 Nobel Prize in Physics would go to Wolfgang Pauli and that Otto Hahn had been awarded the 1944 Nobel Prize in Chemistry for his discovery of fission. (The award had been delayed by the war.)

But Lise Meitner, the colleague to whom Hahn turned to explain his findings, was not honored. The decision to exclude Lise Meitner from any prize that year shocked many in the scientific community. Lise herself thought it was "unjust" and "almost insulting" that she was referred to in the press as Hahn's junior associate.

The award ceremony wouldn't take place until December 1946. Earlier that year, Lise had traveled to the United States, giving seminars and meeting friends. At a dinner of the Women's National Press Club, Lise was honored as The Woman of the Year and met President Truman. "So," Truman reportedly said, "you're the little lady who got us into all this." Lise later attended a cocktail party at which she met General Groves for the first time, where another guest reported the pair had little to say to each other. She recoiled at a script she saw for the 1947 MGM film *The Beginning or the End*, which she said was "nonsense." She believed the film perpetuated the fabrications made earlier about the manner of her departure from Germany, depicting Lise escaping with, as she said, "the bomb in my purse."

The Nobel ceremonies were held December 10, 1946, in Stockholm, and Lise attended. During Hahn's time in Stockholm, Lise was portrayed in the press as a student, an assistant, further diminishing her role in the fission discovery. After Hahn and his wife left Sweden, Lise wrote to a friend:

"I found it quite painful that in his interviews [Hahn] did not say one word about me, to say nothing of our thirty years together."

Lise Meitner was not the only woman whose contributions to the discovery of fission remained obscured. In 1989, Emilio Segrè, a key member of Enrico Fermi's team in Rome, wrote the following in *Physics Today:*

> Another error was in not paying enough attention to a 1934 article by Ida Noddack in Berlin, who criticized our chemistry and pointed to the possibility of fission. Much has been said of her prescience. Her article was certainly known to us in Rome, to Hahn and Meitner in Berlin and to Joliot and Curie in Paris. If any of us had really grasped its importance, it would have been easy to discover fission in 1935.

★   ★   ★

In the months and years that followed the war, the ebullient mood of victory became tempered by the emerging reality that international relations would never be the same and neither would Oak Ridge. With the revelation of the technology that had created the bomb, the worlds both within and beyond CEW's still-standing fences oscillated between fear of atomic war and the anticipation of new scientific frontiers.

Oak Ridge was a city in flux. By the end of 1946, its population had dropped to 42,465 from a peak of nearly 75,000 in 1945. Dorm services were reduced and rents increased. Employment dropped to 28,737 from 82,000. Much of this was due to the shutdown by the end of 1946 of all of Y-12's calutrons except for the pilot units and those in the Beta-3 building. This alone left roughly 20,000 people with no jobs. S-50, the thermal diffusion plant, was shut down on September 9, just one month after the bombing of Nagasaki. The vacated plant was used initially to research the possibility of nuclear-powered aircraft.

As the nuclear arms race ramped up, K-25 became the primary uranium enrichment facility and would continue to produce weapons-grade uranium until 1964, when the large U-shaped icon of Oak Ridge was finally shut down and smaller facilities such as K-27 focused on enriching uranium to only around 3 to 5 percent, enough for nuclear power reactors. This uranium fueled reactors in a number of countries, among them Japan.

The X-10 plant (which became known as the Oak Ridge National Lab in 1948) began to grow its role in scientific research, notably in the field of radioisotopes. On August 2, 1946, a ceremony was held at Oak Ridge's graphite reactor in honor of a shipment of one millicurie of Carbon-14 from Oak Ridge bound for the Barnard Free Skin and Cancer Hospital in St. Louis, Missouri. It was the first-ever shipment of a radioisotope for medical purposes.

One day earlier, August 1, 1946, President Truman signed the Atomic Energy Act, which outlined the development and regulation of military *and* civilian use of nuclear matter and provided for government control of fissionable material. "It is reasonable to anticipate, however," it stated, "that tapping this new source of energy will cause profound changes in our present way of life." This act also meant that a new civilian commission was taking over from the Manhattan Engineer District, a change that officially went into effect January 1, 1947.

Oak Ridge continued experiencing growing pains, as the people who lived there worked to build a future never anticipated by the Project.

★   ★   ★

Three years after the AEC came to be, smoke billowed and a miniature mushroom cloud hovered above Elza Gate at the Clinton Engineer Works. The throng surged en masse toward the gate where the ceremonial ribbon—flammable magnesium tape—had just been ignited. Everyone wanted to be among the first to walk through Elza Gate freely: no inspection, badge-free.

It was March 19, 1949. Crowds had gathered for a street-busting parade that marched down Tennessee Avenue near Jackson Square, through Townsite, along the heart of the outpost-cum-town. President Truman did not attend, but Alben Barkley, his Kentucky-bred vice president, did, alongside congressional representatives, military brass, and Hollywood starlets.

Opening the gates and eliminating the badges and the guards elicited mixed reactions. Security checks that had once seemed a nuisance had for many become a comfort. Many residents had grown to like the idea that anyone who did not *belong* in Oak Ridge was not permitted to enter. In a sense, the gates lent a feeling of belonging and exclusivity, the kind gated communities of the future would purport to offer. Inside the gates there were rules. There were jobs. Opening them meant Oak Ridge might become like any other town.

Opening the gates was the first step the AEC took toward transforming Oak Ridge into a self-governing municipality. This effort began in 1948 and was not initially popular. In 1953, after the gates had been down roughly four years, a town meeting vote regarding incorporation was roundly rejected by a margin of nearly four to one. Nevertheless, Oak Ridge was entering a new phase, moving toward a future few had planned for.

"Oak Ridge is a city without a past not destined for a future," District Engineer Kenneth Nichols had written. The Manhattan District's plans never included a blueprint for the post-Gadget Oak Ridge. But even if the plan in 1942 had been to close up shop, it would likely have been abandoned in the face of the Cold War. Now the great transition had begun.

The postwar housing plan for Oak Ridge had fallen again to the architectural firm of Skidmore, Owings, and Merrill, as it had when CEW first began. The firm anticipated the need for many new neighborhoods once some of the hastily constructed housing was torn down or simply ceased to be usable any longer.

★   ★   ★

In 1954, the Atomic Energy Act of 1946 had been amended to include a greater focus on nuclear power and allowed for the private ownership and management of nuclear power plants.

But President Eisenhower soon passed another act, one that did not garner the same attention but that directly affected Oak Ridge. The Atomic Energy Community Act of 1955 provided for the self-governing of Oak Ridge and private ownership of homes and land. Control of the town of Oak Ridge began to more fully leave the hands of the military.

Residents began purchasing land and building homes or simply buying the ones they had been renting from the government. The A, B, C, and D houses that lined the streets began to take on individual style: garden beds, sun porches, a touch of masonry flesh adhered to prefab bones. But the challenges of living under military supervision were replaced by the challenges of living without it: the possibility of unemployment, the need for police, jails, more schools, public transportation, and local elections. As the mantle passed, yet another vision of the city had to be born. The pioneer spirit that had carried residents through the war now had to evolve into an entrepreneurial one.

Frustrations with the "new" Oak Ridge were played out in private, in the press, and even onstage. On March 20, 1957, Oak Ridge took another step toward independence when Governor Frank Clement signed the Oak Ridge Law into effect, providing for the town's incorporation. Then finally, on May 5, 1959, Oak Ridgers elected to incorporate. The vote was 5,552 for, 395 against. The military and the AEC reduced its role in administration of the community, and by June of 1960, Oak Ridge was a fully independent, "normal" town.

★　　　★　　　★

"The Atom Bomb! Is it a blessing, or will it smash humanity? . . . Can Enemies Strike America? . . . Slave—or Destroyer? . . . Magic of Uranium . . . Atom Power in Your Home! . . ."

With the advent of the Atomic Age came both trepidation and fascination, as evidenced on this cover of one of Jane's 25-cent serial magazines. And as the cloud of mystery lifted—or at least dissipated a bit—from the Manhattan Project, a new darkness fell. Dread of "the bomb" combined with the promise of the power of the atom in your kitchen or garage. Uranium mining by private companies with government contracts took off. The AEC set uranium prices, and hungry prospectors, speculators, and mine workers came out of the woodwork, swarming to places like Moab, Utah.

Schools in Oak Ridge—and across the country—grew accustomed to disaster drills as the Cold War descended upon the country like a blackout curtain. Information about the US Atomic program had made its way to the Soviet Union via Klaus Fuchs; David Greenglass, a.k.a. "Kalibr"; and George Koval among others. Greenglass and Koval had both spent time in Oak Ridge during the war, Koval for nearly a year. Greenglass was the brother of Ethel Rosenberg and passed information to her and Julius Rosenberg with the help of his wife, Ruth. When his role was uncovered in 1950, Greenglass's eventual testimony resulted in the death penalty for the Rosenbergs and no charges for Ruth. He served a 15-year sentence. The Soviet Union had detonated its first nuclear bomb on August 29, 1949, in Semipalatinsk, Kazakh. It was an implosion-type bomb, like Fat Man, sketches of which Greenglass had provided the Soviets.

In 1950, the Federal Civil Defense Administration gave us "Bert the Turtle," who taught folks how to "Duck and Cover." The atomic bomb inspired everything from Pernod-infused cocktails—first served at the Washington Press Club within hours of the announcement of the bombing of Hiroshima—to music and movies, air-raid drills to luxury fallout shelters. *The Beast from 20,000 Fathoms* had landed in movie theaters in 1953, kicking off an age of movie monster madness and featuring as a major plot point the "only isotope of its kind this side of Oak Ridge," humanity's only hope of killing the beast. Oak Ridge had gone from secret to the center stage of a new world, which both enthralled and frightened people. Fear of the newer, far more powerful hydrogen bomb coexisted with the warm, fuzzy Walt Disney production "Our Friend the Atom." There was an edge to existence in this new age that the end of World War II was unable to soften.

By the time Oak Ridge earned its independence in 1960, J. Robert Oppenheimer, lead scientist of the Manhattan Project, had been deemed a security risk and stripped of his clearance. The Korean War had come and gone, and with it the threat of another atomic bombing, this time under the leadership of President Eisenhower. Shortly after the end of that Cold War conflict, President Eisenhower addressed the United Nations, saying:

> But let no one think that the expenditure of vast sums for weapons and systems of defense can guarantee absolute safety for the cities and citizens of any nation. The awful arithmetic of the atomic bomb does not permit of any such easy solution. . . .

In 1961, the Soviets detonated the largest nuclear weapon in history over the Arctic island of Novaya Zemlya. It was a 58-megaton explosion, 4,000 times as powerful as the bomb that leveled Hiroshima. Almost 18 years to the day after the first wartime use of an atomic bomb, August 5, 1963, representatives of the United States, the Soviet Union, and Britain signed the Limited Nuclear Test Ban Treaty, prohibiting nuclear tests and explosions under water, in the atmosphere, or in outer space. Underground testing was still permitted. President John F. Kennedy ratified the treaty on October 7, 1963, shortly before his assassination on November 22.

Oak Ridge, a city born of a secrecy now long revealed, a reservation once under military control and now fully independent, had played a role in altering the course of history, warfare, power, and technology. The Cold War would prevail for a time and eventually pass into memory as Oak Ridge's place on the atomic landscape evolved further still, history and public opinion perpetually shifting beneath it.

★　　★　　★

Change came also for the Girls of Atomic City.

Jane had married Jim Puckett, the man who had carried her suitcase up the stairs of the Guest House that very first day she arrived in Oak Ridge. She had found other work at Y-12 and continued to work there as a statistician. Uranium was still being enriched, weapons stockpiled, and an entirely new industry in Oak Ridge was growing as scientists sought to put the tiny atom to big use beyond nuclear material for the bomb it had helped create.

Physics. Chemistry. Biology. The kind of research that was once relegated to underfunded university labs benefitted now from monies directed toward the burgeoning military industrial complex. The first light ever generated by atomic power. Advances in plutonium reactors. Submarine propulsion, pressurized water reactors, production of radioactive and stable isotopes, neutron diffraction, thermonuclear fusion, heavy ion nuclear research, investigations into bone marrow transplants and medical isotope scanning, and more found a home in the laboratories of Oak Ridge, along with the continued focus on research into the effects of ionizing radiation on human and other living beings. When President John F. Kennedy was assassinated in 1963, bullet fragments and paraffin casts were sent to Oak Ridge National Lab for neutron activation analysis.

At work, Jane noticed many things were still under wraps. Although the Secret may have been out, others had taken its place. Though the greater purpose of Oak Ridge was now known, revealing details about one's job was still forbidden. Not too long after the war, Jane had watched as a young couple who worked near her in Y-12 was quietly escorted out one day. Jane soon learned that they had been paying closer attention to what was going on at Y-12 than she had realized, and sharing what they had learned with people outside the fences. Jane did not know whom. She did not ask. You still did not ask.

Soon babies came. Jim took a job in Tullahoma, Tennessee, home of Arnold Engineering Development Center, the University of Tennessee's Space Institute, and Dickel Whisky. Jane left the lab behind, where Marchant and Monroe calculators and her "human comput-ers" had been replaced by advancements such as the Oak Ridge Au-tomatic Computer and Logical Engine (ORACLE) which, when it was created in 1953, was the most advanced computer in the world.

Virginia continued working at Y-12 as well. One of her lab proj-ects involved new developments from the Dow Chemical Company. Discussing uranium openly hadn't made extracting and purifying it any easier. Tiny little pellets were supposed to absorb different forms of the now-freely-mentioned element, making recovery simpler. Vir-ginia found the results murky at first, but results improved.

A new man had arrived in the lab: Charles Coleman, a physi-cal chemist with a PhD from Purdue, who specialized in separation chemistry. Virginia found him to be brilliant, his problem-solving ability eminently creative. The two soon went from coworkers to friends. Charles was a real match, someone who valued Virginia's mind as well as her potential as a partner in life. The career chemist married at 29. She continued working but transferred to a different lab in an effort to keep her personal and professional lives separate. Babies followed soon after, along with Charlie's many patents.

Kattie and Willie decided to stay in Oak Ridge, though once the war ended many people they knew were moving on. They were finally able to bring their children from Alabama to Tennessee to live with them, where the couple had secured new jobs for the foreseeable fu-ture.

One of the new postwar neighborhoods had been designated for black families and was located in the old Gamble Valley Trailer Camp, an area later called Scarboro. Scarce family-style housing had become available for black couples in 1945, but many lived in hut-ments until 1950.

"It is the first community I have ever seen with slums that were deliberately planned," Enoch P. Waters wrote in 1945 in the *Chicago Defender*, describing the planning of Oak Ridge "as backward socio-logically as the atomic bomb is advanced scientifically."

Kattie, Willie, and their children moved into a home in the Scar-boro area and were finally able to live again as a family. But change came slowly for the black community. Black residents still sat atop the hill overlooking the drive-in movie theater that remained off-limits, angling for a view of the far-off screen. In 1946, an elementary school for black students was organized. Older children still faced a long bus ride to Knoxville, which had a black high school, until 1950, when volunteers began teaching high school grades at the Scarboro School.

In 1955, Oak Ridge became the first city in the state of Tennessee to follow the 1954 Supreme Court ruling against school segregation. It wasn't without strife: Oak Ridgers for Segregation encouraged parents to keep their children home from school. Obscenities were scrawled across the sidewalk leading up to the school's doors. (They were removed before the first day of classes.) Initially, only the school itself was integrated—black students had their own *classes*—but complaints raised by white and black members of the community soon changed that and classes began to be mixed as well.

The spring before Oak Ridge integrated its schools, Kattie's daughter Dorothye graduated as the last-ever valedictorian of Scarboro High School.

With work no longer available to her as a cubicle operator at Y-12—K-25 was now the dominant and more efficient uranium separation plant at postwar CEW—**Helen** began working at Y-12's library. There, one of her responsibilities was to help disseminate declassified information to other approved labs and libraries across the country. She had been asked to help keep secrets, she had been recruited to spy, and now she was being asked to help spread those words that had been cleared by Washington. Phrases and memos and techniques never known to her now passed through her fingertips on their way to be viewed by new and eager eyes of researchers and visiting scientists. Her focus stayed on the courts and ball fields, though. Lucky that. Helen's softball team had found a softball coach: Lloyd Brown. But while impressed with Helen's fielding abilities, Lloyd had other designs on the athlete. On their first date, the pair grabbed a bite at the cafeteria and spent the rest of the evening hitting buckets of golf balls at the driving range. Helen soon married Lloyd in the Chapel on the Hill.

Rosemary was searching for suture material when her life took a turn. A young man had wandered down the hall from one of the research labs and into her office. His name was John Lane and he was recently discharged from the Navy. After working in the sick bay of an aircraft carrier in the South Pacific, he now worked in a lab assisting research into permissible doses of radiation. Suture material was a must-have for his day-to-day responsibilities. Did she have any?

"Where are you from?" John asked.

"Holy Cross, Iowa," Rosemary answered nonchalantly, and handed him a bit of catgut to tide him over until his next shipment arrived.

"I'm from *Cascade!*" he said. "We used to play Holy Cross in baseball!"

And so Rosemary met John in the clinic of a plant in Southern Appalachia, though they had grown up a mere 15 miles away from each other in a small Catholic corner of Iowa—he among the Irish, she, the Germans. The coincidence made an impression on the pair. They were soon married and moved into an E-2 apartment, followed by a B house when the children arrived. After a few years, John was transferred to Germantown, Maryland, and the couple moved their family to what would be their home for many years to come.

Toni also married at the Chapel on the Hill, in November 1945. It had been a Lutheran wedding. Chuck's mother would have approved of that much—but neither she nor Chuck's father were invited.

Chuck kept imagining his father leaping up the moment the minister said, "If any one here has any reason that these two should not be joined together, let him speak now or forever hold his peace." Chuck didn't want to risk that kind of outburst, and Toni certainly wasn't going to complain that Chuck's parents weren't present. To avoid any discussion, Chuck kept one more secret in Oak Ridge. He did not tell his parents about the wedding until it was over: vows exchanged, reception finished, deal legally and spiritually sealed.

Chuck's work continued at K-25 and he then moved over to Y-12. Shortly after the war, Chuck discovered that one of his associates had been a member of the Counter Intelligence Corps—an official creep. It unnerved and angered him that a friend would keep that kind of information from him. Toni was relieved that nothing ever came of it. She was proud that Chuck excelled at work and began racking up quite a few patents of his own.

He was transferred for a short time to Three Mile Island, a nuclear power plant outside Harrisburg, Pennsylvania, located approximately 160 miles from Chuck's parents' home in Queens, New York City. This was technically in violation of the 300-mile "do not live" buffer zone that Toni had established when she issued her Empire State ultimatum. His work foray to Three Mile Island was thankfully a short one. Toni made a short visit then, and returned back down to the safety and seclusion of Oak Ridge.

★ ★ ★

Over the years, Oak Ridgers who had been there since the early pioneer days of 1943 had begun to feel a shift in attitude toward the work they had done during World War II. Three Mile Island eventually became known across the United States and the world when the nuclear power plant suffered a partial core meltdown. This, the worst nuclear accident in American history, occurred March 28, 1979, not two weeks after the release of *The China Syndrome,* the Jane Fonda thriller about dangers at a nuclear plant that garnered four Oscar nominations. Cleanup of the No. 2 reactor would last 14 years, and reluctance toward embracing nuclear energy reached an all-time high. A year before the accident, Oak Ridge's science museum, dubbed the Museum of Atomic Energy when it first opened in 1949, was renamed the American Museum of Science and Energy, striking the word "atomic" and any of its perceived baggage from the name.

Once her kids were a bit older, **Dot** took a job at the museum as a docent. She had enjoyed it at first, being able to share the work she had done as a cubicle operator. Veterans and civilians alike were proud of their contributions to World War II. Why shouldn't she be?

But times had changed. She was never quite sure what to say when asked how she "felt" about her work. Simple answers seemed hard to come by in those moments. And Dot eventually decided to quit her job as a volunteer at the museum.

She could still hear the voice of the woman who was, perhaps, the final straw. Dot was standing at the Y-12 display, next to the replica of the calutron panels, where she would show visitors how she operated the knobs and dials. Most people would ask:

"What's it like to work on something you don't know anything about?"

"What's a calutron?"

"What was it like to live in a secret city?"

But one woman in particular strode up to Dot, glaring, and asked, "Aren't you ashamed you helped build a bomb that killed all those people?"

The truth was, Dot *did* have conflicting feelings. There was sadness at the loss of life, yes, but that wasn't the only thing she felt. They had all been so happy, so thrilled, when the war ended. Didn't any of these people remember that? And yes, Oak Ridgers felt horrible when they saw the pictures of the aftermath in Japan. Relief. Fear. Joy. Sadness. Decades later, how could she explain this to someone who had no experience with the Project, someone who hadn't lived through that war, let alone lived in Oak Ridge?

Dot knew the woman wanted a simple answer, so she gave her one.

"Well," she said, "they killed my brother."

★　　★　　★

After dutifully attending their Catholic "instructions," **Colleen** and Blackie were married November 29, 1945, also at the Chapel on the Hill. They made a striking pair: Colleen in her wedding gown from Cain-Sloan Department Store in Nashville, Blackie walking down the aisle in his Army uniform. Blackie had agreed to raise their children Catholic and, though he did not convert before the wedding ceremony, told Colleen he eventually would, though Colleen never asked. To her mind, he had done enough. The newlyweds went to Washington, DC, for their honeymoon, the first of many travels in their future.

Colleen's fears that she and Blackie would be transferred or that her new husband would decide to move them up north never came to pass. Instead, Blackie was formally discharged from the Army in March of 1946 and went to work for the newly formed Atomic Energy

Commission (AEC), and Colleen had another acronym to add to her arsenal. She got to stay in Oak Ridge, where she was close to home, close to family. Colleen's brother Jimmy had made it home safely from the war and moved up to Kentucky, where he found work in Paducah. Not long after, he died in a car accident.

Funny how life turns out, Colleen would think when Jimmy came to mind. Her mother had prayed for him all through the war, and then assuming the worst was over, she thought it was safe to stop. Jimmy had been saved. Now Jimmy was gone.

Colleen well remembered she hadn't always been fond of Oak Ridge. She had recoiled at the thought of living here when she and her family first came to visit relatives in 1943. The women in dresses, shoes in hand, walking barefoot through the mud. The sight of her uncle's tiny, one-room hutment.

Her mother's words came back to her once more: "It'll be just like camping . . ." It was funny to think about now, after living here for so many years. Camping indeed.

Temporary was the last thing that Oak Ridge turned out to be. When houses became available, she and Blackie bought one for their growing brood. There were eight of them now, five boys and three girls, just one shy of the nine Colleen's mother had raised.

Since the end of the war, Colleen had heard her town referred to as a lot of things, including a social experiment by anthropologist Margaret Mead. Colleen didn't feel she was just part of some experiment. She was part of a very unique, unexpected community, one the Project never anticipated.

Colleen's pride in her home grew with each passing year as she added to the collage of pictures and memories of her time in Oak Ridge. She wanted to share what she had done with future generations and newcomers who came to town. She spoke at schools, telling stories to students about her job at the plant and about the war that Oak Ridge worked to win. Inevitably she, too, was asked what she thought about the destruction and death that the bomb caused. She never knew quite what to say, but tried to explain that in her mind, war was different. That war, in particular, had touched the lives of nearly every person in the entire country. All Americans wanted was to bring their loved ones home. Colleen hoped never to see the bomb she helped fuel used again. She continued to hope that the first time was the last.

The relationship between the United States and Japan had changed dramatically since the days when Colleen first came to Oak Ridge and the prime mission was to defeat the "Japs." Now Japanese scientists regularly came to Oak Ridge to do research, exchange ideas. The wife of one such scientist became one of Colleen's students when Colleen volunteered as a teacher of English as a second language at the YWCA. The two women struck up an easy friendship. Colleen had no knowledge of her student's past when they first met, but soon learned that the woman, Kisetsu Yamada, was a *hibakusha*, a survivor of the Hiroshima bombing. She had been 10 years old at the time of the bombing and had stayed home sick that day, avoiding the center of the city. As the two women worked together, Colleen encouraged Kisetsu to write about her experiences.

From opposite sides of an ocean and a war, Colleen and Kisetsu shared a bond few outside either community could understand. There was not only scientific collaboration but growing cultural exchange as well, an effort that has manifested itself in myriad ways over the years. The most symbolic of these is the bell that stands in the middle of Oak Ridge's public green, hanging within a small, wooden structure vaguely reminiscent of an arts-and-crafts take on a small pagoda. The International Friendship Bell.

When this traditional bonshoo-style Japanese bell—designed in Oak Ridge and cast in Japan—was first proposed, it was one of several cultural exchange programs that had launched over the years between Oak Ridge and various Japanese cities and towns. The driving force behind the bell was Kyoto-born Shigeko Uppuluri and her husband, Ram. But this particular effort struck a nerve with some citizens. Letters flooded the local paper, pro and con. Some believed that creating a site for this bell was too close to offering an apology to Japan for the bombings, though the committee organizers insisted it was not. Others argued that there was nothing wrong with embracing peace as a common goal.

In 1998, two years after the bell was dedicated, Robert Brooks sued the City of Oak Ridge, alleging, "the Friendship Bell erected in a public park on the fiftieth anniversary of the city's founding is a Buddhist symbol whose presence results in an endorsement of the Buddhist religion." According to this logic, continued Brooks, the bell violated the laws of Tennessee and the US Constitution.

"They're praying to a god when they ring that bell," he proclaimed angrily on the nightly news. The City of Oak Ridge prevailed and the bell remains. Japanese children and scientists flew to Oak Ridge for the inaugural ringing. There was no praying, there was no chanting. The bell is free for all to ring and people of all backgrounds do so on many occasions, official or not, August 6 among them.

★ · ★ ★

The ride on the Navy shuttle was a brief one. The memorial itself was long, rectangular, white, and concave in the middle, as if pulled downward by what rested beneath. The ship's rusted gun turret protruded up through the surface of the water.

After docking, Dot disembarked along with the rest of the passengers, making her way toward the narrow structure in the water.

What had started with Pearl Harbor resulted in the development of a technology that ended a war and recast the political and emotional landscape of the world. Dot had moved from rural, post-Depression Tennessee to a secret government city, to the biggest wartime development in modern history and now here to where it had all begun.

The waters of the Pacific acted as a blanket of stillness covering the remnants of the violence that once was, seeds of history now buried in the sea floor. They were over the middle of the ship now, its mammoth form lurking upside down beneath them. Dot looked out over the harbor. The barnacled and algae-ensconced outline of the remains of the ship was visible through the greenish-blue water.

He was in there, somewhere, her brother Seaman Willard Worth Jones. Shorty. She began to cry. After a few moments, she turned to see an older Japanese woman standing next to her.

"Did you lose someone here?" the woman asked Dot in a heavy accent, her own eyes brimming with tears.

"Yes, I did," Dot answered. "My brother."

The woman nodded. "I am so sorry for you," she said.

She moved toward Dot, and Dot held out her arms. The two women embraced. Dot knew this stranger somehow understood. She did not know why, she did not know how, and she did not care to ask.

The woman did not linger, simply said good-bye and walked away.

Dot took the lei she had carried with her and tossed the ring of blossoms out into the open water, knowing it was not only the first but likely the last time she would ever place flowers on her brother's grave.

E p i l o g u e

Heading northwest on Highway 62, I cross over the Clinch River. No gates. No guards. Signs for the Y-12 National Security Complex loom large, nothing hidden about them. Streets and sites that flank the road into town recall what once was: Scarboro Road. Bear Creek Road. New Hope Cemetery. A small wooden sign marks the former location of Elza Gate.

Since the first time I visited Oak Ridge years ago, I have been reminded of the Army bases I knew as a child. Though the town has been out from under military control for decades, its prefab origins still lurk beneath modern-day structures. If you look closely, you can spot them. An office for the National Oceanic and Atmospheric Administration on South Illinois Avenue once served as a field hospital. The Midtown Community Center— a.k.a. the Wildcat Den—remains, now home to the Oak Ridge Heritage and Preservation Association. The site of the former bus terminal houses a Mail Boxes Etc. and a Cash Express. Jackson Square is still here, though the businesses have come and gone and come again. The Center Theater that once showed movies like 1942's *In Which We Serve* is now home to the Oak Ridge Playhouse. Nearby, the Chapel on the Hill continues to host interdenominational religious services and weddings, while the Guest House (which later became the Alexander Inn) is a dilapidated mess, grassy and overgrown. Many younger residents remember the structure as an inn only, knowing nothing of its history as a place where people like J. Robert Oppenheimer, Enrico Fermi, Ernest Lawrence, a young senator John F. Kennedy, among others, lay their heads. A number of A, B, C, and D houses dot the town, many of them refurbished with carports and clapboard, porches, and porticos. Slap a forest green awning on a government prefab and you've got yourself a chiropractor's office. Oak Ridge's history remains, in many ways, still hidden in plain sight.

My first trip here, I half expected some sort of Googie-esque signage, starbursts, and atomic symbols beaming out at me from every surface, a "Home of the Manhattan Project" billboard welcoming visitors to town.

Not so. Some of the most noticeable nods to Oak Ridge's past are found on menus in various bars and eateries, where chicken wings provide a natural outlet for kitschy atomic humor, and sauces range from "Y-12" to "Nuclear."

Now with a population hovering around 28,000, Oak Ridge straddles its future and past. It's a town of science and progress, where researchers continue to discover new elements and neutrons continue to fire away, only now they do so at the Spallation Neutron Source, a facility at the Oak Ridge National Laboratory (ORNL). ORNL is occasionally home to the world's fastest computer, a title it relinquishes and regains periodically in an ongoing battle against similar computing giants in China, Japan, and elsewhere in the US, like Big Ten gridiron rivals meeting each other on a field of competition determined by data transfer rates.

The Secret City Festival is held here in June each year, showcasing that tango between what was and what shall be. The two-day event is part history, part technology, with everything from WWII reenactments and dunking booths to reactor tours. In a day you can go from calutrons to inflatable bouncy houses, taking in Buffett cover bands and bluegrass, fission, and funnel cakes.

At a recent festival, I join Joel Walker, director of education and outreach at the National Archives regional facility outside Atlanta, Georgia (NARA Southeast), in the lobby of the American Museum of Science and Energy. The last time I was at AMSE—which boasts a permanent and in-depth exhibit of Oak Ridge's role in the Manhattan Project—was for Ed Westcott's 90th birthday celebration. Many spoke in honor of and on Ed's behalf. He did not speak. He suffered a stroke years back, and though his physical recovery was substantial—he still scales tall scaffolding to get just the right shot—his speech remains largely impaired. There is, however, no one who helps "tell" the story of this just-add-water town created from scratch 70 years ago better than the Photographer, Ed Westcott.

The bulk of historic—and now declassified—documents available on the Manhattan Engineer District and the Atomic Energy Commission (AEC) are housed at NARA Southeast. On one of my research trips, Joel, who has a particular interest in this collection, took me behind the "Big Door" into the room where archivists and interns scurry about for patrons who have requested research files. The bay containing the AEC files is roughly 100 feet long and just over 22 feet high, and entering it I felt like I was in the final scene of *Raiders of the Lost Ark*. Here are roughly 5,000 cubic feet of AEC files, the majority of which have yet to be fully catalogued. There are, no doubt, many more secrets trapped in those boxes of onionskin paper and typewritten memos.

This is one of the more striking wrinkles to the story of the Project and Oak Ridge: how much is still unknown. And what's more, our ambassadors to that era, the men and women who are our window into that moment in time, are rapidly leaving us, and the structures they once inhabited may soon be gone. K-25 is currently being torn down, but a recently historic preservation agreement with the DOE will provide for the construction of a replica equipment building and history center to help interpret K-25's role during and after the war. Y-12 remains behind gates and is still part of the National Security Complex, but many of its original buildings and remnants remain off-limits, except on special days of the year (the Secret City Festival among them). The dorms are long gone, as is the Castle on the Hill. The Guest House, though in disrepair, recently got a $500,000 grant as part of K-25's preservation agreement.

When these people and what's left of the original town and plants are finally gone, who and what will be left to interpret the origins of one of the most significant moments in world history—the birth of the nuclear age?

The challenge in telling the story of the atomic bomb is one of nuance, requiring thought and sensitivity and walking a line between commemoration and celebration. Opening history up to discussion and debate is the kind of tightrope walk that created years of controversy at the Smithsonian Air and Space Museum, for example. When the museum sought to create an exhibit on the *Enola Gay,* a controversy ensued and eventually came to a head on the eve of the 50th anniversary of the end of World War II.

"When we began discussions of the exhibit, there were two points everyone agreed on," Martin O. Harwit, then the museum's director, was quoted as saying. "One, this is a historically significant aircraft. Two, no matter what the museum did, we'd screw it up."

Unable to create an exhibit that satisfied all parties, curators canceled the exhibit in its original form and Harwit resigned.

There is currently a movement to create a Manhattan Project National Park, led in no small part by Cynthia Kelly and the Atomic Heritage Foundation (AHF) in Washington, DC. Introduced in June 2012 in the Senate by Jeff Bingaman (S. 3300) and in the House by Doc Hastings (H.R. 5987), the Manhattan Project National Historical Park Act would establish National Park Service sites at Oak Ridge, Los Alamos, New Mexico, and Hanford, Washington.

Locally in Oak Ridge, efforts are being made to preserve and restore

some of the town's history. Ray Smith, Y-12's historian, spearheaded creation of the New Hope Center, which houses a curated display space featuring historic artifacts from the electromagnetic separation plant, and helped
establish limited tours of the complex's remaining Manhattan Project facilities. Oak Ridge historian Bill Wilcox—aided by the AHF and others—has
been fighting for nine years to preserve a piece of K-25 that could remain
open to the public, ideally as part of the National Park. But there are challenges. Waste remains an issue, one legacy of the nuclear age that cannot
simply be given a cursory mop-up in advance of any renovation. And, of
course, money is hard to find.

Debates concerning how to present information about this moment in
history will likely continue. Meanwhile, the legacy of the Manhattan Project
continues to impact the social, environmental, and political landscape of
the world. How things turn out in Oak Ridge remains to be seen. For now,
visitors to the Secret City Festival can meet people like Colleen and Marty
Rom, another fascinating woman I interviewed, at the Oak Ridge Heritage
and Preservation Association table. Celia sits nearby at the Center for Oak
Ridge Oral History's booth, sharing her experiences as a woman who was
told she would be here only six to nine months and who is now going on 70
years as an Oak Ridge resident.

After leaving the museum, I drive by John Hendrix's resting place on
my way to Celia's house. The grave of the man once called the Prophet is
located between two modern homes on a suburban street. No matter any
visions he did or did not have, he most likely could not have imagined this,
a subdivision swelling up around him. Later that evening, I bring Celia
with me to Greenfield Assisted Living, where we enjoy some wine with Dot
and Colleen, in an apartment where Colleen's giant Manhattan Project
collage takes up an entire wall. Rosemary is still living with her husband,
John, in Maryland. Jane is in an assisted living facility in Tennessee. Kattie lives on her own in Scarboro and is the oldest member of her church.
Yes, she still cooks on her K-25 biscuit pans. Helen lives in her D house
and remains an ardent basketball fan, rarely missing a UT Volunteers
game. She started writing—by hand—her own book, detailing growing
up during the Depression. Her hands are now quite arthritic, which has
slowed her down considerably. Toni passed away during the writing of this
book, rather unexpectedly. The brief time I spent with her was filled with
as much laughing as note taking. I finish my weekend by visiting and dining with Beverly Puckett, Jane's daughter, and Virginia. Virginia tells me
over dinner that she is taking a class on the History of Transuranic Waste

at the Oak Ridge Institute for Continued Learning, her scientific mind still working hard at age 90.

In remembering his time in Oak Ridge as head psychiatrist, Dr. Eric Clarke later wrote that, "Those who survive Oak Ridge from its beginnings are better for the experience." I know I am better for knowing them.

As I drive away from Oak Ridge, I cross back over the Clinch, the sheer curtain of a pinkish-gray evening settling on its waters, no pearls sleeping in its beds. I leave my dinner with Virginia behind, thinking of her and other women's journeys across the river in a much different time during a very different war. I have no answers as I head east deeper into the secret-shrouded shadow of the mountains. I roll down the window and wash my hands in the clouds.

Notes

I cannot come close to expressing how challenging it was to decide which women I was going to feature most prominently in this book, and how difficult it was to leave the others on the cutting room floor (or in digital research folders, as it were). There were many interviews that I found extremely helpful in writing this book, even if the people who shared their stories with me were not featured in its pages. A list of primary individuals interviewed follows these notes.

Where not otherwise noted, information regarding Celia (Szapka) Klemski, Toni (Peters) Schmitt, Kattie Strickland, Jane (Greer) Puckett, Helen (Hall) Brown, Virginia (Spivey) Coleman, Dot (Jones) Wilkinson, Colleen (Rowan) Black, and Rosemary (Maiers) Lane comes from author interviews conducted between 2009 and 2012.

A note about dialogue: The use and/or creation of dialogue is based on either author interviews, oral histories, or meeting minutes.

A number of texts, original documents, and audio and video resources were consulted during the researching and writing of this book. In addition to the primary works cited here, a suggested "reading, watching, and listening" list is available at girlsofatomiccity.com.

Introduction, Cast of Characters
Description of the region from author's visits to the area, interviews with longtime residents, and from the "History and Architectural Resources of Oak Ridge, Tennessee" (National Register of Historic Places Multiple Property Documentation Form, National Park Service, US Department of the Interior, January 1987) and from "Report on Proposed Site for Plant Eastern Tennessee," Formerly Declassified Correspondence, 1942–1947; Records of the Atomic Energy Commission, Record Group 326, National Archives at Atlanta; National Archives and Records Administration.

More specific details regarding the arrival of the Manhattan Project to the East Tennessee area come from numerous sources and original documentation, many of which will be cited throughout the book. H. G. Wells's book *The World Set Free: A Story of Mankind* was originally published in 1914 (London: MacMillan). It is available in the public domain from the Project Gutenberg and other sources. The book eventually fascinated many scientists, including Manhattan Project physicist Leo Szilard, as mentioned in Richard Rhodes's *The Making of the Atomic Bomb* (New York: Simon & Schuster, 1986), among others. Wells's prediction of the atomic bomb is still referenced today, in places like *Wired* ("Rise of the Machines: Why We Keep Coming Back to H. G. Wells' Visions of a Dystopian Future," by Matthew Lasar, October 8, 2011). Chris Keim, who worked at Y-12 during the war and went on to be division director of technical information at Oak Ridge National Laboratory, shared a wonderful anecdote about Wells's book in his essay, "A Scientist and His Secrets" from *These Are Our Voices: The Story of Oak Ridge, 1942–1970* (Oak Ridge: Children's Museum of Oak Ridge, 1987). He and other scientists bought out all the copies of *The World Set Free* from a Berkeley, CA, bookstore until the store owner got curious about the popularity of the title. Military intelligence approached the shop owner, asked him to keep quiet, and then unsuccessfully tried to find out who had bought the books. On August 18, 1945, just 12 days after the Hiroshima bombing, *The Nation*'s Freda Kirchwey wrote a fantastic essay for that magazine, titled "When H. G. Wells Split the Atom." Wells died in 1946, just one year after the bombs he foresaw were used to end World War II. Information regarding code names: The origin of the word "tubealloy" or "tuballoy" comes from the "Tube Alloys" project, which was the code name the British used for their early work on the atomic bomb. Both "tubealloy" and "Tube Alloy" are also mentioned in several texts, including Rhodes (previously cited). Both spellings are also used in various memos and declassified material, and were used repeatedly by a variety of individuals interviewed by the author. I have chosen the spelling "tubealloy" as opposed to "tuballoy" to reflect the name's origin and its pronunciation (TOOB-uh-loy). 49 and 94 were for plutonium, as was "copper," though that presented some confusion. Both 49 and 94 can be found in various declassified materials and are referenced in *The Plutonium Story: The Journals of Professor Glenn T. Seaborg, 1939–1946*, by Glenn T. Seaborg, edited by Ronald L. Kathren, Jerry B. Gough, Gary T. Benefiel (Columbus: Battelle Press, 1994), and in *The Plutonium Files*, by Eileen Welsome (New York: Random House, 1995).

1. *Everything Will Be Taken Care Of:* Train to Nowhere, August 1943
I first met Celia Klemski through Colleen Black. The two still know each other after having crossed paths at Father Siener's mass during the war. I have interviewed Celia many times and have had the pleasure of just sitting in her living room on many occasions. Already in her early 90s when I first met her, she is fit, healthy, and lively, much like the young woman who jumped on a train with little to no information about where she was headed.

Description of Celia Klemski from author's visits, interviews, and historic photographs (courtesy of Celia Klemski). Descriptions of Shenandoah, Pennsylvania, from Celia Klemski and also George Ross Leighton's portrayal of the town in his essay "Shenandoah, Pennsylvania: Rise and Fall of an Anthracite Town," from his book *Five Cities: The Story of Their Youth and Old Age* (New York: Harper & Brothers, 1936). Stories of rations and scrap-metal drives from author interviews with men and women. I first learned of the remembrance flags featuring blue stars for loved ones who had served and gold stars for those who had passed away from Colleen Black. The Blue Star Mothers of America and Gold Star Mothers of America still exist today. The last Sunday of September is Gold Star Mother's Day. ("Blue Star Mothers of America," by Deborah Tainsh, www.military.com. October 17, 2006; "Proclamation 2196: Gold Star Mother's Day," *Code of Federal Regulations: The President*, Office of the Federal Register.) An image of both stars can be seen in the World War II poster ". . . Because Somebody Talked!" by Wesley, 1943 (Government Printing Office for the Office of War Information, NARA Still Picture Branch).

Information regarding the Manhattan Engineer District's first headquarters from Leslie M. Groves's *Now It Can Be Told: The Story of the Manhattan Project* (New York: Da Capo Press, 1962) and K. D. Nichols's *The Road to Trinity: A Personal Account of How America's Nuclear Policies Were Made* (New York: Morrow, 1987). Locations of Manhattan Project sites in the New York metropolitan area: *A Guide to Manhattan Project Sites in Manhattan*, by Cynthia C. Kelly and Robert S. Norris (Washington, DC: Atomic Heritage Foundation, 2008). Charles Vanden Bulck, disbursement officer and procurement manager for the Manhattan Project, Corps of Engineers (David Ray Smith, "Historically Speaking," *The Oak Ridger*, July 5, 2011.) Description of *Saturday Evening Post* cover from September 4, 1943, issue. Regas restaurant description from author interviews with Celia Klemski and others; also "Regas Closing After Nine Decades," by Carly Harrington, *Knoxville News Sentinel*, December 12, 2010; vintage postcards and photos. Moving of MED offices to Oak Ridge, from War Department memo dated 29 June 1943, "Moving

District Office to Oak Ridge, Tennessee," Formerly Declassified Correspondence, 1942–1947; Records of the Atomic Energy Commission, Record Group 326; National Archives at Atlanta; National Archives and Records Administration.

Author note: "All in the same boat" is possibly the most oft repeated phrase I heard while conducting interviews for this book, from both men and women.

Tubealloy: The Bohemian Grove to the Appalachian Hills, September 1942

Information on a Bohemian Grove meeting from both attendee Kenneth Nichols, who refers to the September 1942 meeting in his book (previously cited), and also Groves, Rhodes (previously cited), and Stephane Groueff's *Manhattan Project: The Untold Story of the Making of the Atomic Bomb* (Boston: Little, Brown, 1967). Additional information about the history and lore of the Bohemian Grove from "Masters of the Universe Go to Camp: Inside the Bohemian Grove," by Philip Weiss, *Spy Magazine*, November 1989; "The Truth About The Bohemian Grove," by Alexander Cockburn and Jeffrey St. Clair, *Counterpunch*, June 19, 2001; "Bohemian Tragedy," by Alex Shoumatoff, *Vanity Fair*, May 2009; "A Guide to the Bohemian Grove," by Julian Sancton, *Vanity Fair*, April 2009. "A Relative Advantage: Sociology of the San Francisco Bohemian Club," by Peter Martin Phillips, dissertation, University of California, Davis, 1994. Additional information on uranium procurement, Edgar Sengier, and the Union Minière du Haut Katanga mining holdings from *Road to Trinity*, previously cited, and Groueff (previously cited). *Road to Trinity* by Nichols (previously cited) and *Now it Can Be Told*. Reference to "fruit that scalds" from Tom Zoellner's *Uranium: War, Energy, and the Rock that Shaped the World* (New York: Penguin Books, 2009). McKellar anecdote from author interviews, also *Remembering the Manhattan Project: Perspectives on the Making of the Atomic Bomb and its Legacy*, edited by Cynthia C. Kelly (Hackensack: World Scientific Publishing, 2004), citing William Frist and J. Lee Annis Jr.'s *Tennessee Senators, 1911—2001: Portraits of Leadership in a Century of Change* (Lanham, MD: Madison Books, 1999).

Author note: Senator McKellar's story is one of the most popular associated with the site of Oak Ridge and is repeated to this day in articles and by word of mouth. Author personally feels it has been "enhanced" by time, considering that the initial estimated cost of the Manhattan Project in 1942 was not yet near $2 billion. Note: General Leslie Groves officially acquired the Tennessee site on September 19, 1942, still considered Oak Ridge's "birthday." Then-colonel Kenneth Nichols was not yet District Engineer at this meeting, but would become so in August of 1943. Information regarding early days of MED from Groves, Nichols, and *Atomic Energy for Military Purposes (The Smyth Report): The Official Report on the Development of the Atomic Bomb Under the Auspices of the United States Government*, by H. D. Smyth (York, PA: Maple Press, 1945).

2. Peaches and Pearls: The Taking of Site X, Fall 1942

I first met Toni Schmitt at the VJ Day celebration at the Oak Ridge Historical Preservation Association in August of 2010. She had an incredible energy, dazzling smile, and incredibly detailed memories. I first interviewed her on September 14, 2010, but unfortunately, she died while I was still working on this book. I had the pleasure of meeting her daughter, Kathy Schmitt Gomez, who shared some of her mother's additional documents and memories with me. These included a letter written by Toni's younger sister Joyce—"Dopey"—who wrote about the peach sales of their youth.

Description of Clinton from author visits and interviews. *"Everything's goin' in and nothin's comin' out . . ."* from multiple author interviews. Information about fish gigs from author visits to the Museum of Appalachia, Clinton, TN. Market Street, Clinton, and its role in the pearling industry from author visits to the site and interviews; also author visits to the Museum of Appalachia (previously cited), the historical marker erected by the State of Tennessee, Market Street, Clinton, TN. Information on the history of the Clinch River pearls and the effect of Norris Dam on those pearls also from *Natural Histories: Stories from the Tennessee Valley*, by Stephen Lyn Bales (Knoxville: University of Tennessee Press, 2007).

Description of and information pertaining to Manhattan Engineer District's (MED) original scouting of sites in East Tennessee from Nichols's essay "My Work In Oak Ridge," from *Voices* (previously cited); original document "Second Visit to T.V.A. Looking for Available War Plant Sites," July 13, 1942, Formerly Declassified Correspondence, 1942–1947; Records of the Atomic Energy Commission, Record Group 326; the National Archives at Atlanta; The National Archives and Records Administration; *A City is Born: The History of Oak Ridge Tennessee*, by Fred W. Ford and Fred C. Peitzch (Oak Ridge: Atomic Energy Commission, Oak Ridge Operations, 1961); Vincent C. Jones's *Manhattan: The Army and the Atomic Bomb* (Washington: Department of the Army, December 31, 1985).

Descriptions of eminent-domain seizures, including notifications, appraisals, displaced families, parcels, payments, and site clearing from *Road to Trinity, Now It Can Be Told*, and *A City is Born* (all previously cited); "A Nuclear Family: I've Seen It" (Y-12 Video Services, Y-12 National Security Complex, 2012); Peter Bacon Hales's *Atomic Spaces: Living on the Manhattan Project* (Urbana: University of Illinois Press, 1997); Charles W. Johnson and Charles O. Jackson's *City Behind a Fence: Oak Ridge, Tennessee 1942–1946* (Knoxville: University of Tennessee Press, 1981); Nichols descriptions of the Norris Dam and Tennessee Valley Authority from the Tennessee Valley Authority, www.tva.gov; relocation of families due to the dam from all of the above and *Tennessee's Dixie Highway: The Cline Postcards*, by Lisa R. Ramsay and Tammy L. Vaughn (Charleston: Arcadia Publishing, 2011).

Parlee Raby letter from document collection at the Y-12 National Security Complex New Hope Center History Center Exhibits, Oak Ridge, TN; stories of Van Gilder and John Rice Irwin from *Voices* (previously cited); John Rice Irwin's "Oak Ridge Displacement" (NARA, College Park: Archive Booklet 62, no date listed). Reference to children being sent home from school to tell their parents they had to move from author interviews and anecdote of Lester Fox shared by Ray Smith. Fox was skipping school when he was called into the Oliver Springs telephone bank and told to get the principal for an important call, which reportedly came from a senator. The principal returned and gathered all students together and told them to go home and tell their families they had to move. The government needed their land.

Stories of John Hendrix, "the Prophet," from *The Oak Ridge Story: The Saga of a People Who Share in History*, by George O. Robinson Jr. (Kingsport, TN: Southern Publishers, 1950); "John Hendrix and the Y-12 National Security Complex in Oak Ridge, Tennessee," by David Ray Smith, www.SmithDRay.net; *Back of Oak Ridge*, by Grace Raby Crawford, edited by David Ray Smith (Oak Ridge, TN: 2003).

Author's note: One of the spared structures, a stone house built just months prior to the land acquisition by an Owen Hackworth, is currently on the National Register of Historic Places stating that it served as housing for General Groves prior to the completion of the administration building and Guest House. Information on the Luther Brannon House from "History and Architectural Resources of Oak Ridge, Tennessee" (previously cited); "Brannon, Luther, House," from the National Register of Historic Places, National Park Service, US Department of the Interior. However, additional references to Groves having used this structure for lodging have not yet been found.

Information on peaches and their role in the region from author interviews with Toni Schmitt, personal papers of Kathy Schmitt Gomez, and "The Wheat Community," by Patricia A. Hope, in *Voices* (previously cited).

Rosie the Riveter and Geraldine (Hoff) Doyle information from "Geraldine Doyle, 86, dies; one-time factory worker inspired Rosie the Riveter and 'We Can Do it!' Poster," by T. Rees Shapiro, *Washington Post*, December 29, 2010; *Saturday Evening Post* (cover image May 29, 1943); *Norman Rockwell: My Adventures as an Illustrator* by Norman Rockwell and Thomas Rockwell (Garden City, NY: Doubleday, 1960). Information about James Edward "Ed" Westcott from author interviews and from *Through the Lens of Ed Westcott: A Photographic History of World War II's Secret City*, edited by Sam Yates (Knoxville: University of Tennessee, 2005).

Tubealloy: Ida and the Atom, 1934

"Ida Noddack: Proposer of Nuclear Fission," by Fathi Habashi, from *A Devotion to Their Science: Pioneer Women of Radioactivity*, by Marelene F. Rayner-Canham and Geoffrey Rayner-Canham (Quebec, Canada: McGill-Queens University Press; Philadelphia: Chemical Heritage Foundation, 1997); "Ida Noddack and the Missing Elements," by Fathi Habashi, *Education in Chemistry*, March 2009; "The Discovery of Nuclear Fission," by Emilio Segrè, *Physics Today*, vol. 42, July 1989. "Enrico Fermi—Biography," Nobelprize.org, June 10, 2012; "Possible Production of Elements of Atomic Number Higher than 92," by Prof. E. Fermi, *Nature*, pp. 898–899, June 16, 1934; "Über Das Element 93 (On Element 93)," by Ida Noddack, *Zeitschrift für Angewandte Chemie*, vol. 47, September 1934, p. 653.

3. Through the Gates: Clinton Engineer Works, Fall 1943

Interviews conducted with Kattie Strickland, Celia Klemski (previously cited), Toni Schmitt (previously cited), and Jane Puckett. Additional documentation (badges, invitations of work, telegrams) courtesy of the private papers of Celia Klemski and Jane Puckett. Repurposing of fencing from old farms from *Atomic Spaces* (previously cited).

I first met Kattie after interviewing her granddaughter Valeria Steele Roberson. Kattie is lively and friendly and very patient with repeated questions about what must have been a trying time in her life.

Jane Puckett is a force of nature, and still friends with Virginia Coleman and Rosemarie Waggener, another interviewee who is not featured in this book.

Author note: Many interviewees had tales of hacking and coughing dust. This particular anecdote about the "Oak Ridge croup" and orientation films comes from interviewee Joanne Gailar, and from her essay "Impressions of Early Oak Ridge," in *These Are Our Voices* (previously cited).

All *Oak Ridge Journal* clips as cited within text.

The constant shuffling and dividing of dorm rooms and the need for space comes from author interviews, notably with Celia Klemski and Colleen Black, *Road to Trinity, City is Born, City Behind a Fence,* and *Atomic Spaces* (all previously cited).

Relocation of MED headquarters to Tennessee from author interviews and Groves, Nichols, and Smyth (all previously cited).

Information regarding recruitment, including labor piracy and segregation, from Russell B. Olwell's *At Work in the Atomic City: A Labor and Social History of Oak Ridge, Tennessee* (Knoxville: University of Tennessee Press, 2004); *City Behind a Fence* and *Atomic Spaces* (previously cited); *Victory at Home: Manpower and Race in the American South During World War II*, by Charles D. Chamberlain (Athens, GA: University of Georgia Press, 2003); Challenges in recruitment and need for workers from *Road to Trinity, Atomic Spaces, At Work in the Atomic City, City Behind a Fence*, and *Now it Can Be Told* (all previously cited), and *The Manhattan Project: Making the Atomic Bomb*, F. G. Gosling (Washington, DC: US Department of Energy, 2005).

Dedication of the Chapel on the Hill from *City Behind a Fence* (previously cited).

SED description from interviews with William Tewes, Colleen Black, and "Scientists in Uniform: The Special Engineer Detachment" (Los Alamos National Security, LLC, U.S. 2010–2011); "Special Engineer Detachment" (Y-12 National Security Complex, US Department of Energy); "The Unsung Heroes of the Manhattan Project," by Beverly Majors, *The Oak Ridger*, December 27, 2010. Executive Order 8802: "Prohibition of Discrimination in the Defense Industry" was issued by President Roosevelt. Executive Order 8802 dated June 25, 1941, General Records of the United States Government; Record Group 11; National Archives.

Description of black hutment area from author interviews with Kattie Strickland, Valeria Steele Roberson, also *Atomic Spaces, City Behind a Fence* (previously cited). Regarding J. Ernest Wilkins Jr.: Letter from Edward Teller to Harold Urey, dated September 18, 1944. Formerly Declassified Correspondence, 1942–1947; Records of the Committee on Fair Employment Practice, Record Group 228; National Archives at Atlanta; National Archives and Records Administration.

Additional information about Christmas toy rations from *It's a Wonderful Christmas: The Best of the Holidays 1940–1954*, by Susan Waggoner (New York: Stewart, Tabori & Chang, 2004); and the Lionel Corporation.

Tubealloy: Lise and Fission, 1938

There are two comprehensive biographies of Lise Meitner: *Lise Meitner: A Life in Physics*, by Ruth Lewis Sime (Berkeley and Los Angeles: University of California Press, 1996); *Lise Meitner and the Dawn of the Nuclear Age*, by Patricia Rife (Boston: Birkhauser, 1999). Also "Looking Back," by Lise Meitner, *Bulletin of the Atomic Scientists*, November 1964; "A Nobel tale of wartime injustice," by Elisabeth Crawford, Ruth Lewin Sime, and Mark Walker, *Nature*, vol. 382, August 1, 1996. Meitner's excursion with her nephew is described in Rhodes (previously cited), and *The Uranium People*, by Leona Marshall Libby (New York: Crane, Russak. Charles Scribner's Sons, 1979).

Information regarding Hahn's dismissal of Noddack's theory from *Proposer of Nuclear Fission* and *Devotion to Their Science* (both previously cited). Hahn and Strassmann's paper: "Concerning the Existence of Alkaline Earth Metals Resulting from Neutron Irradiation of Uranium," O. Hahn and F. Strassmann, *Naturwissenschaften*, Jan. 1939, vol. 27, p. 11. Meitner and Frisch's paper: "Disintegration of Uranium by Neutrons: A New Type of Nuclear Reaction," Lise Meitner and Otto R. Frisch, *Nature*, Feb. 11, 1939, 143, 239–240. Information regarding Leo Szilard, Eugene Wigner, Albert Einstein and letter to Roosevelt from Groves, Nichols, and many others. This letter, from Einstein to President Roosevelt, is widely considered to be the crucial piece of correspondence that started the United States research into atomic weapons. Evolution of Manhattan Project names and designations and funding from Smyth and Jones (both previously cited).

4. Bull Pens and Creeps: The Project's Welcome for New Employees

I met Virginia Coleman through Bobbie Martin, an active member of the Oak Ridge Heritage and Preservation Association (ORHPA). I took to her immediately and was moved by both her brilliance and kindness. She opened her home to me, gave her time to me. I am constantly amazed when I hear of the latest class she's taking, often science-based and intimidating to people who are a third her age.

Information regarding the "bull pen" comes from author interviews and "Manhattan Project Autobiography," by John Googin, *For Your Information*, vol. 6, Issue 1 (Oak Ridge: Y-12 Pride in Development, April 1994). Resident Handbook courtesy of personal papers of Jane Puckett.

Information regarding background checks from Groves, Nichols, *At Work*, and *City Behind a Fence* previously cited. Locksmith anecdote and admonition for asking questions during training from "A Scientist and his Secrets" (Keim, previously cited).

Training questions and vague consequences from author interviews and Gailar (previously cited).

I first met Dot in the lobby of Greenfield Retirement in Oak Ridge, the same day I met Colleen. Dot is hilarious and has a tremendous self-deprecating sense of humor about both her upbringing and her time at Oak Ridge. Evenings spent with her and Colleen have been some of my favorites.

Helen, too, was one of the earlier women I interviewed. She has a dry, no-nonsense sense of humor and a scrapbook full of photos of her in her basketball uniform and news articles from her many games.

Information about ACME insurance Company envelopes from author interviews, notably William J. Wilcox Jr.

Tubealloy: Leona and Success in Chicago, December 1942

Information regarding the party at the Fermi home, the day of the reaction, past information about the Fermi family, and Leona Woods from *The Uranium People* (previously cited), and *Atoms in the Family: My Life With Enrico Fermi*, by Laura Fermi (Chicago: University of Chicago Press, 1954). There are numerous descriptions of the events of December 2, 1942, and most books already cited here include descriptions and were consulted.

For descriptions of the size and scope of CP-1 from "Piglet and the Pumpkin Field," Argonne National Laboratory, US Department of Energy, http://www.ne.anl.gov/About/legacy/piglet.shtml; "The First Reactor" (Washington, DC: US Department of Energy, December 1982); and from *Making of the Atomic Bomb* (previously cited). Description of Leona Woods's contribution to the pile from *Uranium People*. Fermi description of fission from *The Manhattan Project: The Birth of the Atomic Bomb in the Words of Its Creators, Eyewitnesses, and Historians*, edited by Cynthia C. Kelly (New York: Black Dog & Leventhal, 2007).

5. Only Temporary: Spring into Summer, 1944

I first met Colleen in the lobby of Greenfield Retirement Living. I was there with Ray Smith, who had brought me to meet former Y-12 Supervisor Connie Bolling, who passed away not long after our interview. When we met, Colleen was wearing a blinking Christmas light necklace. She is dynamic and nonstop.

Colleen and others provide recipes—one which she got that very day on line at the shower—in *Cooking Behind the Fence: Recipes and Recollections from the Oak Ridge '43 Club,* Cookbook Chairman, Colleen Black (Oak Ridge: Oak Ridge Heritage & Preservation Association, 5th edition, 2009). If you were a decent shot, squirrels made for a quick meal in those days of meat rations. Four legs and two back pieces got a quick dredging in flour, salt, and pepper. Brown the lot in a cast-iron pan with a touch of shortening. Maybe make a little gravy from the drippings.

Description of Happy Valley from author interviews, predominantly with Colleen Black, also "Oak Ridge's Lost City," by William J. Wilcox Jr. Location and layout of Clinton Engineer Works as a whole, and Townsite specifically, including maps, construction progress, and contractual relations with Stone & Webster and Skidmore, Owings, and Merrill, and the Pierce Foundation from the Department of Energy's *The Manhattan Project* (previously cited). Construction and planning of the Clinton Engineer Works from Groves, Nichols, Rhodes, US Department of Energy, Hales, and Johnson/Jackson (all previously cited).

Certificate of Availability program (sometimes referred to as Statement of Availability) information from author interviews with Colleen Black, and *Code of Federal Regulations of the United States of America: 1944 Supplement, Titles 11–32,* by Office of the Federal Register (Washington, DC: US Government Printing Office).

Regarding phone calls: Colleen told a very funny story about visiting the home of a woman privileged to have her own phone. She had taken to hiding her phone under a small cardboard box to avoid constant requests from neighbors and friends to use it. During Colleen's visit, the phone rang.

And rang.

And rang.

The hostess tried in vain to ignore the sound until finally, one of the other guests chirped, "Your box is ringing."

Demand for workers, War Power Commission demands, and worker turnover rates from *At Work in the Atomic City, Atomic Spaces,* and *City Behind a Fence.* Information on the Brown-Patterson Agreement and International Brotherhood of Electrical Workers is from Groves, Jones, and Hales (all previously cited). Description of housing—all, including trailers, barracks, dorms, and homes—from author interviews, and *Early Oak Ridge Housing: Photographs, Floor Plans and General Descriptions* (no date), Robinson, and *City Behind a Fence* (both previously cited). Information on services, including laundry, is from author interviews, *Resident Handbook* (previously cited),

Robinson, and *City Behind a Fence.* Information on Roane-Anderson from author interviews, Groves, Nichols, *City Behind a Fence*, Hales, and Robinson (all previously cited).

Dr. Eric Kent Clarke's perspectives from "Report on Existing Psychiatric Facilities and Suggested Necessary Addition," Dr. Eric Kent Clarke, chief psychiatrist, Formerly Declassified Correspondence, 1942–1947; Records of the Atomic Energy Commission, Record Group 326; National Archives at Atlanta: National Archives and Records Administration.

Negro Village information from author interviews and *City Behind a Fence*, *At Work in the Atomic City*, and *Atomic Spaces*, all previously cited. Treatment of black residents and complaints of mistreatment from Formerly Declassified Correspondence, 1942–1947; Records of the Committee on Fair Employment Practice, Record Group 228; National Archives at Atlanta; National Archives and Records Administration. Anecdote about "good girls" and "bad girls" from Nichols (previously cited).

Tubealloy: The Quest for Product

Sources of uranium from Nichols and Groves, previously cited. Regarding Eldorado, Mallinckrodt, Westinghouse, Ames, and Harshaw, from Smyth Report, Groves and Nichols (previously cited), from Office of Legacy Management, United States Department of Energy. Letter from United States Atomic Energy Commission from Glenn Seaborg, chairman, to Mr. Harold E. Thayer, president, Mallinckrodt Chemical Works, from "Mallinckrodt Chemical works: The Uranium Story," collection, The Manhattan Project Heritage Preservation Association, Inc. http://www.mphpa.org/classic/CP/Mallinckrodt/Pages/MALK_Gal lery_01.htm, last accessed June 2012. Regarding Harshaw, from "Nuclear Fallout in Cleveland," by James Renner, *The Independent*, March 3, 2010. Additional companies involved in the processing of various uranium compounds at different stages include Metal Hydrides Co., Electromet, Linde, DuPont, ALCOA, and others, via Smyth and Groves (previously cited).

Description of various incarnations of uranium from author interviews, notably with William J. Wilcox Jr., also the Smyth Report (previously cited). Descriptions of sites, their purposes, construction timetables from Groves, Nichols, Rhodes (all previously cited); "An Overview of the History of Y-12: 1942–1992: A Chronology of Some Noteworthy Events and Memoirs" (The Secret City Store, 2001); "The Role of Oak Ridge in the Manhattan Project," by William J. Wilcox Jr. (Oak Ridge: 2002); "K-25: A Brief History of the Manhattan Project's 'Biggest' Secret," by William J. Wilcox Jr. (Oak Ridge, 2011).

Information regarding uranium slugs and the Aluminum Company of America from "A Short History of Oak Ridge National Laboratory (1943–1993)," by the Office of Science, Oak Ridge National Lab Laboratory, US Department of Energy; http://www.ornl.gov/info/swords/swords.shtml, last accessed June 2012.

Status of Project, expenses, and construction timetable from Nichols and Groves (previously cited), and description of K-25 from Nichols, Groves, and Wilcox. Information regarding gaseous diffusion process and difficulties with barrier material from Groves. The path of the uranium through the K-25 structure, according to Wilcox: Uranium started in the Feed Building and was pumped first into the east wing of the U-shaped structure.

Information regarding electromagnetic separation process and Ernest Lawrence from author interviews, the Smyth Report, Wilcox, Smithsonian Institution Archives, Record Unit 9531, Nichols, Groves, Groueff, Rhodes, and Googin. Code names for various compounds from author interviews, Smithsonian, and Googin (previously cited). Additional information regarding uranium recovery from the calutrons via Groves, Nichols, and Wilcox. Bill Wilcox walked me through this process, and Jane Puckett's notes helped as well. Uranium was recovered from the boxes by washing with a nitric acid solution. It then had to be extracted from the poisonous, acidic blue-green solution, then put through the chemical paces to turn it into uranium tetrachloride (UC14) for the Beta process. It was eventually oxidized into UO4 (which looks a lot like cheesecake), then 723 (UO3, a yellowish powder); then eventually chlorine found its way back into the recipe. This resulted initially in 745 (UC15), and then after sublimation—going from solid to gas without passing through a pesky liquid phase, like dry ice in a Halloween punch—the uranium was UC14 again. This, in time for round two, the Beta process.

Purchasing of silver from US Treasury from author interviews, Nichols, Groves, and *Making the Atomic Bomb*, by the DOE (previously cited), Rhodes, and "14,700 tons of silver at Y-12," by the Y-12 National Security Complex, US Department of Energy. As the calutrons were taken out of commission and dismantled, the silver borrowed from the U.S. Treasury was returned bit by bit to the government, with the final repayment arriving in 1970. Only about four hundredths of 1 percent was missing. Cameron Reed's article "From Treasury Vault to the Manhattan Project," in the January-February 2011 issue of *American Scientist* offers a detailed look at the story of Oak Ridge's silver. Information regarding Tennessee Eastman and lack of workers from Nichols, Groves, Wilcox, and *Making the Atomic Bomb* (DOE). Doubling of Y-12, shutting down of Y-12 in 1943, increased estimates of

U-235 needed for the bomb, catering anecdote from Groves. Board feet used for Y-12 from *Making the Atomic Bomb*, DOE (previously cited). Information regarding naming plants from Letter to Gus Robinson from Leslie Groves, dated October 14, 1949, Formerly Declassified Correspondence, 1942–1947; Records of the Atomic Energy Commission, Record Group 326; National Archives at Atlanta; National Archives and Records Administration.

Background information on Evelyn Handcock Ferguson and Harold Kingsley Ferguson from "Ferguson Builds War Plants Fast," by the Associated Press, as seen in *Charleston News and Courier*, November 22, 1942; "Rites Tomorrow for H. K. Ferguson," *Cleveland Plain Dealer*, December 10, 1943. Information regarding Phil Abelson and decision to pursue liquid thermal diffusion from Groves, and *Making the Atomic Bomb* (DOE). Information regarding meeting between Evelyn Ferguson and Groves from Groves, Smyth, and Groueff.

6. To Work

Y-12 contest information and efficiency of female workers from author interviews and Nichols (previously cited).

Description of roles of women workers, PSQs, workplace activity from author interviews. Y-12 information, including bus fare and rates, from author interviews, *Oak Ridge Journal*, Robinson and Googin. Additional information regarding commuting times for cubicle operators to Y-12 from George Akin's paper "Eastman at Oak Ridge," published in 1981 and found in box 7, folder 27 of the "Club" collection in the Department of Rare Books, Special Collections and Preservation at the University of Rochester. Anecdotes regarding buses from author interviews. Description of badges and guards from author interviews, *City Behind a Fence, At Work in the Atomic City*, and Robinson. Changing house information from author interviews. Description of cubicle control rooms from author interviews, photographs by Ed Westcott (NARA Still Pictures Division, Washington, DC), and *At Work in the Atomic City*. Number of women in control room and description of panels from author interviews, photographs by Ed Westcott (previously cited), author visits to Y-12, cubicle exhibit, American Museum of Science and Energy (Oak Ridge), Smithsonian Oral Histories (previously cited).

Description of Es, Qs, Rs, etc. from author interviews, Googin, Smithsonian (previously cited), papers of Jane Puckett, "Lawrence and His Laboratory: A Historian's View of the Lawrence Years, Episode 2: The Calutron," by J. L. Heilbron, Robert W. Seidel, and Bruce R. Wheaton, *Newsmagazine*, Lawrence Berkeley National Laboratory, US Department of Energy, 1981.

Information about cleaning out of E boxes from author interviews with Wilcox; yellowcake from Virginia Coleman. Anecdote regarding *Mellor's Handbook of Inorganic Chemistry* from Googin. Codes from author interviews, Smithsonian, and Googin. Information regarding preparation 38 from *Heavy Water and the Wartime Race for Nuclear Energy*, by Per F. Dahl (London: Institute of Physics, 1999). Number of buildings in Y-12 complex from Rhodes.

Information regarding calculators from author interviews, notably Jane Puckett. Description of Jane's process notes, job description, pay rate and titles from personal papers of Jane Puckett.

Information regarding Clock Alley from author interviews, *At Work in the Atomic City*, and *Atomic Spaces*.

Author note: I have read in several places that Clock Alleys were segregated. However, Kattie clearly remembers being on line to clock in with both white and black workers. Work song from interview with Kattie Strickland and from *Negro Work Songs and Calls*, edited by B. A. Botkin (Washington, DC: Archive of Folk Song, Folk Music of the United States, Music Division, Recording Laboratory AFS L8, Library of Congress). Information regarding transfer of train personnel at Reservation boundary from Robinson.

K-25 pipe conditioning information from author interviews with Colleen Black. Description of the floor from author interviews and photographs by Ed Westcott (previously cited). Glyptal information from author interview and Glyptal/General Electric magazine ad (1943).

The gas that Colleen's probe was emitting was helium, though she did not know that, and the gauge she was eyeing was that of a mass spectrometer, which she also did not know at the time.

Jellico train wreck information from author interviews and *Troop Train Wreck*, by David Ray Smith (Oak Ridge: September 2007); "Death Toll in Troop Train Wreck Reaches 33," *Kingsport Times*, July 9, 1944; "Troop Train Wreck Toll Set at 40," Associated Press, *Milwaukee Sentinel*, July 8, 1944. Details regarding deaths per month from memo titled "Number of Deaths at the Oak Ridge Hospital" and dated September 20, 1944, from Formerly Declassified Correspondence, 1942–1947; Records of the Atomic Energy Commission, Record Group 326, National Archives at Atlanta; National Archives and Records Administration.

Tubealloy: The Couriers

Description of courier route from Rhodes, Groueff. Information regarding container and form of contents from author interviews, notably with David Ray Smith and Wilcox. Contents as well as silo also described in Rhodes.

First shipment quality from Groves and Y-12 production specifics from Groves. Y-12 shipping receipts from Formerly Declassified Correspondence, 1942–1947; Records of the Atomic Energy Commission, Record Group 326; National Archives at Atlanta; National Archives and Records Administration.

Description of courier travel and route from author interviews, also Rhodes, Groueff, and *The New World: A History of the United States Atomic Energy Commission, vol. I, 1939–1946*, by Richard G. Hewlett and Oscar E. Anderson Jr. (University Park: Pennsylvania State University Press, 1962); and "Operations and shipments begin," from Y-12 National Security Complex, US Department of Energy.

7. Rhythms of Life

Descriptions of Roane-Anderson meeting of December 1943 and the need for recreation, especially among young women, from Clarke and *Spaces* (previously cited), also "Minutes of Meeting of Executive Committee, Recreation and Welfare Association, Held at Town Hall, Oak Ridge, Tennessee, 12/31/43, at 2:00 PM," memo from the War Department, US States Engineer Office, dated January 4, 1944. State of mind of housewives from author interviews, notably Rosemary Lane. Lists of activities from Robinson, *Oak Ridge Journal*, and author interviews. Information regarding Waldo Cohn, from author interviews, also "the Symphony Orchestra," by June Adamson, from *Voices* (previously cited).

Information regarding dances from author interviews, *Oak Ridge Journal* (as cited within text). "Parachute dresses" seen online and on exhibit at the Behring Center of the Smithsonian, National Museum of American History, Washington, DC.

Average age of Oak Ridge from author interviews and "New High School in '51 Talk of the Town—and state," by D. Ray Smith, *Oak Ridger*, August 11, 2008. Regarding "Where are you from": Colleen loves to sing "Where are you from, Mr. Oak Ridger?" which was from the musical "A Thousand Suns," written by Betty Clayton Osborn on the occasion of Oak Ridge's 25th anniversary.

Author note: Virtually everyone I interviewed described going on "dates" to the cafeteria. Chapel on the Hill schedules from *Oak Ridge Journal*. Reference to Methodist church at movie theater from Robinson. Story of kicking bottles out of the way to have services in the rec hall from Viola Lockhart Warren Papers (Collection 1322). Department of Special Collections, Charles E. Young Research Library, University of California, Los Angeles. Number of church groups from Robinson.

Happy Valley recreation description from author interviews, notably with Helen Jernigan, also "Happy Valley," by Helen C. Jernigan, in *Voices*. 3.2 percent beer ad from Brewing Industry Foundation "The American Soldier and Sobriety," *Life* magazine, April, 19, 1943. Tales of bribing gate guards and hoarding of booze from author interviews, notably Paul Wilkinson, Toni Schmitt, and *Please God, US First*, by John C. Pennock (Charlottetown: TWiG Publications, 2003). Hiding contraband booze and how to make fake wine from author interviews. Swimming pool statistics from Oak Ridge Visitor Center and "History and Architectural Resources of Oak Ridge, Tennessee" (previously cited).

Segregated recreation information from *At Work in the Atomic City, Atomic Spaces, City Behind a Fence*, and author interviews, notably with Valeria Steele Roberson and Kattie Strickland. Also "A New Hope," by Valeria Steele, from *Voices* (previously cited). Hal Williams information from "Scarboro: The Early Days" exhibit at Scarboro Community Center, Oak Ridge, Tennessee; "A Tribute to Hal Williams," by Rose Weaver, *Oak Ridger*, February 9, 2010. Colored Camp Council meeting from *City Behind a Fence*.

Tensions with Knoxville inhabitants from author interviews. Bacon Hosiery Mills information from *City Behind a Fence*.

Tubealloy: Security, Censorship, and the Press

Information about the Met Lab meeting from "Behind the Decision to Use the Atomic Bomb: Chicago 1944–45," by Alice Kimball Smith, *Bulletin of the Atomic Scientists*, October 1958. Information on compartmentalization and "sticking to knitting" from Groves.

Censorship information and War Department Counterintelligence Unit information from Groves and Robinson. Approach to screening and hiring from Groves and from *An Exceptional Man for Exceptional Challenges: Stafford L. Warren*, vol. 1. Interviewed by Adelaide Tusler. Oral History Program, University of California at Los Angeles, Regents of the University of California, 1983.

Presidential Executive Order from "Franklin D. Roosevelt: 'Executive Order 8985. Establishing the Office of Censorship,' December 19, 1941." Courtesy of Gerhard Peters and John T. Woolley, The American Presidency Project, http://www.presidency.ucsb.edu/ws/?pid=16068, last accessed June 2012.

U.S. Government Office of Censorship. "Code of Wartime Practices: For American Broadcasters" (Washington: United States Government Printing Office, 1942). June 15, 1942 ed. by Clarence W. Griffin Papers, North Carolina State Archives, Raleigh, NC.

Additional information about censorship, including the June 28, 1943, memo and Mutual Broadcasting Company from Robinson (previously cited).

8. The One about the Fireflies . . .

All jokes included in this chapter were told to the author throughout the researching of this book. There are many, many more . . .

Women's stories from author interviews.

Information about the newspaper, vis-à-vis Francis Gates stories from "From Bulletin to Broadside," by June Adamson from *Voices* (previously cited).

Additional information regarding Celia's brother Clem from official military record of Clement P. Szapka, NARA office of Military Personnel Records, National Personnel Records Center, St. Louis, MO. Censoring of letters was a common occurrence based on author interviews, including Celia Klemski and Helen Hall.

Use of incomplete ideas to increase rumors from author interviews, notably Joanne Gailar. Information regarding Superman censorship from Robinson and "Fatal Fiction: A Weapon to End All Wars," by H. Bruce Franklin, *Bulletin of the Atomic Scientists*, Nov. 1989.

Jim Ramsey, longtime resident of Oak Ridge and son of one of the "oldtimers," said that native Gullah speakers from the Low Country of South Carolina were also hired to empty garbage, ostensibly because of their limited reading skills. Propaganda images from photographs taken by Ed Westcott (previously cited). While visiting with Ed Westcott at his home, I noticed the Norman Rockwell calendar he had in his kitchen. Many of Westcott's pictures had that "Rockwell" feel to them, and some were staged as well. The juxtaposition of lines at the butcher shop and comic book sales with the fences, guards, and towering industry have always struck me as interesting, and I find this one of the more engaging aspects of Westcott's work. Additional information on "creeps" and informants from author interviews, also predominantly Groves, as well as *City Behind a Fence* and Hales. June 14, 1944, memo and seditious dismissals from *Spaces*. Additional information about guard harassment in the black hutment area from Formerly Declassified Correspondence, 1942–1947; Records of the Committee on Fair Employment Practice, Record Group 228; National Archives at Atlanta; National Archives and Records Administration.

Tubealloy: Pumpkins, Spies, and Chicken Soup, Fall 1944

Kramish story from "Hiroshima's First Victims," by Arnold Kramish, *The Rocky Mountain News*, August 6, 1995. Kramish described uranium as a "bone-seeker" and suffered for many years as a result of his accident. Tibbets information from Groves and from "Wendover's Atomic Secret," by Carl Posey, *Air & Space Magazine*, March 2011.

List of Project scientists from Groves, Rhodes, and Smyth. Difficulty of checking background on academic scientists and comments on Communism from Groves. Oppenheimer information from Groves and also *American Prometheus: The Triumph and Tragedy of J. Robert Oppenheimer*, by Kai Bird and Martin J. Sherwin (New York: Alfred A. Knopf, 2005).

Niels Bohr anecdote from *The Manhattan Project*, Kelly (previously cited). Information about David Greenglass, including code name, from memos dated September 21, 1944 and November 14, 1944, from VENONA program records of the US Army Signal Intelligence Service (now the National Security Agency) and from "The Atom Spy Case," by the Federal Bureau of Investigation, and *The Brother: The Untold Story of the Rosenberg Case*, by Sam Roberts (New York: Random House, 2001).

9. The Unspoken: Sweethearts and Secrets

Jane's stapler box message courtesy of author interviews and personal papers of Jane Puckett. Story regarding "ocean paint" from *Cooking Behind the Fence* (previously cited); urine story from author interviews; molasses story from "Citizens of Oak Ridge describe Life in the Secret City during World War II," by Frank Munger, *Knoxville News Sentinel*, August 7, 2005, http://www.knoxnews.com/news/2005/aug/07/citizens-of-oak-ridge-describe-life-in-the-city/, last accessed June 2012.

Information regarding Bill Pollock and the Pollock Wired Music System from "Bill Pollock . . . Music Man," by June M. Boone, from *Voices*, and *61-11 & Olio*, by Charles R. Schmitt (Oak Ridge: C&D Desktop Publishing and Printing Company, 1995).

"Sleepy Time Gal": music by Ange Lorenzo, Raymond B. Egan, words by Joseph R. Alden, Richard A. Whiting. Copyright EMI Music Publishing.

Vi and Stafford Warren story from Stafford Warren oral history and Viola Lockhart Warren papers (previously cited).

ACME Insurance Company information from author interviews. Story of clandestine coffee klatsch being busted from *Cooking Behind the Fence* (previously cited).

Dr. Clarke's perspectives from "Report on Existing Psychiatric Facilities and Suggested Necessary Additions," as cited in text (1944) from NARA Southeast, RG 326; "Psychiatric Problems at Oak Ridge," by Eric Kent Clarke, *American Journal of Psychiatry*, Jan 1, 1946, vol. 102, p. 437–444.

Tubealloy: Combining Efforts in the New Year
Progress on Y-12 from Groves and Nichols.

Information regarding Truman not seeking nomination as vice presidential candidate from Senate Historical Office, US Senate, Hart Senate Office Building, Washington, DC. Henry Wallace was reportedly not a desirable vice presidential candidate in the eyes of a growing faction of the Democratic Party, who viewed him as having too many eccentricities and Russian connections, among them mystic and philosopher Nicholas Roerich, whom Wallace referred to in his letters as "guru."

Idea to run the plants in tandem from Nichols, Groves, Jones, and DOE (all previously cited).

Mark Fox information from Nichols. Decision to build K-27, and Groves-Nichols New York City meeting from Nichols.

10. Curiosity and Silence
Information regarding psychiatric patient from author interviews, notably Rosemary Lane and Lois Mallet; also from "Psychiatric Problems at Oak Ridge," Clarke (previously cited); "Psychiatry on a Shoestring," by Eric Kent Clarke, ed. by Amy Wolfe, from *Voices* (previously cited); Oak Ridge Hospital memo from Carl A. Whitaker to Maj. Charles E. Rea, regarding conversion of apartment at 207 Tennessee Avenue and state of the patient, dated February 9, 1945; memo from Charles E. Rea to Col. Stafford L. Warren, chief, Medical Section, subject: "Care of Ensign Justin Hugh Allen," regarding apartment conversion, nurse care, and ordering of shock therapy machine, dated February 8, 1945; all from Formerly Declassified Correspondence, 1942–1947; Records of the Atomic Energy Commission, Record Group 326; National Archives at Atlanta; National Archives and Records Administration. Information regarding the "occasional homosexual gang" from "Psychiatric Problems at Oak Ridge," Clarke (previously cited). Information regarding electroshock therapy from *Pushbutton Psychiatry: A Cultural History of Electroshock in America*, by Timothy W. Kneeland and Carol A. B. Warren (Walnut Creek, CA: Left Coast Press, 2002); "A Science Odyssey: People and Discoveries—Electroshock therapy introduced, 1938" (WGBH, 1998), http://www.pbs.org/wgbh/aso/databank/entries/dh38el.html, last accessed June 2012; "Neuropsychiatry in World War II," Office of Medical History, U. S. Army Medical Department, http://history.amedd.army.mil/booksdocs/wwii/NeuropsychiatryinWW IIVolI/chapter10.htm, last accessed June 2012.

K-25 start-up from Nichols, Groves, and Wilcox. Steam plant information from Robinson and Wilcox.

Tubealloy: The Project's Crucial Spring

Status of Y-12, K-25, and S-50 production from Nichols, Groves, and Wilcox. Concept of cost and redundancy of plants and sites from Nichols. Cost of Y-12 from Wilcox. Electrocution shock at Y-12 story from author interview and from video interview of Agnes Houser (Y-12 National Security Complex, Oral History video).

Regarding courier travel and treatment: Stafford Warren oral history (previously cited). Courier health memo from Friedell: Formerly Declassified Correspondence, 1942–1947; Records of the Atomic Energy Commission, Record Group 326; National Archives at Atlanta; National Archives and Records Administration. Memos regarding physiological hazards, tracer experiments, method of administration, from US Department of Energy, including "Physiological Hazards of Working with Plutonium"; "Memo to members of the advisory committee on human radiation experiments, Oct. 18, 1994"; also *Final Report Advisory Committee on Human Radiation Experiments* (New York, Oxford: Oxford University Press, 1996).

11. Innocence Lost

Information regarding Ebb Cade's case from: ACHRE Report, Part II, Chapter 5: The Manhattan District Experiments. Department of Energy, http://www.hss.doe.gov/healthsafety/ohre/roadmap/achre/chap5; sf2.html; Memorandum Report, Atomic Energy Commission, Jon D. Anderson, director, Division of Inspection, July 15, 1974; memorandum, "Shipping of Specimens," from Hymer L. Friedell to commanding officer, Santa Fe Area, April 16, 1945, Formerly Declassified Correspondence, 1942–1947; Records of the Atomic Energy Commission, Record Group 326; National Archives at Atlanta; National Archives and Records Administration; *Plutonium Files* (previously cited), "Human Radiation Studies: Remembering the Early Years: Oral History of Healthy Physicist Karl Z. Morgan, PhD." Conducted January 7, 1995 (US Department of Energy, Office of Human Radiation Experiements, June 1995).

Morgan's oral history regarding Cade is quite stunning. More here:

YUFFEE: You knew that the injection was going to take place prior to it?
MORGAN: No.
YUFFEE: Do you know who performed the injections?
MORGAN: No. Do you want me to tell you what I know about it?
CAPUTO: Sure.
MORGAN: Bob Stone—the associate director [for Health] under
   Compton—had his office next to mine at X-10. One morning, he

came in all excited and upset. You will have to put this in context of the time and the location that we were in. We were in the South, and it's no reflection on the African Americans, but they were called "[racial epithet]." I'm only telling you as I recall; my memory is far from perfect.

As I recall, he said, "Karl, you remember that [racial epithet] truck driver that had this accident sometime ago?" I said "Yes," I knew about it. He said, "Well, he was rushed to the military hospital in Oak Ridge and he had multiple fractures. Almost all of his bones were broken, and we were surprised he was alive when he got to the hospital; we did not expect him to be alive the next morning. So this was an opportunity we've been waiting for. We gave him large doses by injection of plutonium -239."

Of course, when you say "-239," it has some [plutonium] -238 and -240 mixed in, but [it is] primarily -239. [For security reasons, the word "plutonium" was never used in 1943–44. Stone continued] "We were anticipating collecting not just the urine and feces but a number of tissues, such as the skeleton, the liver, and other organs of the body. But this morning, when the nurse went in his room, he was gone. We have no idea what happened, where he is, but we've lost the valuable data that we were expected to get." I had not even heard of the experiment. I learned later that Stafford Warren and Hymer Friedell and the others apparently knew about the study, but my project was primarily with physics not with medical or biological studies. So this was the first I heard of the situation.

I heard nothing more about this till some years later. I happened to see a little notice in the Knoxville paper, the *News-Sentinel*, stating that this man, "a black man"—our society had evolved a little more at that time—had died someplace in eastern North Carolina, as I recall they must have given enough information that I could tie it in with the same fellow. Then I heard nothing about it till recently. Only recently, more recently in the past few weeks, I have heard the name of the fellow and more information about his family, etc.

CAPUTO: Who would have had the authority to provide the plutonium for the experiment?

MORGAN: Who would have the authority? That's a good question. In spite of our security, in some ways it was provided in a very ridiculous manner. I think I could have gotten all the plutonium that could be provided for anything I wanted to do, if it could be spared. Joe Hamilton got a dribbling amount to supplement his studies that he had done with plutonium -238, [which] he had gotten from the accelerator. I'm sure, confident, that if I'd put the request in, I could have gotten it. But, I suppose, all I would have had to do is walk in Martin Whittaker's office and say, "Martin, we want to do this experiment. We need so many, two or three microcuries." He would have provided it.

CAPUTO: So Martin Whittaker decided, since there was such a little amount of plutonium [available at that time], what had priority—

MORGAN:—In that period, it was very informal. We knew that we had to follow very stringent restrictions to prevent useful information from getting out. You have to keep in mind that during the first several months—this was in the early period [of the Manhattan Project]—health physicists, seniors [like me], were primarily physicists, and the doctors and surgeons were primarily doctors and surgeons, not people working with plutonium. So with all of us, we did the best we knew how, and I think we did a tremendously good job considering our background, and what we were trying to do, and what our major job was.

I don't think it would be any problem in getting the plutonium. Probably—my guess would be that Hymer Friedell or Stafford [Warren] were brought intimately into the earlier stages of [this study]. I say that without any great knowledge, but only because I knew both parties quite well at the time and knew what their interests were and what one of their main goals was: to get information on the risks of plutonium [and uranium]. Was it as hazardous as radium or more hazardous, [was] the essential question.

Updated information on size and scope of Oak Ridge from Robinson, *City Behind a Fence*. Information regarding Spam and Edward R. Murrow at Christmas, 1944, from Hormel Foods Corporation. Flattop description and specs from Robinson, *City Behind a Fence*, and "Early Oak Ridge Housing" (ORHPA, no date given); American Museum of Science and Energy (Oak Ridge, TN) and "Original Flat-top house on display at Oak Ridge museum," by Amy McRary, *Knoxville News Sentinel*, March 22, 2009.

Information regarding *Sunday Punch* from author interviews, also "Sunday Punch finds a new home," *Oak Ridger*, August 10, 2010; "Weekend warrior:

B-25J bomber connected East Tennesseans," by Fred Brown, *Knoxville News Sentinel*, March 21, 2010.

Tubealloy: Hope and the Haberdasher, April–May 1945
Secretary of war's visit to Oak Ridge, including quotes, from Nichols and Groves. Groves learning of Roosevelt's death, and subsequent briefings, from Groves. Henry Stimson letter to Harry S. Truman, April 24, 1945, and "moon and stars" references from the document collection at the Harry S. Truman Library & Museum, including Henry Stimson to Harry S. Truman, April 24, 1945; CF; Truman Papers, Truman Library. Information regarding Truman Committee from Nichols.

Russians march on Berlin from "The Battle for Berlin in World War Two," by Tilman Remme, BBC, March 10, 2011. Information regarding Hitler's death from "Official: KGB chief ordered Hitler's remains destroyed," by Maxim Tkachenko, CNN, December 11, 2009.

Interim Committee Notes and Reports of Informal and Formal meetings from May 9, May 14, and May 31: Notes of Meeting of the Interim Committee, 1945 (May 9, May 14, and May 31), Miscellaneous Historical Document Collection, Truman Papers, Harry S. Truman Library & Museum. Attendees to the first informal meeting of the Interim Committee were Secretary Henry Stimson (chairman), Hon. Ralph A. Bard, Dr. Vannevar Bush, Hon. James F. Byrnes, Hon. William L. Clayton, Dr. Karl T. Compton, Mr. George L. Harrison, and, by "invitation," Mr. Harvey H. Bundy.

Farm Hall information from Farm Hall transcripts published in *Operation Epsilon: The Farm Hall Transcripts*, introduced by Sir Charles Frank, OBE, FRS (Berkeley and Los Angeles: University of California Press, 1993).

Life continuing on at CEW after VE Day from author interviews. Post-VE Day billboards from photographs by Ed Westcott (previously cited). Attack and impact of Japan firebombing from "U.S. Army Air Forces in World War II: Combat Chronology, March 1945," Air Force Historical Studies Office. B-29 Superfortress information, Tinian, from Groves. Groves opinion about whether to proceed with using the bomb, from Groves.

12. Sand Jumps in the Desert, July 1945
Description of the General's trip back to Washington and office location from Groves. Westcott's meeting with Groves from author interviews and Robinson. Joan Hinton information from "Joan Hinton, Physicist Who Chose China Over Atom Bomb, Is Dead at 88," by William Grimes, *New York Times*, June 11, 2010; *Silage Choppers and Snake Spirits: The Lives & Struggles of Two Americans*

in Modern China, by Dao-yuan Chou (Quezon City, Philippines: Ibon Books, 2009); *Their Day in the Sun: Women of the Manhattan Project*, by Ruth H. Howes and Carolina L. Herzenberg (Philadelphia: Temple University Press, 1999).

Elizabeth Graves information from *Day of Trinity*, by Lansing Lamont (New York: Athenum, 1985); *Women* (previously cited); "Draft Final Report of the Los Alamos Historical Document Retrieval and Assessment (LAH-DRA) Project, Chap. 10: Trinity," prepared for the Centers for Disease Control and Prevention, National Center for Environmental Health Division of Environmental Hazards and Health Effects Radiation Studies Branch, June 2009; "Proving Ground," by Sid Moody, Associated Press (An *Albuquerque Journal* Special Reprint, July 1995).

Choosing test site and description of Trinity test from Groves, Lansing, LAHDRA. "Batter my heart, three-person'd God," anecdote from *American Prometheus*. "Now I am become Death . . . ," and "Now we are all sons of bitches . . . ," from Lansing, also *Day After Trinity*, directed by Jon Else (United States: 1980).

Additional Trinity information from "Proving Ground," by Sid Moody, Associated Press (An *Albuquerque Journal* Special Reprint, July 1995; LAHDRA report, previously cited). There are numerous statistics and personal reactions from the day of the Trinity test, many of which are mentioned in *Day After Trinity*.

Potsdam meeting and diary notes from Harry S. Truman on the Potsdam Conference, July 16, 1945. President's Secretary's File, Truman Papers, Harry S. Truman Library & Museum; also *Racing the Enemy: Stalin, Truman, and the Surrender of Japan*, by Tsuyoshi Hasegawa (Cambridge: Harvard University Press, 2005); *Truman*, by David McCullough (New York: Simon & Schuster, 1992).

Groves's relaying of Trinity report and timeline from Groves and Nichols.

Scientist petitions and counter petitions of July 3, 1945, and July 17, 1945, from NARA, RG 77; "Behind the Decision to Use the Atomic Bomb," the *Bulletin of Atomic Scientists*, October 1958, p. 304, and Petition to the President of the United States, July 17, 1945; MHDC, Truman Papers, Truman Library. July 23, 1945, meeting between Compton and Nichols from Nichols (previously cited) and from *Atomic Quest: A Personal Narrative*, by Arthur Holly Compton (New York: Oxford University Press, 1956). Description of Graves photosession from author interviews and Robinson.

Calutron numbers and statistics from Smith and Wilcox, also "Public glimpses machines that fueled bomb," by Duncan Mansfield, Associated Press, seen in *USA Today*, June 14, 2005.

Groves's orders for bombing, from Groves. Regarding target choices, plans to bomb: "No communiqués on the subject or releases of information will be issued by Commanders in the field without specific prior authority," he wrote. "Any news stories will be sent to the War Department for special clearance." Nick Del Genio and courier information from AMSE (previously cited), Groves, Nichols, and author interviews.

Route and dates of travel of couriers, Truman order, and Spaatz orders from Groves. Information and quotes regarding Truman-Stimson meeting in Germany from *Atomic Tragedy: Henry L. Stimson and the Decision to Use the Bomb Against Japan*, by Sean Langdon Malloy (Ithaca: Cornell University Press, 2008) and *Mandate for Change, 1953–1956: The White House Years, A Personal Account* by Dwight D. Eisenhower (New York: Doubleday, 1963). Information regarding delivery of petitions to Groves and Truman from Nichols. Farm Hall transcript from *Operation Epsilon*.

Information regarding Westcotts's photos and the press packets of July 27, 1945, from *The Oak Ridge Story*, Robinson (previously cited). Ebb Cade information from previously cited materials (Chap. 11).

All information on women from author interviews.

13. The Gadget Revealed

All women's anecdotes and reaction to bombing news from author interviews.

Timing of release of statement regarding bombing of Hiroshima from *By the Bomb's Early Light: American Thought and Culture at the Dawn of the Atomic Age*, by Paul Boyer (Chapel Hill, NC: University of North Carolina Press, 1985).

Truman address from "Press release by the White House," August 6, 1945. Subject File, Ayers Papers, Harry S. Truman Library & Museum. Truman location, selection of targets, journey of remaining parts of bomb, and U-235 from Groves, Nichols, and Lansing. Description of attack and mission from Groves.

Information about Miriam White Campbell from the Los Alamos Historical Society podcasts: http://www.losalamoshistory.org/podcasts/campbell. mp3. Estimates of Hiroshima injuries from Rhodes (previously cited); *Hiroshima*, by John Hersey (New York: Alfred A. Knopf, [1946] 1985). Estimated numbers of immediately killed range widely depending on the source, from 66,000 initially killed to more than 70,000. Estimated deaths by the end of 1945 are often cited as 140,000, but real loss and death as a result of the bombings are still virtually impossible to estimate when taking into account the amount of time it took for some individuals to die as a result of their injuries or exposure to radiation.

Text of leaflets dropped on Japanese cities from Truman Papers, Miscellaneous Historical Document File, no. 258, Harry S. Truman Library & Museum. Text of Stimson address from "Press release by Henry Stimson, August 6, 1945." Subject File, Ayers Papers. Harry S. Truman Library & Museum.

Elizabeth Edwards story from author interviews and Waldo Cohn information from *Voices* (previously cited); Bill Wilcox anecdote from author interview and personal papers of William J. Wilcox Jr. Meitner information from Sime (previously cited). Farm Hall transcripts from *Operation Epsilon*. Jacqueline Nichols anecdote from Nichols.

14. Dawn of a Thousand Suns

All women's anecdotes from author interviews.

Information about job loss fear from author interviews. Letter from under secretary of war, as seen in the *Oak Ridge Journal* and personal papers of Jane Puckett. Letter from Jane Greer's sister from personal documents of Jane Greer.

Additional Nagasaki information: The mission endured more challenges than the flight of the *Enola Gay* that dropped Little Boy only three days earlier. *Bock's Car*, which carried the bomb nicknamed Fat Man, faced fuel transfer valve problems and bad weather. Fuel levels endangered the mission, cloud cover made it difficult to see the target that, according to orders, had to be attacked by "visual means." Once the bomb was away, the crew felt three aftershocks rather than the expected two (one from the initial blast and one reflected from the ground). The plane's commander, Major Charles Sweeney, thought perhaps the third, unexpected shock had been reflected off a hill banking the Urakami Valley, and worried that they had missed their target completely. But they had not. One trip around the mushroom cloud and *Bock's Car* landed in Okinawa on fumes. Anecdote of young woman crying in her dorm room from Atomic Heritage Foundation, http://www.atomicheritage.org/index.php/ahf-updates-mainmenu-153.html, last accessed 8-28-2012.

Information regarding VJ Day in Oak Ridge, from author interviews and photographs by Ed Westcott (previously cited). Bill Wilcox letter and anecdote from author interviews and personal documents of William J. Wilcox Jr. *Oak Ridge Journal* selections from the paper as cited in text.

15. Life in the New Age

All women's anecdotes from author interviews.

Oak Ridge Journal from paper as cited.

Vi Warren comments from "Mission to Japan," by Jane Warren Larson, from *Voices* (previously cited). Stafford Warren account of Japan from Stafford Warren oral history (previously cited) and from "Mission to Japan," by Jane Warren Larson, from *Voices* (previously cited).

Nancy Farley Wood information from Stafford Warren oral history (previously cited) and from "Nancy Farley Wood, 99," by Ana Beatriz Cholo, *Chicago Tribune*, May 17, 2003.

Information regarding Masao Tsuzuki from Stafford Warren oral history and from *Suffering Made Real: American Science and the Survivors at Hiroshima*, by M. Susan Lindee (Chicago: University of Chicago Press, 1994).

Information regarding Nakamura and *Asahi Shimbun* from "The media: nuclear secrecy vs. Democracy," by Robert Karl Manoff, *Bulletin of the Atomic Scientists*, January 1984.

Bernard Hoffman photos from *Life* magazine, October 15, 1945. Information regarding Truman wanting to keep the bomb a secret, from "In the Matter of J. Robert Oppenheimer," PBS's *American Experience*, http://www.pbs.org/wgbh/americanexperience/features/transcript; shoppenheimer-transcript/.

Details regarding Wilfred Burchett from "Hiroshima Cover-up: How the War Department's Timesman Won a Pulitzer," by Amy Goodman and David Goodman, *CommonDreams*, August 10, 2004, http://www.common dreams.org/views04/0810-01.htm, last accessed 8-28-2012, and "66 Years Ago: Wilfred Burchett Arrives in Hiroshima—as a New Era of Nuclear Censorship Begins," by Greg Mitchell, *The Nation*, September 2, 2011, http://www.thenation.com/blog/163115/66-years-ago-wilfred-burchett-arrives-hiroshima—new-era-nuclear-censorship-begins#, last accessed 8-28-2012, "1945: A Rain of Ruin from the Air," *BBC: On this Day, 1950–2005*, http://news.bbc.co.uk/onthisday/hi/witness/august/6/newsid—4715000/4715303.stm, last accessed 8-28-2012, and "Atomic Truths Plague Prize Coverup," by Juan Gonzalez, *New York Daily News*, August 9, 2005.

Regarding the Smyth Report: author interviews, and announcement of the Smyth report for sale in *Oak Ridge Journal*.

Regarding Truman and Oppenheimer's meeting: *Prometheus* (previously cited); *Truman*, by David McCullough (New York: Simon & Schuster, 1992).

Ebb Cade information from previously cited materials and also the memorandum to Mr. Wright Langham, Santa Fe, New Mexico, from David Goldbring, for the District Engineer, regarding E.C.'s medical history and shipment of 15 teeth. Dated September 19, 1945, Formerly Declassified Correspondence, 1942–1947; Records of the Atomic Energy Commission, Record Group 326; National Archives at Atlanta; National Archives and Records Administration and ACHRE report (previously cited).

Information regarding Lise Meitner from Sime (previously cited). Emilio Segrè quote about Ida Noddack from "The Discovery of Nuclear Fission," by Emilio G. Segrè, *Physics Today*, July 1989.

Oak Ridge statistics following war from *A City is Born* (previously cited); Y-12 National Security Complex, US Department of Energy; Wilcox-K-25 (previously cited); "Oak Ridge National Laboratory: The First Fifty Years," *Oak Ridge National Laboratory Review*, produced by UT-Battelle, LLC, for the US Department of Energy.

Regarding isotope production from "Oak Ridge National Laboratory Research and Radioisotope Production," by W. E. Thompson (Oak Ridge, TN: Oak Ridge National Laboratory, January 1952). Atomic Energy Act of 1946, excerpted from "Legislative History of the Atomic Energy Act of 1946" (Public Law 585, 79th Congress) US Atomic Energy Commission (Washington, DC: 1965). Further amended in 1954: "Drawing Back the Curtain of Secrecy: Restricted Data Declassification Policy. 1946 to the Present," Office of Scientific and Technical Information, US Department of Energy, June 1, 1994. Atomic Energy Community Act of 1955, 42 U.S.C. 2301, et seq., which provides for termination of government ownership and management of communities owned by the Atomic Energy Commission. Other information regarding history of the Atomic Energy Commission from *A City Is Born, City Behind a Fence, ORNL: The First 50 Years*, and "A History of the Atomic Energy Commission," by Alice L. Buck (Washington, DC: US Department of Energy, July 1983).

Elza Gate opening in March 1949 from *History of AEC, A City Is Born*, and *City Behind a Fence* (previously cited). Nichols's comments on Oak Ridge from "My Work in Oak Ridge," by K. D. Nichols, from *Voices* (previously cited).

Building of new housing, including those for black families, from *City Behind a Fence*. Information regarding education options for black students after the war from "Before Clinton of Little Rock, Oak Ridge integration made history," by Bob Fowler, *Knoxville News Sentinel*, February 16, 2009; "Education in Oak Ridge—Pre-Oak Ridge and Early Oak Ridge Schools, Part 2," by D. Ray Smith, *Oak Ridger, November 21, 2006;* "A 1950s' letter & the integration of area schools," by D. Ray Smith, *Oak Ridger*, January 21, 2011; "A New Hope," by Steele, from *Voices* (previously cited).

Information regarding integration of Clinton High School from Green McAdoo Cultural Center, Clinton, TN, and "See it Now: Clinton and the

Law," narrated and produced by Edward R. Murrow and Fred Friendly, CBS Television, 1957.

Vote on Oak Ridge incorporation and transfer of power from Robinson's "Oak Ridge Story" and "The Atom Town Wants to Be Free," by John Bird, *Saturday Evening Post*, vol. 231, March 21, 1959.

Serial magazine quotes from personal papers of Jane Puckett.

Uranium mining information from "Abandoned Uranium Mines: An 'Overwhelming Problem' in the Navajo Nation," by Francie Diep, *Scientific American*, December 30, 2010; "Moab," by Margaret S. Bearnson, from *Utah History Encyclopedia* (University of Utah Press, 1994).

Information regarding David Greenglass and the Rosenbergs from "The Atom Spy Case" and Roberts (previously cited). Information regarding George Koval: "George Koval: Atomic Spy Unmasked," by Michael Walsh, *Smithsonian Magazine*, May 2009.

Atomic Cocktail information from Boyer (previously cited). "Duck and Cover," in public domain, by Archer Productions, 1950. "Our Friend the Atom," Walt Disney Productions, 1957. November 1953 address by Eisenhower to the United Nations from Dwight D. Eisenhower Presidential Library and Museum.

Information regarding Soviet detonation at Novaya Zemlya from "1961: World Condemns Russia's Nuclear Test," *BBC: On This Day 1950–2005*, http://news.bbc.co.uk/onthisday/hi/dates/stories/october/30/newsid_3666000/3666785.stm, last accessed 8-28-2012. Regarding President Kennedy and the test ban, from John F. Kennedy Presidential Library and Museum.

ORACLE as the most advanced computer in the world from *Voices*, p. 361 (previously cited). Kennedy assassination research from ORNL: *The First 50 Years* (previously cited). Kisetsu Yamada information from author interviews and correspondence with Colleen Black. Information on the International Friendship Bell from author visits to site, interviews, and "2008 Historically Speaking International Friendship Bell," by Ray Smith; Robert Brooks's lawsuit for peace bell from United States Court of Appeals for the Sixth Circuit 222 F.3d 259: Robert Brooks, Plaintiff-appellant, v. City of Oak Ridge, Defendant-appellee, Argued: March 16, 2000, Decided and Filed: July 21, 2000. Also "Oak Ridge International Friendship Bell—Part 1 of casting ceremony," by D. Ray Smith, *Oak Ridger*, July 8, 2008.

Epilogue

Information regarding the *Enola Gay* exhibit controversy: "From The Enola Gay Controversy: History, Memory, and the Politics of Presentation," by

Michael J. Hogan, ed., *Hiroshima in History and Memory* (Cambridge: Cambridge University Press, 1996).

Information on Manhattan Project National Park from author interviews and from "Manhattan Project National Historical Park Act," Atomic Heritage Foundation, June 21, 2012.

Information regarding proposed Manhattan National Parks sites from Atomic Heritage Foundation http://www.atomicheritage.org/index.php/component/content/article/40-preservation-tab-/518-doi-transmits-recommendations.html, last accessed 8-28-2012.

Details regarding K-25 preservation from "Community celebrates K-25 historic preservation agreement," by John Huotari, *Oak Ridge Today*, Aug. 10, 2012.

List of Author Interviews

Interviews were conducted between 2009 and 2012. This list is not comprehensive; repeated subsequent visits resulted in countless conversations of a less formal, yet often informative, nature.

Celia Klemski, Colleen Black, Dorothy Wilkinson, Helen Brown, Virginia Coleman, Toni Schmitt, Jane Puckett, Kattie Strickland, Rosemary Lane, Helen Jernigan, Rosemarie Waggener, Marty Rom, Elaine Buker, Lois Mallett, Betty and Harlan Whitehead, Dorothy Spoon, Martha Nichols, Anne Voelker, Helen Schwenn, Ardis and George Leichsenring, Jeanie Wilcox, Earline Banic, Carolyn Stelzman, Madge Newton, Dee Longendorfer, Lilian Johns Ross, Helen and Red Lynch, Bobbie Martin, Louise Walker, Liane Russell, Joanne Gailar, Georgia Marie Cloer Bailey, Louise Warmley, Mira Kimmelman, D. Ray Smith, William J. Wilcox Jr., William Tewes, Steven Stow, John Lane, Paul Wilkinson, Connie Bolling, Valeria Steele Roberson, Kathy Schmitt Gomez, Nannette Bissonnet, Martin McBride, Anne McBride, Rose Weaver, Ed Westcott (with D. Ray Smith and Don Hunnicutt), Jim Ramsey, Fred Strohl.

Vi Warren's columns from *Oak Ridge Journal* as cited in text.

Thanks

During the seven years since I first came across this project, an astounding number of people offered their time, insights, and expertise. They have not only been helpful, but have given me, whether they realized it or not, motivation and inspiration when I needed it most. Every one of them deserves a heartfelt thank-you.

My tireless agent, Yfat Reiss Gendell, hung in there with me as this idea endured various incarnations and false starts, and did not stop until it found a good home. Her loyalty, intelligence, and compassion are a rare mix in this business. I also thank Yfat's assistants, present and past, Erica Walker and Cecilia Campbell-Westlind, and the rest of the team at Foundry Literary + Media, including Yfat's partner, Peter McGuigan, David Patterson, and Stephanie Abou.

I am indebted to my remarkable editor, Michelle Howry. Her enthusiasm for this project, combined with her dedication, tenacity, and thoughtfulness, have made this book much better than it would have been had I been left to my own devices. I am well aware that I hit the editorial jackpot when my proposal landed on her desk. She is part of an exceptional team at Touchstone that includes her assistant, Kiele Raymond; publisher Stacy Creamer; editorial director Sally Kim; associate publisher David Falk; the marketing and publicity team of Marcia Burch, Justina Batchelor, and Meredith Vilarello; also Josh Karpf and his production and copyediting squad, including copy editor Toby Yuen, and proofreaders Tricia Tamburr and Judy Myers and compositor Meghan Day Healey; cover designers Cherlynne Li and Ervin Serrano; and interior designer Ruth Lee-Mui. Molly Puldon wrote the wonderful Reading Group Guide. I feel very fortunate to have had all of you helping out along the way.

There are a number of organizations and people that I have tapped as resources throughout the researching and writing of this book. I truly enjoyed the brief time I spent with Cindy Kelly at the Atomic Heritage Foundation. She is the driving force behind the nationwide preservation efforts of the

Manhattan Project sites. Several organizations helped with oral histories, including Courtney Esposito at the Smithsonian Institution Archives, and Brandon Barton, Stella Zhu, and especially Alva Moore Stevenson with the Center for Oral History Research at the Charles E. Young Research Library at UCLA. Also thanks to librarian Geneva Holiday at the Davis Library at the University of North Carolina at Chapel Hill for locating critical Joan Hinton resources; and Ted McCafferty, Cleveland Public Library, who located resources pertaining to Evelyn Handcock Ferguson. Several branches of the National Archives and Records Administration have been instrumental in helping me navigate the overwhelming sea of documents and photos that this irreplaceable national treasure offers every American citizen. At College Park, Maryland, Edward McCarter and Nick Natanson assisted me as I waded through the thousands of Ed Westcott photos that are preserved there. Susan Clifton, Douglas Swanson, and Dennis Braden at Archives I in Washington, DC, have provided advance support for this book, offering valuable advice for outreach and lectures. David Satterfield at NARA's personnel records office helped me locate World War II service records. I must give many thanks to National Archives public affairs specialist Miriam Kleiman, who has been a sort of National Archives tour guide and first responder, always managing to introduce me to the right people at the right time, and pointing me in the right direction.

The National Archives at Atlanta is the primary home to the Atomic Energy Commission records and much more; this facility has played a key role in the researching of this book. Everyone at that facility went out of their way to help me find what I was looking for, including Guy Hall, John Whitehurst, Kevin Baker, Maureen Hill, and Catherine Farmer. A very special thank-you goes out to Joel Walker. Joel's contagious excitement about the Atomic Energy Commission collection made my work not only easier but also much more enjoyable. He is a tremendous asset to both the National Archives and the legacy of the Manhattan Project.

I would like to give the biggest of thank-yous to the city of Oak Ridge. Countless individuals there have taken time to talk and visit with me, suggest potential interviewees, or simply offer friendly advice and encouragement. I have enjoyed attending several events hosted by the Oak Ridge Heritage and Preservation Association. The Oak Ridge Public Library has a wonderful "Oak Ridge Room," and Teresa Fortney and especially Anne Marie Hamilton-Brehm have assisted me there. There are two museums in particular to which I would like to give credit: the Children's Museum of Oak Ridge, where I was assisted by Margaret Allard, and the American

Museum of Science and Energy, where I have had the good fortune of getting to know Deputy Director Ken Mayes.

Many individuals in the Oak Ridge community provided time, information, and contacts. Many others submitted to interviews, and though they may not have been highlighted in the book, they were nonetheless invaluable. For their time and energy I thank Rose Weaver, Martin and Anne McBride, Henry Perry, Ethel Steinhauer, Emily and Don Hunnicut, Rosemarie Waggener, Marty Rom, Elaine Buker, Lois Mallett, Betty and Harlan Whitehead, Dorothy Spoon, Martha Nichols, Anne Voelker, Helen Schwenn, Ardis and George Leichsenring, Earline Banic, Carolyn Stelzman, Madge Newton, Dee Longendorfer, Lilian Johns Ross, Helen and Red Lynch, Bobbie Martin, Louise Walker, Joanne Gailar, Georgia Marie Cloer Bailey, Louise Warmley, Steven Stow, John Lane, Paul Wilkinson, Connie Bolling, Nannette Bissonet, Jim and John Klemski, Jim Ramsey, Fred Strohl, Valeria Steele Roberson, Liane Russell, Mira Kimmelman, Helen Jernigan, Kathy Schmitt Gomez, Suzanne and Peter Angelini, and Beverly and HalliBurton Puckett.

I have a special place in my heart for certain "Men of Atomic City": Bill Tewes has provided wonderful stories not only about Oak Ridge, but also concerning the experiences of women there during the war, thanks to his willingness to share remembrances of his wife, Audrey. Without Ed Westcott's photos, I very likely would never have begun looking into Oak Ridge's World War II history. He is an irreplaceable window into this world. I always light up at the indefatigable Bill Wilcox, whose dedication to preserving history and living a meaningful life is truly inspiring. His wife, Jeanie, never fails to have a joke and a smile for me. And dear Ray Smith has introduced me to countless contacts, provided numerous resources, and keeps me in the loop about everything going on in and around Oak Ridge. He is a one-man historical society, and I have enjoyed getting to know him and his lovely wife, Fanny. Ray Smith and Bill Wilcox are unique, selfless and driven, working for a cause with little recognition. I adore them.

This book would not exist in any meaningful way, shape, or form without the generosity of time and spirit offered up so freely and joyfully by the women featured in this book: Colleen Black, Rosemary Lane, Dot Wilkinson, Helen Brown, Kattie Strickland, Jane Puckett, Celia Klemski, Toni Schmitt, and Virginia Coleman. Knowing them has enriched my life and work in ways I am still discovering.

There is nothing more important than the support of family and friends throughout the long process of writing a book, and I have been ridiculously fortunate in this arena. My local bookstore in Asheville, North Carolina,

Malaprop's, is an author's best friend. Emoke B'Racz and Linda Barrett Knopp have created and nurtured a lasting and valuable institution—a true haven for those who love books. Alsace Walentine in particular has helped me with events, signings, publicity, and so much more. George Fleming kept my spirits up. Buncombe County Library's Lyme Kedic helped track down the untrackable in the book world. Drake Witham was not only a valuable set of eyes, but also boots on the ground in Los Angeles when I needed them. I can't say enough about the luminous spirit and rigorous mind of Kathryn Temple, whose assistance kept me sane.

And finally, this book would never have been possible without the support, patience, sharp eyes, and kind heart of my husband, Joseph D'Agnese.

Thank you.

Index

A

Abelson, Phil, 107
ACME Insurance Company, 74,
    168, 184
Advisory Committee on Human
    Radiation Experiments
    (ACHRE), 293
Alamogordo, N.Mex., Trinity test
    at, 233–38, 239, 241, 242,
    244, 251, 275
alcohol, 143–44, 154
Allison, Sam, 236
Aluminum Company of America,
    100
American Journal of Psychiatry, 201
American Museum of Science and
    Energy (AMSE), 304, 312
Anderson, Herb, 77
Archer Daniels Midland
    warehouses, 10
Arizona, USS, 71
Army, U.S., 49, 145
    Corps of Engineers, 21, 291
    Counter Intelligence Corps,
        275, 303–4
Asahi Shimbun, 290
atom, 32, 56
    Bohr's model of, 60

neutrons in, 32–34
    bombardment of
        Tubealloy with, 33,
        58–59
    fission and, 61, 76, 100
    nucleus of, 32, 60
    splitting, 34
atomic bomb ("the Gadget"), xvii,
    100, 230–31, 298
    Eisenhower and, 246
    Germany's research on, 62,
        119, 228, 252–53, 258
    gun version of, 207, 226–27,
        251
    implosion version of, 207, 226,
        235, 272
    Interim Committee and,
        227–28, 230
    Jumbo container for, 235
    Limited Nuclear Test Ban
        Treaty and, 299
    news of CEW's involvement
        in, 249, 256–57, 259–62,
        264–68, 270–71, 273
    in popular culture, 298–99
    Soviet Union and, 243, 298,
        299
    Stimson on, 258
    test of, 233–38, 239, 241, 242,
        244, 251, 275

About the Author

DENISE KIERNAN is an author and journalist whose work has appeared in *The New York Times, The Wall Street Journal, The Village Voice, Ms. Magazine, Discover,* and many other national publications. Her previous history titles include *Signing Their Lives Away* and *Signing Their Rights Away.* She lives in North Carolina.